Business and Post-disaster Management

This book provides a comprehensive examination of the effects of a natural disaster on businesses and organisations, and on a range of stakeholders, including employees and consumers. Research on how communities and businesses respond to disasters can inform policy and mitigate the cost and impacts of future disasters. This book discusses how places recover following a disaster and the vital roles that business and other organisations play.

This volume gives a detailed understanding of business, organisational and consumer responses to the Christchurch earthquake sequence of 2010–2011, which caused 185 deaths, destroyed over 70 per cent of buildings in the city's CBD, inflicted major infrastructure damage, and severely affected the city's image. Despite the devastation, the businesses, organisations and people of Christchurch are now undergoing significant recovery.

The book sheds significant new light not only on business and organisation response to disaster but also on how business and urban systems may be made more resilient.

C. Michael Hall is a Professor with the Department of Management, Marketing & Entrepreneurship, University of Canterbury, New Zealand, and Docent in Geography, University of Oulu, Finland. He also holds positions at the School of Business and Economics, Linneaus University, Sweden, and School of Business, University of Johannesberg, South Africa. He has published widely in the areas of tourism, environmental change, regional development and sustainability.

Sanna Malinen is a Senior Lecturer in Human Resource Management and Organisational Behaviour at the University of Canterbury. Her research interests are in the fields of organisational behaviour, organisational psychology and human resource management. She is a lead researcher in the Employee Resilience Research group.

Rob Vosslamber is a Senior Lecturer in Accounting at the University of Canterbury. His research interests include accounting theory, accounting history and taxation.

Russell Wordsworth is a Senior Lecturer in Human Resource Management at the University of Canterbury. His research interests are in the fields of human resource development, employee attraction and retention and ethics in human resource management.

Business and Post-disaster Management

Business, organisational and consumer resilience and the Christchurch earthquakes

Edited by C. Michael Hall, Sanna Malinen, Rob Vosslamber and Russell Wordsworth

Routledge
Taylor & Francis Group

LONDON AND NEW YORK

First published 2016 by Routledge

2 Park Square, Milton Park, Abingdon, Oxforshire OX14 4RN
711 Third Avenue, New York, NY 10017

Routledge is an imprint of the Taylor & Francis Group, an informa business

First issued in paperback 2018

British Library Cataloguing-in-Publication Data
A catalogue record for this book is available from the British Library

Library of Congress Cataloging-in-Publication Data
   Business and post-disaster management : business, organisational and consumer resilience and the Christchurch earthquakes / edited by C. Michael Hall, Sanna Malinen, Rob Vosslamber and Russell Wordsworth.
      pages cm
   Includes bibliographical references and index.
   ISBN 978-1-138-89085-5 (hkb) — ISBN 978-1-315-64021-1 (ekb)
   1. Christchurch Earthquake, N.Z., 2011—Economic aspects.
2. Disasters—Economic aspects—New Zealand.   3. Disaster relief—
Economic aspects—New Zealand.   4. New Zealand—Economic
conditions—1984– I. Hall, Colin Michael, 1961– editor.
   HV600 2011 .C47 B87 2016
   363.34'95099383—dc23   2015033987

ISBN: 978-1-138-89085-5 (hbk)
ISBN: 978-1-138-31795-6 (pbk)

Typeset in Galliard
by Apex CoVantage, LLC

Contents

List of figures   viii
List of tables   ix
Contributors   x
Acknowledgements   xiii

PART I
Context

1 Introduction: the business, organisational and
   destination impacts of natural disasters – the
   Christchurch earthquakes 2010–2011   3
   C. MICHAEL HALL, SANNA MALINEN, ROB VOSSLAMBER AND
   RUSSELL WORDSWORTH

PART II
Business and organisational responses and relationships

2 Why stay? the resilience of small firms in
   Christchurch and their owners   23
   HUIBERT P. DE VRIES AND ROBERT T. HAMILTON

3 Dynamics of organisational response to a disaster:
   a study of organisations impacted by earthquakes   35
   VENKATARAMAN NILAKANT, BERNARD WALKER, JOANA KUNTZ,
   HUIBERT P. DE VRIES, SANNA MALINEN, KATHARINA NÄSWALL
   AND KATE VAN HEUGTEN

4 After the shock: employee turnover decision-making
  in a post-crisis context   48
  RUSSELL WORDSWORTH AND VENKATARAMAN NILAKANT

5 Survival strategies of cultural service providers
  in a post-earthquake context   65
  ABANTI ANTARA, JÖRG FINSTERWALDER AND MICHAEL C. SHONE

6 I do (not) want you back! (Re)gentrification of the
  arts centre, Christchurch   79
  ALBERTO AMORE

7 Earthquake impacts, mitigation, and organisational
  resilience of business sectors in Canterbury   97
  GIRISH PRAYAG AND CAROLINE ORCHISTON

PART III
Consumer and communication responses

8 From brand love to brand divorce: the effect of a
  disruption in supply on consumer–brand relationships   121
  SUSSIE MORRISH, GIRISH PRAYAG AND MATTHEW NGUYEN

9 Customer relationships and experiences during
  times of disaster: a case study of Ballantynes   132
  JÖRG FINSTERWALDER AND HANNAH GREY

10 It's not all dark! Christchurch residents' emotions
   and coping strategies with dark tourism sites   155
   GIRISH PRAYAG

11 Telling tales: some implications for response
   agencies from stories of informal personal
   communication in the aftermath of a devastating
   earthquake   167
   COLLEEN E. MILLS

PART IV
Learning from 'the new normal'

12 **'Regeneration is the focus now': anchor projects
and delivering a new CBD for Christchurch**   181
ALBERTO AMORE AND C. MICHAEL HALL

13 **The governance of built heritage in the
post-earthquake Christchurch CBD**   200
ALBERTO AMORE

14 **Disasters, insurance and accounting**   219
ROB VOSSLAMBER

15 **Disasters, urban regeneration and the temporality
of servicescapes**   230
JÖRG FINSTERWALDER AND C. MICHAEL HALL

PART V
Conclusions

16 **Undertaking business, consumer and organisational
research in a post-disaster setting**   251
C. MICHAEL HALL, SANNA MALINEN, VENKATARAMAN NILAKANT,
ROB VOSSLAMBER, BERNARD WALKER AND RUSSELL
WORDSWORTH

17 **Putting ecological thinking back into disaster
ecology and responses to natural disasters:
rethinking resilience or business as usual?**   269
C. MICHAEL HALL

Index   293

Figures

2.1 Business turnover 2010–2013   25
4.1 Decision process for *new beginnings*   54
4.2 Decision process for *reluctant departures*   57
4.3 Decision process for *tragic endings*   58
4.4 Decision process for *deliberate departures*   60
7.1 Theoretical framework   98
8.1 Analogy of a brand divorce for Marmite   128
9.1 A message from Ballantynes   139
9.2 Girls' Day Out   140
9.3 A customer update from Ballantynes   142
9.4 M·A·C is back in Christchurch   144
9.5 Back where we belong   146
12.1 Relationships between urban regeneration as usual and
     post-disaster regeneration   182
13.1 Pre-earthquake factors at the basis of the subsequent crisis
     of built heritage in Christchurch CBD   205
15.1 Re:Start Mall   236
15.2 Relocated Re:Start Mall   237
15.3 Pallet Pavilion and arches   238
15.4 Transitional football field servicescape   239
15.5 Smash Palace at its second location   240
15.6 Dance-o-Mat transitional servicescape   240
15.7 Damaged Christchurch Cathedral (above) and transitional
     servicescape Cardboard Cathedral (below) in different spaces   241
17.1 Equilibrium model of single island biota   273
17.2 Representations of dominant factors in island species turnover   274
17.3 Relationships between biogeographical processes and island
     characteristics   275
17.4 Characteristics of disturbance: intensity, scale and frequency   276
17.5 Island biogeographical perspectives on business endemism,
     immigration, emigration and extinction   277

Tables

1.1 Lexical analysis of abstract, keywords and title of articles and reviews in Scopus related to natural disasters 1975–2014   6
2.1 Impact of earthquake   26
5.1 Earthquake impacts and substitute cultural and heritage services post-earthquake   74
6.1 Overview of literature on retail gentrification   81
6.2 List of long-established tenants and relocation following the earthquake of February 2011   87
6.3 The proposed vision for the Arts Centre   90
7.1 Earthquake impacts on organisational resources   102
7.2 Earthquake impacts on an organisation's basic infrastructure   105
7.3 Mitigation strategies of organisations   108
7.4 Organisational resilience   111
12.1 Key buildings in the Christchurch CBD and their status after the earthquakes of February 2011 as of March 2015   185
12.2 Chronology of events from the earthquake of 2010 until the release of the cost-sharing agreement   186
13.1 Conservation approaches in post-disaster contexts: findings from the literature   201
13.2 List of key heritage buildings in Christchurch CBD   203
13.3 Listed heritage buildings before and after the earthquakes of 2010 and 2011   207
15.1 Perspectives on the role of servicescapes in marketing   232
17.1 Ontologies and epistemologies of ecological systems   282

Contributors

Alberto Amore is with the Department of Management, Marketing and Entrepreneurship, University of Canterbury, Christchurch, New Zealand. Alberto's main research interests include tourism planning and policy, spatial planning and governance and practices of urban regeneration in Europe, North America and Australasia.

Abanti Antara was formerly a graduate student in the Department of Management, Marketing and Entrepreneurship, University of Canterbury, Christchurch, New Zealand, and is now a PhD Candidate in the Department of Tourism, Sport and Society at Lincoln University, New Zealand. Her research interests include tourism management, tourism sustainability, re-branding tourism, cultural heritage tourism, disaster studies and indigenous tourism.

Huibert P. de Vries is with the Department of Management, Marketing and Entrepreneurship, University of Canterbury, Christchurch, New Zealand. Herb's research interests are in the field of management practices in small and medium-sized enterprises (SMEs) and minority entrepreneurship.

Jörg Finsterwalder is with the Department of Management, Marketing and Entrepreneurship, University of Canterbury, Christchurch, New Zealand. His research interests include co-creation of services, group services and consumer tribes, value networks and service (eco) systems, service consumer behaviour, customer experiences, and disasters and services.

Hannah Grey was formerly a graduate student in the Department of Management, Marketing and Entrepreneurship, University of Canterbury, Christchurch, New Zealand. She is now a Marketing Specialist at BP.

C. Michael Hall is a Professor with the Department of Management, Marketing and Entrepreneurship, University of Canterbury, New Zealand and Docent in Geography, University of Oulu, Finland. He also holds positions at the School of Business and Economics, Linneaus University, Sweden, and School of Business, University of Johannesberg, South Africa. He has published widely in the areas of tourism, environment change, regional development and sustainability.

Robert T. Hamilton is with the Department of Management, Marketing and Entrepreneurship, University of Canterbury, Christchurch, New Zealand. His main research interests are in the areas of small business growth and development, including internationalisation and the life-cycle of high growth firms.

Joana Kuntz is with the Department of Psychology and Resilient Organisations Research Programme, University of Canterbury, Christchurch, New Zealand. Her research interests include resilience, change management and leadership development.

Sanna Malinen is a Senior Lecturer in Human Resource Management and Organisational Behaviour at the University of Canterbury. Her research interests are in the fields of organisational behaviour, organisational psychology and human resource management. She is a lead researcher in the Employee Resilience Research group.

Colleen E. Mills is with the Department of Management, Marketing and Entrepreneurship, University of Canterbury, Christchurch, New Zealand. Colleen's research interests focus on times of equivocality and ambiguity, particularly the periods of change accompanying natural disasters, organisational restructuring, CEO succession and business startup.

Sussie Morrish is with the Department of Management, Marketing and Entrepreneurship, University of Canterbury, Christchurch, New Zealand. Sussie's research interests revolve around the interface between marketing and entrepreneurship in various strategic contexts, including the effect of natural disasters such as the Canterbury earthquakes on entrepreneurial businesses.

Katharina Näswall is with the Department of Psychology and Resilient Organisations Research Programme, University of Canterbury, Christchurch, New Zealand. The primary focus of her research is on work-related stress and wellbeing, with a special interest for uncertainty in the workplace, balance between work and life outside work, as well as factors which aid coping with work-related stress, such as social support and leadership factors.

Matthew Nguyen was formerly a graduate student in the Department of Management, Marketing and Entrepreneurship, University of Canterbury, Christchurch, New Zealand.

Venkataraman Nilakant is with the Department of Management, Marketing and Entrepreneurship and Resilient Organisations Research Programme, University of Canterbury, Christchurch, New Zealand. Nilakant specialises in organisational resilience, organisational change and management of change and is the co-editor of *Managing Responsibly: Alternative Approaches to Corporate Management and Governance* (2012).

Caroline Orchiston is with the Centre for Sustainability, University of Otago, Dunedin, New Zealand. Her main research interests are tourism business recovery and resilience, community preparedness and planning for natural hazards events.

Girish Prayag is with the Department of Management, Marketing and Entrepreneurship, University of Canterbury, Christchurch, New Zealand. Girish's research interests are related to organisational resilience in the tourism industry and consumer behaviour in a post-disaster context related to tourism activities.

Michael C. Shone is with the Department of Tourism, Sport and Society, Faculty of Environment, Society and Design, Lincoln University, Lincoln, New Zealand. Michael's research interests include tourism policy and planning, destination management and regional development.

Kate van Heugten is with the Department of Human Services and Social Work, School of Language, Social and Political Sciences, University of Canterbury, Christchurch, New Zealand. Kate's research draws on sociological theory to research the organisation of work and she is the author of *Human Service Organizations in the Disaster Context* (2014).

Rob Vosslamber is a Senior Lecturer in Accounting at the University of Canterbury. His research interests include accounting theory, accounting history and taxation.

Bernard Walker is with the Department of Management, Marketing and Entrepreneurship and Resilient Organisations Research Programme, University of Canterbury, Christchurch, New Zealand. He is involved in major projects focused on improving the performance and resilience of organisations, as well as working in the areas of non-standard employment, leadership, conflict and teamwork.

Russell Wordsworth is a Senior Lecturer in Human Resource Management at the University of Canterbury. His research interests are in the fields of human resource development, employee attraction and retention and ethics in human resource management.

Acknowledgements

Writing a book on the aftermath of a natural disaster that you have lived through is a strange experience. On the one hand there is an attempt to retain a sense of distance and detachment that is the hallmark of much academic writing and research. On the other, it is also extremely personal, with the potential to arouse not only memories of the events themselves but also one's feelings towards what has happened since and lives and places interrupted. These are feelings that arguably only researchers who have been through such events understand. Nevertheless, they provide an important reality for conducting research on natural disasters, no matter what disciplinary background one is coming from.

This book has its origins in the major earthquake sequence that affected the Canterbury region of the South Island of New Zealand, and especially the city of Christchurch, in 2010–2011. The earthquakes and their impacts provided the catalyst for a wide range of research to chart the response and recovery of the city and region. This book provides one strand of such research that focuses on the business and organisational dimensions of response to natural disaster as well as some of the consumer, communication and destination elements. The opportunity to host an internal earthquake seminar at the College of Business and Law, University of Canterbury, in November 2013 where researchers could present their earthquake-related research provided an important staging point for the development of the present volume. Researchers from a wide range of disciplines were invited to attend and present their work. Although a number of colleagues chose to publish their research elsewhere, they provided valuable feedback and discussion. Nevertheless, following the event it was clear that there was a need to bring together much of the work being done on business, organisations, tourism and consumers in the post-earthquake environment, especially as these areas are generally underrepresented in the natural disaster literature. And it is from that decision that this volume was born.

There are a number of personal and professional acknowledgements that we would like to provide without which this volume would not have been possible. At a personal level we would like to thank our families and friends for their support since the earthquakes.

Michael would like to thank Jody, Cooper and JC for their love and support and coping with yet another book and would also especially like to offer very grateful thanks to Peter and Jane Finch, Keith and Pauline Orevich, and Tim Baird in Christchurch and Jim and Nita Cowper in Tauranga for helping with work and personal accommodation while he was an earthquake refugee.

Rob wishes to thank his wife Andy for her constant love and support – even when the earth moved!

Russell would like to thank his wife Izel for love and support throughout earthquakes and the process of putting this book together. He would also like to thank each of the participants who contributed to the research reported in Chapter 4. The stories touched him deeply.

Sanna wishes to thank Jason, Samu, äiti and iskä for their love and support, and all the participants who so willingly participated in our research.

At a professional level we would like to thank the School of Business Research Committee who helped financially support the original business and law earthquake research seminar and especially Catherine Woods, the committee secretary. At a departmental and administrative level the support of Paul Ballantine, Irene Joseph, Irene Edgar and Donna Heslop-Williams has also been extremely helpful. Thanks also to Jody Cowper-James for help in checking referencing and formatting. Finally, we would like to convey our thanks to Yong Ling Lam, Samantha Phua and Aletheia Heah of Taylor & Francis in Singapore for their encouragement and support for the book.

Michael Hall
Sanna Malinen
Rob Vosslamber
Russell Wordsworth

Part I
Context

1 Introduction

The business, organisational and destination impacts of natural disasters – the Christchurch earthquakes 2010–2011

C. Michael Hall, Sanna Malinen,
Rob Vosslamber and Russell Wordsworth

Introduction

A disaster is 'a serious disruption of the functioning of a community or a society involving widespread human, material, economic or environmental losses and impacts, which exceeds the ability of the affected community or society to cope with its own resources' (UN International Strategy for Disaster Reduction (UNISDR) 2009: 9). Disasters have always been significant for economies and societies. However, population growth, economic change and restructuring, increased urbanisation which attracts more people and leads to greater infrastructure growth, and environmental change have all served to make the threats posed by natural disasters greater than ever (Pelling 2003; Swiss Re 2014). According to Swiss Re (2015a), there were more natural catastrophe events in 2014 than in any single year yet recorded in the period 1970–2014. Concurrently, economic development, population growth, a higher concentration of assets in exposed areas and a changing climate are increasing the economic cost of natural disasters (Swiss Re 2015a: 8).

Yet despite the growing literature on natural disasters and disaster management and impact (e.g. Cavallo et al. 2013; Meyer et al. 2013; North and Pfefferbaum 2013; Lazzaroni and van Bergeijk 2014), especially at a time of increasing concern with respect to global environmental change (Hall 2013, 2015; Neumayer et al. 2014), there is a relative paucity of literature on the business and broader organisational dimensions of natural disasters and the following response and recovery stages (McManus et al. 2008; Corey and Deitch 2011; De Mel et al. 2012; Park et al. 2013). This book is, in part, a response to some of the 'unanswered questions' of the relationship between business and disasters (Webb et al. 2000: 83). It addresses the call for studies that explore how disaster creates impact and business recovery varies across and within sectors and firms, while some of the chapters also take a more longitudinal research on businesses and organisations in the context of disaster.

This book provides research on the business, organisation and destination impacts of post-disaster environments from multiple perspectives. The research reported in this volume was undertaken in the post-disaster context following the earthquakes which struck between September 2010 and December 2011 in Canterbury, New Zealand, causing severe damage to the city of Christchurch. However, the various chapters do not just treat the Christchurch experience in isolation, but seek to relate local research to the international research literature and agenda. Although the focus is primarily on business and organisations, the research is not approached through a narrow lens. Clear connections are also made to broader community and governance issues as well as marketing, strategy and planning and wider concerns regarding disaster resilience (Patton and Johnson 2001). Therefore, as well as seeking to understand what businesses and organisations do in post-disaster situations, the book also indicates how some of the disciplinary approaches and frames used within business studies can also help inform our knowledge of natural disasters and their impacts.

This chapter provides an introduction to the book and is divided into three sections. The first section provides a broad overview of some of the literature on natural disasters and positions some of the business and organisation-related contributions to the literature. The second section then briefly outlines the impacts of the Canterbury earthquake sequence and why it is significant not just for Christchurch and New Zealand but in an international context. The final part of chapter then provides an outline of the book.

Researching natural disasters: an overview

Notwithstanding the argument that 'there is no such thing as a natural disaster' (Hartman and Squires 2006; Mora 2009: 101), in the sense that the effects of a disaster are a product of social, economic and environmental vulnerabilities as well as natural hazards (Blaikie et al. 1994), a natural disaster may be defined as:

> . . . a serious disruption to a community or region caused by the impact of a naturally occurring rapid onset event that threatens or causes death, injury or damage to property or the environment and which requires significant and coordinated multi-agency and community response. Such serious disruption can be caused by any one, or a combination, of the following natural hazards: bushfire; earthquake; flood; storm; cyclone; storm surge; landslide; tsunami; meteorite strike; or tornado.
> (Council of Australian Governments 2004: 4)

In addition to the examples noted above, other types of disaster events often included in international disaster databases or studies, as well as in lay people's understanding of a natural disaster, include drought, epidemics, extreme temperatures, insect infestations, volcanic eruptions, wildfires and windstorms (Cornall 2005; Leroy 2006; Bellamere 2015). Nevertheless, for the purposes of this book it is useful to distinguish between a natural hazard, which is a geophysical, atmospheric or hydrological event (e.g. earthquake, landslide, tsunami, flood or drought) that has the potential to cause harm or loss, and a disaster which is 'the occurrence of an extreme hazard event that impacts on communities causing damage, disruption and casualties, and leaving the affected communities unable to function normally without outside assistance' (Benson and Twigg 2007: 126). An earthquake event fits into both categories; the difference between the two is that in the latter the potential of a natural hazard to cause severe harm and loss has actually happened. As Leroy (2006) emphasises, natural hazards are an integral part of life on Earth. The disaster element, which includes measurable human and economic costs (e.g. death, infrastructure destruction, cultural impact, financial loss) is more a function of vulnerable people and systems than severity in the natural hazard. Yet use of terminology clearly is extremely important as it arguably affects whether a disaster is regarded as "natural" – or not – and the responses to it, while the human dimension of disasters also highlights the importance of a social science perspective on disaster, risk and natural hazards.

One of the difficulties in assessing the impacts of natural disasters is that the definition being used can change according to the aim of the study (Petrucci 2012). However, the notion of impact is broadly understood as including the direct, indirect and intangible economic, environmental and social losses caused by a natural disaster event (Lindell and Prater 2003; Swiss Re 2014). Direct losses include physical effects such as destruction and changes that reduce the functionality of an individual, system or structure. This includes damage to people (death/injury), buildings, their contents, as well as clean-up and disposal costs. Indirect losses include the effects of disrupted or damaged utility services and local businesses, including loss of revenue; cost increases; expenses connected to the provision of assistance, such as lodging, food and drinking water; and costs associated with the need to drive longer distances because of blocked or damaged roads. Intangible losses include psychological impairments caused by both direct and intangible losses that individuals personally suffer during the disaster and over the longer-term (Petrucci 2012).

In examining the disaster literature it is useful to distinguish between the effects of crisis events arising from the human system, such as economic and financial crises, or the impacts of rapid economic or regulatory change on the one hand, and those arising from natural hazards on the other (Hall 2010). Of course, the two may be interrelated, and some of their effects – and human and political responses – may be similar (Gotham and Greenberg 2008, 2014; see Amore and Hall, Chapter 12, this volume).

Table 1.1 presents a lexical analysis of the titles, abstracts and keywords in the Scopus bibliographic database for the period 1974–2014 for journal articles and reviews related to natural disasters. The table illustrates the substantial growth of publications on natural disasters and associated themes with relevance for the present book. According to the Scopus disciplinary categories the natural disaster literature is dominated by the medical and health sciences, which accounts for approximately a third of journal publication output with the natural sciences accounting for slightly less. Engineering accounts for just under 10 per cent of all outputs. Just under 20 per cent of publications are described as social science.

Table 1.1 Lexical analysis of abstract, keywords and title of articles and reviews in Scopus related to natural disasters 1975–2014

Term	1975–1979	%	1980–1984	%	1985–1989	%	1990–1994	%	1995–1999	%	2000–2004	%	2005–2009	%	2010–2014	%	Total	%
Natural Disaster	172	100	237	100	363	100	792	100	1 024	100	1 894	100	4 701	100	4 494	100	13 677	100
Management	15	8.7	40	16.9	85	23.4	258	32.6	232	22.7	562	29.7	1 536	32.7	1 423	31.7	4 151	30.4
Planning	24	14.0	59	24.9	81	22.3	221	27.9	239	23.3	335	17.7	1 138	24.2	702	15.6	2 799	20.5
Economy	15	8.7	23	9.7	29	8.0	79	10.0	152	14.8	249	13.1	616	13.1	887	19.7	2 050	15.0
Organisation	13	7.6	34	14.3	82	22.6	235	29.7	173	16.9	272	14.4	959	20.4	499	11.1	2 267	16.6
Vulnerability/Vulnerable	2	1.2	3	1.3	8	2.2	20	2.5	75	7.3	172	9.1	421	9.0	645	14.4	1 346	9.8
Strategy	0	0.0	4	1.7	14	3.9	32	4.0	39	3.8	151	8.0	376	8.0	494	11.0	1 110	8.1
Rebuild/recovery	6	3.5	6	2.5	6	1.7	23	2.9	47	4.6	112	5.9	401	8.5	403	9.0	1 004	7.3
Business	0	0.0	1	0.4	1	0.3	8	1.0	15	1.5	30	1.6	243	5.2	372	8.3	670	4.9
Resilience	0	0.0	0	0.0	0	0.0	0	0.0	5	0.5	22	1.2	96	2.0	278	6.2	401	2.9
Consumer/customer	0	0.0	1	0.4	1	0.3	5	0.6	9	0.9	16	0.8	74	1.6	75	1.7	181	1.3
Accounting	0	0.0	0	0.0	1	0.3	2	0.3	3	0.3	5	0.3	37	0.8	47	1.0	95	0.7
Marketing	0	0.0	0	0.0	0	0.0	3	0.4	2	0.4	11	0.6	20	0.4	20	0.4	56	0.4

Note: Data from Scopus obtained 1 August 2015.

However, business, management and accounting are the focus of less than four per cent of publications, and economic, econometrics and finance less than three per cent. Although these categories are not mutually exclusive, they do provide some idea of the relative disciplinary emphasis in natural disaster studies.

A more detailed analysis of journal articles and reviews related to natural disasters also highlights the use of business studies–related terms in abstracts, keywords and titles, and the relative mismatch between the terminology used and the actual contribution from business studies. For example, almost a third of all publications mention management. However, the vast majority of these, including the very highly cited papers (with the notable exception of Kleindorfer and Saad (2005) on supply chain disruption risk), do not focus on business management. Where management is an issue, papers tend to examine the activities of disaster relief organisations and operations. Similarly, there is a significant mismatch between recognition of the economic significance of natural disasters and publications either by economists or in economics and finance journals, although influential papers here include those of Kahn (2005), Skidmore and Toya (2002) and Noy (2009). Nevertheless, much of the extant economic literature on natural disasters tends to examine national and regional implications rather than the activities of individual businesses or sectors (although see Xiao (2011) for a study of the local economic impact of a disaster). Cavallo and Noy (2011) provide a review of the economic literature on disasters, as do the valuable integrative papers by Klomp and Valckx (2014), and Lazzaroni and van Bergeijk (2014). Similar disciplinary gaps also occur in the study of organisations and strategy in natural disasters (Fussell and Elliott 2009), where much of the literature is not informed by research in organisational studies or business strategy (but notable exceptions include Chopra and Sodhi (2004) on supply chain breakdown, Birkland (1998) on agenda setting, and Mitroff and Alpaslan (2003) and Vargo and Seville (2011) on corporate strategy and preparedness in response to disasters).

In addition to some of the papers previously noted, especially with respect to supply chain security and natural disasters, business research has been focussed on risk (e.g. Sarasvathy et al. 1998); and on business vulnerability, recovery and survival (e.g. Dahlhamer and Tierney 1998; Chang and Falit-Baiamonte, 2002; Webb et al. 2002; Zolin and Kropp 2007; Zhang et al. 2009; Asgary et al. 2012; Xiao and van Zandt 2012; Atkinson and Sapat 2014; Xiao and Peacock 2014; Marshall et al. 2015), including mobility and relocation (Wasileski et al. 2011). Several papers also have a specific focus on small business and natural disasters, including Runyan (2006) on specific barriers faced, Yoshida and Deyle (2005) on determinants of hazard mitigation, and Brewton et al. (2010) on family firm resilience.

Despite calls for a crisis-based view of the firm, and of small business in particular (Herbane 2010), there is only a limited connection between business response to natural disasters and the innovation and entrepreneurship literature (Johannisson and Olaison 2007; Chamlee-Wright and Storr 2010). Arguably, some of this relationship is being approached via the increased interest in business, organisational and supply-chain resilience in the context of crises and natural disasters (e.g. McManus et al. 2008; Lam et al. 2009; Ponomarov and Holcomb 2009; Brewton et al. 2010; Parsons 2010; Burnard and Bhamra 2011; Sullivan-Taylor and Branicki 2011; Biggs, Ban, et al. 2012; Biggs, Hall, et al. 2012; Orchiston 2013; Miles et al. 2015).

Marketing and consumer behaviour has surprisingly small presence in the literature on natural disasters, especially given the potential role of social marketing in understanding how people perceive disasters and in communicating disaster-related information (Guion et al. 2007; Baker 2009; Baker et al. 2014; Hall 2014; Okazaki et al. 2015), post-disaster actions (Raggio and Folse 2011), and better understanding business networking and disaster-induced crises (Grewal et al. 2007). Several papers have examined issues of loss and consumer response (e.g. DeLorme et al. 2004; Sneath et al. 2009; Kennett-Hensel et al. 2012), while there is also growing interest in post-disaster consumer agency (e.g. Pavia and Mason 2014).

As this brief overview of some of the key themes in the business and natural disaster literature has indicated, there are a number of areas where business disciplines have contributed to understanding post-disaster recovery and the impacts of disasters on business. Increasingly this literature is also starting to intersect with some of the wider environmental and social science literature, and with debates on vulnerability, resilience and risk (O'Brien et al. 2004; O'Brien et al. 2007; Turner 2010; Hayward 2013; Cutter et al. 2014). This is especially due to concerns not only about emerging natural hazards, such as climate change, and the reality of increased global business and economic interconnectedness, but also changes in governance and the perceived role that business may have in disaster preparedness and post-disaster recovery (Gotham and Greenberg 2014). Therefore, this volume seeks to add to the literature and debates through a range of analyses of the post-disaster situation in Christchurch, New Zealand. However, before introducing the contents of the volume, it is appropriate to briefly outline the impacts of the 2010–2011 earthquakes.

The impacts of the Canterbury earthquake sequence 2010–2011

The first of the earthquakes in Canterbury sequence struck at 4.35am on 4 September 2010 with its epicentre approximately 40 kilometres west of the city of Christchurch near the town of Darfield. This first earthquake measured 7.1 on the Richter scale, with intense shaking lasting for approximately 40 seconds. The Darfield Earthquake (as it became known) caused widespread damage and business disruption across the Canterbury region; however, surprisingly, given its relative proximity to urban areas, no lives were lost in this initial event. In the four months remaining in 2011 the Darfield earthquake was followed by several hundred aftershocks, the most significant of these being the 'Boxing Day' earthquake on 26 December 2011 which, while only measuring a magnitude of 4.9 on the Richter scale, was centred beneath the CBD (Central Business District) and resulted in additional damage to the city's infrastructure and the temporary closure of the CBD.

Then on 22 February 2011 at 12.51pm, the city of Christchurch was struck by another major aftershock centred directly beneath the CBD at a very shallow depth of five kilometres. Although measuring only magnitude 6.3 on the Richter scale, the peak ground acceleration of 2.2g was the highest ever recorded in the world and four times that experienced in the Haiti earthquake. Unlike the September 2011 earthquake, this event resulted in enormous devastation and loss of life.

Apart from the tragic loss of 185 lives (associated with the 22 February 2011 event), the earthquake sequence had a significant and sustained impact on organisations and individuals in the Canterbury region. Large-scale devastation of the CBD of Christchurch meant that most inner-city businesses had to relocate their operations either temporarily or permanently, since 50 per cent of the buildings in the CBD were severely damaged. Over 3,000 businesses in the CBD, along with their 50,000 employees, were either permanently or temporarily displaced. Nearly a third of CBD businesses were unable to operate in the six-month period immediately following the February 2011 earthquake. Key infrastructure around the region was also significantly damaged, interrupting water and sewerage, power supply, roading, public transport, and educational systems. The extent of the disaster is indicated by the need to rebuild 895km of roads; damage sustained to 124km of water mains and 300km of sewer pipes, resulting in 30,000 chemical toilets being distributed to households; the partial or complete relocation of twelve schools, resulting in 55 per cent of high school students sharing a school; and damage to recreational facilities across the city, most notably the AMI Stadium, which forced organisers of the 2011 Rugby World Cup to relocate all seven games scheduled for Christchurch to elsewhere in New Zealand. The earthquakes did not have a pronounced impact on the aggregate national economy, with the more significant economic effects found at the regional level. Doyle and Noy (2015) suggest that the earthquakes reduced consumer price index inflation moderately, and the first earthquake had a small, but short-lived, adverse effect on the real gross domestic product growth. There was also a short-term effect on international tourism arrivals, especially with respect to the Japanese and Korean markets, but other events, such as an ash cloud from a volcano in Chile and the Japanese Tōhoku earthquake and tsunami of March 2011, had a much greater effect on visitor arrivals.

Over 100,000 residential houses were damaged and required to be repaired or rebuilt. Of these homes, 7,000 required complete demolition, and the land upon which the property stood was 'red zoned' (a term used to describe land which is so badly damaged that it is likely to take a prolonged period of time before it can be built on again). As a result a large-scale urban relocation took place in parts of Christchurch. An estimated 400,000 insurance claims were lodged with the Earthquake Commission (EQC), a Crown Entity established to provide natural disaster insurance for residential property (contents, dwellings and some coverage of land). By the end of 2014, over 93 per cent of these claims had been settled. However, the rebuilding and repair of homes and other infrastructure continues to this day.

As a result of damage to residential dwellings, many families had to leave their homes either temporarily or permanently, with over one-third of Christchurch residents changing address at least once between September 2010 and September 2014. In terms of population displacement, the Canterbury Earthquake Recovery Authority (CERA) estimates that within the first week after the February 2011 earthquake, approximately 55,000 residents left the city, although the majority of these returned following a short period away. Over the longer term Statistics New Zealand estimates that the population of Christchurch decreased by approximately 3.5 per cent, or 13,500 people, in the two years from June 2010 to June 2012 (CERA 2014b), but it has since recovered, partly due to employment opportunities as a result of the post-disaster rebuild.

It is important to highlight the sustained nature of the earthquake and aftershock sequence that characterised the Canterbury earthquakes. Unlike many earthquakes, which have a significant initial quake and then a short period of aftershocks, the Canterbury aftershock sequence continued for several years and included numerous significant earthquakes. By mid-2014 the region had experienced over 13,000 aftershocks, of which 55 were above magnitude 5 and 496 above magnitude 4 on the Richter Scale. The ongoing aftershocks resulted in increased uncertainty for insurers and underwriters, delaying insurance settlements and rebuild processes. This sustained disruption to businesses and households had a significant impact on employment levels in the region. A 2011 study by the then Department of Labour indicated that of 1,750 employers interviewed, 28 per cent experienced difficulties in retaining employees due to the earthquakes (Department of Labour 2011). This figure rose to nearly 50 per cent for larger organisations (those employing 50 or more employees). Figures from the New Zealand Inland Revenue Department (IRD) for the period following the February 2011 earthquake showed that more than 1,000 employees left the region each month for six consecutive months (see Wordsworth and Nilakant, Chapter 4, this volume). The extent to which these departures were voluntary cannot be discerned from the IRD data, and there is no publicly available information on voluntary turnover rates for the period following the earthquakes. Anecdotal evidence suggests, however, that for several large employers in the region, such as the Canterbury District Health Board (Robertson 2012), Christchurch City Council (Cairns 2012), and the University of Canterbury (Mathews 2012), voluntary turnover rates increased in the first two years following the earthquakes.

The ongoing earthquake sequence also had a significant impact on the mental wellbeing of the city's residents. CERA's Canterbury Wellbeing Index, which uses multiple indicators to track individual wellbeing and social recovery, demonstrated that immediate increases in stress, anxiety and uncertainty due to the earthquakes themselves were compounded by ongoing housing problems, delayed property repairs and insurance settlements, and loss of social networks, which kept stress levels in the region at highly elevated levels for a sustained period. Prior to the September 2010 earthquake, 90–95 per cent of Canterbury residents reported having a good or extremely good quality of life. In 2014 this figure had fallen to 74 per cent (CERA 2014a). Data from the Canterbury

Wellbeing Index suggests that stress resulting from earthquake-related issues peaked in 2012 and dropped significantly by the end of 2014, although for many residents day-to-day life remains difficult.

While recovery is evident, it is far from complete. By September 2014, residents of Christchurch City still perceived their quality of life to be lower than that outside of the city (such as in the neighbouring Selwyn and Waimakariri districts), and over a fifth of residents reported feeling stressed most or all of the time (CERA 2014a). The combined impact of continuous aftershocks, and the dislocation and relocation of businesses, homes and schools, is arguably yet to be fully realised. Evidence suggests that mental health issues are still of concern (Spittlehouse et al. 2014), and new challenges such as traffic disruption and noise are emerging as the rebuild continues. Some employees are likely to be unwilling to return to the CBD, particularly to multi-storey buildings, posing yet further challenges to both employers and employees. Although the earthquakes lasted seconds, the recovery and rebuilding of Canterbury will take many years.

The above synopsis does not, and cannot, fully capture the complexity of the circumstances endured by the residents, organisations and businesses of Canterbury. It does, however, provide an overview of the salient features of the post-crisis context which served to delimit the timing, design and parameters of the research context of the chapters in this book.

Outline of the book

This book is not the first set of publications to emerge on the Christchurch earthquakes. As of the time of writing (August 2015) there had been 444 refereed articles or reviews that specifically referred to the earthquakes in their title, abstract or keywords, with undoubtedly more to come as the evaluation of the earthquake and post-disaster effects occur in a range of different fields. Of the journal literature over half was from the earth and planetary sciences, well over a quarter from engineering and just under a quarter from medicine, nursing and psychology. Much of the business and organisation literature that has emerged on the impacts of the earthquakes has focused on issues of disruption, resilience and recovery (e.g. Bowden 2011; Fischer-Smith 2013; Whitman et al. 2013; Brown et al. 2014; Nilakant et al. 2014; Whitman et al. 2014; Kachali et al. 2015); and address themes that emerge throughout the chapters of this book. Changed work (Donnelly and Proctor-Thompson 2015) and consumer practices (Ballantine et al. 2014) have also been one of the effects of the loss of CBD offices and retail, with these themes taken up by Finsterwalder and Gray (Chapter 9, this volume) in particular. Issues of accounting and natural disasters have been addressed by Miley and Read (2013) in a comparative historical context, but Vosslamber (Chapter 14, this volume) focuses more on the immediate implications of the Christchurch earthquakes for insurance and accounting. Similarly, Noy (2015) also places the impacts of the Christchurch experience into a comparative context.

This book is divided into three main sections which reflect some of the key themes that emerge out of research on the impacts of the Christchurch earthquakes and natural disasters in general. The first section, on business and organisational responses and relationships, has six chapters that examine a range of issues. Chapter 2 by de Vries and Hamilton poses the obvious question of 'Why stay?' with respect to small firms following the earthquakes and uses this as a means of introducing the reader to broader issues of resilience. Chapter 3 by Nilakant et al. takes a wider perspective to look at organisational response, thereby also helping the reader gain an appreciation of the post-quake actions of public agencies as well as private firms. Chapter 4 by Wordsworth and Nilakant examines the individual-level impacts of the earthquakes on employees' decisions to remain in or leave their employment. Chapters 5 and 6 discuss the strategies and actions of cultural services organisations, which are a significant part of Christchurch's economy, especially for tourism. Antara et al. examine organisational recovery strategies (Chapter 5) and Amore provides a case study of changes at the city's Arts Centre and how the earthquakes hastened pre-existing development trajectories (Chapters 6). The final chapter of the section by Prayag and Orchiston (Chapter 7) provides a comparative account of business sector resilience and earthquake response.

The second section discusses consumer and communication responses to the earthquakes. Chapter 8 by Morrish et al. provides a case study of the effect of the earthquakes on consumer–brand relationships, in this case Marmite (an iconic New Zealand brand), while Chapter 9 by Finsterwalder and Grey is a case study of relationship marketing in the retail sector. In Chapter 10 Prayag uses the lens of dark tourism to discuss how particular locations are important for Christchurch residents' post-earthquake coping strategies. Chapter 11 by Mills concludes the section by looking at the important role of informal communication in the earthquake aftermath.

The third section discusses what general lessons might be learned from "the new normal", the terminology that was adopted following the February 2011 earthquake which bought such damage to the city (McColl and Burkle 2012). Chapter 12 by Amore and Hall discusses the nature of the Christchurch rebuild and the government's regeneration strategy and its similarity to other economic regeneration strategies around the world. Chapter 13 by Amore further develops the regeneration theme and discusses the role of heritage buildings in the rebuild, which is also a major focus of recovery programmes elsewhere in the world. In the aftermath of the earthquakes Chapter 14 by Vosslamber looks at financial statement disclosures concerning insurance cover for disasters, noting that it would help users of such statements to assess the ability of an organisation to endure the shock of a disaster. The last chapter in this section by Finsterwalder and Hall discusses how transitional servicescapes have become an important part of the urban regeneration process.

Two more chapters conclude the book. Chapter 16 by Hall et al. provides an account of the research issues that arise from working in a post-disaster setting and brings together a number of the research challenges that the authors faced. In the final chapter Hall discusses the different ways in which disaster ecology and post-disaster resilience are framed and how they need to be better informed by the ecological systems understanding of resilience from which they originated. According to Hall, such an approach has potentially significant implications for future business and organisational studies on natural disasters.

Conclusion

The Christchurch post-disaster experience is important not just in a regional or national setting but also internationally. Three main reasons can be provided. First, as of mid-2015 the cost from the Christchurch earthquake for the insurance sector was put at USD$17.2 billion for the February 2011 event and close to USD$25 billion for all three major earthquake events combined (Swiss Re 2015b). This cost 'took the insurance industry by surprise. Over the last 50 years, the only higher earthquake related insurance losses globally have been those from the 9.0 M event in Japan in 2011 (USD$37.7 billion indexed to 2013) and the 6.7 M event in Northridge (California) in 1994 (USD$22.9 billion indexed to 2013)' (Swiss Re 2015b: 1). The lesson of the Christchurch experience for insurers, and extending to governments and businesses in other jurisdictions, is that a relatively small natural hazard event (by global standards) in a developed country can cause exceptional levels of damage and cost. Moreover, 'a small magnitude earthquake could hit virtually anywhere and trigger unexpectedly large losses . . . It is possible that Christchurch is not an exception but that similar loss developments beyond current risk perceptions could also happen in other cities' (Swiss Re 2015b: 5). Worldwide seismic risk in city centres is underestimated by the insurance industry (Swiss Re 2015b), and therefore almost certainly by business and government as well.

A second important aspect of the book is that it is part of a slowly emerging set of more comprehensive studies of post-disaster recovery that examine a specific urban location, e.g. the extensive writing on post-Katrina New Orleans (e.g. Gotham and Greenberg 2014; Fields et al. 2015; Gotham 2015; Hobor 2015; Tierney 2015). However, the present book differs from some of these other studies because although there are some comparative elements, especially with respect to regeneration strategies, this volume has a much stronger business and organisational emphasis. Indeed, this last factor is arguably a further significant aspect of the book as it not only adds to the literature on how business responds to natural disasters, but also provides examples of the range of topics that business and management researchers can bring to the wider natural disaster literature, especially in urban situations.

Finally, although this book has a business and organisation focus, we cannot forget that business and other organisations should not, indeed cannot, exist in isolation from the communities in which they are embedded. From a resilience perspective it is vital that not only governments seek to enhance the wellbeing of all the citizens that they serve, but that business does as well. In focusing on businesses and organisations we are therefore trying to better understand one dimension, among several, that will better promote public wellbeing and the common good, and reduce vulnerability to future natural hazards. We hope that this book will be one small step towards achieving this goal.

References

Asgary, A., Anjum, M. I. and Azimi, N. (2012) 'Disaster recovery and business continuity after the 2010 flood in Pakistan: Case of small businesses', *International Journal of Disaster Risk Reduction*, 2: 46–56.

Atkinson, C. L. and Sapat, A. K. (2014) 'Hurricane Wilma and long-term business recovery in disasters: The role of local government procurement and economic development', *Journal of Homeland Security and Emergency Management*, 11(1): 169–192.

Baker, S. M. (2009) 'Vulnerability and resilience in natural disasters: A marketing and public policy perspective', *Journal of Public Policy & Marketing*, 28(1): 114–123.

Baker, S. M., Hill, R. P., Baker, C. N. and Mittelstaedt, J. D. (2014) 'Improvisational provisioning in disaster the mechanisms and meanings of ad hoc marketing exchange systems in community', *Journal of Macromarketing*, doi:0276146714550994

Ballantine, P. W., Zafar, S. and Parsons, A. G. (2014) 'Changes in retail shopping behaviour in the aftermath of an earthquake', *International Review of Retail, Distribution and Consumer Research*, 24(1): 1–13.

Bellemare, M. F. (2015) 'Rising food prices, food price volatility, and social unrest', *American Journal of Agricultural Economics*, 97(1): 1–21.

Benson, C. and Twigg, J. with Rossetto, T. (2007) *Tools for Mainstreaming Disaster Risk Reduction: Guidance Notes for Development Organisations*. International Federation of Red Cross and Red Crescent Societies, Geneva: ProVention Consortium.

Biggs, D., Ban, N. and Hall, C. M. (2012) 'Lifestyle values, resilience, and nature-based tourism's contribution to conservation on Australia's Great Barrier Reef', *Environmental Conservation*, 39(4), 370–379.

Biggs, D., Hall, C. M. and Stoeckl, N. (2012) 'The resilience of formal and informal tourism enterprises to disasters – reef tourism in Phuket', *Journal of Sustainable Tourism*, 20(5): 645–665.

Birkland, T. A. (1998) 'Focusing events, mobilization, and agenda setting', *Journal of Public Policy*, 18(1): 53–74.

Blaikie, P., Cannon, T., Davis, I. and Wisner, B. (1994) *At Risk: Natural Hazards, People's Vulnerability and Disasters*, London: Routledge.

Bowden, S. (2011) 'Aftershock: Business relocation decisions in the wake of the February 2011 Christchurch earthquake', *Journal of Management & Organization*, 17(6): 857–863.

Brewton, K. E., Danes, S. M., Stafford, K. and Haynes, G. W. (2010) 'Determinants of rural and urban family firm resilience', *Journal of Family Business Strategy*, 1(3): 155–166.

Brown, C., Stevenson, J., Giovinazzi, S., Seville, E. and Vargo, J. (2014) 'Factors influencing impacts on and recovery trends of organisations: Evidence from the 2010/2011 Canterbury earthquakes', *International Journal of Disaster Risk Reduction*, doi:10.1016/j.ijdrr.2014.11.009

Burnard, K. and Bhamra, R. (2011) 'Organisational resilience: Development of a conceptual framework for organisational responses', *International Journal of Production Research*, 49(8), 5581–5599.

Cairns, L. (2012) 'Marryatt defends extra council leave', *The Press*, 15 November. Online. Available HTTP: <http://www.stuff.co.nz/the-press/news/7951478/Marryatt-defends-extra-council-leave>.

Canterbury Earthquake Recovery Authority (CERA) (2014a) *Canterbury Wellbeing Index: Mental Wellbeing*. Christchurch: CERA.

——(2014b) *Canterbury Wellbeing Index: Population*. Christchurch: CERA.

Cavallo, E., Galiani, S., Noy, I. and Pantano, J. (2013) 'Catastrophic natural disasters and economic growth', *Review of Economics and Statistics*, 95(5): 1549–1561.

Cavallo, E. and Noy, I. (2011) 'Natural disasters and the economy – A survey', *International Review of Environmental and Resource Economics*, 5(1): 63–102.

Chamlee-Wright, E. and Henry Storr, V. H. (eds.) (2010) *The Political Economy of Hurricane Katrina and Community Rebound*, Cheltenham: Edward Elgar.

Chang, S. E. and Falit-Baiamonte, A. (2002) 'Disaster vulnerability of businesses in the 2001 Nisqually earthquake', *Environmental Hazards*, 4(2–3): 59–71.

Chopra, S. and Sodhi, M. S. (2004) 'Managing risk to avoid: Supply-chain breakdown', *MIT Sloan Management Review*, 46(1): 53–61, 87.

Corey, C. M. and Deitch, E. A. (2011) 'Factors affecting business recovery immediately after Hurricane Katrina', *Journal of Contingencies and Crisis Management*, 19(3): 169–181.

Cornall, R. (2005) 'New levels of government responsiveness for 'all-hazards': The management of natural disasters and emergencies', *Australian Journal of Public Administration*, 64(2): 27–30.

Council of Australian Governments (2004) *Natural Disasters in Australia*, produced by the Australian Government Department of Transport and Regional Services on behalf of the Council of Australian Governments (COAG), Canberra: Commonwealth of Australia, High Level Group on the Review of Natural Disaster Relief and Mitigation Arrangements.

Cutter, S. L., Ash, K. D. and Emrich, C. T. (2014) 'The geographies of community disaster resilience', *Global Environmental Change*, 29: 65–77.

Dahlhamer, J. M. and Tierney, K. J. (1998) 'Rebounding from disruptive events: Business recovery following the Northridge earthquake', *Sociological Spectrum*, 18(2): 121.

DeLorme, D. E., Zinkhan, G. M. and Hagen, S. C. (2004) 'The process of consumer reactions to possession threats and losses in a natural disaster', *Marketing Letters*, 15(4): 185–199.

De Mel, S., McKenzie, D. and Woodruff, C. (2012) 'Enterprise recovery following natural disasters', *The Economic Journal*, 122(559): 64–91.

Department of Labour (2011) *A Changing Landscape: The Impact of the Earthquakes on Christchurch Workplaces*, Wellington: Department of Labour.

Donnelly, N. and Proctor-Thomson, S. B. (2015) 'Disrupted work: home-based teleworking (HbTW) in the aftermath of a natural disaster', *New Technology, Work and Employment*, 30(1): 47–61.

Doyle, L. and Noy, I. (2015) 'The short-run nationwide macroeconomic effects of the Canterbury earthquakes', *New Zealand Economic Papers*, 49(2): 134–156.

Fields, B., Wagner, J. and Frisch, M. (2015) 'Placemaking and disaster recovery: Targeting place for recovery in post-Katrina New Orleans', *Journal of Urbanism: International Research on Placemaking and Urban Sustainability*, 8(1): 38–56.

Fischer-Smith, R. (2013) 'The Earthquake Support Subsidy for Christchurch's small and medium enterprises: Perspectives from business owners', *Small Enterprise Research*, 20(1): 40–54.

Fussell, E. and Elliott, J. R. (2009) 'Introduction: social organization of demographic responses to disaster: studying population – environment interactions in the case of Hurricane Katrina', *Organization & Environment*, 22(4): 379–394.

Gotham, K. F. (2015) Limitations, legacies, and lessons post-Katrina rebuilding in retrospect and prospect. *American Behavioral Scientist*, 59(10): 1314–1326.

Gotham, K. F. and Greenberg, M. (2008) 'From 9/11 to 8/29: post-disaster recovery and rebuilding in New York and New Orleans', *Social Forces*, 87: 1039–1062.

——(2014) *Crisis Cities: Disaster and Redevelopment in New York and New Orleans*, Oxford: Oxford University Press.

Grewal, R., Johnson, J. L. and Sarker, S. (2007) 'Crises in business markets: Implications for interfirm linkages', *Journal of the Academy of Marketing Science*, 35(3): 398–416.

Guion, D. T., Scammon, D. L. and Borders, A. L. (2007) 'Weathering the storm: A social marketing perspective on disaster preparedness and response with lessons from Hurricane Katrina', *Journal of Public Policy & Marketing*, 26(1): 20–32.

Hall, C. M. (2010) 'Crisis events in tourism: Subjects of crisis in tourism', *Current Issues in Tourism*, 13(5): 401–417.

——(2013) 'Climate change and human security: The individual and community response', in M. Redclift and M. Grasso (eds.) *Handbook on Climate Change and Human Security*, Cheltenham: Edward Elgar.

——(2014) *Tourism and Social Marketing*, Abingdon: Routledge.

——(2015) 'Global change, islands and sustainable development: Islands of sustainability or analogues of the challenge of sustainable development?', in M. Redclift and D. Springett (eds.) *Routledge International Handbook of Sustainable Development*, Abingdon: Routledge.

Hartman, C. and Squires, G. (eds.) (2006) *There Is No Such Thing as a Natural Disaster: Race, Class, and Hurricane Katrina*, New York: Routledge.

Hayward, B. M. (2013) 'Rethinking resilience: Reflections on the Earthquakes in Christchurch, New Zealand, 2010 and 2011', *Ecology and Society*, 18(4): 37.

Herbane, B. (2010) 'Small business research: Time for a crisis-based view', *International Small Business Journal*, 28(1): 43–64.

Hobor, G. (2015) '"New Orleans" remarkably (un)predictable recovery developing a theory of urban resilience', *American Behavioral Scientist*, 59(10): 1214–1230.

Johannisson, B. and Olaison, L. (2007) 'The moment of truth – reconstructing entrepreneurship and social capital in the eye of the storm', *Review of Social Economy*, 65(1): 55–78.

Kachali, H., Whitman, Z., Stevenson, J., Vargo, J., Seville, E. and Wilson, T. (2015) 'Industry sector recovery following the Canterbury earthquakes', *International Journal of Disaster Risk Reduction*, 12: 42–52.

Kahn, M. E. (2005) 'The death toll from natural disasters: The role of income, geography, and institutions', *Review of Economics and Statistics*, 87(2): 271–284.

Kennett-Hensel, P. A., Sneath, J. Z. and Lacey, R. (2012) 'Liminality and consumption in the aftermath of a natural disaster', *Journal of Consumer Marketing*, 29(1): 52–63.

Kleindorfer, P. R. and Saad, G. H. (2005) 'Managing disruption risks in supply chains', *Production and Operations Management*, 14(1): 53–68.

Klomp, J. and Valckx, K. (2014) 'Natural disasters and economic growth: A meta-analysis', *Global Environmental Change*, 26(1): 183–195.

Lam, N. S., Pace, K., Campanella, R., LeSage, J. and Arenas, H. (2009) 'Business return in New Orleans: Decision making amid post-Katrina uncertainty', *PloS One*, 4(8): 1–10.

Lazzaroni, S. and van Bergeijk, P. A. (2014) 'Natural disasters' impact, factors of resilience and development: A meta-analysis of the macroeconomic literature', *Ecological Economics*, 107: 333–346.

Leroy, S. A. (2006) 'From natural hazard to environmental catastrophe: Past and present', *Quaternary International*, 158: 4–12.

Lindell, M. K. and Prater, C. S. (2003) 'Assessing community impacts of natural disasters', *Natural Hazards Review*, 4(4): 176–185.

Marshall, M., Niehm, L., Sydnor, S. and Schrank, H. (2015) 'Predicting small business demise after a natural disaster: An analysis of pre-existing conditions', *Natural Hazards*, doi:10.1007/s11069-015-1845-0

Mathews, P. (2012) 'Canterbury University's post-quake struggles', *The Press*, 6 October. Online. Available HTTP: <http://www.stuff.co.nz/the-press/news/christchurch-earthquake-2011/7777550/Canterbury-Universitys-post-quake-struggles>.

McColl, G. J. and Burkle, F. M. (2012) 'The new normal: Twelve months of resiliency and recovery in Christchurch', *Disaster Medicine and Public Health Preparedness*, 6(1): 33–43.

McManus, S., Seville, E., Vargo, J. and Brunsdon, D. (2008) 'Facilitated process for improving organizational resilience', *Natural Hazards Review*, 9(2): 81–90.

Meyer, V., Becker, N., Markantonis, V., Schwarze, R., Van den Bergh, J., Bouwer, L., Bubeck, P., Ciavola, P., Genovese, E., Green, C., Hallegatte, S., Kreibich, H., Lequeux, Q., Logar, I., Papyrakis, E., Pfurtscheller, C., Poussin, J., Przyluski, V., Thieken, A. and Viavattene, C. (2013) 'Review article: Assessing the costs of natural hazards–state of the art and knowledge gaps', *Natural Hazards and Earth System Science*, 13(5): 1351–1373.

Miles, M., Lewis, G., Hall-Phillips, A., Morrish, S., Gilmore, A. and Kasouf, C. (2015) 'The influence of entrepreneurial marketing processes and entrepreneurial self-efficacy on community vulnerability, risk, and resilience', *Journal of Strategic Marketing*, doi:10.1080/0965254X.2015.1035038

Miley, F. and Read, A. (2013) 'After the quake: The complex dance of local government, national government and accounting', *Accounting History*, 18(4): 447–471.

Mitroff, I. I. and Alpaslan, M. C. (2003) 'Preparing for evil', *Harvard Business Review*, 81(4): 109–115, 124.

Mora, S. (2009) 'Disasters are not natural: Risk management, a tool for development', in M. Culshaw, H. Reeves, I. Jefferson and T. Spink (eds.) *Engineering Geology for Tomorrow's Cities*. Geological Society, London, Engineering Geology Special Publications, Vol. 22, London: Geological Society.

Neumayer, E., Plümper, T. and Barthel, F. (2014) 'The political economy of natural disaster damage', *Global Environmental Change*, 24: 8–19.

Nilakant, V., Walker, B., van Heugten, K., Baird, R. and de Vries, H. (2014) 'Conceptualising adaptive resilience using grounded theory', *New Zealand Journal of Employment Relations*, 39(1): 79–86.

North, C. S. and Pfefferbaum, B. (2013) 'Mental health response to community disasters: A systematic review', *JAMA The Journal of the American Medical Association*, 310(5): 507–518.

Noy, I. (2009) 'The macroeconomic consequences of disasters', *Journal of Development Economics*, 88(2): 221–231.

——(2015) 'Comparing the direct human impact of natural disasters for two cases in 2011: The Christchurch earthquake and the Bangkok flood', *International Journal of Disaster Risk Reduction*, 13: 61–65.

O'Brien, K., Eriksen, S., Nygaard, L. and Schjolden, A. (2007) 'Why different interpretations of vulnerability matter in climate change discourses', *Climate Policy*, 7: 73–88.

O'Brien, K., Sygna, L. and Haugen, J. (2004) 'Vulnerable or resilient? A multi-scale assessment of climate impacts and vulnerability in Norway', *Climatic Change*, 64: 193–225.

Okazaki, S., Benavent-Climent, A., Navarro, A. and Henseler, J. (2015) 'Responses when the earth trembles: The impact of community awareness campaigns on protective behavior', *Journal of Public Policy & Marketing*, 34(1): 4–18.

Orchiston, C. (2013) 'Tourism business preparedness, resilience and disaster planning in a region of high seismic risk: The case of the Southern Alps, New Zealand', *Current Issues in Tourism*, 16(5): 477–494.

Park, Y., Hong, P. and Roh, J. J. (2013) 'Supply chain lessons from the catastrophic natural disaster in Japan', *Business Horizons*, 56(1): 75–85.

Parsons, D. (2010) 'Organisational resilience', *The Australian Journal of Emergency Management*, 25(2): 18–20.

Paton, D. and Johnston, D. (2001) 'Disasters and communities: Vulnerability, resilience and preparedness', *Disaster Prevention and Management*, 10: 270–277.

Pavia, T. and Mason, M. (2014) 'Vulnerability and physical, cognitive, and behavioral impairment model extensions and open questions', *Journal of Macromarketing*, 34(4): 471–485.

Pelling, M. (ed.) (2003) *Natural Disaster and Development in a Globalizing World*, London: Routledge.

Petrucci, O. (2012) 'Assessment of the impact caused by natural disasters: Simplified procedures and open problems', in J. P. Tiefenbacher (ed.) *Managing Disasters, Assessing Hazards, Emergencies and Disaster Impacts*, INTECH, Open Access Publisher. Online. Available HTTP: <http://www.intechopen.com/books/approaches-to-managing-disaster-assessing-hazards-emergencies-and-disaster-impacts>.

Ponomarov, S. Y. and Holcomb, M. C. (2009) 'Understanding the concept of supply chain resilience', *International Journal of Logistics Management*, 20(1): 124–143.

Raggio, R. D. and Folse, J. (2011) 'Expressions of gratitude in disaster management: An economic, social marketing, and public policy perspective on post-Katrina campaigns', *Journal of Public Policy & Marketing*, 30(2): 168–174.

Robertson, G. (2012) 'DHB staffing turnover up since quake', *Insight*, director K. Brown, Radio New Zealand, Wellington.

Runyan, R. C. (2006) 'Small business in the face of crisis: Identifying barriers to recovery from a natural disaster', *Journal of Contingencies and Crisis Management*, 14(1): 12–26.

Sarasvathy, D. K., Simon, H. A. and Lave, L. (1998) 'Perceiving and managing business risks: Differences between entrepreneurs and bankers', *Journal of Economic Behavior and Organization*, 33(2): 207–225.

Skidmore, M. and Toya, H. (2002) 'Do natural disasters promote long-run growth?', *Economic Inquiry*, 40(4): 664–687.

Sneath, J. Z., Lacey, R. and Kennett-Hensel, P. A. (2009) 'Coping with a natural disaster: Losses, emotions, and impulsive and compulsive buying', *Marketing Letters*, 20(1): 45–60.

Spittlehouse, J. K., Joyce, P., Vierck, E., Schluter, P. and Pearson, J. (2014) 'Ongoing adverse mental health impact of the earthquake sequence in Christchurch, New Zealand', *Australian and New Zealand Journal of Psychiatry*, 48(8): 756–763.

Sullivan-Taylor, B. and Branicki, L. (2011) 'Creating resilient SMEs: Why one size might not fit all', *International Journal of Production Research*, 49(18): 5565–5579.

Swiss Re (2014) *Mind the Risk: A Global Ranking of Cities under Threat from Natural Disasters*, Zurich: Swiss Re.

——(2015a) *Natural Catastrophes and Man-made Disasters in 2014: Convective and Winter Storms Generate Most Losses*, Sigma 2/2015, Zurich: Swiss Re.

——(2015b) *Small Quakes, Big Impact: Lessons Learned from Christchurch*, Zurich: Swiss Re.

Tierney, K. (2015) 'Resilience and the neoliberal project discourses, critiques, practices – and Katrina', *American Behavioral Scientist*, 59(10): 1327–1342.

Turner, B. L. (2010) 'Vulnerability and resilience: Coalescing or paralleling approaches for sustainability science?' *Global Environmental Change*, 20(4): 570–576.

UN International Strategy for Disaster Reduction (UNISDR) (2009) *2009 UNISDR Terminology on Disaster Risk Reduction*, Geneva: UNISDR.

Vargo, J. and Seville, E. (2011) 'Crisis strategic planning for SMEs: Finding the silver lining', *International Journal of Production Research*, 49(18): 5619–5635.

Wasileski, G., Rodríguez, H. and Diaz, W. (2011) 'Business closure and relocation: A comparative analysis of the Loma Prieta earthquake and Hurricane Andrew', *Disasters*, 35(1): 102–129.

Webb, G. R., Tierney, K. J. and Dahlhamer, J. M. (2000) 'Businesses and disasters: Empirical patterns and unanswered questions', *Natural Hazards Review*, 1(2): 83–90.

——(2002) 'Predicting long-term business recovery from disaster: A comparison of the Loma Prieta earthquake and Hurricane Andrew', *Environmental Hazards* 4(2–3): 45–58.

Whitman, Z., Stevenson, J., Kachali, H., Seville, E., Vargo, J. and Wilson, T. (2014) 'Organisational resilience following the Darfield earthquake of 2010', *Disasters*, 38(1): 148–177.

Whitman, Z., Wilson, T., Seville, E., Vargo, J., Stevenson, J., Kachali, H. and Cole, J. (2013) 'Rural organizational impacts, mitigation strategies, and resilience to the 2010 Darfield earthquake, New Zealand', *Natural Hazards*, 69(3): 1849–1875.

Xiao, Y. (2011) 'Local economic impacts of natural disasters', *Journal of Regional Science*, 51(4): 804–820.

Xiao, Y. and Peacock, W. (2014) 'Do hazard mitigation and preparedness reduce physical damage to businesses in disasters? Critical role of business disaster planning', *Natural Hazards Review*, doi:10.1061/(ASCE)NH.1527-6996.0000137, 04014007

Xiao, Y. and van Zandt, S. (2012) 'Building community resiliency: Spatial links between household and business post-disaster return', *Urban Studies*, 49(11): 2523–2542.

Yoshida, K. and Deyle, R. E. (2005) 'Determinants of small business hazard mitigation', *Natural Hazards Review*, 6(1), 1–12.

Zhang, Y., Lindell, M. K. and Prater, C. S. (2009) 'Vulnerability of community businesses to environmental disasters', *Disasters*, 33(1): 38–57.

Zolin, R. and Kropp, F. (2007) 'How surviving businesses respond during and after a major disaster', *Journal of Business Continuity & Emergency Planning*, 1(2): 183–199.

Part II

Business and organisational responses and relationships

2 Why stay?

The resilience of small firms in Christchurch and their owners

Huibert P. de Vries and Robert T. Hamilton

Introduction

The Canterbury earthquakes of 2010 and 2011 and the long series of major after-shocks have had a huge social and economic impact on the people of the region. Some impacts were immediate and dramatic, while others were longer-term reper-cussions. This chapter tracks events four years on from the initial earthquakes.

The chapter contributes to the systematic body of evidence on the fate of small businesses following major natural disasters, those involving 'physical threats and the destruction of property, life and the systems needed for a community to function' (Herbane 2010: 46). It focuses on small firms because, according to Brown (1993, cited in Penrose 2000), up to 80 per cent of businesses without a comprehensive plan may disappear within two years of a major disaster. There is a need to document the reactions and coping mechanisms of small firm owners caught up in disasters, such as the destructive tremor on 22 February 2011 that killed 185 people in Christchurch, destroying most of the central city and much of Christchurch's eastern suburbs.

Literature review

Significant research has been undertaken on alternative approaches to disaster management (Baker 2009), especially on how large firms deal with organisational crises and natural disasters (Pearson and Clair 1998; McEntire, Fuller, Johnston and Weber 2002). However, crisis management in small businesses remains relatively unexplored (Herbane 2010). Understanding the resilience of small business owners in the wake of natural disasters is complex and multi-levelled. Although the two domains of small business and crisis management have exten-sive literatures, Herbane (2010) affirms that their nexus requires closer attention. He reflects on the importance of such research, as crisis must be measured not only in lost revenue but also in terms of the damage to services, local communi-ties, supply chain capacity and business capability. Biggs, Hall and Stoeckl (2014) assert that resilience is an important framework for understanding society's ability to cope with crises. They define resilience as a business's ability to maintain and adapt in the face of disturbance while maintaining its identity (Biggs et al. 2014). Doern (2014) analysed small business owners' resilience during the London riots of 2011. She considered the preparedness and immediate impact of a major crisis, and referred to small business resilience as a mindset that is both anticipatory and containment oriented. However, a major earthquake cannot be anticipated – the Canterbury earthquake sequence was estimated to be a one-in-ten-thousand-year event. Furthermore, depending on the epicentre, depth and magnitude, the implications of 'containment' are also unknown.

Research by Runyan (2006) investigated small business response to the USA's 2005 Hurricane Katrina. He interviewed owners and support agencies within three months of the event and concluded that there is a "double impact" on small business owners who are also local citizens. He concludes that small businesses cannot be prepared for all disasters, which leaves the question: How do small business owners cope? The effects on Britain's small rural tourism firms of the 2001 outbreak of foot and mouth disease are reported in Irvine and Anderson (2004). A longitudinal quantitative study was undertaken with data collected two years apart. They considered the impacts on the local businesses in Grampian and Cumbria and concluded that these were severe but not as bad as anticipated. They argued that media exaggeration was particularly damaging to businesses. Although useful, two quantitative snapshots in time cannot explain the nuances and variability of individual owner/manager experiences and resilience. As Doern (2014) points out, there is a limited understanding of the firm-level experiences of enduring a major unforeseen disaster such as a sequence of strong earthquakes. While hurricanes, floods and even riots can be both foreseen and presumed to be short-lived, earthquake aftershocks can persist for several years.

The closest parallel to the Canterbury earthquakes, and one extensively studied, is the Northbridge earthquake that afflicted the Los Angeles area in January 1994, killing 57 people and damaging some 200,000 homes and 39,000 businesses (Tierney 1997). In a survey conducted some 16 months after this earthquake, 23 per cent of respondent businesses remained worse off relative to their pre-earthquake state; 53 per cent were back to how they were; and 24 per cent were by then in a better condition than they had been pre-quake. Smaller firms were more likely to be in the worst off group because of a loss of customers and/or a local economic recession in their area. The smaller firms were also less well prepared for such a disaster and in a poorer financial condition. Those large firms that were better off were also better prepared and able to benefit from the post-earthquake economic stimulus and a more buoyant local economy. Interestingly, physical damage and local shaking intensity were not associated with business recovery (Dahlhamer and Tierney 1998). The main influence on recovery was the off-site infrastructure damage that affected in particular the movement of goods, staff and customers to and from the business. It was the ancillary damage affecting the ability to trade normally that had the greatest impact on recovery prospects. These prior learnings have informed the present study.

Method

The extant literature provides no detailed accounts of owner-managers' experiences beyond the immediate disaster. We address this using an emergent research design (Charmaz 2008) featuring the owners of eight Christchurch SMEs. The fieldwork was undertaken in 2014, some three years after the most devastating earthquake. These eight businesses are profiled in Figure 2.1. In 2013, four of these businesses were trading on lower sales turnover than in the pre-disaster 2010 financial year [2, 3, 7, 8 – See Figure 2.1], while the other four were trading above their 2010 sales levels [1, 4, 5, 6]. Table 2.1 summarises the situation of these businesses as a consequence of the earthquakes.

Face-to-face interviews identified the how's and why's of the business owner-managers navigation through the immediate survival and longer-term implications for their businesses in Christchurch. The narratives were collected and examined according to four broad analytical questions: (1) What were the consequences of and response to the prominent quake events of 2010–2011? (2) How did business owners restart their businesses? (3) Why have they stayed? (4) What events, changes and learning occurred in these ensuing four years? In applying the emergent approach, we adopted the governing principles of grounded theory to the collection and analysis of data (Glaser and Strauss 1967; Goulding 2005). The transcripts were open coded, line by line, to identify key and repeating properties (Urquhart 2013). Each transcript was subsequently coded to examine similarities and differences (Goulding 2002). A coding template evolved which was then used to form coding trees (de Vries 2008) and subsequent coding categories and the identification of themes. Coding was conducted manually and used NVivo simply as a storage and handling tool, thus also allowing note taking in the form of memos (Glaser 1998). This was followed by further theoretical sampling and data collection to inform and expand on emerging themes (Glaser 1992).

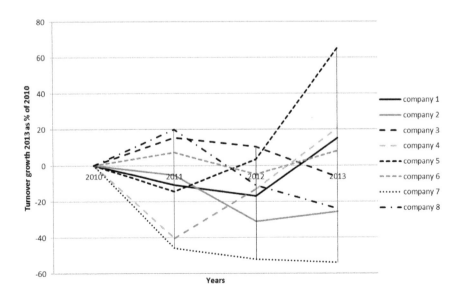

Figure 2.1 Business turnover 2010–2013

Table 2.1 Impact of earthquake

Company	Industry Sector	Firm Age (years, 2010)	Employee numbers (2010)	Physical damage to own premises	Ancillary damage/ ability to trade	Turnover 2013 as % of 2010
1	Manufacturing (B2B)	47	6	Yes	No	+15
2	Retail	24	20	Yes	Yes	−26
3	Manufacturing/ Retail	25	8	No	Yes	−7
4	Hospitality (B2B)	14	3	No	Yes	+21
5	Construction (B2B)	46	98	No	No	+65
6	Retail	10	4	No	No	+8
7	Retail	4	5	Yes	Yes	−54
8	Retail	18	10	No	No	−24

The 2013 recovered companies

The four companies that have recovered their 2010 sales levels are from different sectors: manufacturing, hospitality/wholesale, construction, and retail. Three of these companies suffered no ancillary damage that compromised their ability to operate, but one did: Company 1.

> Very lucky. What we lost was not enough to claim for. Less than our excess. But I will say one thing, that our suppliers were all very good and a number of them came back to us and said we will give you some free stock to cover what you have lost. So between ourselves and the handful of suppliers it minimised a bit of the costs as well. It wasn't a huge amount.
>
> (Company 4)

> Structurally above the ground was fine. There was some liquefaction in the factory and all the guys helped out to clean out the liquefaction and they were pretty much back to work in a couple of days, and we needed to be. They understood that and it was good.
>
> (Company 5)

As opposed to Company 1:

> The warehouse was damaged but operational. However, our main manufacturing building was severely damaged. The concrete slab floor collapsed in many sectors of the factory which meant some of our machines fell over and the rest needed to be re-levelled. Really, the factory was stuffed.

Given the significance of ancillary damage to businesses in earthquakes – for example, as identified in the 1994 Northridge earthquake in California (Dahlhamer and Tierney 1998) – company 4 is a case of unexpected survival. Company 4 is a business to business (B2B) operator supplying the hospitality trade predominantly in the city's central business district, an area laid waste by the February 2011 earthquake. Sales plummeted between 2010 and 2011: 'We lost 50 per cent of our business overnight – well, over the two earthquakes. So it put a lot of pressure on' (see Figure 2.1). What saved this company was the speed with which it changed its business focus by expanding B2B sales outside of Christchurch and expanding their product range to further boost sales – 'For a long time the out-of-town was carrying us through really.' By 2013, sales were at 140 per cent of their 2010 levels and being boosted further by the gradual revitalisation of the central city:

> It's been a whole lot of things I guess. It's been tough but it's been exciting, and it's been fun along the way. I think dealing with hospitality and just seeing it in Christchurch, seen it start from almost scratch and seeing what's happening with some of the bars and restaurants around town is quite exciting.
>
> (Company 4)

Unlike Company 4, Company 1 suffered severe damage to its manufacturing plant and premises, coupled with a downturn in demand from local business clients. They moved quickly into makeshift production facilities and embarked on what became an 18-month legal battle with their insurance company: 'The factory was a complete rebuild but the insurance didn't want to play ball and mucked us around, so after 9 months of getting nowhere we had to get our lawyers involved.' However, this B2B manufacturer resolved the dispute and repaired an existing production facility to meet growing demand from a larger client base as a number of competitors had not survived the disaster. Both of these companies made quick decisions in the immediate aftermath of the earthquakes and then survived long enough to benefit from the eventual upturn in local demand from their business customers.

Neither of Companies 5 or 6 experienced serious physical damage to premises or to their ability to trade. Both were companies that were in the right place at a bad time. Company 5 is a construction business that had been suffering due to the global financial crisis which affected bank lending and commercial building activity:

> The earthquake saved the construction industry throughout New Zealand I believe. We were heading for serious decline in construction and probably building companies would have been downscaling to a huge degree if the earthquake hadn't happened. And also subcontractors, plumbers, painters, brick layers. It was looking quite grim.
>
> (Company 5)

Company 5 initially gained sales from the need to make ongoing urgent repairs and support structures for damaged buildings – some damaged multiple times.

> Engineers came to our office and said what steel have you got lying around as we need to build a structure immediately. Right we've got this, and this,

where previously engineers would use their knowledge to design something, now it was actually designing around what we had sitting there to make it work. We worked day and night to have that up and the end result was that it crumpled around the structure anyway after the next quakes. We had resources and ability and equipment.

(Company 5)

Thereafter it was also able to expand as the rebuild got underway:

The biggest lesson is be prepared. You can't be prepared for the unprecedented action but be able to multi-task and adapt. It's about adaption really and everything all the knowledge we have built up about the business for the last 49 years has suddenly changed. The business model, the costing structures, everything changed overnight. The engineering designs have changed, they have become complex. So the business is the same but the model has changed a bit, and that's for a lot of businesses.

(Company 5)

Company 6 is an electronics retailer who was able to grow sales in the immediate post-quake period:

Pretty much straight away our business boomed. Mainly because a lot of emergency products were being sold. . . . And I think people found that this side of town became the only side of town you could go and get anything. Yeah moved ahead reasonable well.

(Company 6)

Company 6 decided to source and stock the range of emergency products that most people never expected to need: 'We were selling batteries and radios and all sorts of things to the public. And for about a month or so our business probably tripled in customer count and turnover.' What these recovered companies have in common is a sequence of rapid responses to the initial adversity and a determination to survive until the post-disaster recovery gained enough momentum for them to benefit from this.

Updating Figure 2.1 into 2014, the most recent year for which data are available, Company 4's sales were almost double their 2010 level; Company 1 was up 30 per cent on 2010; Company 5 continued to hold revenue up 60 per cent in a local construction sector made more competitive by new entrants; and Company 6 was up around 18 per cent from 2010 sales. It is worth noting that the most successful recoverers (companies 1, 4, 5) were all B2B operators, and this may have facilitated their recovery.

The 2013 non-recovered companies

The sample also included four firms which, in 2013, had not recovered to the level of their 2010 turnovers. The first point to note is that all of these are retailers and so location is critical to how well they perform. Three of the four non-recovering businesses also suffered major ancillary damage that inhibited their ability to trade following the disaster.

> It's a nightmare [roads in Christchurch] and I've just chosen not to care about things I can't control. So it is as bad as it is. In fact one day I left my shop to go to the local school and I had to come back to the mall to get there. So customers who don't want to be bothered have terrible issues and won't be coming here, but I treat it as part of the whole experience.
>
> (Company 2)

In Company 2, the store also had some minor physical damage that was quickly repaired, but in 2012 the entire section of the mall in which the store was located was vacated to allow for major structural repairs. They were forced to move to an unsatisfactory location, with no frontage and very limited space. This caused the drop in sales over the 2011–2012 period. 'We don't have the regular walk-in customers, so we currently rely on existing customers. A very, very, loyal customer base. People I have known for 20 years – it's just how it is.' Thus the business was barely sustainable with the loyal customer base; turnover was down significantly because of the loss of the walk-in customers. They were only able to move back to their original site at the end of 2013. The owner used the 2012–2013 period to restructure the business, reducing costs and retiring debt.

> It's a crazy thing but we have been out of our shop now for 62 weeks and I'm at a point where I am closer to paying my bills than I have ever been in my life. Everything has diminished – business has diminished, wage bill has diminished, rents – quarter of a million dollars per year, and it's gone. And that's net you save out. Our margins are enormously squeezed at the moment because of the competition and parallel import, that sort of thing. There's no margin in the hardware – the good stuff. So I think history will show we had the perfect time to be out of the shop really. If we were still in the damaged shop and paying rent I'd go as far as to say I would be battling by now.
>
> (Company 2)

At the time of writing (late 2014) this owner is still in dispute over some insurance claims.

Company 3 was doing quite well through 2010–2011 but the neighbourhood infrastructure was damaged. In 2013, major road reconstruction commenced outside of his premises, compromising the shop's location and having the expected severe effect on sales and profits.

> They started major road works for the damaged sewers down the main arterial root to our business and right outside our shop. And they did that from January right through June. . . . It cost us a lot of money which is having a negative effect on us at the moment. But I think we will fight back. It was really difficult for customers to come in. They couldn't get to us and even

though we do pride ourselves on the high quality and customers can be quite loyal, that's our challenge now to get our market share back.

(Company 3)

Company 7 was the worst affected by the earthquakes, with its location destroyed and its residential area severely damaged. The owners located a shipping container store on the original site, now levelled, hoping to preserve their location. But their suburb continued to depopulate and the demographic changed dramatically.

The environment they are now working in there are lots of containers down the main street. They have lost their building and they are working out of a container at the back of the property. Once the original building was torn down they put up a Marquee which has become their bar and deli area.

(Company 7)

Company 8 had very little material or ancillary damage. It had, however, been struggling against increased international competition. Sales rose by some 20 per cent from 2010 to 2011, but this was short-lived. Sales and margins began to fall after 2011 as fixed costs such as rent and insurance premiums rose dramatically.

So our rent before the earthquakes was around $40,000 plus GST and the current rent [has increased to] $90,000 within a two-year period. So that has just gone ridiculously high. Our insurances went from say four and a half thousand to twenty thousand a year for insurances. Again just not realistic.

(Company 8)

This company was struggling in the pre-disaster period but the other three under-performing retailers were hugely affected by the loss of their original location advantages as a result largely of the collateral damage from the earthquakes.

In 2014, Company 2 continued to recover its sales level but had yet to reach its 2010 level. Once the road reconstruction ended, Company 3's location recovered its value and sales are now back to their pre-earthquake level. Both Company 7 and Company 8 closed down in 2014. The owners of Company 7 left the region, while those involved with Company 8 took the initiative to move into a new but unrelated business.

Personal resilience: why they stayed

Most participants admitted considering leaving Christchurch, but this was not a palatable option. While all respondents had business imperatives and stated that their businesses needed to remain viable, the major rationale for staying in Christchurch was family obligations and commitments: 'I've got a dad and [wife] has got a mum and they don't want to shift. And they don't have anybody else much to support them.' Some spoke too of their obligations to employees and the personal challenge of helping rebuild the city. Their Christchurch business was so intertwined with their lives that they would lose part of themselves by leaving:

But I'm bound to Christchurch because of family and my children working for me; and the worst thing is because I've been there for 27 years it's not just selling the business it's selling part of me. That's a decision you can't take lightly.

(Company 3)

This "intertwined" or embedded characteristic was also evident with the two respondents that ceased operation as both admitted that they delayed making the decision to shut down and in hindsight this had been financially costly:

. . . the biggest headache for me was six months of thinking do I close this thing down or is it going to turn around, what other things can I do to make it right . . . I mean we should have put the signs up years ago.

(Company 8)

Although the immediate aftermath saw an increase in sales for Company 8, the long-term upshot was a decline in turnover and increased costs, which worsened their already precarious financial position and accelerated the decision to cease trading.

Commercial obligations were also factors in the decision to stay, including long term leases, commercial property ownership, and the management of insurance claims and remediation. Most respondents also believed in the future value of their businesses, and the loyalty and adaptability of their staff. However, as with Companies 7 and 8, the financial imperative must be met. So when a company reaches a tipping point, no level of commitment to Christchurch, family or other sense of obligation can sustain the business.

The respondents with continuing businesses were nevertheless faced with significant barriers in moving their businesses forward, including higher costs and ongoing disruption to roads and infrastructure from the city's rebuild. They were also frustrated by what they perceived was an increase in bureaucracy within the city, but more importantly the indecision and inertia at official levels was hindering business activity.

But that was the way it was and we can only move from it and get better really. The Government needs to step in as they are doing, and it's high time they do and get things sorted.

(Company 5)

Respondents referred to a changing competitor profile and a more challenging and demanding customer base. To offset this they referred to the changing customer demographic as opening up new opportunities and the positive relationships they had with other stakeholders in the city:

I think everybody is here with one common goal to see it through for the benefit of the city. And it will eventually be a great city but it does take time.

(Company 5)

Respondents of continuing businesses reflected on many factors contributing to their personal resilience: 'Sounds tragic [loss of store] but in a lot of ways it's been quite good.' They had a high level of self-belief and internal locus of control, were very "hands-on" with their businesses, and referred to positive or personal relationships with their staff. They were dedicated to living in Christchurch and optimistic about the city's future. Although the last four years had been extremely stressful, they now had coping mechanisms. Sport and exercise were the most common stress relievers identified in the study. Taking time out through driving or spending time with family and friends were also mentioned. Some referred to stress as just part of life and noted the need to 'just deal with it'. Some respondents seemed to imply that the quakes were just another dimension of the typical fluidity of the business environment:

> I think looking back, anybody in Christchurch looking around would probably have the same sort of viewpoint. What our city is going to develop into is – whether it is our lifetime or not, I don't know – but it is going to be a pretty vibrant new city, I think, in how many years. So I mean it's been a bit of everything I think.
>
> (Company 4)

Conclusion

Participants reported using this disaster as a catalyst for changing their business model, including closure. Some suggested that change was inevitable and may have occurred regardless, but in a more gradual manner:

> I don't know if this is because of the quakes, or because our business has actually grown, but we are looking to try and create a more professional image and becoming better planned as well.
>
> (Company 4)

In some cases respondents referred to poor decision-making on their part before the quakes and that the crisis highlighted some personal business weaknesses or flaws in their business model:

> [The] main lesson is growth hides a multitude of ills. When you are growing you do some stupid stuff, really, really stupid stuff. Too many staff, sign on for things you don't really need to sign on for, advertise in publications that have no common sense . . .
>
> (Company 2)

Hence the quakes were a catalyst for exacting change which had been put off or covered over in such areas as debt levels, staffing levels, and market positioning. One respondent spoke of implementing a completely new operational model as it had previously been top heavy with excessive staffing and unnecessary expenditure lines. Another took the opportunity to reconfigure the family ownership structures of the businesses. These issues may not have been dealt with without the impetus of the quake environment which forced the owner-managers to rethink their business strategies:

> I guess one positive of the quakes – if you can talk about positives! – was that once we had the insurance sorted we could sit down and look at how we should structure the ownership now that the family had changed over that last 20 years.
>
> (Company 1)

Major changes highlighted in this study included moving to new locations; changing staffing strategies, including decreasing and increasing staff; revising mission and vision statements; and implementing new growth and customer strategies. Many respondents spoke of overcoming the immediate impact of the quakes quite quickly and effectively. However, it was the ongoing effects that impacted on their decisions to change business models. Firstly, in location and layout strategy, those businesses that were leasing their premises have experienced dramatic increases in rents which have caused them to review their location, layout and exit strategies, such as a smaller footprint, moving location or closure:

> But the last couple of years our business has really bounced back to grow and we have had to change our business model. Employing somebody, moving into premises and that sort of thing.
>
> (Company 4)

Respondents who owned their own premises experienced increased building and compliance costs in their efforts to remediate their existing buildings or extend their buildings to grow their businesses, as well as delays in construction.

Secondly, competitive strategy saw some respondents refer to large national or overseas competitors arriving in Christchurch. This had caused them to rethink their stand-alone operations and look to business-networked strategies by working with former local competitors as a means of competing. For example, Company 4 referred to corporates trying to squeeze out the smaller players in a re-establishment of the hospitality industry in Christchurch, and Company 5 discussed the international and national competitors coming into the buoyant Christchurch construction environment where previously the market was not viewed large enough by these companies.

The findings confirm that the crisis raised huge challenges but also numerous opportunities for respondents to change their businesses for the better. Factors such as loss or damage to buildings, rising cost structures, altered customer base, new corporate competitors, changes in the Christchurch environment, and business decline and growth in combination over the last four years has driven the need for change and ultimately survival, for some.

References

Baker, S. M. (2009) 'Vulnerability and resilience in natural disasters: A marketing and public policy perspective', *Journal of Public Policy & Marketing*, 28(1): 114–123.

Biggs, D., Hall, C. M. and Stoeckl, N. (2014) 'The resilience of formal and informal tourism enterprises to disasters: Reef tourism in Phuket, Thailand', *Journal of Sustainable Tourism*, 20(5): 645–665.

Charmaz, K. (2008) 'Grounded theory as an emergent method', in S. N. Hesse-Biber and P. Leavy (eds.) *Handbook of Emergent Methods*, New York: The Guilford Press.

Dahlhamer, J. M. and Tierney, K. J. (1998) 'Rebounding from disruptive events: Business recovery following the Northridge earthquake', *Sociological Spectrum*, 18(2): 121–141.

de Vries, H. P. (2008) 'The influence of migration, settlement, cultural and business factors on immigrant entrepreneurship in New Zealand', unpublished thesis, Department of Management, University of Canterbury, Christchurch.

Doern, R. (2014) 'Entrepreneurship and crisis management: The experiences of small businesses during the London 2011 riots', *International Small Business Journal*, doi:10.1177/0266242614553863

Glaser, B. G. (1992) *Emerging vs Forcing: Basics of Grounded Theory Analysis*, Mill Valley, CA: Sociology Press.

———(1998) *Doing Grounded Theory: Issues and Discussions*, Mill Valley, CA: Sociology Press.

Glaser, B. G. and Strauss, A. L. (1967) *The Discovery of Grounded Theory*, New York: Aldine.

Goulding, C. (2002) *Grounded Theory: A Practical Guide for Management, Business and Market Researchers*, London: Sage.

———(2005) 'Grounded theory, ethnography and phenomenology: A comparative analysis of three qualitative strategies for marketing research', *European Journal of Marketing*, 39(3): 294–308.

Herbane, B. (2010) 'Small business research: Time for a crisis-based view', *International Small Business Journal*, 28(1): 43–64.

Irvine, W. and Anderson, A. R. (2004) 'Small tourist firms in rural areas: Agility, vulnerability and survival in the face of crisis', *International Journal of Entrepreneurial Behavior & Research*, 10(4): 229–246.

McEntire, D. A., Fuller, C., Johnston, C. W. and Weber, R. (2002) 'A comparison of disaster paradigms: The search for a holistic policy guide', *Public Administration Review*, 62(3): 267–281.

Pearson, C. M. and Clair, J. A. (1998) 'Reframing crisis management', *The Academy of Management Review*, 23(1): 59–76.

Penrose, J. M. (2000) 'The role of perception in crisis planning', *Public Relations Review*, 26(2): 155–171.

Runyan, R. C. (2006) 'Small business in the face of crisis: Identifying barriers to recovery from a natural disaster', *Journal of Contingencies and Crisis Management*, 14(1): 12–26.

Tierney, K. J. (1997) 'Business impacts of the Northridge earthquake', *Journal of Contingencies and Crisis Management*, 5(2): 87–97.

Urquhart, C. (2013) *Grounded Theory for Qualitative Research*, London: Sage.

3 Dynamics of organisational response to a disaster

A study of organisations impacted by earthquakes

Venkataraman Nilakant, Bernard Walker,
Joana Kuntz, Huibert P. de Vries,
Sanna Malinen, Katharina Näswall and
Kate van Heugten

Introduction

There is a relative dearth of empirical studies on how organisations respond to a major disaster, recover from it, and renew themselves in a new post-disaster environment. We refer to this as *adaptive resilience*. This chapter discusses the adaptive resilience of "lifelines" organisations in Christchurch following the devastating earthquakes of 2010 and 2011. Lifelines organisations are utilities that provide essential infrastructure services to the community, such as water, wastewater, transport, energy and telecommunications, but the term also includes financial institutions and local government organisations. Qualitative, and when possible quantitative, data were collected from 11 such organisations in Christchurch between 2012 and 2014. Using grounded theory methods (Charmaz 2014; Bryant and Charmaz 2007), this chapter identifies four major themes that characterise the post-disaster response of organisations, and these are: (a) employee needs, wellbeing and engagement; (b) collaboration; (c) leadership; and (d) learning from experience. Findings from quantitative survey data supported these themes. This chapter offers a processual framework, consisting of the four themes, to build resilience in organisations. The chapter suggests that organisational resilience is a process, not an organisational trait. Employee wellbeing and engagement, collaboration and learning from experience together contribute to organisational resilience. However, building adaptive resilience requires first paying attention to staff wellbeing and then to both external and internal collaboration. Finally, organisations must create explicit mechanisms for learning from experience. The role of leadership in developing resilience is to foster wellbeing, collaboration and learning, in that order.

The chapter is organised as follows. The first section provides an overview of organizational adaptation to disasters. The chapter then discusses the research methodology underlying the study. This is followed by the major qualitative and quantitative findings and results. The chapter concludes by suggesting an integrative framework for adaptive resilience.

Organisational adaptation to disasters

The disaster management literature differentiates between three temporal but inter-connected phases: (1) pre-crisis, which is the period prior to the adverse event, (2) crisis, which is immediately after the adverse event, and (3) post-crisis, which is a period of positive recovery to a pre-event state or a new altered state (Lettieri, Masella and Radaelli 2009). The pre-crisis phase is characterised by mitigation and preparedness processes, whereas the crisis and post-crisis phases involve response and recovery processes (Lettieri, Masella and Radaelli 2009). Cognitive limitations and decision-making under stressful conditions can impair the effectiveness of crisis and post-crisis activities. Stress, surprise and the imperative for a quick response can lead to dysfunctional processes (Smart and Vertinsky 1977). In addition, the impaired cognitive, emotional and behavioural responses of organisational members, coupled with an eroded social structure, can also make it hard to respond effectively to an adverse event (Pearson and Clair 1998). Organisational leaders may have to reframe the organisation's mission and core values, restore individual and collective sense making, and re-create new shared meanings and roles. Pearson and Clair (1998) suggest that team-based responses, partnerships between stakeholders, effective information dissemination, and positive media exposure will enhance the probability of a successful outcome.

Effective adaptation to disasters is also referred to as resilience. The concept has been widely used in other fields, such as developmental psychology (Masten, Best and Garmezy 1990; Bonanno 2005), disaster management (Paton et al. 2000; Bruneau et al. 2003; Manyena 2006; Paton and Johnston 2006), ecology (Holling 1973; Gunderson 2000; Klein, Nicholls and Thomalla 2003), global environmental change (Cutter et al. 2008), and community health (Coles and Buckle 2004; Norris et al. 2008). In the social sciences, the literature on resilience is extensive, although mostly focused on individual, family or community resilience (Egeland et al. 1993).

Within organization theory, the concept of resilience has received attention from the areas of positive organisational scholarship (Sutcliffe and Vogus 2003), and high-reliability organisations (Roberts 1990). Norris et al. (2008) view resilience as a process that links resources to a positive trajectory of performance following a disaster. In this literature, *resilience* is defined as positive adjustment under challenging conditions such that the organisation is stronger after the adverse event (Vogus and Sutcliffe 2007). Resilient organisations are less likely to fail, have fewer negative consequences as a result of disaster, and are likely to recover more quickly compared to a vulnerable organisation (Bruneau et al. 2003). Despite a growing interest in organisational resilience, there is very little empirical evidence of what organisations actually do in the face of disasters. This study is interested how organisations responded, recovered and achieved positive renewal in a post-disaster environment. We were also interested in the recovery process of employees in this environment, and examined the role that organisations can play in facilitating this recovery.

Research methodology

What made the Christchurch scenario unique were the continuing aftershocks that created a volatile, uncertain and dynamic context of organisational adaptation. This study employed both qualitative and quantitative research methods. Given that the effects of the earthquakes and their aftershocks were uncharted, contingent and dynamic, we needed an emergent method which was inductive and open-ended. The grounded theory method was selected because it is inductive, comparative, interactive and systematic (Charmaz 2008, 2014). More importantly, as an emergent method it was well-suited to the evolving post-disaster context. There are different methodological strategies for generating grounded theory, although they all emphasise emergence (Strauss and Corbin 1994,1997; Glaser 1998; Bryant and Charmaz 2007; Charmaz 2008). Despite methodological differences, the different approaches to grounded theory share common features. They aim to minimise preconceived ideas, collect and analyse data simultaneously, are open to varied explanations, and focus on data analysis to construct middle-range theories (Charmaz 2008). All of them involve coding data, writing theoretical memos during data collection, constant comparisons, theoretical sampling and theoretical saturation. The study is based on the approach of Charmaz (1990, 2002, 2014) for data collection and analysis. The accompanying quantitative survey content was based on the themes derived from the interview phase.

Senior leader interviews

The study began in October 2011. Initially, organisations in the traditional physical infrastructure sector were approached; however, this expanded to include the newer, broader definitions of infrastructure, including financial institutions and local government organizations. By the end of 2013, ten organisations had agreed to participate in the study. In each of these, a cross-section of senior executives involved in post-disaster management was interviewed. Initially the questions were open-ended and focused on what happened in the immediate aftermath and the first months of the disaster. Respondents talked about the immediate context, organisational challenges, people's reactions, decision-making processes, and communication. Since these organisations were charged with immediately rebuilding the damaged infrastructure, the respondents also talked about operational activities and community involvement. Simultaneous analysis of data through open coding and memo writing led to common themes that were explored further in successive organisations. No new themes were uncovered in the tenth organisation, suggesting that theoretical saturation had been reached.

Data was collected from a total of 147 individuals through face-to-face interviews. Some individuals were interviewed more than once. The interviews were recorded and transcribed verbatim, producing more than 3,000 pages of text. Interview transcripts were initially open coded, then subjected to focused coding using NVivo (Saldana 2009). Leximancer was used to elicit concept maps from the data. Both initial and focused coding was done by multiple researchers working independently. The codes were uploaded to a common database and compared. Researchers involved in data collection and analysis also wrote theoretical memos that were uploaded to the common database. Initial open coding and theoretical memos identified general themes. Focused coding then led to four categories and their properties that were implicated in post-disaster adaptation. Subsequent memos focused on comparing the organisations across specific categories. These categories were presented to some of the organisations involved in the study. There was support from the respondents, suggesting face validity for the concepts generated.

The eleventh organisation served as a separate setting to test the framework generated from the previous analysis. This was an organisation created after the February 2011 earthquakes to rebuild the city's damaged horizontal infrastructure. It was a unique organisation called the Stronger Christchurch Infrastructure Rebuild Team (SCIRT) (2015), established as an alliance between three funding agencies (Canterbury Earthquake Recovery Authority, New Zealand Transport Agency and Christchurch City Council) and five construction-contractor businesses (City Care, Downer, Fletcher, Fulton Hogan and McConnell Dowell). As a new-start organisation that began in a volatile and uncertain post-disaster environment, it incorporated some unique design principles. Data was collected from a vertical cross-section of staff in 18 individual face-to-face interviews and five focus groups made up of a total of 41 individuals. Both individual interviews and focus group discussions covered the categories identified from earlier data. However, the interviews and discussions were open-ended to allow for new data to emerge. The process of memo-writing, transcription and analysis was similar to the earlier organisations, with coding addressing the four themes. Although this analysis identified additional organisation-specific issues, it did not suggest new major themes relating to organisational practices; the four earlier themes were strongly supported.

Workshops

Discussion-based workshops were conducted with middle managers and front-line staff from a Christchurch-based financial institution. The aim of the workshops was twofold: to offer information to leaders on coping, wellbeing and change management strategies in a post-disaster environment, and to gather information on the challenges facing and recovery process of front-line staff and their leaders.

Manager and front-line staff surveys

Quantitative surveys were distributed in several of the organisations that had previously participated in the interview process of senior leaders. The surveys were completed by managers and their staff, and 206 individuals (from six samples) participated in this phase of the research. We included measures of various attitudinal constructs, including organisational support (Eisenberger et al. 1986), supervisor support (Eisenberger et al. 2002), family support (perceptions of supervisor's concern for family; Clark 2001), organisation's learning culture (Bess, Perkins and McCown 2011), job satisfaction (Cammann et al. 1983), affective commitment (Meyer, Allen and Smith 1993), work engagement (Saks 2006), turnover intentions (Vendenberghe and Bentein 2009), trust in senior management (Champ 2007) and employee wellbeing (energy, sleep and concentration (Arnetz et al. 2008). In addition, a measure of employee resilience was developed specifically for this research (Näswall et al. 2013). This measure assesses an employee's capability, enabled by the organisation, to utilise resources to continually adapt and flourish at work, even when faced with challenging circumstances. In the survey, each question block was followed by open-ended fields, allowing participants to elaborate on their ratings.

Senior leader interviews: findings and discussion

We categorised the phases of the disaster aftermath as immediate response, recovery, and long-term renewal. While each organisation faced its own separate challenges, certain issues were common across the ten organisations. The dominant themes throughout the phases of the disaster included: (a) employee needs, wellbeing and engagement; (b) collaboration; (c) leadership; and (d) learning from experience.

Employee needs, wellbeing and engagement

In the immediate aftermath of the disaster, organisations focused on the immediate safety and wellbeing of employees. Residents throughout the city needed essentials such as food, water and sanitation. Many homes were damaged or uninhabitable. Employers assisted by providing these tangible forms of support for their employees. In addition, free counselling services and financial support were also offered, while distressed employees were given time off to recover and to deal with urgent quake-related issues.

A significant feature was the changing nature of employee needs over the course of the disaster. In the early stages, employees often did not explicitly articulate their needs; later, however, they began to seek assistance with those needs as well as other types of needs that subsequently emerged. This created a trajectory of changing employee needs for organisations to monitor and manage. The extent to which middle managers exhibited emotional intelligence influenced their ability to identify and respond to needs. Where a lack of empathy among middle managers was evident in a small number of cases, it was associated with increased employee stress and negative attitudes to the organisation and work.

With the transition from the initial response phase to the longer-term recovery, differences in the way organisations attended to employee wellbeing became more apparent. Communication was critical. Ongoing communication, including active listening by managers in order to monitor changing needs, boosted organisational resilience. This included managing employee workloads and fostering employee wellbeing. Since these were infrastructure organisations, employees worked long hours and risked fatigue to assist the recovery. Organisations that did attend to staff needs learned to provide flexibility in order to assist employees in managing their workloads, as well as dealing with pressing needs outside of work concerning their family, insurance and mental health matters. As the city moved to a "new normal", some organisations became less attentive to wellbeing and engagement. Later, these organisations gained insight into the problems caused by this inattention and this resulted in them entering into a subsequent catch-up, introducing a specific focus on wellbeing.

The content of the longer-term support included developing comprehensive personal wellbeing programmes and workshops. Some organisations also extended this support to families, adopting family-friendly practices which included hosting social gatherings and family picnics as well as providing families with access to support workshops. Apart from formal support, there was also widespread informal support with employees talking to each other, sharing experiences and offering mutual support. Managers fostered this informal type of assistance in many organisations that were studied. Overall, in the post-disaster situation, customised human resource practices were more effective than a one-size-fits-all approach.

Collaboration

Collaboration was a second major theme. In a post-disaster situation, an organisation is forced to respond to a new context, often with only limited experience and resources. Organisations in our study had to acquire resources from elsewhere or re-distribute existing resources. In addition, immediately after the earthquakes, quick decisions had to be made to respond effectively. All this necessitated people from different functions and departments working together. In some instances, organisational silos, i.e. traditional functional boundaries and authority structures, were temporarily broken to enable cross-functional collaboration and teamwork. More important was the quality and strength of external ties. External collaboration provided organisations with information, ideas and resources that were critical to effective recovery.

Local leadership

The role of the local leadership was a third major theme. Leaders who were perceived to be effective were seen to be self-aware, empathetic and valuing people over profits. These leaders were also perceived as being visible, caring, honest and authentic in their communication. Effective local leaders empowered their staff by delegating authority. They were also sensitive to the evolving context. They were more situationally aware; they did not get caught in the immediate crises, balanced risk with opportunity, were clear about their goals, shared information and collaborated readily, and were open to new approaches. A number of these leaders talked about their personal growth in the post-quake environment. They talked about being more understanding and less judgemental of people after the earthquakes. Effective leaders were also conscious of the increasing workloads of staff in the post-disaster environment and actively managed these workloads.

Learning from experience

Organisations in the study responded well to the February 2011 earthquakes as they had learnt useful lessons from their response to the September 2010 earthquake. They learnt to pay attention to staff wellbeing and external collaboration. For some organisations, the learning from disasters resulted in new ways of functioning and was also disseminated to other parts of the organisation. These organisations instituted processes for systematically learning from their experiences. However, for most of the organisations in our study, the initial lessons learnt did not endure. The earthquakes resulted in significant opportunities for some organisations but they did not become better at reflecting and learning from their experience.

Acquisition and deployment of resources coupled with management of environmental uncertainty were the major challenges facing organisations in a post-disaster environment. Our findings indicate that staff wellbeing and engagement are critical for survival. Both collaboration and learning are required for acquiring and pooling resources, monitoring the environment, generating new ideas and initiating new ways of working in a changed environment. Post-disaster management requires leadership that is explicitly focused on promoting staff wellbeing and engagement, internal and external collaboration and continuous learning within the organisation.

Workshops: findings and discussion

Discussion-based workshops were conducted with middle managers and front-line staff from a Christchurch-based financial institution. Workshop discussions suggested that, two years after the initial event, the staff recovery process was still underway. Participants commented that performance expectations were a major stressor – targets were quickly raised to pre-disaster standards, despite infrastructural damage to the workplace, resource depletion, and significant changes to the organisation's client base and service needs. Three main themes emerged, which largely mirror the findings in the interviews, but also elucidate the perspective of managers and their staff: lack of resourcing, organisational support and leadership, and commitment.

Lack of resourcing

The workshops corroborated interview findings where expressions of goodwill and support from upper management immediately following the disaster quickly transitioned to business as usual expectations. However, new and increasingly complex customer demands – including customers' need for support – proved emotionally taxing to front-line staff. Increased emotional labour had a detrimental impact on staff wellbeing. Managers also saw their roles expand to include a counselling component, due to emotional support needs expressed by customers and staff.

Organisational support and leadership

The initial response phase to the earthquakes was described as "fantastic" and largely driven by perceptions of support and visibility of senior management. The organisation offered various types of support, from washing machines at work to financial assistance. However, this support was not continued past the first few months, even though it was still required, and it was suggested that the executive team based outside of Christchurch lacked understanding of the local situation and its challenges. Increased visibility of and communication from leadership was desired. Participants felt that their extra-role efforts went unrecognised by the executive team.

Commitment

Many of the participants had long organisational tenure. Regardless of the challenges, managers and front-line staff showed high levels of commitment to their teams, and in particular to their customers. This sense of team commitment was a key driver of discretionary performance and continued tenure with the organisation, despite the challenges.

The workshops underscore the importance of continuous, long-term support, ensuring that employees do not feel they have been forgotten. Worker experiences of a disaster and its impact are disparate, and recovery is a drawn-out process, with unique trajectories for the individuals affected. Hence, it is vital to survey workers throughout the recovery process and to understand their changing needs. The Canterbury experience suggests that workers are still in need of support from the organisation years after a disaster, and that this support can positively impact employee resilience, workplace attitudes and wellbeing.

Managers and front-line staff surveys: findings and discussion

The findings presented below are based on analyses of the relationships between organisational factors (organisational and supervisory support, family support and learning culture) and wellbeing and attitudinal outcomes (employee resilience, job satisfaction, affective commitment, work engagement, turnover intention, trust towards senior leaders, and wellbeing). Context for the findings is derived from the comments provided by the respondents in the open-ended fields.

Across all the samples, employees who felt their organisation valued their contributions, considered their goals and cared about their wellbeing, reported higher levels of wellbeing and more positive attitudes, particularly higher levels of satisfaction with one's job and trust towards senior leaders. Support from immediate managers surfaced as a key driver of positive attitudes. Staff perceptions of managerial concern for the team were associated with higher job satisfaction, lower intentions to leave the organisation, higher levels of resilience, and higher work engagement. Perceptions of supervisory support can be strengthened by consideration of employee input, concern for their wellbeing, understanding of their goals and values, and availability to engage with staff.

The surveys also indicated that learning culture was positively related to all wellbeing and attitudinal outcomes, particularly to job satisfaction, employee resilience and trust in senior management. Being able to discuss mistakes without the fear of retribution, being rewarded for thinking innovatively, and exchanging feedback openly and honestly are ways in which leaders can influence their staff members' perceptions of the workplace. The findings further suggest that performance management systems should not only address poor performance, but reinforce behaviours that are in line with organisational values and direction, and make allowances for a trial-and-error approach. This is particularly relevant in recovery environments, where mistakes are more frequent due to changing requirements and additional emotional pressures both at work and at home, and where new ways of working and conducting business must be devised to ensure survival and competitive advantage.

The findings suggest that line managers play a key role in supporting their team members, which is likely to lead to more positive perceptions of the organisation. It is noteworthy that supervisor support was particularly valued when it comprised concern for staff members and for their families. Staff support during a recovery process should therefore transcend workplace boundaries and target areas that may be extraneous to, but potentially have a significant impact on, the workplace.

Participants' qualitative comments in the surveys highlighted another important role that immediate managers played. Managers were seen as "buffering" incompatibilities between organisational mandates and the everyday challenges faced by front-line staff in the post-disaster environment. While returning to 'business as usual' was required by some organisations' headquarters (located outside of Christchurch), often within a few months after the major disaster, staff members were better able to cope with work demands when their managers took practical steps to safeguard their wellbeing.

The survey results also highlight the importance of providing an environment where employees can act in a resilient manner. Organisations that enable employees to engage in reflective learning, to make mistakes without fear of retribution, and ask for support when needed, are well-positioned to promote resilient behaviours. Employee resilience and wellbeing comprise important elements of overall organisational resilience, as reflected in the interviews with senior leaders.

The results obtained are consistent with, and provide significant support for, the findings from the senior leader interviews, and highlight the importance of immediate managers as recovery enablers. It is noteworthy that our survey results also indicated that, in virtue of their responsibility for staff and business recovery processes, line managers' wellbeing was significantly affected. Considering their critical role in recovery, it is absolutely vital that organisations in post-disaster environments provide the necessary support tools and structure to assist these middle-level leaders.

Conclusion

While there have been a number of conceptual papers on organisational resilience, there is little empirical evidence to support such conceptual arguments (Lengnick-Hall and Beck 2005, 2009). It is now accepted that organisational resilience may be a continuum, ranging from bouncing back to bouncing forward – that is, from surviving a crisis to thriving in the new environment (Lengnick-Hall and Beck 2005). It is useful to view resilience as consisting of two aspects: (a) inherent resilience that enables an organisation to function well in the absence of any adverse events, and (b) adaptive resilience, which refers to flexibility in response during adverse events (Cutter et al. 2008). Inherent resilience reduces the probability of failure and reduces negative consequences of failures, whereas adaptive resilience that enables the organisation to recover quickly after an adverse event. This study provides insight into the specific dynamics involved in adaptive resilience.

The findings suggest that effective post-disaster adaptation requires ensuring staff wellbeing, enhancing collaborative relationships and fostering learning within the organisation. Leadership spans these three aspects. Effective leaders are empathetic, caring and authentic in their communication. In a disaster situation: they empower their staff, are appreciative and are able to reflect and learn from their own experiences.

All the organisations in the study were able to attend to staff wellbeing and engagement. Most of them were able to utilise their external networks for recovery and renewal. Only a few, however, were able to apply the learning from the disaster experience to modify their mind-sets and functioning. This suggests that there might be a three-step maturity process for adaptive resilience. Organisations must first attend to employee needs and wellbeing; they must subsequently foster collaboration, both external and internal; and, finally, they need to explicitly pay attention to knowledge acquisition and integration from ongoing experiences. Organisational learning cannot be effective without first managing staff wellbeing and, subsequently, collaboration. Both wellbeing and collaboration foster learning. The distinctive contribution of this study is that, based on empirical evidence from a real disaster, it suggests that adaptive resilience is a three-step process. The processual framework of adaptive resilience indicates that the role of leadership is to initially attend to changing employee needs and ensure to their wellbeing. Subsequently, leaders must foster both external and internal collaboration and, then, create explicit mechanisms for learning from experience.

References

Arnetz, B. B., Frenzel, L., Åkerstedt, T. and Lisspers, J. (2008) 'The brief fatigue syndrome scale: Validation and utilization in fatigue recovery studies', in Y. Watanabe, B. Evengård, B. H. Natelson, L. A. Jason and H. Kuratsune (eds.) *Fatigue Science for Human Health*, Tokyo: Springer.

Bess, K. D., Perkins, D. D. and McCown, D. L. (2011) 'Testing a measure of organizational learning capacity and readiness for transformational change in human services', *Journal of Prevention & Intervention in the Community*, 39(1): 35–49.

Bonanno, G. (2005) 'Clarifying and extending the construct of adult resilience', *American Psychologist*, 60(3): 265–267.

Bruneau, M., Chang, S. E., Eguchi, R. T., Lee, G. C., O'Rourke, T. D., Reinhorn, A. M., Shinozuka, M., Tierney, K., Wallace, W. A. and Winterfeldt, D. V. (2003) 'A framework to quantitatively assess and enhance the seismic resilience of communities', *Earthquake Spectra*, 19(4): 733–752.

Bryant, A. and Charmaz, K. (2007) 'Grounded theory research: Methods and practices', in A. Bryant and K. Charmaz (eds.) *The Sage Handbook of Grounded Theory*, London: Sage.

Cammann, C., Fichman, M., Jenkins, D. and Klesh, J. R. (1983) 'Assessing the attitudes and perceptions of organizational members', in S. Seashore, E. Lawler III, P. Mirvis and C. Cammann (eds.) *Assessing Organizational Change: A Guide to Methods, Measures, and Practices*, New York: Wiley.

Champ, M. (2007) 'Another perspective on the talent challenge: Motivational forces for leaving the public sector', paper presented at 7th Australian Industrial and Organisational Psychology Conference, Adelaide, Australia, 28 June – 1 July.

Charmaz, K. (1990) "'Discovering' chronic illness: Using grounded theory', *Social Science & Medicine*, 30(11): 1161–1172.

——(2002) 'Qualitative interviewing and grounded theory analysis', in J. F. Gubrium and J. A. Holstein (eds.) *Handbook of Interview Research: Context and Method*, Thousand Oaks, CA: Sage.

——(2008) 'Grounded theory as emergent method', in S. N. Hesse-Biber and P. Leavy (eds.) *Handbook of Emergent Methods*, New York: The Guilford Press.

——(2014) *Constructing Grounded Theory* (2nd ed.), London: Sage.

Clark, S. C. (2001) 'Work cultures and work/family balance', *Journal of Vocational Behavior*, 58(3): 348–365.

Coles, E. and Buckle, P. (2004) 'Developing community resilience as a foundation for effective disaster recovery', *The Australian Journal of Emergency Management*, 19(4): 6–15.

Cutter, S. L., Barnes, L., Berry, M., Burton, C., Evans, E., Tate, E. and Webb, J. (2008) 'A place-based model for understanding community resilience to natural disasters', *Global Environmental Change*, 18(4): 598–606.

Egeland, B., Carlson, E. and Sroufe, L. (1993) 'Resilience as process', *Development & Psychopathology*, 5(4): 517–528.

Eisenberger, R., Huntington, R., Hutchison, S. and Sowa, D. (1986) 'Perceived organizational support', *Journal of Applied Psychology*, 71(3): 500–507.

Eisenberger, R., Stinglhamber, F., Vandenberghe, C., Sucharski, I. L. and Rhoades, L. (2002) 'Perceived supervisor support: Contributions to perceived organizational support and employee retention', *Journal of Applied Psychology*, 87(3): 565–573.

Glaser, B. G. (1998) *Doing Grounded Theory: Issues and Discussions*, Mill Valley: Sociology Press.

Grant, R. M. (1996) 'Prospering in dynamically-competitive environments: Organizational capability as knowledge integration', *Organization Science*, 7(4): 375–387.

Gunderson, L. (2000) 'Ecological resilience-in theory and application', *Annual Review of Ecology and Systematics*, 31: 425–429.

Holling, C. S. (1973) 'Resilience and stability of ecological systems', *Annual Review of Ecology and Systematics*, 4: 1–23.

Klein, R., Nicholls, R. and Thomalla, F. (2003) 'Resilience to natural hazards: How useful is this concept?', *Environmental Hazards*, 5(1–2): 35–45.

Lengnick-Hall, C. A. and Beck, T. E. (2005) 'Adaptive fit versus robust transformation: How organizations respond to environmental change', *Journal of Management Studies*, 31(5): 738–757.

——(2009) 'Resilience capacity and strategic agility: Prerequisites for thriving in a dynamic environment', in C. Nemeth, E. Hollnagel and S. Dekker (eds.) *Resilience Engineering Perspectives: Preparation and Restoration*, Vol. 2, Aldershot: Ashgate.

Lettieri, E., Masella, C. and Radaelli, G. (2009) 'Disaster management: Findings from a systematic review ', *Disaster Prevention and Management*, 18(2): 117–136.

Manyena, S. B. (2006) 'The concept of resilience revisited', *Disasters*, 30(4): 433–450.

Masten, A., Best, K. and Garmezy, N. (1990) 'Resilience and development: Contributions form the study of children who overcome adversity', *Development & Psychopathology*, 2(4): 425–444.

Meyer, J. P., Allen, N. J. and Smith, C. A. (1993) 'Commitment to organizations and occupations: Extension and test of a three-component conceptualization', *Journal of Applied Psychology*, 78(4): 538–551.

Näswall, K., Kuntz, J., Hodliffe, M. and Malinen, S. (2013) *Employee Resilience Scale (EmpRes): Technical Report*, Resilient Organisations Research Report 2013/06, Christchurch: University of Canterbury.

Norris, F. H., Stevens, S. P., Pfefferbaum, B., Wyche, K. F. and Pfefferbaum, R. L. (2008) 'Community resilience as a metaphor, theory, set of capacities, and strategy for disaster readiness', *American Journal of Community Psychology*, 41(1–2): 127–150.

Paton, D. and Johnston, D. (2006) *Disaster Resilience: An Integrated Approach*, Springfield: Charles C. Thomas,.

Paton, D., Smith, L. and Violanti, J. (2000) 'Disaster response: Risk, vulnerability and resilience', *Disaster Prevention and Management*, 9(3): 173–180.

Pearson, C. M. and Clair, J. A. (1998) 'Reframing crisis management', *Academy of Management Review*, 23(1): 59–76.

Roberts, K. H. (1990) 'Some characteristics of one type of high reliability organization', *Organization Science*, 1(2): 160–176.

Saks, A. M. (2006) 'Antecedents and consequences of employee engagement', *Journal of Managerial Psychology*, 21(7): 600–619.

Saldana, J. (2009) *The Coding Manual for Qualitative Researchers*, London: Sage.

Smart, C. and Vertinsky, I. (1977) 'Designs for crisis decision units', *Administrative Science Quarterly*, 22(4): 640–657.

Strauss, A. and Corbin, J. (1994) 'Grounded theory methodology: An overview', in N. K. Denzin and Y. S. Lincoln (eds.) *Handbook of Qualitative Research*, Thousand Oaks: Sage.

——(eds.) (1997) *Grounded Theory in Practice*, London: Sage.

Stronger Christchurch Infrastructure Rebuild Team (SCIRT) (2015) *SCIRT Rebuilding Infrastructure*. Online. Available HTTP: <http://strongerchristchurch.govt.nz/> (Accessed 1 April 2015).

Sutcliffe, K. and Vogus, T. (2003) 'Organizing for resilience', in K. S. Cameron, J. E. Dutton and R. E. Quinn (eds.) *Positive Organizational Scholarship: Foundations of a New Discipline*, San Francisco: Berrett-Koehler.

Vandenberghe, C. and Bentein, K. (2009) 'A closer look at the relationship between affective commitment to supervisors and organizations and turnover', *Journal of Occupational and Organizational Psychology*, 82(2): 331–348.

Vogus, T. J. and Sutcliffe, K. M. (2007) 'Organizational resilience: Towards a theory and research agenda', paper presented at ISIC, IEEE International Conference on Systems, Man and Cybernetics, 7–10 October.

4   After the shock

Employee turnover decision-making in a post-crisis context

Russell Wordsworth and Venkataraman Nilakant

Introduction

Employee turnover, be it voluntary or otherwise, is a natural part of the employ-ment cycle and eventually all employees leave an organisation, either of their own volition or otherwise. Employee turnover is therefore not a necessary consequence or outcome of a crisis. The etymology of the word 'crisis' reveals, however, that its origin lies in late Middle English denoting the turning point of a disease and derives from the Ancient Greek words *krinein,* meaning to decide and *krisis* mean-ing a decision (Oxford English Dictionary 2015). By their nature crises require individuals, and organisations, to be decisive and to take decisions. It is therefore not unreasonable to expect employee turnover to be one of the potential conse-quences of a crisis or natural disaster. Indeed, a 2011 study by the Department of Labour indicated that 28 per cent of the 1,750 employers interviewed experi-enced difficulties in retaining employees as a direct consequence of the Christch-urch earthquake sequence (Department of Labour [DoL], 2011). This figure was closer to 50 per cent for larger organisations (those employing 50 or more employees). Additionally, figures from the Inland Revenue Department (IRD) for the period directly following the February 2011 earthquake showed that more than 1,000 employees left the region each month for six consecutive months. The extent to which these departures were voluntary cannot be discerned from the IRD data, and there is no publicly available information on voluntary turnover rates for the period following the earthquakes. Anecdotal evidence suggests, how-ever, that for several large employers in the region, such as the Canterbury District Health Board (Robertson 2012), Christchurch City Council (Cairns 2012), and the University of Canterbury (Mathews 2012), voluntary turnover rates increased sharply in the first two years following the earthquakes.

From a crisis management perspective, sustained turnover of staff following a disaster can significantly erode the recovery of the organisation and its ability to restore its performance to pre-disaster levels, ultimately threatening the survival of the organisation (Byron and Peterson 2002). The post-crisis context therefore provides an important and unique setting within which to study voluntary turno-ver decision-making. To date, however, there has been a dearth of research in this area (Davis 2008). Voluntary turnover scholarship has long been dominated by an analytical mindset devoted to the prediction and control of the turnover phenomenon, and the production of grand and generalisable theories that transcend situational contexts (Allen, Hancock, Vardaman and Mckee 2014). While strong arguments have been made to suggest that turnover decisions are influenced by contextual and relational complexities (Morrell, Loan-Clarke and Wilkinson 2001), limited research has taken place outside of the predominant organisational, and often Western, context (Guthrie 2001; Boxall, Macky and Rasmussen 2003; Maertz, Stevens and Campion 2003; Morrison 2003; Morrell and Arnold 2007). As a consequence, context-specific explanations of turnover are not common. Additionally, studies that seek to understand actual decision processes by retrospectively interviewing leavers do not feature strongly in the turnover literature.

In addressing these gaps, this chapter presents a leaver-centric account of voluntary turnover decision-making in the context of a major disaster. The data is grounded in first-person accounts of 32 leavers from four organisations that were affected by the ongoing sequence of earthquakes between September 2010 and December 2011.

Theoretical background

Much of the current research on voluntary turnover derives from early models proposed by March and Simon (1958); Mobley (1977); Mobley, Griffeth, Hand and Meglino (1979); Price and Mueller (1981) and Steers and Mowday (1981). Inherent in these attitudinal path models are several presuppositions. Firstly, they assume a rational decision process influenced primarily by desirability of movement (as manifest in job dissatisfaction) and ease of movement (seen as a function of the availability of alternatives). They are further premised on the assumption that quitting is largely an individual decision based on the interaction between the individual and the work environment. Lastly, they construe turnover decisions as a step-by-step sequential process derived from dissatisfaction that progress in a relatively predictable order. Countless studies have sought to validate and build on these early models through the addition of distal antecedents, mediators, moderators, and proximal antecedents of turnover (Holtom, Mitchell, Lee and Eberly 2008). The net result is a large body of empirical support for a somewhat modest relationship between job dissatisfaction, perceived alternatives, turnover intentions, and turnover (Griffeth, Hom and Gaertner 2000). Much of the criterion variance remains unexplained by existing turnover models, with most models explaining between 15 and 20 per cent of the variance in turnover (Hom and Griffeth 2013; Russell 2013). The dominance of these early models, together with a seemingly unwavering focus on prediction, has constrained theoretical development in the field, and placed limitations on the ability to understand the nuanced and complex nature of turnover decisions (Allen, Hancock and Vardaman 2013).

In seeking to advance turnover theory and understand actual turnover decision-making processes, Lee and Mitchell's (1994) "Unfolding Model" represented a refreshing departure from the above research paradigm. Drawing on image theory, they argued that leavers follow varied turnover paths, several of which are initiated by a "shock" and subsequent image violation. Numerous studies have provided support for the basic tenets and paths of the unfolding model (Lee, Mitchell, Holtom, McDaniel and Hill 1999; Donnelly and Quirin 2006; Holtom et al. 2008; Morrell, Loan-Clarke, Arnold and Wilkinson 2008; Kulik, Treuren, and Bordia 2012), while several others have been less confirmatory (Holt, Rehg, Lin, and Miller 2007; Niederman, Sumner and Maertz 2007; Morrell et al. 2008), thereby leaving scope for additional inquiry. There is no disputing the fact that the addition of shocks as key "drivers" of turnover has advanced our understanding of turnover decision-making considerably. Indeed, Holtom et al. (2005) demonstrated that shocks trigger voluntary departures more often than accumulated job dissatisfaction; however, the causal mechanisms by which shocks lead to turnover remain understudied. Part of the reason for this lies in the way in which shocks have been defined to date. Shocks are typically construed as a static and one-off jarring event experienced by an individual. This definition is overly restrictive and does not consider the dynamic nature of shocks, the cumulative impact of multiple shocks, or the impact of a large extra-organisational shock that is commonly experienced by all employees – all of which are characteristic of a post-crisis context. The possibility that a commonly experienced shock, such as the Christchurch earthquakes, may be perceived to hold a different event magnitude, and therefore differentially impact turnover decision-making, has yet to be explored fully.

Additionally, shocks have commonly been defined as the 'initiating mechanism' engendering the turnover decision-making process. Indeed, Holtom et al. (2005: 341) go as far as to state that unless an event leads directly to job-related deliberations that involve leaving, it cannot be considered a shock. As a result very few studies have sought to examine the level of influence "initial shocks" exert on the actual final decision to leave (Morrell, Loan-Clarke and Wilkinson 2004; Kulik et al. 2012). As Morrell et al. (2004: 166) note, most studies of the unfolding model fail to acknowledge that an initial shock does not necessarily have to directly influence the final decision to leave. It is, for example, quite plausible that a single shock could initiate a process of decision-making but, on its own, is insufficient to result in leaving. Additional shocks, or a set of circumstances experienced after the initial shock, may be what ultimately results in leaving and thereby constitute the actual motives for leaving (Bergman, Payne and Boswell 2012). Such reasoning does not negate, however, the impact of the original shock as a salient part of the decision sequence, albeit somewhat distal from the actual decision to leave. Rather, it suggests there are temporal, contextual and processual differences in the way in which shocks might lead to turnover. Studies exploring such possibilities are, however, not prevalent in the turnover literature and the interplay between initial shocks, subsequent shocks and actual reasons for leaving is therefore in need of closer examination. To this end, the post-crisis context of the Christchurch earthquakes provided a unique setting in which to examine the role shocks play in turnover decisions. More specifically the study sought to understand:

- How turnover decisions get made in an environment of repeated external shocks and continuing uncertainty following a major disaster.
- The major determinants of voluntary turnover decisions within this context.
- The outcomes of voluntary turnover decisions in a post-disaster context and how organisations might influence these outcomes.

Methodology

The study adopted a grounded theory approach to achieve the above research aims (Charmaz, 2014; Corbin and Strauss, 2008), thus answering the repeated calls for more qualitative and in-depth studies of turnover (Maertz and Campion 1998; Morrell and Arnold 2007; Allen, Bryant and Vardaman 2010; Hom, Mitchell, Lee and Griffeth 2012). The study's focus on post-disaster decision necessitated collecting data retrospectively, an approach which is not uncommon in disaster-related research (Norris and Kaniasty 1992; Norris et al. 2002). Additionally it was decided to delay initial data collection until 18 months following the first earthquake in order to account for the cumulative impact of additional shocks and stressors. Doing so raised some initial concerns regarding memory decay and recall bias; however, these concerns were attenuated by several studies which demonstrated that delayed self-reports of traumatic events showed remarkable stability and reliability over time (Norris and Kaniasty 1992; Lee et al. 1999; Krinsley, Gallagher, Weathers, Kutter and Kaloupek 2003).

To be included in the study, participants had to meet three criteria: they had to be in paid employment at the time of the September 2010 earthquake, had to have experienced the September 2010 and/or February 2011 earthquakes, and had to have left their jobs of their own volition in the 18 months following the initial earthquake. Data was collected through in-depth interviews with 32 leavers from four large organisations in the Canterbury region. Participants included 19 females and 13 males, ranging in age from 22 to 57 years. All interviews were conducted by the first author, recorded, and transcribed verbatim. Transcripts were returned to participants for checking and verification prior to commencing data analysis. Data collection and analysis took place simultaneously and iteratively with open coding commencing after the first interview. This allowed the interview protocol to be adapted to emerging concepts, thereby guiding subsequent data collection. Following a grounded theory process of theory building, all new data were compared with emergent concepts utilising the constant comparison method and memoing. This process continued until all concepts were fully developed and the relationship between the concepts fully specified.

Findings

A departure from tradition

For one group of participants (n = 6), a degree of job dissatisfaction was present prior to the crisis, and leaving was attributed, at least in part, to this dissatisfaction.

The analysis suggests, however, that for the majority of participants, traditional antecedents of turnover, such as dissatisfaction with the job or organisation, did not play a significant role in their decision-making. Most leavers described being highly satisfied with their jobs prior to the crisis, and for many this satisfaction was still present at the time of leaving. Several participants in this category explained that they would have happily continued to work at their organisation had the earthquake sequence not occurred. Also contrary to existing turnover literature, most participants had not entertained thoughts of quitting and did not hold any plans for leaving prior to the crisis. Findings suggest that for many their decision to leave was not contingent on securing alternative employment. In fact, fewer than half of the participants (n = 13) had a job offer in hand when they left their organisation. The analysis suggests temporal differences in coming to the decision to quit and the actual effectuation of that decision.

All 32 participants in the study experienced the earthquakes and the circumstances that followed, and for most (n = 28) this extra-organisational shock played a substantial role in their decision to leave. While turnover models incorporating shocks commonly construe them as initial triggering events, the analysis suggests that shocks have differential impacts on turnover decision-making. The remainder of the chapter examines these differential impacts. Based on the existing concept of dissatisfaction, as well as five emergent concepts of latent disquiet, critical reflection, hiatus, watershed, and job search and evaluation, participants were classified into four distinct groups: (1) *New beginnings,* (2) *Reluctant departures,* (3) *Tragic endings,* (4) *Deliberate departures.* The following sections describe the decision-making processes typical of leavers in each of these classifications.

New beginnings (n = 9)

Participants classified as 'new beginnings' were mainly satisfied employees who had not seriously entertained thoughts of leaving or engaged in active job search behaviour prior to the earthquakes. Rather, these participants described having periodic "back of the mind thoughts" or a sense of unease and restlessness. Most commonly this centred on feelings of "underutilisation of self" or the pursuit of an "unanswered calling". Such thoughts did not represent scripted plans for leaving at some point in the future, and did not drive active dissatisfaction with the job. As such they were seldom acted upon or subjected to much conscious deliberation; hence, we conceptualise these thoughts as *latent disquiet.* Rosemary (56, a senior manager), illustrates the concept of latent disquiet:

> . . . and it was always in the back of my mind that I was not going to want to be with [the organisation] to the end of my days, because I have seen other people do that, and I thought – no, I want to do other things as well as [senior management role within the organisation].

The findings reveal that, in addition to directly triggering turnover deliberations, shocks indirectly influence turnover by surfacing latent disquiet. Participants described back of the mind thoughts becoming far more salient following the earthquakes. This surfacing of latent disquiet is illustrated by Aubrey (52, a horticulturalist), who left his job several months after the February earthquake:

> I guess in a way it's like the anecdote. You put a frog in a saucepan of water and you heat it and the frog don't do nothing, but you drop the frog into hot water and it does everything in its power . . . I could have stayed at [the organisation]. I suspect strongly if nothing had happened like it did I might well have stayed, because . . . I don't know. Because something did happen . . . I knew when I went into town that day [as part of an urban search and rescue first response team] everything changed – changed everybody's life around me and I knew I couldn't escape those "I need to do something's".

The surfacing of latent disquiet initiated a process of conscious deliberation and deep reflection addressing the very assumptions that held people to the organisation or, in many cases, the city. This is conceptualised as *critical reflection*. The ability of participants to surface disquiet and engage in critical reflection appeared to be influenced by the presence of a period of downtime brought about by the disruption of organisational routine or forced absence from the workplace as a consequence of the earthquakes. This is conceptualised as "hiatus". The findings offer support to Mezirow's (1990) assertion that premise reflection can occur only after a significant event and requires hiatus from activity in which to reassess one's assumptions. The findings also suggest that critical reflection was typically directed at the participant's attachment to one of three things, either a relationship (people), their jobs (profession), or a physical location (place). For *new beginnings* critical reflection mostly focused on the participant's attachment to their profession or career and involved a deep questioning of the assumptions which they perceived to be holding them back from pursuing more meaningful work or, in some cases, from a personal relationship. Critical reflection lead to the realisation that leaving represented a desirable outcome and a conscious decision to leave followed. An active job search formed part of the decision process for many *new beginnings*, although most (6/9) left their jobs having not secured future employment. The basic decision process for *new beginnings* is depicted in Figure 4.1.

Reluctant departures (n = 9) and tragic endings (n = 5)

As discussed earlier, shocks are typically construed as one-off static events that lead directly to job-related deliberations. The Canterbury earthquakes were, however, neither one-off nor static, with the aftershock sequence continuing for several years. Unlike *new beginnings* discussed above, the analysis suggests that in the case of *tragic endings* and *reluctant departures* it was cumulative impact of multiple shocks, in combination with numerous of intra- and extra-organisational stressors, which ultimately necessitated a decision to quit. Although the stressors

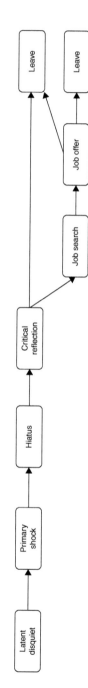

Figure 4.1 Decision process for *new beginnings*

described by each individual varied, participants in both of these categories described reaching a *tipping* point or watershed where they felt compulsion to make a decision to leave in order to regain a sense of control over their situation. Wendy (51, a librarian) illustrates the reaching of a tipping point:

> The situation was sort of hard to manage. And then my father was diagnosed with dementia, which of course, sort of was – I think everybody had got so stressed that every sort of weak link just broke . . . So on top of everything else I had to make a decision about my father because his doctors were insisting that he would be put into care, and of course, we just resisted the idea and trying to manage the situation at hand and it was just too much and one day I just felt like [long pause] you know I just couldn't carry on any more . . .

Although reaching a tipping point was common to both *reluctant departures* and *tragic endings*, participants in these two categories differed in a number of ways. For *reluctant departures* the reaching of a tipping point was commonly followed by a self-imposed hiatus or period of downtime in which to engage in a process of critical reflection similar to that of *new beginnings*. For participants classified as *reluctant departures,* stressors were almost always extra-organisational and were exacerbated by uncertainty and anxiety related to the ongoing earthquake sequence. Critical reflection therefore centred mostly on attachment to place or people and to a far lesser extent attachment to the job, as illustrated by Robby (35, network assistant) an immigrant who left New Zealand following the earthquakes:

> . . . as the months unfolded it became very clear to us that we were just trying to make it work for the sake of it and trying to hold onto something that had actually left. And something that had kind of buggered off over the horizon for us. So once we realised that the Christchurch we were trying to hold onto and the lifestyle we were trying to hold onto was no longer there it wasn't that hard or painful a decision.

In cases where critical reflection did centre on the person's job, the focus of the reflection was very often on achieving a higher purpose or pursuing greater meaning or utilisation of self, as illustrated by Aubrey (52, horticulturalist):

> But in here [points to his heart] there was a detachment that I had never experienced before and I could not understand how that happened. And then, after a week or two weeks, I started to think to myself, "Well, look if this is going to have marked effect on how I do things with my life, where is my life? Is everything in order?" My marriage is good, click, ticked. Family's fine. Phone, house, got a job. The future, mmm? And that's basically how it started.

Most participants in the *reluctant departures* category were highly satisfied employees and thus were not planning to leave their jobs prior to the earthquake;

however, the process of critical reflection led to an acceptance that, although not desirable, leaving represented the most appropriate outcome given their altered circumstances. Contrary to existing turnover models, job search and securing alternative employment had very little impact on the decision-making process for *reluctant departures*. Rather, the findings suggest that turnover decisions may encompass separate phases of "detachment" and "effectuation". All participants in this category stated that they commenced job search activity only once their decision to leave had crystalised, and only 4/9 left having secured alternative employment. For these participants job search appeared to impact the execution and timing of their decision, but not the decision itself. Participants also stated that once the decision to leave had been made, employer mitigation was highly unlikely. The basic decision process for *reluctant departures* is depicted in Figure 4.2.

Participants in the *tragic endings* category were also highly satisfied employees who held no plans for leaving prior to the earthquakes. Unlike *reluctant departures*, however, none of these participants described experiencing a period of hiatus or downtime in which to engage in a process of critical reflection. Rather, they attempted repeatedly and unsuccessfully to manage the consequences of the primary shock (earthquake) in order maintain or regain control of their work and personal lives. All participants in this category described experiencing considerable extra- and intra-organisational stressors, although they all identified a dominant intra-organisational stressor as their primary reason for leaving. Most commonly this took the form of interpersonal conflict (secondary shock) brought about as a consequence of reorganisation following earthquakes. This, coupled with accumulating uncertainty, stress, anxiety and extra-organisational stressors related to the earthquake, resulted in a tipping point being reached. A final, and often benign shock, served as the "final straw" which pushed participants over the tipping point. In the absence of hiatus and critical reflection, reaching a tipping point was followed by the rapid execution of a decision to quit, often with little planning and without undertaking any form of job search, as illustrated by Brenda (48, a programme coordinator):

> I didn't feel good about it [leaving], but it was sink or swim for me and I said to [senior manager], nobody else is going to do this for me. Nobody is there for me. Nobody else has stood up for me. I'm the only one that can do this and I have to do this and I have to do it today.

The findings help explain the interaction between initial shocks, secondary shocks and final straw shocks, and how the cumulative impact of shocks can lead to turnover decisions. Although their decision to leave was voluntary, all participants in the *tragic endings* category described feeling compelled to make a decision in order to regain control. Where *reluctant departures* described a collective, and often consultative, decision process, *tragic endings* described a very individual decision and one in which they felt quite isolated. Decisions were thus associated with a high degree of emotional strain, and in some cases regret. Several participants in this category explained that it was only once they

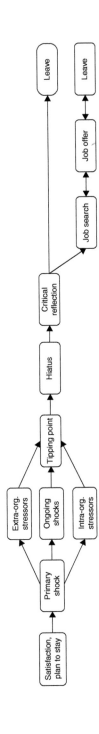

Figure 4.2 Decision process for *reluctant departures*

EO: extra-organisational (stressors external to the organisational setting – for example, dealing with Earthquake Commission (EQC), insurance)

IO: intra-organisational (stressors within the organisational setting – for example, team conflict, role overload, organisational disruption)

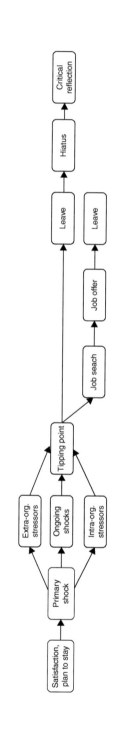

Figure 4.3 Decision process for *tragic endings*

EO: extra-organisational (stressors external to the organisational setting – for example, dealing with Earthquake Commission (EQC), insurance)

IO: intra-organisational (stressors within the organisational setting – for example, team conflict, role overload, organisational disruption)

had executed their decision to leave that they were able to create time and space to reflect critically. The basic decision process for *tragic endings* is depicted in Figure 4.3.

Deliberate departures (n = 9)

In support of existing turnover theory, the findings demonstrate that shocks can also lead to quitting without necessitating critical reflection or causing a tipping point to be reached. For participants categorised as *deliberate departures*, leaving was viewed as a positive outcome and was not associated with much emotional strain or cognitive dissonance, thereby reducing the need for critical reflection. The main extra-organisational shock (earthquake) was not the primary reason for their leaving; rather, it served one of two secondary purposes. First, it altered the local labour market through increased labour demand in certain industries and the creation of new organisations or roles that had not existed prior to the earthquakes. This enabled a number of participants to enact predetermined plans (referred to as "scripts" in traditional turnover literature) for leaving that they were unable to enact prior to the crisis because of a low availability of alternatives. Alec (34, a lifeguard) who had always wanted to get into teaching illustrates this point:

> I never actually had a definite point when I was going to leave, it was always a, "When a teaching position comes up for teaching aiding, or a role that works with kids came up that was when I was going to go" . . . and so after the quakes, funding came through the Ministry [of Education] for more teacher aides to go into schools, and then that gave me a role into a school.

In a similar fashion, increased demand for certain jobs made it easier for already dissatisfied employees to find alternative employment. Second, the earthquake(s) eroded community embeddedness and people's attachment to place (see also Chapter 2, this volume), which in turn served to either expedite the enactment of predetermined plans or reduce the decision strain associated with enacting these plans or accepting unsolicited job offers. Most participants in the *deliberate departures* category described their decision as a rational choice between employment alternatives. Consequently, an active job search formed part of the decision process for most of the participants (n = 6) in this category. Unlike the other three categories, deliberations about leaving were very much directed at the organisation (attachment to profession). The basic decision process for *deliberate departures* is depicted in Figure 4.4.

Theoretical contribution and practical implications

This chapter offers a rich and nuanced view of the process of decision-making associated with voluntary turnover in a post-crisis context. In doing so it advances understanding of how shocks lead to quitting, particularly in instances of turnover

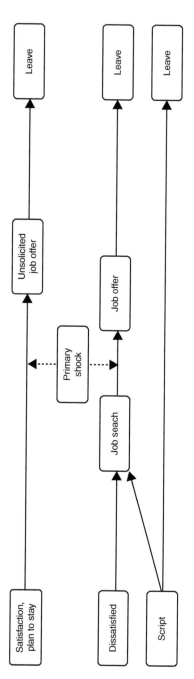

Figure 4.4 Decision process for *deliberate departures*

where decisions are not derived from dissatisfaction with the job or organisation. The findings lend support to the view that shocks play an important role in turnover decision-making. However, unlike most models which posit that turnover deliberations are a direct consequence of shocks (Lee et al., 1999; Holtom et al. 2005), it is suggested there are several intervening factors which ultimately lead to the decision to quit. The study proposes that latent disquiet, critical reflection, hiatus, and tipping points are significant causal mechanisms through which shocks get translated into leaving. This finding has important organisational implications. First, managers need to recognise that significant extra-organisational shocks can lead to turnover, even if they do not directly impact the organisation. Second, the findings identify several phases in the decision-making process during which managers may be able to mitigate leaving.

The chapter expands the traditional definition of shocks beyond their initial and direct impact on turnover deliberations. Evidence is provided to suggest that construing shocks as a single distinguishable event that jars an employee toward deliberate judgments about his/her job is overly simplistic (Holtom et al. 2005), and that in fact a complex relationship exists between initial, subsequent, and final straw shocks. This has important implications for organisations seeking to mitigate employee turnover in a post-crisis context. Managers should be aware that crises affect employees in multiple ways, and that those employees who come through the strongest at the start of a crisis may well be at the highest risk of leaving during later stages of the recovery or post-recovery period. Assisting employees in identifying and managing extra-organisational stressors, not only following the initial shock, but throughout the recovery stages is therefore essential.

Organisational downtime and disruption to routine were also found to have a significant impact on employee turnover by providing satisfied employees the mental space to surface latent disquiet and critically reflect on their attachment to place, person or profession. Managers need to keep employees engaged during such times and be aware that crises have the potential to magnify feelings of underutilisation of self or the pursuit of unanswered callings. The findings further demonstrate that crises can trigger or necessitate decision-making, in the form of critical reflection, which goes well beyond rational choice between alternative employment options. Additionally, the degree to which critical reflection forms part of the decision-making process is dependent on decision magnitude, such that decisions of a high magnitude (long tenure, senior position, main breadwinner) are associated with substantial critical reflection. Contrastingly, in situations where decision magnitude was low (short tenure, part-time role, not main breadwinner) a rational choice between two organisations was the focus of the decision. These findings are an important contribution to the turnover literature, which historically has treated all turnover decisions as equal. Finally, crises are likely to have differential impacts on labour markets; employers should understand how labour supply is affected in their specific industry and adapt retention strategies accordingly.

References

Allen, D. G., Bryant, P. C. and Vardaman, J. M. (2010) 'Retaining talent: Replacing misconceptions with evidence-based strategies', *Academy of Management Perspectives*, 24(2): 48–64.

Allen, D. G., Hancock, J. and Vardaman, J. M. and Mckee, D. N. (2014) 'Analytical mindsets in turnover research', *Journal of Organizational Behavior*, 35(S1): S61–S86.

Bergman, M. E., Payne, S. C. and Boswell, W. R. (2012) 'Sometimes pursuits don't pan out: Anticipated destinations and other caveats: Comment on Hom, Mitchell, Lee, and Griffeth (2012)', *Psychological Bulletin*, 138(5): 865–870.

Boxall, P., Macky, K. and Rasmussen, E. (2003) 'Labour turnover and retention in New Zealand: The causes and consequences of leaving and staying with employers', *Asia Pacific Journal of Human Resources*, 41(2): 196–214.

Byron, K. and Peterson, S. (2002) 'The impact of a large-scale traumatic event on individual and organizational outcomes: Exploring employee and company reactions to September 11, 2001', *Journal of Organizational Behavior*, 23(8): 895–910.

Cairns, L. (2012) 'Marryatt defends extra council leave', *The Press*, 15 November. Online. Available HTTP: <http://www.stuff.co.nz/the-press/news/7951478/Marryatt-defends-extra-council-leave>.

Charmaz, K. (2014) *Constructing Grounded Theory* (2nd ed.), London: Sage.

Corbin, J. M. and Strauss, A. L. (2008) *Basics of Qualitative Research: Techniques and Procedures for Developing Grounded Theory* (3rd ed.), Los Angeles: Sage.

Davis, A. (2008) 'The impact of natural disasters on employee turnover: The shocks and aftershocks of Hurricane Katrina on IT professionals', unpublished thesis, Louisiana State University, Alabama.

Department of Labour (DoL) (2011) *A Changing Landscape: The Impact of the Earthquakes on Christchurch Workplaces*, Wellington: Department of Labour.

Donnelly, D. P. and Quirin, J. J. (2006) 'An extension of Lee and Mitchell's unfolding model of voluntary turnover', *Journal of Organizational Behavior*, 27(1): 59–77.

Griffeth, R. W., Hom, P. W. and Gaertner, S. (2000) 'A meta-analysis of antecedents and correlates of employee turnover: Update, moderator tests, and research implications for the next millennium', *Journal of Management*, 26(3): 463–488.

Guthrie, J. P. (2001) 'High-involvement work practices, turnover, and productivity: Evidence from New Zealand', *Academy of Management Journal*, 44(1): 180–190.

Holt, D. T., Rehg, M. T., Lin, J. H. S. and Miller, J. (2007) 'An application of the unfolding model to explain turnover in a sample of military officers', *Human Resource Management*, 46(1): 35–49.

Holtom, B. C., Mitchell, T. R., Lee, T. W. and Eberly, M. B. (2008) 'Turnover and retention research: A glance at the past, a closer review of the present, and a venture into the future', *Academy of Management Annals*, 2(1): 231–274.

Holtom, B. C., Mitchell, T. R., Lee, T. W. and Inderrieden, E. J. (2005) 'Shocks as causes of turnover: What they are and how organizations can manage them', *Human Resource Management*, 44(3): 337–352.

Hom, P. W. and Griffeth, R. W. (2013) 'What is wrong with turnover research? Commentary on Russell's critique', *Industrial and Organizational Psychology-Perspectives on Science and Practice*, 6(2): 174–181.

Hom, P. W., Mitchell, T. R., Lee, T. W. and Griffeth, R. W. (2012) 'Reviewing employee turnover: Focusing on proximal withdrawal states and an expanded criterion', *Psychological Bulletin*, 138(5): 831–858.

Krinsley, K. E., Gallagher, J. G., Weathers, F. W., Kutter, C. J. and Kaloupek, D. G. (2003) 'Consistency of retrospective reporting about exposure to traumatic events', *Journal of Traumatic Stress*, 16(4): 399–409.

Kulik, C. T., Treuren, G. and Bordia, P. (2012) 'Shocks and final straws: Using exit-interview data to examine the unfolding model's decision paths', *Human Resource Management*, 51(1): 25–46.

Lee, T. W. and Mitchell, T. R. (1994) 'An alternative approach – the unfolding model of voluntary employee turnover', *Academy of Management Review*, 19(1): 51–89.

Lee, T. W., Mitchell, T. R., Holtom, B. C., McDaniel, L. S. and Hill, J. W. (1999) 'The unfolding model of voluntary turnover: A replication and extension', *Academy of Management Journal*, 42(4): 450–462.

Lee, T. W., Mitchell, T. R., Wise, L. and Fireman, S. (1996) 'An unfolding model of voluntary employee turnover', *Academy of Management Journal*, 39(1): 5–36.

Maertz, C. P. and Campion, M. A. (1998) '25 Years of voluntary turnover research: A review and critique', in C. L. Cooper and I. T. Robertson (eds.) *International Review of Industrial and Organizational Psychology*, Vol. 13, New York: Wiley.

Maertz, C. P., Stevens, M. J. and Campion, M. A. (2003) 'A turnover model for the Mexican maquiladoras', *Journal of Vocational Behavior*, 63(1): 111–135.

March, J. G. and Simon, H. A. (1958) *Organizations*, New York: Wiley.

Mathews, P. (2012) 'Canterbury University's post-quake struggles', *The Press*, 6 October. Online. Available HTTP: <http://www.stuff.co.nz/the-press/news/christchurch-earthquake-2011/7777550/Canterbury-Universitys-post-quake struggles>.

Mezirow, J. (1990) 'How critical reflection triggers transformative learning', in J. Mezirow and Associates (eds.) *Fostering Critical Reflection in Adulthood: A Guide to Transformative and Emancipatory Learning*, San Francisco: Jossey-Bass.

Mobley, W. H. (1977) 'Intermediate linkages in relationship between job satisfaction and employee turnover', *Journal of Applied Psychology*, 62(2): 237–240.

Mobley, W. H., Griffeth, R. W., Hand, H. H. and Meglino, B. M. (1979) 'Review and conceptual analysis of the employee turnover process', *Psychological Bulletin*, 86(3): 493–522.

Morrell, K. and Arnold, J. (2007) 'Look after they leap: Illustrating the value of retrospective reports in employee turnover', *International Journal of Human Resource Management*, 18(9): 1683–1699.

Morrell, K., Loan-Clarke, J., Arnold, J. and Wilkinson, A. (2008) 'Mapping the decision to quit: A refinement and test of the unfolding model of voluntary turnover', *Applied Psychology-an International Review-Psychologie Appliquee-Revue Internationale*, 57(1): 128–150.

Morrell, K., Loan-Clarke, J. and Wilkinson, A. (2001) 'Unweaving leaving: The use of models in the management of employee turnover', *International Journal of Management Reviews*, 3(3): 219–244.

——(2004) 'Organisational change and employee turnover', *Personnel Review*, 33(2): 161–173.

Morrison, R. (2003) 'Informal relationships in the workplace: Associations with job satisfaction, organisational commitment and turnover intentions', *New Zealand Journal of Psychology*, 33(3): 114–128.

Niederman, F., Sumner, M. and Maertz, C. P. (2007) 'Testing and extending the unfolding model of voluntary turnover to it professionals', *Human Resource Management*, 46(3): 331–347.

Norris, F. H., Friedman, M. J., Watson, P. J., Byrne, C. M., Diaz, E. and Kaniasty, K. (2002) '60,000 disaster victims speak: Part I. An empirical review of the empirical literature, 1981–2001', *Psychiatry: Interpersonal and biological processes,* 65(3): 207–239.

Norris, F. H. and Kaniasty, K. (1992) 'Reliability of delayed self-reports in disaster research', *Journal of Traumatic Stress,* 5(4): 575–588.

Oxford English Dictionary (2015) 'Crisis', *OED Online,* Oxford University Press, June 2015. Online. (Accessed 25 July 2015).

Price, J. L. and Mueller, C. W. (1981) 'A causal model for turnover for nurses', *Academy of Management Journal,* 24(3): 543–565.

Robertson, G. (2012) 'DHB staffing turnover up since quake', in K. Brown (ed.) *Insight,* Wellington, New Zealand: Radio New Zealand.

Russell, C. J. (2013) 'Is it time to voluntarily turn over theories of voluntary turnover?', *Industrial and Organizational Psychology-Perspectives on Science and Practice,* 6(2): 156–173.

Steers, R. M. and Mowday, R. T. (1981) 'Employee turnover and post-decision justification', in L. L. Cummings and B. M. Straw (eds.) *Research in Organizational Behavior,* Vol. 3, Greenwich: JAI Press.

5 Survival strategies of cultural service providers in a post-earthquake context

Abanti Antara, Jörg Finsterwalder
and Michael C. Shone

Introduction

This chapter presents research that examines the impact of the 2010–2011 Canterbury earthquakes on cultural service providers (for example, museums, art galleries) in the city of Christchurch, New Zealand. As a consequence of these earthquakes, Christchurch lost many of its unique cultural and heritage attractions during the period of rebuild which is significant both for the city as a destination as well as tourist and local visitation and use. Like many cultural service providers visitation provides important income streams. For the purposes of this chapter the terms *tourism* and *cultural tourism* are used to encompass all forms of visitation whether it be from people from inside the region, who often make up the bulk of the users of cultural services, or by domestic and international travellers from outside the region. This study investigates the impact of the earthquakes on cultural heritage visitation; the post-quake representation of cultural and heritage sites, features and activities; and the implementation of "substitute" cultural and heritage attractions. Taken together, these investigations provide knowledge about substitute heritage attractions and alternative ways to encourage visitation in this post-disaster context.

Cultural tourism in Christchurch

As a consequence of a series of devastating and costly earthquakes in Christchurch during 2010 and 2011, the city is struggling to re-establish its cultural attractions in the period of "rebuild" and "replace" for the future (Swaffield 2013). Swaffield (2013) identifies three main stages for disaster response in the city: immediate response (crisis/rescue); recovery (aftermath/relief); and reconstruction (rehabilitation/rebuild or replace/closure). Christchurch has lost much of its heritage architecture, arts and cultural facilities as buildings have been damaged, ruined, destroyed and demolished. For example, a number of unique heritage sites in the city, such as historic and culturally significant churches (including the Anglican and Roman Catholic cathedrals) and the Christchurch Arts Centre, were badly damaged and will take years to be repaired, rebuilt or in some cases demolished (New Zealand Federation of Historical Societies 2013)

(See also Amore, Chapter 6, this volume). At the time of writing, four years on from the 2010–2011 earthquakes, the city's heritage attractions are in various stages of rebuild or repair. Of the heritage attractions which remain standing, some, such as the Christchurch Arts Centre, are reasonably well advanced in the repair process. Final decisions on the future of both of the city's cathedrals, and the nature of any rebuild or replacement, are yet to be made. Consequently, local people and visitors to Christchurch are surrounded by constant reminders of the devastating power of the earthquakes and significant impact on the city's suite of cultural attractions.

Heritage is particularly relevant to the economic and social wellbeing of communities in destination areas (Hall and McArthur 1993), including with respect to post-disaster urban regeneration (see Amore, Chapter 13, and Amore and Hall, Chapter 12, in this volume). Cultural heritage tourism utilises the cultural and historic capital of a region and contributes to the growth of a cultural services sector that, in many areas, has replaced traditional resource-based industries (Silberberg 1995; Pitchford 2008). The significance of culture and heritage is further reinforced by Cooper and Hall (2013), who note its importance for some forms of international tourism. With some heritage attractions, such as museums and historic sites, this type of cultural service may motivate visitors to stay longer in, or revisit, destination areas (Kirshenblatt-Gimblett 1998), which in turn promotes a range of downstream economic benefits for the conservation of heritage areas, especially those located in urban environments (Pitchford 2008).

As with many tourism and other businesses, cultural services are susceptible to natural disasters because these events impact negatively on security, transportation facilities and visitor mobility, which are all essential for visitation (Laws and Prideaux 2005). These natural disasters can result in a drastic reduction in visitation because of media coverage and the rapid spread of negative stories through social media (Sharpley 2005; de Saumarez 2007; Scott, Laws and Prideaux 2008; Hall 2010; Orchiston 2012). Where regular utilities, road networks and critical services are cut off, businesses and public organisations are forced to close temporarily or even permanently (Laws and Prideaux 2005; Platt 2012). As a result, the financial sustainability of cultural service providers is called into question with any return to pre-disaster visitation levels taking place often over highly variable time frames (Orchiston 2012).

Although the role of cultural and heritage services in improving community resilience has been recognised (McHenry 2011), there is relatively limited knowledge of the effect of disasters on cultural service providers and their response strategies (Matthews, Smith and Knowles 2009). Christchurch therefore provides a potentially useful case study of the approaches utilised by cultural service organisations as they sought to adapt to severely changed operating environment.

Research methods

This research utilises a case study approach to investigate the post-disaster responses and strategies of cultural service providers in Christchurch, New Zealand.

Qualitative research methods with an exploratory focus were employed in this study – namely, semi-structured, in-depth interviews conducted in August and September 2013 with managers of cultural service providers, supplemented by document analysis. Both public and private sector organisations were included in this sample.

Using this purposive sampling approach, a total of 12 in-depth interviews, two from each provider, were conducted. The interview questions were informed by the post-disaster management framework developed by Faulkner and Viku-lov (2001). These questions included the topics of pre-disaster planning; actions immediately following the earthquakes; short-term recovery strategies; long-term recovery strategies; and post-disaster resolution, such as the development of substitute attractions/activities and collaborative practices. The organisations represented in this research included the Christchurch Arts Centre, the Christchurch Tram, the Christ Church Cathedral, Christchurch and Canterbury Tourism (the region's tourism marketing organisation), and Canterbury Museum. In addition to these, one organisation from the private sector that wished to remain anonymous was also included and has been given the pseudonym "Heritage-1".

Research findings

The research participants universally agreed that the earthquakes have had a significant and detrimental impact on cultural and heritage services in Christchurch, and that cultural and heritage service providers suffered particularly large losses in terms of their attraction base (due to physical damage) and visitation. Analysis of the interviews shows that the concept of disaster impact can be subdivided into four themes: reduced numbers of visitors; infrastructural damage; visitor perception; and safety and security.

Reduced numbers of visitors

The interviewees considered the main impact of the disaster to be a reduction in the number of international tourists visiting the city following the earthquakes. As noted by the Canterbury Museum, visitor numbers to Christchurch were significantly down on pre-earthquake levels:

> In the period immediately before the earthquakes we were receiving about 650,000 visitors a year. That is an extremely high number in a city of 350,000 people. When we reopened after the earthquakes that visitor number had dropped to around two-thirds (450,000 of 650,000) of pre-earthquakes levels.

This loss of visitor arrivals was also reported in a number of other interviews, including Christchurch Tram, whose interviewee noted that the main impact on its business, and Christchurch more generally, was that the international market had 'more or less dried up; stopped'. The financial impact on this business was also considerable. This interviewee reported that prior to the earthquakes, approximately NZ$400,000 per annum worth of business was in the form of international visitors. Immediately following the earthquakes this figure dropped to NZ$30,000 per annum.

After the earthquakes the number of domestic New Zealand tourists to Christchurch was also down considerably compared to pre-earthquake levels. This loss of domestic tourists is also noted by the Christchurch Tram informant:

> Pre-earthquake our visitor number breakdown was approximately 60 per cent international tourists, 15 per cent domestic tourists and the rest locals, but now it is more like between 30–40 per cent international, around 10 per cent domestic and the rest [approximately 50 per cent] are actually local Christchurch people.

Infrastructural damage

Another large impact identified by interviewees was damage to facilities and infrastructure both of the cultural service organisations as well as other sectors, such as accommodation and hospitality, that worked closely with cultural services. Most notable among these was the loss of accommodation immediately following the earthquakes. The comments of Christchurch and Canterbury Tourism succinctly capture this concern:

> We actually did not have hotels to house people in, and finding them accommodation of any type was a hugely difficult thing to do – there was just nothing around. You have to remember that we, as a city, lost approximately 80 per cent of hotel accommodation after the earthquake. Add to that the lack of other types of accommodation – motels, backpackers, B&Bs – as well as restaurants, attractions and activities, and you have a city whose tourism sector is in crisis.

All of the interviewees were unable to get in their offices in the immediate aftermath of the earthquakes. Some of their offices were destroyed, computer systems collapsed, and equipment damaged. After getting over the first shock of the disaster and infrastructure damages, all of the participants did their office work from home. This loss of office space was noted by Heritage-1:

> We did not have an office anymore. We gave up as our offices kept falling down. So we, the staff that remained, worked from home. Apart from the operation staff, as sales and marketing person, I worked at home, my boss and the directors worked at home, as did the receptionist for booking our products . . . because we could not get back to Heritage-1 for a long time. Our computer systems were down about four months. I was running the organisation from my home office for probably about three months on and off before fully operational back in here.

From a broader city perspective, the damage to, or loss of, infrastructural capacity as a consequence of the earthquakes was an extremely difficult challenge to overcome. Interviewees noted specifically that damage to core infrastructure such as power, water, and sewerage was considerable:

> The effect was that the museum site had no power, water, light, sewerage – no service at all – and being at the edge of the red zone [large area in the central city heavily damaged and cordoned off from public access] made the museum largely inaccessible.
>
> (Canterbury Museum)

Visitor perception

The interviewees believed that the infrastructure damage, as well as the difficult living conditions experienced in some parts of the city, influenced the perception of the visitors in a negative way. Christchurch Tram commented:

> All the infrastructures for our products are now almost fully repaired, but this is not the case for the wider Christchurch environment in which we operate. So, for example, the tram experience for the visitor who is taking a ride in October [2013] will be reduced because we are travelling through a broken city. It's just not as pretty as it used to be, and although interesting, is in the long term a less appealing thing for people to do.

Several interviewees noted this point, and reflected on the perception that Christchurch had changed from a quaint and attractive city into a city characterised by demolition and construction zones. This overarching perception of Christchurch as a damaged and/or broken city was identified as one of the most significant challenges for the city's cultural and heritage service providers leading to a reconsideration of marketing strategies and target markets – for example, a shift from international to local visitors.

Safety and security

Natural disasters such as earthquakes can have a significant impact on visitor safety and security. This has certainly been the case for the cultural and heritage tourism sector in Christchurch. The interviewees described the disasters' effect on safety and security in several ways. For example, Christchurch Tram's interviewee explained:

> We had a big job to do, just to make the building fundamentally safe again and recover and check the structure. The most concerning impact, in this regard, has been the safety and security of the staff and safety of customers who were using our products at the time.

This has been an ongoing concern for cultural service providers, most notably because of the nature of either their buildings or location of operations (often historic and, therefore, sometimes less structurally sound than modern buildings), or the nature of their attractions/activities (viewing and/or touring cultural and heritage sites as a core component of their offering). This point was raised by Heritage-1:

> In terms of personal safety, because we were in an old building we were lucky that nobody was hurt. We were able to vacate the building between the initial earthquake and the first big aftershock (a period of approximately 20 minutes). When the aftershock hit a section of our internal stairs [they] actually fell down. We were closed again about six months later by our board who were worried about structural strength and safety of the Heritage-1 building. It required an acceleration programme of building safety checks which revealed the need for structural strengthening of the building.

Responses to these challenges

In response to the four challenges identified above, a number of actions and initiatives were undertaken by cultural and heritage service providers to adjust to post-earthquake operating conditions. These have been categorised as follows: short-term emergency response, long-term recovery planning, and operational responses.

Short-term emergency response

Most of the interviewees acknowledged that the implementation of safety plans, such as evacuation plans, was a priority in the immediate aftermath of the earthquake. Heritage-1 noted:

> We would normally have 50 people in the building; some of them were not in the building on the day but others were. The safety planning worked as near about 60 or 70 people were in the building and thankfully we evacuated them all.

Safety and emergency planning was also a high priority for Christchurch and Canterbury Tourism, which assumed a high level of responsibility and trans-organisational coordination with emergency services to ensure visitor safety and the provision of visitor information services during this time:

> We had i-site [visitor information centre] staff finding out if all visitors were okay, especially the international ones who spoke different languages, explaining where to go, what to do.

As an immediate response, so-called telephone trees, i.e. a network of people organised to quickly and simultaneously convey information to overcome compromised and over-stretched communication networks, was successfully utilised by a number of interviewees. Other interviewees, such as Heritage-1, noted that short-term emergency response was also concerned with securing sites, maintaining public safety, and securing buildings. In the mid-term emphasis was placed on commencing restoration planning, resizing or "right-sizing" organisations in terms of structure and staffing, and placing an emphasis on the people performing restoration work within the organisation.

Long-term recovery planning

All of the interviewees indicated they were engaged in longer-term planning which focused on the recovery of visitation levels and visitor experience, as well ensuring a safe operating environment for their staff and visitors. The earthquakes also provided a catalyst for significant change in some organisations and for clarifying their focus. This was noted explicitly by the Christchurch Arts Centre (2015) (see also Amore, Chapter 6, this volume):

> For the longer term, the board decided to change the senior leadership of the Arts Centre and reduce the number of activities we engage in. We've modified the Arts Centre's vision statement accordingly and have taken this new "master plan" to the public for feedback. We are also doing a lot of work in relation to our facility reconstruction programme in terms of costs and procurement options – looking at how we might restore the site exactly. After having made changes to the management team and modifying the Arts Centre's vision, acknowledging community interests and the heritage value of the site, as well as restoration costs, potential uses and, most importantly, stability, the organisation is approaching financial sustainability in a way that we weren't really able to achieve in pre-earthquake Christchurch.

Cultural and heritage operators placed a greater emphasis on communication with the visitors, staff, the local community and other stakeholders. This need for a longer-term recovery plan is reflected in the comments of Christchurch and Canterbury Tourism (CCT):

> For long-term recovery, we are trying to get involved with different lobby groups to ensure the tourism voice is being heard throughout the Christchurch rebuild process. Sometimes it is difficult as people are so focused on their own specific areas of concern and aren't necessarily looking at the larger recovery picture. We need to ensure that the recovery plan works for tourism because tourism is number two in terms of Christchurch's significant industries.

Operational responses and strategies

In light of the impact of the disasters and the subsequent recovery activities, the interviewees mentioned several operational dimensions of long-term planning. The most important of these, in the eyes of the interviewees, was the need to overcome operational complacency; that is, to be aware of, and be prepared to respond appropriately and swiftly to a sudden change in operating conditions due to natural disasters. As noted by Christchurch Tram's informant, 'it taught us to be more flexible and probably not as complacent'.

Another response identified by interviewees was the need to improve the structure of the organisation so that decisions could be made in a swift and reflexive manner if required. Canterbury Museum's interviewee commented that:

> Our response to the earthquakes has been that we are now able to make very quick decisions, and to move very quickly on many fronts. We have tried to cut down on bureaucracy within our organisation so that decision-making is a lot more straightforward and action-oriented than it used to be prior to the earthquakes. And we've also tried to cut our expenditure as much as possible as a response to reduced income from visitors.

Some interviewees also noted that they reduced the number of staff within their organisations in response to the loss of business due to the earthquakes. This was undertaken not only for financial purposes, but also so that new staff members with alternative skill sets in alignment with the post-earthquake operating environment and conditions could be recruited. This sentiment was expressed, for example, by the Christchurch Arts Centre (see also Amore, Chapter 6, this volume):

> As an organisation, and because our focus changed a great deal, we changed our Arts Centre staff team. In fact, we changed it a lot. Our Board made the decision to make changes to the senior management along with the venues department and the marketing department in order to help get us through the next phase of our earthquake recovery.

Another operational response and resolution was to work more collaboratively with other organisations (see also Nilakant et al., Chapter 3, this volume). This was noted by the Christchurch Arts Centre, which has been engaged in considerable levels of collaboration with its "physical neighbours", local and central government, its tenants, art cultural education entities, as well as Christchurch and Canterbury Tourism. This collaboration has centred on the development of a new operational vision for the Arts Centre. The need for collaboration was also raised by Christchurch and Canterbury Tourism, which has been working more closely with a range of organisations since the earthquakes, including the Christchurch City Council (its major funding body), in order to develop a recovery and regeneration strategy for the tourism industry.

The interviewees also identified the use of substitute attractions as a medium-term response to the disruption to their operations caused by the earthquakes (see Table 5.1). For example, the Christchurch Arts Centre interviewee described the substitute attractions and activities utilised to regenerate interest in the city's cultural heritage via a market place approach to public spaces. This included a range of art works being created throughout the city to add vibrancy and interest to the city's transitional street scape. This approach to substitute attractions was also utilised by Christchurch Tram, which used a range of new and old technologies to allow customers to experience the history of the tram ride while at the same time being able to view, via video screens within the carriage, what the street view of Christchurch used to be like:

> The tram will be as it used to be in terms of the antique character of the tram experience. It will include the use of manual tickets for passengers and other authentic features like that, but there will also be video screens in the interior of the tram. So, customers can see what the view out the window used to be like pre-earthquakes and compare it to what they can see now. We can't hide the fact that there is now nothing of real value or interest to see during some parts of the ride, but we can show them what used to be there. So then we can enhance their overall experience.

The concept of substitute attractions was also raised by Christchurch and Canterbury Tourism, which described the use of transitional cultural and heritage attractions that utilise the renewed focus on the city's damaged and/or "lost" heritage:

> We also now talk about the new and transitional elements of the city because they also play an important part of the visitor experience to the city – these would include the Transitional Cardboard Cathedral and Re:START Mall.

The importance of substitute attractions as a recovery response was noted universally by the interviewees, many of whom identified two specific substitute cultural and heritage attractions for tourists: Red Bus Tour (a "red zone" area tour) and Quake City (an earthquake exhibition with disaster elements):

> Both the Red Zone Bus Tour and Quake City are supplement to any attractions . . . They are another way [to tell] the heritage stories [of] the community, but with the added economic benefit [of] tourists being able [to] do two or three [earthquake-related activities] rather than . . . just the one visit to the museum [Canterbury Museum].

Both tourists and locals alike were curious to explore the city's earthquake-related damage (see also Prayag, Chapter 10, this volume). The Red Bus Tour, in collaboration with Canterbury Museum, became an extremely popular visitor attraction, which showed some 37,000 visitors around the Red Zone until end of June 2013. Red Bus Tours was then rebranded to Red Bus Rebuild Tour to continue its success, now focusing on the rebuild activities in the city and showing Christchurch's transitional projects, including "Greening the Rubble", "Gap Filler", Street Art and the Cardboard Cathedral (see also Finsterwalder and Hall, Chapter 15, this volume). The tour's focus was on technology incorporated into

Table 5.1 Earthquake impacts and substitute cultural and heritage services post-earthquake

Service provider	Major impact	Promotional activities including substitute attractions
Christchurch Arts Centre	Closed for a period Lost tenancies	Events in market square near the Arts Centre (art works, mirror paintings, Art Festival 2013), free Theatre premieres 2014, SCIRT World Buskers Festival 2015
Canterbury Museum	Closed for 3 months Lost several artefacts and art works (188 items on display; 2,000–3,000 items in storage)	Educational tours for school students to encourage resilience, free shows (to encourage the community and locals to visit and make the place lively), Street Art, Red Zone Bus Tours, Quake City Exhibition
Heritage-1	Lost the venue	New innovative venue in former warehouse, earthquake cultural event
Christchurch Tram	Lost office, infrastructure, damage to trams and tramways	Christchurch of the past theme video operating in trams
Christchurch and Canterbury Tourism	Accommodation, attractions, and transport infrastructure that serve as the basis for Christchurch as a destination and which the body promotes	Support for Re:START Mall, Gap Filler, a project to populate empty spaces in the city, New Convention Centre (in progress)
Christ Church Cathedral	Building severely damaged	Cardboard Cathedral

the new city (e.g. the Enterprise Precinct Innovation Centre (EPIC), http:// epicinnovation.co.nz/) as well as providing historical and future focused information on specific points of interest along the route, including earthquake impacts, developments, and earthquake damaged buildings that were under repair (Red Bus 2013).

Quake City followed an earlier exhibition by Canterbury Museum on the impact of the Christchurch earthquakes and was located to the Re:START Mall, the container-based retail precinct in Christchurch's CBD. Quake City is a multi-sensory attraction aimed at informing, engaging and educating visitors about the Canterbury earthquakes. This exhibition, in combination with increased Canterbury Museum visitor numbers, appears to be another successful venture. The public and tourist response to the museum's reopening as well as to Quake

City has been remarkable. Over 680,000 people visited Canterbury Museum and the Quake City exhibition in Christchurch's Re:START mall during 2014 alone (Christchurch and Canterbury Tourism 2015), which is a record in the museum's 148 year history. The exhibition is scheduled to continue until at least 31 March 2017 (Canterbury Museum 2015). From these examples it is apparent that operators and service providers were and are still trying to create new inno-vative activities and strategies to regain visitor numbers along with changing the perception of the city post-earthquakes.

Discussion

Post-disaster recovery adjustment to infrastructural damage at both a destination and operational level is obviously one of the most immediate challenges for the participants in this research (see also Faulkner and Vikulov 2001). Participants identified and utilised a range of innovative strategies to the earthquakes, includ-ing, for example, establishing mobile or remote offices, incorporating video stories into their attraction mix, and utilising telephone trees as an alternative communication network. In addition, changes to organisation structures and strategies were used to create a more vibrant, functioning and action-oriented business than they used to have in the pre-earthquake conditions.

The findings of this research also point towards the need for improved disaster assessment (and response) planning. In the post-disaster context, there needs to be assessment of the likely impact of the disaster as well as an informed assess-ment of the probability of further occurrence (Chacko and Marcell 2008). This research revealed that in order to assist with this disaster assessment planning, participants placed considerable importance on the personal experience of the pre-earthquake preparation and restoration process. Indeed, personal experi-ence of destructive earthquakes can influence whether or not people make efforts to prepare for future earthquake events (Lindell and Whitney 2000; Orchiston 2010).

The research also identified that short-term emergency planning for visitors and staff is regarded by participants as being an essential response in a post-disaster context. This is also noted by Faulkner (2001), who sees short-term emergency planning as the first step in a recovery response to natural disasters. This is complemented over time by a longer-term focus which concentrates on developing strategic, rather than immediate, responses to regenerating tourism in destination areas (Chacko and Marcell 2008; Hall 2008). The transition from (short-term) emergency planning to (long-term) recovery planning was noted by all participants in this research. It should be noted, however, that many of these planning responses were focused strongly on marketing and promotional activities, and as such reinforce the findings of Faulkner and Vikulov (2001) who suggest that disaster recovery plans mostly focus on promotional activities for further outcomes.

Another key feature of the participant organisations' responses to the earth-quakes was the development of substitute cultural and heritage attractions and activities. In the recovery planning of participants, new and innovative experiences were identified and created to substitute for those lost, damaged or impaired in the post-disaster context. The participants in this research supported the idea that they should develop new and innovative attractions which may substitute for or help to resist decline in temporary conditions. Moreover, substitute attractions can sometimes be offered at a lower cost, with fewer transportation and/or logistical challenges, with greater personal safety, and with a higher level of assurance of a quality visitor experience. This notion of substitute attractions represents a key component of the Tourism Disaster Management Framework developed by Faulkner and Vikulov (2001), in which the use of substitute elements helps to ensure the long-term survival of cultural and heritage service providers, particularly during the transitional post-disaster recovery context. The use of such substitute attractions, such as Quake City being located in the Re:Start Mall, has been a key feature of the post-earthquake cultural and service provision in the Christchurch context (see also Finsterwalder and Hall, Chapter 15, this volume).

Conclusion

The cultural and heritage service providers who participated in this research faced a range of challenges regarding the physical setting within which they operate (for example, damaged buildings and cityscape) as well as visitor perceptions regarding Christchurch as an earthquake-ruined city. In response, service providers have adopted a reflexive approach to this post-disaster operating environment via a number of mechanisms noted above. Included in this reflexive approach has been a recognition of the need to overcome operational complacency and to streamline organisational decision-making. As a corollary to this, many service providers have sought to "right-size" their staffing levels and competencies for improved organisational alignment, as well as work more collaboratively with other service providers across the sector. Perhaps most pragmatically, they have utilised a range of substitute cultural and heritage attractions while the city of Christchurch transitions into post-disaster recovery and rebuild.

These actions taken by service providers have, in turn, fostered an operating environment of innovation and creativity in decision-making, as well as encouraged greater strategic planning at the organisational level. Moreover, the steps taken by service providers appear to have also strengthened the cultural and heritage sector's overall social capital with respect to coordination and collaborative working relationships. In doing so the sector is arguably now better positioned to respond positively to both external and internal operational pressures than it was pre-earthquake. Taken together, this research has highlighted the need for the cultural and heritage services to develop providers' resilience and preparedness for natural disaster and unforeseen events. By developing this resilience capacity, cultural and heritage services can significantly reduce their individual and collective vulnerability to such events.

References

Canterbury Museum (2015) *Exhibitions*. Online. Available HTTP: <http://www.canterburymuseum.com/events/> (Accessed 12 May 2015).

Chacko, H. E. and Marcell, M. H. (2008) 'Repositioning a tourism destination', *Journal of Travel & Tourism Marketing*, 23(2–4): 223–235.

Christchurch Arts Centre (2015) *Crafting a vision*. Online. Available HTTP: <http://www.artscentre.org.nz/looking-ahead.html> (Accessed 12 May 2015).

Christchurch & Canterbury Tourism (2015) *2014 visitor numbers set Museum record*, 19 January. Online. Available HTTP: <http://www.christchurchnz.com/media/newsroom/2014-visitor-numbers-set-museum-record/> (Accessed 12 May 2015).

Cooper, C. and Hall, C. M. (2013) *Contemporary Tourism: An International Approach*, Oxford: Goodfellow Publishers.

de Saumarez, N. (2007) 'Crisis management, tourism and sustainability: The role of indicators', *Journal of Sustainable Tourism*, 15(6): 700–714.

Faulkner, B. (2001) 'Towards a framework for tourism disaster management', *Tourism Management*, 22(2): 135–147.

Faulkner, B. and Vikulov, S. (2001) 'Katherine, washed out one day, back on track the next: A post-mortem of a tourism disaster', *Tourism Management*, 22(4): 331–344.

Hall, C. M. (2008) *Tourism Planning* (2nd ed.), Harlow: Prentice-Hall.

Hall, C. M. (2010) 'Crisis events in tourism: Subjects of crisis in tourism', *Current Issues in Tourism*, 13(5): 401–417.

Hall, C. M. and McArthur, S. (1993) 'Heritage management: An introductory framework', in C. M. Hall and S. McArthur (eds.) *Heritage Management in New Zealand and Australia: Visitor Management, Interpretation, and Marketing*, Auckland: Oxford University Press.

Kirshenblatt-Gimblett, B. (1998) *Destination Culture: Tourism, Museums, and Heritage*, Los Angeles: University of California Press.

Laws, E. and Prideaux, B. (2005) 'Crisis management: A suggested typology', in E. Laws and B. Prideaux (eds.) *Tourism Crises: Management Responses and Theoretical Insight*. New York: Haworth Hospitality Press.

Lindell, M. K. and Whitney, D. J. (2000) 'Correlates of household seismic hazard adjustment adoption', *Risk Analysis*, 20(1): 13–26.

Matthews, G., Smith, Y. and Knowles, G. (2009) *Disaster Management in Archives, Libraries and Museums*, Cheltenham: Ashgate.

McHenry, J. A. (2011) 'Rural empowerment through the arts: The role of the arts in civic and social participation in the Mid-West region of Western Australia', *Journal of Rural Studies*, 27(3): 245–253.

New Zealand Federation of Historical Societies (2013) 'Preliminary work started on Akaroa's damaged War Memorial', *Keeping in Touch*, 7(1): 1–8.

Orchiston, C. (2010) 'Tourism and seismic risk: Perceptions, preparedness and resilience in the zone of the Alpine Fault, Southern Alps, New Zealand', unpublished doctoral thesis, University of Otago, Dunedin, New Zealand.

——(2012) 'Seismic risk scenario planning and sustainable tourism management: Christchurch and the Alpine fault zone, South Island, New Zealand', *Journal of Sustainable Tourism*, 20(1): 59–79.

Pitchford, S. (2008) *Identity Tourism: Imaging and Imagining the Nation*, Bingley: Emerald.

Platt, S. (2012) *Reconstruction in New Zealand Post 2010–11 Christchurch Earth-quakes*, Cambridge: University of Cambridge, Cambridge Architectural Research.

Red Bus. (2013) *Media Release for Red Bus Tour Launch, 31 July*. Online. Available HTTP: <http://www.redbus.co.nz/christchurch/articles/index.cfm/2013/07/media-release-for-red-bus-tour-launch/> (Accessed 12 May 2015).

Scott, N., Laws, E. and Prideaux, B. (2008) 'Tourism crises and marketing recovery strategies', *Journal of Travel & Tourism Marketing*, 23(2–4): 1–13.

Sharpley, R. (2005) 'The tsunami and tourism: A comment', *Current Issues in Tourism*, 8(4): 344–349.

Silberberg, T. (1995) 'Cultural tourism and business opportunities for museums and heritage sites', *Tourism Management*, 16(5): 361–365.

Swaffield, S. R. (2013) 'Place, culture and landscape after the Christchurch earthquake', in H. Sykes (ed.) *Space, Place and Culture*, Melbourne: Future Leaders.

Wood, A. (2015) 'Visitor numbers to Christchurch rocking post-quake', *The Press*, 9 January. Online. Available HTTP: <http://www.stuff.co.nz/business/industries/64785264/Visitor-numbers-to-Christchurch-rocketing-post-quake> (Accessed 12 May 2015).

6 I do (not) want you back!

(Re)gentrification of the arts centre, Christchurch

Alberto Amore

Introduction

This chapter examines the strategies that are shaping the recovery of the Arts Centre of Christchurch (ACC) through the lens of gentrification. It is argued here that the Arts Centre of Christchurch Trust Board (hereafter the Trust) took advantage of the climate of emergency following the earthquakes of 2010 and 2011 to accelerate the process of site development that was interrupted on the eve of the first quake, when the commission appointed by the Christchurch City Council (CCC) refused the Trust's project for the National Conservatorium of Music. The current Arts Centre development plan (released in August 2013) (ACC 2013a, 2014a) identifies creative businesses and upmarket hospitality businesses as the desired tenants for the site and does not foresee clauses for former tenants to return to Arts Centre.

This study utilises theories of gentrification and links them to the emerging paradigm of crisis-driven urbanisation. It argues that the decisions of the Trust following the earthquakes of 2010 and 2011 are framing a market-led recovery of the Arts Centre that move beyond its original community focus. While mainstream literature has hitherto discussed the process of retail gentrification at the neighbourhood level, this study illustrates the phenomenon of retail displacement within a site of historic relevance, thus providing an insight which has been overlooked.

Literature

Investment in the historic urban fabric has become a widespread practice of urban regeneration in many developed countries (Ashworth and Tunbridge 2000). In several cases, the safeguarding and retention of historic places results in a new use of heritage premises. Such physical 'rehabilitation of old structures' (Smith 1982: 139), however, is likely to stimulate an inexorable process of gentrification. The notion of gentrification used here applies to a wide spectrum of city users, who represent the main targets of urban strategies in the contemporary city (Harvey 1989). That is, the re-use of old buildings can encourage a process of capital reinvestment (Smith 2000) for the creation of spatially embedded places designed for a more affluent class of people with distinctive cultural consumption characteristics (Zukin 1990). Particularly with respect to heritage buildings, 'the establishment of legally-protected landmark historic districts confirms the selective construction [of] both monopoly rents and a monopoly of consumption rights' (Zukin 1990: 42).

Gentrification is 'a global urban strategy that is densely connected into the circuits of global capital and cultural circulation [under] the leading edge of neoliberal urbanism' (Lees, Slater and Wyly 2008: 132). The study of gentrification is useful to understand the roots of urban development as the outcome of highly political processes (Betancur 2002) following market-driven and market-obeying policies of urban development (Porter 2009) whose ultimate aim is the increase of rent values 'for the right to use land' (Lees et al. 2008: 51), which may not be commensurate with some of the original roles of publicly owned properties. While most works on gentrification address the phenomenon of residential displacement, its effects 'on neighbourhood attributes such as retail remains an underrepresented area of study' (Greenberger 2013: 1) (Table 6.1). Only a limited set of works discusses the displacement of commercial activities as result of upscale retail diversification in historic neighbourhoods (Zukin et al. 2009). The latter goes hand-in-hand with tourism, as the establishment of leisure shops and restaurants contributes to the transformation of a given site 'into a relatively affluent and exclusive enclave marked by a proliferation of corporate entertainment and tourism venues' (Gotham 2005: 1099). To date, however, the process of retail and tourist gentrification within historic sites has been overlooked. The work by Gonzalez and Waley (2013) is one of the very few contributions that illustrate the process of retail gentrification within a site of historic relevance (i.e. the Kirkgate Market in central Leeds, UK). Nevertheless, this work does not illustrate a context of crisis following a natural or human-induced disaster.

To address this gap, studies on retail gentrification have emerged to illustrate how urban redevelopment policies use disasters as pretext 'to initiate or consolidate gentrification projects' (Glück 2013: 3). Studies from Manchester (Massey 2005), New York and New Orleans (Gotham and Greenberg 2014) show how key stakeholders seized the opportunity to implement neoliberal policy responses to transform cities through projects 'previously off the table due to bureaucratic inertia, lack of funding' (Gotham and Greenberg 2014: 95) or opposition by the existing community.

The relationship between gentrification and disaster is discussed below through a longitudinal review of the dynamics of the recovery of the Arts Centre. This study differs from other research undertaken in the South of Lichfield areas of Christchurch (e.g. McDonagh, Borwing and Perkins 2013, 2014), which illustrates how the earthquake halted the process of gentrification. However, it suggests that the earthquake triggered the displacement of low-rent businesses and that 'the rents demanded for retail space in new buildings appear to preclude small owner-operated businesses' (McDonagh et al. 2014: 1).

Table 6.1 Overview of literature on retail gentrification

City	Scale	Focus	CBD	Post-disaster
New York	Urban	Process of retail gentrification as expression of socio-spatial changes in uses and consumers of the city (Zukin 1990).	–	–
Newcastle upon Tyne	Neighbourhood	Displacement of low-cost retailers as result of regeneration in the historic centre of the city (Diggle and Farrow 1999).	X	–
Sydney	Neighbourhood	Supply-side analysis of trade and retail in four neighbourhoods at the margins of the CBD (Bridge and Dowling 2001).	–	–
London	Neighbourhood	Retail gentrification with strong pro-market policies of displacement and refurbishment of the urban fabric for the night economy (Butler and Robson 2001).	–	–
Manchester	Neighbourhood	Private-led restoration of the retail areas following the IRA bombings of 1996 (Massey 2005).	X	X
New Orleans	Neighbourhood	Retail gentrification as complementary dimension of tourist gentrification in key tourist areas of the city (Gotham 2005).	X	–
New York	Neighbourhood	Longitudinal analysis of retail gentrification in two areas of the city. Rise of upscale restaurants and boutiques as facet of neighbourhood's creative capital and distinctiveness (Zukin et al. 2009).	–	–
Barcelona	Neighbourhood / Site	Retail gentrification in the historic centre of Barcelona, with displacement of low-cost retailers. Analysis of policies to attract new retailers in closed premises (Pascual-Molinas and Ribera-Fumaz 2009).	X	–

(*Continued*)

Table 6.1 (Continued)

City	Scale	Focus	CBD	Post-disaster
Barcelona	Neighbourhood	Analysis of production-led gentrification through the study of business and corporation settlement in clustered neighbourhoods (Dot Jutgla, Cesella and Pallares-Barbera, 2010).	–	–
Seville	Urban	Retail gentrification as triggering agent of users' and residents' displacement (Díaz Parra 2008).	–	–
Portland	Neighbourhood	Retail gentrification and repercussions on black American community (Sullivan and Shaw 2011).	–	–
Toronto	Neighbourhood	Ethnic neighbourhood transformation through the lens of retail gentrification (Murdie and Teixeira 2011).	–	–
Leeds	Site	Process of retail gentrification in central markets as result of market-led policies and real estate interests in renting premises to upmarket tenants (Gonzalez and Waley 2013).	X	–
New York	Neighbourhood	Understanding of retail change as reflex of production-led gentrification through longitudinal study on local retailers (Greenberger 2013).	–	–
Christchurch	Neighbourhood	Retail resilience and displacement as result of the 2010–2011 Canterbury earthquakes (McDonagh et al. 2013).	X	X
St. Catherine	Neighbourhood	Displacement of existing retailers and attraction of creative and tourism businesses (Wierzba 2014).	X	–
Seoul	Neighbourhood	Attitude of long-established businesses towards gentrification of the neighbourhood (Jeong et al. 2015).	–	–

Case study: the Arts Centre of Christchurch

The Arts Centre of Christchurch is a complex of Gothic Revival buildings once home to the University of Canterbury (UC) (New Zealand Historic Places Trust (NZHPT) 2011), and located on the western edge of the Christchurch CBD. The first facilities were built between 1877 and 1882 (ACC 2013c) by English-born architect Benjamin Mountfort, who was also appointed for the design of further buildings through the 1890s (ACC 2013d; 2013f). Since 1990, the 23 buildings of the Arts Centre have been registered as places of special or outstanding historical significance (Heritage New Zealand (HNZ) 2015). Before the earthquakes, the Arts Centre was one of the major tourist attractions of the so-called "cultural precinct" (Christchurch Tourism 2008). Between the late 1950s and the early 1970s, however, the site faced a period of uncertainty following the relocation of the University of Canterbury to the peripheral campus area in Ilam (Strange 1994). This phase heightened the processes of pioneering gentrification (Smith 1986) and 'vulnerability intensification', which refers to the 'increasing vulnerability of urban populations and ecosystems to future disasters' as result of the deepening of vulnerabilities in the aftermath of a disaster (Gotham and Greenberg 2014: 12) that were occurring in relation to the location/site.

1978–2008: pioneering gentrification in a highly vulnerable site

The period between the mid-1970s and the early 1980s illustrates the features of the first wave of gentrification (Hackworth and Smith 2001), with the establishment of arts stakeholders in the vacant premises of the complex. The Court Theatre was the first tenant to relocate to the Arts Centre in 1975 (Strange 1994), followed by the Free Theatre of Christchurch in 1982 (Free Theatre of Christchurch 2014). The presence of cultural attractions and events within the complex fuelled the establishment of cafes and restaurants throughout the early 1980s, with the opening of Dux de Lux restaurant and bar in the old Student Union building (Dux de Lux 2014). Recreation and retail activities were boosted throughout the 1990s with the opening of stores such as Beadz Unlimited (Stewart 2011a) and the establishment of stallholders in the atrium of the complex. By 2003, the Arts Centre was home to 180 small to medium businesses (ACC 2003). In 2004, finally, the site welcomed the first high-end retail tenant with the opening of clothing store Untouched World in the Old Registry building (Clark 2004). Unlike other forms of gentrification, however, the property of the premises remained firmly in the hands of the Trust, as foreseen in the original Trust Deed from 1978. Businesses operated as tenants in the premises for commercial use identified in the original feasibility study of 1974 (Community Arts Centre Steering Committee 1974).

Given the historic relevance of the site, this early phase also reflected some features of the third phase of classical gentrification (Clay 1979) during which the site gains relevant media and community interest, and gentrifiers move in with higher disposable incomes (the first phase is marked by pioneers who complement the existing population; the second by the share of pioneers increasing and changes in the composition of retail and services). The announcement in 1973 that 'the buildings would be given to the people of Christchurch as an arts centre' (Strange 1994: 101) was followed by the statement of the then New Zealand Prime Minister, the Hon. Norman Kirk, who hoped that the use of 'the buildings [would] draw from the threads of all the cultures in New Zealand and attempt to produce something uniquely New Zealand in character' (quoted in Strange 1994: 101). Similarly, the release of the feasibility study plan in 1974 saw the participation and the unanimous support of politicians and community leaders. As Canterbury-based planner Malcolm Douglass later reported, this initiative 'was a rare example of those in the lead being supported by a huge groundswell of public feeling' (quoted in Strange 1994: 103).

The years that preceded the earthquakes of 2010 and 2011 were characterised by increased vulnerabilities and a lack of resources that resembled the crisis-driven urbanisation model (Gotham and Greenberg 2014). Since the establishment of the Trust in December 1978, earthquake strengthening, retention of historic buildings, attraction of high-end tenants and lack of public funding had been major ongoing concerns. The Trust was able to undertake preliminary earthquake strengthening and retention works throughout the 1980s (Strange 1994; Crean 2008), but it soon became clear that further works were going to be needed to make the Arts Centre less prone to medium and strong earthquakes (ACC 2003). However, works only began at the end of 2007 as part of a systematic restoration project of NZD$25 million over a period of 15 years (Crean 2007), with the aim being to strengthen the buildings and then retain them in perpetuity (ACC 2011). However, the real estate market never expressed interest in the Arts Centre as originally expected (Community Arts Centre Steering Committee 1974), and it did not attract high-end retailers. Rather, those expressing interest in relocating to the complex were low-rent arts stakeholders such as the Court Theatre or single-person owned businesses. Nevertheless, the presence of tenants positively contributed to the economy of the Arts Centre. In fact, most of the revenues of the Arts Centre came from the renting of commercial premises (ACC 2010a). Similarly, the presence of a several businesses increased the tourist appeal of the site and thus led directly to the increase in the Arts Centre assets value from NZD$14 million in 2002 (ACC 2003) to $21.2 million in 2008 (ACC 2010a). Finally, the ACC's continued tight financial position made the retention of the Arts Centre in its previous guise, with a substantial community organisation base, problematic. Despite feasibility studies that had recommended that the Trust meet all its expenditure from its income (Community Arts Centre Steering Committee 1974), the Arts Centre had to cope with extraordinary expenditures of earthquake strengthening costing millions of dollars. Given the limited heritage funding in New Zealand (see also Chapter 13, this volume), the CCC was the only major body from which grants could be accessed. However, the Council had progressively reduced its support to the Arts Centre in the early 2000s (ACC 2003). Eventually, the CCC granted the amount of funds requested by the Arts Centre in 2003 (NZ$400,000 per annum) at the end of 2009 (CCC 2013).

This phase of pioneering gentrification took place in the context of the progressive shift of businesses and residents to outside the Christchurch CBD. The slow but inexorable decline of the central city attracted low-rent tenants, such as artists and small hospitality entrepreneurs, to the premises handed to the Arts Centre Steering Committee and, later, the Trust. The site, however, had important structural vulnerabilities that could not be entirely addressed with the tight financial assets available since the establishment of the Trust. Under the pressure of financial sustainability and the need to reinforce the site, seeking for high-end tenants and increasing the commercial space of the centre became the paramount strategies for the Trust to manage the site in quasi-absence of public funds.

2008–2010: second wave of gentrification

This phase is marked by an increasing struggle between owners and tenants (Hackworth and Smith 2001). The pressures around the Trust resulted in an aggressive entrepreneurial approach (Lees et al. 2008) at the expense of the most vulnerable tenants and community groups. The Trust acknowledged that venues such as the National Conservatorium of Music would be crucial in the development of the Arts Centre. This phase, moreover, underpins one of the features of the second wave gentrification highlighted by Gotham (2005), with cultural anchors used to consolidate a new wave of gentrification led by more lucrative tenants. The earthquakes of 2010 and 2011, however, deflected the process of gentrification to a new path.

Early concerns among tenants emerged at the end of 2008, when the Trust asked advisors to review the Arts Centre assets value. The advisors concluded that the tangible assets of the Arts Centre as at December 2009 were worth NZD$100.74 million, with a depreciation rate of 0.2 per cent per annum (ACC 2010a, 2011). The Trust, however, admitted that there would not be 'upward pressure on tenant rentals' (ACC 2010a: 5), as the latter were based on the rental market for retail spaces in the Christchurch CBD (ACC 2010a). As the former Arts Centre Chairman, John Simpson, explained, this new method of site value was:

> a common issue for owners of heritage buildings, in part arising from a difficult fit between the reporting requirements and standards of the governing legislation (written for normal commercial buildings) and the unique characteristics and performance of heritage assets.
>
> (ACC 2010a: 3)

Frictions between the Trust and the tenants reached their peak when the Trust launched a project in collaboration with the University of Canterbury and the Christchurch City Council to build a National Conservatorium of Music within the heritage complex. The lease of the land for the facility would have given 'the Arts Centre the money to maintain, preserve and reconstruct existing buildings' (Conway 2010b) and thus complete the necessary earthquake strengthening works. The project was widely criticised by long-established tenants of the Arts Centre, heritage conservationists and resource management experts. In particular, the Court Theatre considered relocating outside the Arts Centre (van Beynen 2009), while a group of fierce opponents established the Save Our Arts Centre (SOAC) to oppose the Trust and the Council (SOAC 2010a). Other concerns raised by SOAC were the changes to the Trust Deed in 2008, the alleged lack of available funds reported in the Trust reports of 2008 and 2009 (Gorman 2010), the inclusion of clauses blocking objections to consent applications in the new tenancy contracts (Greenhill 2009), and the subdivision of the site into six lots. The latter, in particular, was seen as having a significant adverse effect on the ability to protect recognised heritage values (SOAC 2010b).

The consent to proceed with the building of the conservatorium, in the end, was denied by the CCC hearing commission on March 2010 (CCC 2010) in accordance with the legislation on historic heritage protection established by the *Resource Management Act 1991*. This decision, however, did not stop the Trust from developing an underground car parking area in the heart of the Centre. On 2 September 2010, the Trust team ordered the relocation of 103 stallholders to the Southern edge of the centre in order to empty the area and initiate the works (Conway 2010c). Then the first earthquake struck.

2010–2014: framing the re-gentrification of the arts centre

Following the first major earthquake of 4 September 2010, businesses remained closed for a few days, but none of the buildings leased for commercial use suffered significant damage, and by mid-September most of the activities had reopened (Sachdeva 2010). Nevertheless, 20 stallholders had their licence terminated (Conway 2010a). According to the Stallholder's Association, the Trust used the earthquake 'as a very sad and sorry excuse' (Conway 2010a: A.4) to evict those who were opposed to the parking area project. In early February 2011, the Trust leased part of the Registry building to the Canterbury Cheesemongers, who had lost their previous building in the September earthquake (Stewart 2011b).

In contrast, the earthquake of 22 February 2011 had severe consequences for tenants at the Arts Centre. Following inspection in early March, 22 out of the 23 buildings of the complex were red-stickered (Gates 2011g) and admission to tenants was restricted by civil defence for safety reasons until 8 March. On 23 March the Trust announced that, due to the high uncertainty with the recovery of the Arts Centre, the tenants had 'to consider their own future in alternative spaces' (Gates 2011d: A.3). With the exception of the Canterbury Cheesemongers, all the tenants were unilaterally evicted by the Trust. Nevertheless, long-established businesses decided to fight the eviction. Seven of these businesses took legal action against the Trust and requested the release of engineering reports on their former leased units (Gates 2011j). The hope of these tenants was to return back to their premises (Gates 2011k), but they soon realised that the Trust would not grant them the right of returning to the Arts Centre in the future. Other businesses, instead, relocated to alternative premises immediately following the

Table 6.2 List of long-established tenants and relocation following the earthquake of February 2011

Tenants (as at September 2010)*	Type of business	First established	Status	New location(s)
Academy Cinemas	Movie theatre	1976	Lease terminated	The Colombo Mall
Annie's Wine Bar	Bar	1992	Lease terminated	Shut down
Artisan Fibres	Handcrafted clothing	1985	Lease terminated	Shut down
Arts Centre Bookshop	Bookstore	1991	Lease terminated	Worcester Street
Arts Centre Leather Shop	Handcrafted leather goods	1998	Lease terminated	Shut down
Backstage Bakery	Café	1986	Lease terminated	New business (St Asaph, St Kitchen & Stray Dog Bar)
Beadz Unlimited	Costume jewellery	1993	Lease terminated	New Regent Street
Canterbury Cheesemongers	Cheese shop and dining	2011	Remained	
Cave Rock Gallery	Art shop and gallery	1990	Lease terminated	Shut down
Cloister Cinema	Movie theatre	1986	Lease terminated	Colombo Mall
Coffee Corner	Café	2003	Lease terminated	Upper Riccarton
Connexion Gallery	Cooperative of jewel makers	2000	Lease terminated	Disestablished
Court Theatre	Performing arts	1975	Lease terminated	Shed in Addington
Dux Live	Live music venue	1978	Lease terminated	Addington
Dux de Lux	Restaurant	1978	Lease terminated	Riccarton
Free Theatre	Performing arts	1982	Returned	Temporarily at Arts Centre (until 2016)
Forget me knots	Knitted works	1994	Lease terminated	Akaroa (2011) Halswell (2012 onwards)

(*Continued*)

Table 6.2 (Continued)

Tenants (as at September 2010)*	Type of business	First established	Status	New location(s)
Fudge Cottage	Sweets shop	1990	Lease terminated	Bishopdale Mall
New Zealand Jade & Opal Centre	Jewellery	2001	Lease terminated	Shut down
Palate	Shop and dining	2007	Lease terminated	Shut down
Rutherford's Den	Tourist attraction	1999	Lease terminated	Expected return to the Centre: end of 2015
Salamander Gallery	Gallery and laboratory	1991	Lease terminated	Shut down
SOFA Gallery	Visual arts	1980	Lease terminated	University of Canterbury
Southern Ballet	Performing arts	1975	Lease terminated	Sydenham
Te Puna Toi	Visual arts	1980	Lease terminated	University of Canterbury
Te Toi Mana	Arts shop and gallery (Maori Art)	1985	Lease terminated	Shut down
The Christchurch Carving and Bone Studio	Carving art shop and gallery	1985	Lease terminated	Shut down
The Wool Studio	Knitted wear	1985	Lease terminated	Middleton
Untouched World	Clothing store	2004	Lease terminated	RE:Start Mall Burnside
Visually Maori	Arts shop and gallery (Maori Art)	1980	Lease terminated	Shut down
Woodcraft Gallery	Woodcraft	1986	Lease terminated	Linwood
Wool Yarns and Fibres	Wool clothing	1990	Lease terminated	Woolston
Zander Imaging	Visual arts	2000	Lease terminated	Shut down

*Excludes activities under the Arts Centre Trust and stallholders. All of the above relocations are within the Christchurch region.

eviction. Among these were the Court Theatre, which reopened at the end of 2011 in a new temporary location outside the CBD (Gates 2011e) and expressed interest in eventually relocating to the proposed Performing Arts Precinct (Dally 2012b) (Table 6.2).

Of interest is the fight against eviction carried on by the owner of Dux de Lux, Richard Sinke. According to an engineering report commissioned by Sinke, the building that was home to the Dux de Lux could be re-occupied in a very short period (Yardley 2011a) at a reasonable cost (NZD$390,000) (Gates 2011i). Sinke proposed to personally finance the restructuring works, thus gaining the sympathy of local opinion (Gates 2011c). In June 2011 the Trust agreed to meet Sinke and discuss the future of the restaurant as part of the reconstruction and revitalisation of the Arts Centre (Gates 2011h). Nevertheless, the Trust informed Sinke that the full strengthening of the building would have made the repairs very expensive and unnecessary for a secondary building (Gates 2011f). Finally, Sinke decided to reopen two new facilities outside the CBD between 2011 and 2012 (Greenhill 2011; Turner 2012), with a third restaurant to be opened in 2015 (Dally 2015).

The decision to unilaterally terminate leases and evict tenants from the Arts Centre was justified on safety grounds. However, it soon became clear that the Trust could now concentrate its efforts on the projects of earthquake restoration and re-gentrification of the centre. After the earthquake of 2010, the Trust announced that strengthening of damaged buildings was crucial, the costs of which further affected the financial liabilities of the Arts Centre (Sachdeva 2010). The eviction of tenants following the earthquake of February 2011 was seen as a necessary measure given the 'unclear, yet long, time needed for the recovery' (Gates 2011d: A.3). The Director of the Arts Centre, Ken Franklin, stated that the Trust had the obligation to direct funds to preserve the key heritage buildings, and funding the reopening of businesses was not contemplated as a recovery strategy (Gates 2011l). Similarly, the Chairman of the Trust, Deane Simmonds, asserted that tenants had the right to challenge the Trust with legal actions, but he also noted that this would have taken 'money away from preserving and restoring the buildings' (Gates 2011h: A.9).

In the first months after the February earthquake, the limited funds available to the Trust were allocated to extraordinary works on key buildings (Gates 2011g) and a detailed scanning of the Arts Centre (ACC 2012). The latter was decisive in securing the pay-out from insurers and thus permitted the Trust to obtain more than NZD$350 million between 2011 and 2013 (ACC 2014a). Therefore, the Trust was able to fund the strengthening of buildings to 100 per cent of the revised building code (Gates 2011a). Priority was given to restoring key heritage buildings, but the Trust assured the public that demolition of secondary buildings was out of question (Gates 2011a). In the absence of significant public funding to help restore the Arts Centre and support the tenancy of its previous community organisations, the strategies used to restore the Arts Centre have only served to reinforce the overall direction of the Centre towards high-end retail with its accompanying higher rents. The earthquake has therefore served to accelerate existing gentrification processes.

The intransigence of Trust members towards former tenants seemed to soften with the appointment of Andre Lovatt as Director in October 2012 and the inclusion of new members in the Trust Board. Among them, the newly appointed Chairwoman, Jen Crawford, stated that tenants ousted by the 2011 earthquakes would be "invited" to return (Mann 2012), once the Trust completed the recovery of buildings (scheduled for 2018) and achieved financial sustainability (ACC 2013a). The new Director also welcomed former tenants in March 2013 to discuss the future of the Arts Centre (ACC 2014a). However, their inclusion did not imply a return of old businesses back to the Arts Centre. Rather, it simply engaged people 'to test some ideas and generate some discussion' (Gates 2013b: A.6).

Since May 2013, the Trust established a memorandum of understanding with the Christchurch Arts Festival to host the event in a temporary venue outside the Arts Centre (ACC 2013b), and subscribed to an agreement with the Canterbury Museum for the promotion of heritage and the hosting of joint events (New Zealand Ministry for Culture and Heritage (NZMCH) 2014). The Trust is contributing to the re-initiation of the Cultural Precinct (ACC 2013a). Lovatt also welcomed stakeholders to pick from a shortlist of established international best practices (ACC 2014a) identified by 'a range of experts from the arts, heritage and culture sectors' (ACC 2013e: 11). The resulting *Vision for the Arts Centre* identified a range of anchor uses of the complex, with a range of complementary activities gravitating around them (ACC 2013a, 2014a) (Table 6.3).

Among the complementary activities, the Arts Centre identified 'education retreats, hospitality venues, boutique accommodation [...] the Arts Centre Shop and a Members' area' (ACC 2014a: 7) as the ideal business solutions to turn the Arts Centre into a hub for creative entrepreneurs, general public and tourists (ACC 2013a). The implementation of this new vision is conceived as an opportunity to bring new activities and users to a 21st-century cluster for creative businesses (ACC 2014a). The decisions undertaken since the appointment of the new Director suggest a strong direction towards the arts and the creative businesses. In particular, the Trust allocated the first fully restored building

Table 6.3 The proposed vision for the Arts Centre

Element	Anchor Use	Complimentary Use
Promote	Market Square	Information Centre
		Arts Centre Shop
		Ideas den
Encourage	Arthouse Cinema	Boutique accommodation
	Exhibition space	Hospitality venue
Facilitate	Studio space	Hire spaces
	Co-working hub	
Educate	Children's activities	Leadership Retreat
	Education and outreach	
	Residency Programme	

Source: derived from ACC 2013a, 2014a.

(i.e. the Registry building) to a design company (McDonald 2013). Similarly, the Trust is considering expressions of interests from the hospitality sector for the recently re-opened Gymnasium building (Gates 2013a), which is the temporary home of the Free Theatre (ACC 2014b). At the time of writing, three buildings are scheduled for re-opening (Gates 2014). The University of Canterbury will relocate its music and classics departments to the Old Chemistry building along with a collection of Greek and Roman artefacts (UC 2014), while a 3-D printing laboratory will open in the Common Room (Gates 2014). Lastly, the Boys High School building will be made available to upmarket hospitality and retail operators (McDonald 2013). The reopening of the whole site is scheduled for the end of 2018 (Gates 2014) at a cost of NZD$290 million.

Nevertheless, the persisting shortfall between the costs of recovery and the funds available (Dally 2012a) and the limited fundraising following the major contribution for the rebuild of the Tower and the Great Hall (Gates 2011b) puts the Trust in need of raising approximately NZD$5 million by 2024 (Gates 2014) in order to build back better. This means that, as throughout the CBD, the rents of refurbished buildings will be higher than those agreed before the earthquakes. Not surprisingly, as Lovatt stated, the Arts Centre 'is looking at trying to do things like getting good tenants in there who can pay rent and contribute to the future of the Arts Centre' (Gates 2013a: A2). The expected move of "A-grade tenants" to the Arts Centre has also been welcomed among real estate agents, who suggest that the complex may 'tempt big hospitality businesses from Christchurch' (McDonald 2013) and the rest of the country (Taylor 2013). A complementary strategy may encourage site developments or the demolition of secondary heritage buildings. In fact, the Trust secured the subdivision of the land assets as planned before the earthquakes (ACC 2010b) and recent changes in the heritage legislation (Brazendale 2013) encourage *de facto* the adoption of projects that had been previously rejected.

Conclusions

This chapter illustrated how exogenous events, such as an earthquake, can decisively alter the trajectory of development and positioning of a locally, if not nationally, significant nonprofit cultural organisation responsible for the conservation and management of heritage. The seismic events of 2010 and 2011 created the conditions for a new phase of gentrification that would not have occurred so quickly in a business as usual scenario. Perhaps somewhat ironically, given the physical impacts on the Arts Centre, the earthquakes, via the opportunities made available by insurance funding, have been decisive in providing the Arts Centre a degree of financial sustainability it has sought since first established in late 1978.

Undoubtedly, the earthquakes represented a decisive turning point in giving the Trust the opportunity to conserve the integrity of the buildings while promoting the arts and the creative industries. The recovery of the Arts Centre, however, shows how the earthquakes of 2010 and 2011 heightened the second wave of gentrification that had encountered legal and community opposition between 2009 and the first major earthquake. The decisions of the Trust suggest a strong market-led redevelopment strategy that is supported only thanks to the important insurance pay-outs. Along with the expensive recovery project, the Trust is continuing to seek new uses in addition to the current high-end retail and lifestyle business opportunities for the Arts Centre in order to guarantee financial sustainability in the long term.

At the time of writing, the Arts Centre has revised its internal governance (Nahkies 2012) and a private bill is currently under scrutiny at the New Zealand Parliament (New Zealand Parliament 2015) to retain the site for the public in the event of future earthquakes. Authorities and heritage stakeholders welcome the move to a skills-based Trust board and the upcoming legislation for the site (Lochhead 2014) as ideal solutions to prevent the rise of frictions between the Trust and the community as occurred before the earthquakes. In fact, the decisions of the Trust under the direction of former director Ken Franklin were perceived as abuses of authority from a board which was 'charged with acting in the public interest' (Yardley 2011b: C.4). Arguably, the appointment of new Trust members is expected to establish new forms of engagement between the Trust and the community (New Zealand Parliament 2015). However, it appears that the plans of the current Trust underpin the pre-earthquake projects of up-market development which were fiercely opposed by many in the local community. This inevitably raises concerns as to what extent the community is still the main beneficiary of the Arts Centre, as was originally foreseen in the Trust Deed of 1974.

References

The Arts Centre of Christchurch Incorporated (ACC) (2003) *Proposal to Arts, Heritage and Culture Committee.* Online. Available HTTP: <http://resources.ccc.govt.nz/files/thecouncil/meetingsminutes/agendas/2003/february/artscultureap/clause4attachment1.pdf> (Accessed 12 December 2014).

——(2010a) *Annual Report 2009.* Online. Available HTTP: <http://www.artscentre.org.nz/assets/arts-centre-annual-report-2009.pdf> (Accessed 6 August 2013).

——(2010b) *Proposed Subdivision and Land Use Application.* Online. Available HTTP: <http://resources.ccc.govt.nz/files/ArtsCentreOfChristchurch-SubdivisionAndLanduseApplication.pdf> (Accessed 20 March 2015).

——(2011) *Annual Report 2010.* Online. Available HTTP: <http://www.artscentre.org.nz/assets/arts-centre-annual-report-2010.pdf> (Accessed 6 August 2013).

——(2012) *Annual Report 2011.* Online. Available HTTP: <http://www.artscentre.org.nz/assets/arts-centre-annual-report-2011.pdf> (Accessed 6 August 2013).

——(2013a) *Annual Report 2012.* Online. Available HTTP: <http://www.artscentre.org.nz/assets/ac-annual-report-1213.pdf> (Accessed 6 August 2013).

——(2013b) *Arts Centre newsletter – Issue 1 — April 2013.* Online. Available HTTP: <http://www.artscentre.org.nz/assets/newsletter1.pdf> (Accessed 19 February 2014).

——(2013c) *Arts Centre to Host Christchurch Arts Festival.* Online. Available HTTP: <http://www.artscentre.org.nz/assets/1_christchurch-arts-festival – arts-centre-media-release—31-may-2013.pdf> (Accessed 19 November 2013).

———(2013d) *Clock Tower and College Hall*. Online. Available HTTP: <http://www. artscentre.org.nz/clock-tower – college-hall.html> (Accessed 19 October 2013).

———(2013e) *Engineering Building*. Online. Available HTTP: <http://www. artscentre.org.nz/engineering.html> (Accessed 19 October 2013).

———(2013f) *Observatory, Biology and Physics Buildings*. Online. Available HTTP: <http://www.artscentre.org.nz/observatory%2c-biology-and-physics.html> (Accessed 19 October 2013).

———(2014a) *Annual Report 2013*. Online. Available HTTP: <http://www.artscentre. org.nz/assets/arts-centre-annual-report-2013.pdf> (Accessed 4 April 2014).

———(2014b) *Arts Centre Newsletter – Issue 6 — August 2014*. Online. Available HTTP: <http://www.artscentre.org.nz/assets/arts-centre-newsletter-august-2014. pdf> (Accessed 6 March 2015).

Ashworth, G. and Tunbridge, J. (2000) *The Tourist-Historic City. Retrospect and Prospect of Managing the Heritage City*, London: Routledge.

Betancur, J. (2002) 'The politics of gentrification. The case of West Town in Chicago', *Urban Affairs Review*, 37: 780–814.

Brazendale, N. J. (2013) 'Preservation of heritage buildings in the wake of the Canterbury Earthquakes', *The New Zealand Journal of Environmental Law*, 17: 237–289.

Bridge, G. and Dowling, R. (2001) 'Microgeographies of retailing and gentrification', *Australian Geographer*, 32: 93–107.

Butler, T. and Robson, G. (2001) 'Social capital, gentrification and neighbourhood change in London: A comparison of three south London neighbourhoods', *Urban Studies*, 38: 2145–2162.

Christchurch City Council (CCC) (2010) *Decision on a Publicly Notified Resource Consent Application. RMA 90014850 National Conservatorium of Music*, Christchurch: CCC.

———(2013) *Christchurch City Council Supplementary Agenda 12 September 2013*. Online. Available HTTP: <http://resources.ccc.govt.nz/files/TheCouncil/meetings minutes/agendas/2013/September/CBCouncil12September2013Supplementary-Agenda.pdf> (Accessed 3 March 2015).

Christchurch Tourism (2008) *Cultural Precinct*. Online. Available HTTP: <http://www. christchurchtourism.com/attractions/cultural-precinct/> (Accessed 25 March 2015).

Clark, H. (2004) *Opening New Store for Untouched World, Arts Centre, Christchurch*, Wellington: New Zealand Government. Online. Available HTTP: <http://www. beehive.govt.nz/node/21886> (Accessed 20 February 2015).

Clay, P. L. (1979) *Neighbourhood Renewal: Middle-class Resettlement and Incumbent Upgrading in American Neighbourhoods*, Lexington, MA: Lexington Books.

Community Arts Centre Steering Committee (1974) *Old University Precinct Future Use Feasibility [sic] Study*, Christchurch: Community Arts Centre Steering Committee.

Conway, G. (2010a) 'Arts Centre damage forces some stallholders out', *The Press*, 21 September, A.4.

———(2010b) 'Opponents of music school fail', *The Press*, 3 February, A.1.

———(2010c) 'Stallholders to protest at forced shift',, *The Press*, 3 September, A.7.

Crean, M. (2007) 'Centre of attention', *The Press*, 11 April, D.2.

———(2008) 'Renovations mean best of both worlds', *The Press*, 22 November, D.11.

Dally, J. (2012a) 'Arts Centre faces $50m shortfall', *The Press*, 3 November. Online. Available HTTP: <http://www.stuff.co.nz/the-press/news/7901317/Arts-Centre faces-50m-shortfall> (Accessed 20 April 2015).

———(2012b) 'Arts Centre redux', *The Press,* Supplement, 3 November, 4.

———(2015) 'Richard Sinke's Dux empire expands into Innovation Precinct', *The Press,* 6 March. Online. Available HTTP: <http://www.stuff.co.nz/the-press/christchurch-life/67031347/Richard-Sinkes-Dux-empire-expands-into-Innovation-Precinct> (Accessed 25 March 2015).

Díaz Parra, I. (2008) 'Movimiento vecinales contra la gentrificación y transformaciones en la politica local de Sevilla. Los casos de El Pumarejo y San Bernardo', paper presented at the X Coloquio Internacional de Geocritica. Diez años en el mundo, en la Geografia y en las ciencias sociales, 1999–2008, Barcelona, 26–30 May 2008.

Diggle, R. and Farrow, H. (1999) *What Is the Future of Low Cost Shopping in Grainger Town?: Will It Survive and Does This Matter?* Newcastle upon Tyne: Centre for Research on European Urban Environments.

Dot Jutgla, E., Cesella, A. and Pallares-Barbera, M. (2010) 'Gentificatión productiva en Barcelona: Effectos del nuevo espacio económico', paper presented at the IV Jornadas de Geografia Económica. Grupo de Geografia Económica de la AGE, León, 1–2 July 2010.

Dux de Lux. (2014) *Dux Dine.* Online. Available HTTP: <http://www.duxdine.co.nz/> (Accessed 5 May 2014).

Free Theatre of Christchurch (2014) *A Brief History.* Online. Available HTTP: <http://www.freetheatre.org.nz/a-brief-history.html> (Accessed 15 May 2014).

Gates, C. (2011a) '30m repair plan for Arts Centre', *The Press,* 15 July, A.4.

———(2011b) 'Arts Centre needs $200m rebuild', *The Press,* 20 December, A.1.

———(2011c) 'Battle grows to get Dux open again', *The Press,* 2 June, A.1.

———(2011d) 'Centre evicts tenants, lays off staff', *The Press,* 24 March, A.3.

———(2011e) 'Court's new theatre promises to become landmark for recovery', *The Press,* 8 December, A.2.

———(2011f) 'Dux de Lux fights eviction', *The Press,* 25 March, A.7.

———(2011g) 'Rebuilding Arts Centre may take years, cost $100m', *The Press,* 15 March, A.4.

———(2011h) 'Talks 'positive' but Dux reopening an unknown', *The Press,* 4 June, A.9.

———(2011i) 'Talks on Dux step forward – bar owner', *The Press,* 3 June, A.3.

———(2011j) 'Tenants launch legal challenge', *The Press,* 1 June, A.1.

———(2011k) 'Tenants sue Arts Centre to get access to reports', *The Press,* 18 July, A.5.

———(2011l) 'Wine bar joins eviction battle', *The Press,* 31 March, A.4.

———(2013a) 'Bar to open in former cinema', *The Press,* 5 February, A.2.

———(2013b) 'Step-by-step revival of Arts Centre', *The Press,* 9 February, A.6.

———(2014) 'Students to bring life back into Arts Centre', *The Press,* 25 October, A.9.

Glück, Z. (2013) 'Race, class, and disaster gentrification', *Tidal Blog,* 13 March. Online. Available HTTP: <http://tidalmag.org/blog/race-class-and-disaster-gentrification/> (Accessed 23 December 2014).

Gonzalez, S. and Waley, P. (2013) 'Traditional retail markets: The new gentrification frontier?', *Antipode,* 45: 965–983.

Gorman, P. (2010) 'Arts centre figures flawed', *The Press,* 5 March, A.1.

Gotham, K. F. (2005) 'Tourism gentrification: The case of New Orleans' Vieux Carre (French Quarter)', *Urban Studies,* 42: 1099–1121.

Gotham, K. F. and Greenberg, M. (2014) *Crisis Cities: Disaster and Redevelopment in New York and New Orleans*, Oxford: Oxford University Press.

Greenberger, N. (2013) 'Changing retail dynamics in Greenpoint, Brooklyn', unpublished thesis, Columbia University.

Greenhill, M. (2009) 'New clause will give tenants less say in arts centre development', *The Press*, 13 October, A.3.

———(2011) 'Dux owner sets up music venue', *The Press*, 6 August, A.9.

Hackworth, J. and Smith, N. (2001) 'The changing state of gentrification', *Tijdschrift voor economische en sociale geografie*, 92: 464–477.

Harvey, D. (1989) *The Urban Experience*, Oxford: Blackwell.

Heritage New Zealand (HNZ) (2015) *Arts Centre of Christchurch*, Online. Available HTTP: <http://www.heritage.org.nz/the-list/details/7301> (Accessed 20 March 2015).

Jeong, Y., Heo, J., and Jung, C. (2015) 'Behind the bustling street: Commercial gentrification of Gyeongridan, Seoul', *Procedia – Social and Behavioral Sciences*, 170: 146–154.

Lees, L., Slater, T. and Wyly, E. K. (2008) *Gentrification*, London: Routledge.

Lochhead, L. (2014) *Submission. Arts Centre of Christchurch Trust Bill*. Press release. Online. Available HTTP: <http://historicplacesaotearoa.org.nz/historic-places-canterbury-submission-arts-centre-of-christchurch-trust-bill/> (Accessed 18 November 2014).

Mann, C. (2012) 'Bar owner can't wait for permanent home again', *The Press*, 4 August, A.13.

Massey, J. (2005) 'The gentrification of consumption: A view from Manchester', *Sociological Research Online*, 10(2). Online. Available HTTP: <http://www.socresonline.org.uk/10/2/massey1.html> (Accessed 20 February 2015).

McDonagh, J., Borwing, J. and Perkins, H. (2013) 'Gentrification interrupted – impacts of the Christchurch earthquakes on inner city revitalisation', paper presented at the 20th Annual European Real Estate Society Conference. Vienna, 3–6 July 2013.

———(2014) 'What now? The post disaster experiences of small, inner city retail businesses', paper presented at the 20th Pacific Rim Real Estate Society. Lincoln, 19–22 January 2014.

McDonald, L. (2013) 'Arts Centre opening for hospitality operators', *The Press*, 7 December, A.1.

Murdie, R. and Teixeira, C. (2010) 'The impact of gentrification on ethnic neighbourhoods in Toronto: A case study of Little Portugal', *Urban Studies*, 48: 61–83.

Nahkies, G. (2012) *The Christchurch Arts Centre: A Review of Governance Structure Issues*, Wellington: BroadWorks International. Online. Available HTTP: <http://www.parliament.nz/resource/0000198787> (Accessed 27 February 2014).

New Zealand Historic Places Trust (NZHPT) (2011) *NZHPT Submission to the Canterbury Earthquakes Royal Commission*, Wellington: NZHPT.

New Zealand Ministry for Culture and Heritage (NZMCH) (2014) *Canterbury Museum and the Arts Centre Join Forces*. Online. Available HTTP: <http://www.mch.govt.nz/news-events/news/canterbury-museum-and-arts-centre-join-forces> (Accessed 12 January 2015).

New Zealand Parliament. (2015) *Arts Centre of Christchurch Trust Bill – Second Reading*, Wellington: New Zealand Parliament. Online. Available HTTP: <http://www.parliament.nz/en-nz/pb/debates/debates/51HansD_20150401_00000028/

arts-centre-of-christchurch-trust-bill-%E2%80%94-second-reading> (Accessed 12 April 2015).

Pascual-Molinas, N. and Ribera-Fumaz, R. (2009) 'Retail gentrification in Ciutat Vella, Barcelona', in K. Shaw and L. Porter (eds.) *Whose Urban Renaissance? An International Comparison of Urban Regeneration Strategies*, New York: Routledge.

Porter, L. (2009) 'Whose urban renaissance?', in L. Porter and L. Shaw (eds.) *Whose Urban Renaissance? An International Comparison of Urban Regeneration Strategies*, New York: Routledge.

Sachdeva, S. (2010) 'Arts Centre repair bill in millions', *The Press*, 16 September, A.1.

Smith, N. (1982) 'Gentrification and uneven development', *Economic Geography*, 58: 139–155.

———(1986) 'Gentrification, the frontier and the restructuring of urban space', in N. Smith and P. Williams (eds.) *Gentrification of the City*, London: Allen and Unwin.

———(2000) 'Gentrification', in R. J. Johnston, D. Gregory, G. Pratt and M. Watts (eds.) *The Dictionary of Human Geography*, Oxford: Blackwell.

Save Our Arts Centre (SOAC) (2010a) *Registration decision: Save Our Arts Centre Incorporated*, Christchurch: SOAC.

———(2010b) *Subdivision Will Lead to Inappropriate Development*. Press release. Available HTTP: <http://www.scoop.co.nz/stories/AK1003/S00141/subdivision-will-lead-to-inappropriate-development.htm> (Accessed 18 February 2015).

Stewart, T. (2011a) 'Beads of success in suburbia', *The Press*, 4 June, C.2.

———(2011b) 'Firm moves a couple of blocks', *The Press*, 5 February, C.20.

Strange, G. (1994) *The Arts Centre of Christchurch: Then and Now*, Christchurch: Clerestory Press.

Sullivan, D. and Shaw, S. C. (2011) 'Retail gentrification and race: The case of Alberta Street in Portland, Oregon', *Urban Affairs Review*, 47: 413–432.

Taylor, C. (2013) 'Restaurateur sought for Arts Centre precinct', *The New Zealand Herald*, 27 July, C.10.

Turner, A. (2012) 'Restaurant with a familiar ring opens in Riccarton', *The Press*, 16 November, A.2.

University of Canterbury (UC) (2014) *UC Reconnecting with CBD at the Arts Centre*. Press release. Online. Available HTTP: <http://www.comsdev.canterbury.ac.nz/rss/news/?feed=news&articleId=1479> (Accessed 23 January 2015).

van Beynen, M. (2009) 'Court Theatre mulls quitting Arts Centre', *The Press*, 12 December, A.3.

Wierzba, T. (2014) 'Transforming downtown St. Catharines into a creative cluster', unpublished thesis, Brock University.

Yardley, M. (2011a) 'Dux de Lux fate the new duel du jour', *The Press*, 16 April, C.11.

———(2011b) 'Arts Centre owned by us', *The Press*, 4 June, C.4.

Zukin, S. (1990) 'Socio-spatial prototypes of a new organization of consumption: The role of real cultural capital', *Sociology*, 24: 37–56.

Zukin, S., Trujillo, V., Frase, P., Jackson, D., Recuber, T. and Walker, A. (2009) 'New retail capital and neighbourhood change: Boutiques and gentrification in New York City', *City & Community*, 8: 47–64.

7 Earthquake impacts, mitigation, and organisational resilience of business sectors in Canterbury

Girish Prayag and Caroline Orchiston

Introduction

Business sector is a significant predictor of both the impact of and recovery from disasters (Webb et al. 2002; Brown et al. 2014). The purpose of this chapter is to present the findings from a comparative analysis of perceived earthquake impacts, mitigation strategies, and organisational resilience of three major business sectors (accommodation/food services, manufacturing and education/training) in the region of Canterbury. The importance of these sectors can be seen from their significant contribution to GDP and employment in Canterbury.

The accommodation sector underpins tourism activity in Christchurch and contributes around two per cent of GDP for the region, employing almost 12,000 people (Canterbury Development Corporation (CDC) 2015). The September 2010 and February 2011 earthquakes had a significant impact on this sector and related tourism activities, leading to reduced visitor numbers and damage to built infrastructure. Hotels and backpacker accommodation in the central business district were particularly badly affected (Orchiston et al. 2014).

The manufacturing sector is of strategic importance to the Canterbury region, being the second largest manufacturing centre in New Zealand, and contributes 12 per cent to the GDP of Christchurch. The sector employs around 23,000 people (CDC 2015). However, resource requirements of the earthquake rebuild are shifting employees and certain job categories to the construction sector, driving up wages and posing challenges to the manufacturing sector (CDC 2015).

The education/training sector in Christchurch has the second largest growth rate in international student numbers in New Zealand since the earthquakes and contributes five per cent to Christchurch's GDP. The sector employs around 14,700 people and is expected to be a future growth sector in the region (CDC 2015). Comparing the performance of these sectors on earthquake impacts, mitigation strategies, and organisational resilience offers valuable insights into organisational planning and preparedness for disasters.

The effects of earthquakes on the physical and social environments are well-documented, but the ways in which organisations respond to, adapt, and recover post-disaster are poorly understood (Halvorson and Hamilton 2010). There is a need to understand how different sectors are affected by disasters, and the factors

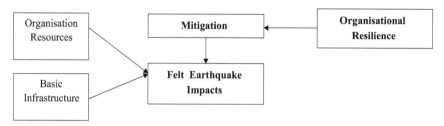

Figure 7.1 Theoretical framework

that influence recovery (Galbraith and Stiles 2006). For example, business sector, business size and age are significant predictors of success and survival post-disaster in some studies but not in others (e.g. Dahlhamer and Tierney 1998; Brown et al. 2014). Also, attempts to understand the factors that influence the impact, mitigation and recovery of organisations in a post-disaster context are limited (Whitman et al. 2013; Mannakkara and Wilkinson 2014).

Disaster management is commonly represented by four phases: mitigation, preparedness, response and recovery (Rubin 1991). Figure 7.1, based on disaster management principles (Faulkner and Vikulov 2001), helps to illustrate the relationships between the three factors of earthquake impacts, mitigation and organisational resilience. Earthquakes can impact organisations' basic infrastructure and resources (Brown et al. 2014). However, the mitigation strategies put in place can, in part, be explained by the level of organisational resilience, with more resilient businesses/sectors showing a stronger emphasis on developing mitigation strategies. The mitigation strategies put in place are also indicative of the level of preparedness of organisations in response to a disaster. This level of preparedness affects response and recovery of not only the organisation, but also the business sector. Mitigation strategies, for example, can also reduce the physical impact of earthquakes on organisations, and improve their ability to recover following disasters (Kachali et al. 2012; Brown et al. 2014). The relationships between the different elements of Figure 7.1 are discussed in more detail below. The chapter then examines the results of a project that examines how the accommodation, education/training and manufacturing sectors responded to the impacts of the Christchurch earthquakes. The chapter concludes with some implications for the various business sectors studied.

Impacts from earthquakes and recovery

The literature on organisational earthquake vulnerability and impacts suggest that several factors account for organisational impact and survival in a post-disaster context. Earthquake impacts on organisations can take the form of direct physical damage to structures, property and inventory; non-structural damage to premises; service interruptions; changes in cash flow; halted or slowed production; changes in suppliers and customers; staff attrition; and psychosocial effects on staff and their family (Kroll et al. 1991; Tierney 1997; Webb et al. 2002; Corey and Deitch 2011; Wasileski et al. 2011; Orchiston et al. 2012; Whitman et al. 2013). Utility disruption in particular can lead to significant financial losses (Tierney 1997; Webb et al. 2000) and reduced productivity (Wasileski et al. 2011). For example, disruption to the transport network can limit customer and supplier access to premises (Tierney 1997). Following the 2010/2011 Canterbury earthquakes, Brown et al (2014) found that "customer issues" impacts were the most disruptive for organisations. The disruption of critical services and organisational size are also symbiotic with sector-specific organisational vulnerabilities (Whitman et al. 2013). For example, Kachali et al. (2012) found that 78 per cent of the hospitality businesses surveyed reported the need to use new suppliers.

Industry sectors tend to respond differently to earthquake effects (Tierney, 1997; Webb et al. 2002). Wholesale and retail businesses generally report significant sale losses, relatively high failure rates and slower rates of recovery (Kroll et al. 1991). In contrast, large disasters can stimulate activity and growth for the manufacturing and construction sectors (Webb et al. 2002). Recovery from a disaster is a complex and interconnected process, and without a guaranteed outcome for affected organisations (Kachali et al. 2012). Organisational recovery in a post-disaster context is dependent on several factors, including industry-sector vulnerabilities (Webb et al. 2002; Whitman et al. 2013), neighbourhood effects (e.g. damage to nearby organisations), and customers' perceptions of an area's damage state (Dahlhamer and Tierney 1996). The relationship between industry sector and recovery is not consistent across all disasters or throughout the recovery period (Brown et al. 2014). Given that organisations work in an increasingly interdependent environment, it is necessary to understand organisational recovery from a dynamic systems perspective. Decisions made by one organisation in the immediate aftermath of a disaster can influence the recovery of other organisations (Corey and Dietch 2011). To this end, understanding the effectiveness of mitigation strategies used by different business sectors may facilitate post-disaster recovery of organisations and of a region in general.

Mitigating earthquake impacts on organisations

The literature on mitigation strategies used to limit earthquake impacts on organisations and boost recovery can at best be described as contradictory. For example, the majority of sectors surveyed after the September 2010 earthquake (the first in the sequence of the Canterbury earthquakes), mentioned that well-designed and well-built buildings and relationships with staff were the most important factors limiting disruption (Whitman et al. 2013). Also, large organisations were more likely to use business continuity plans in mitigating organisational disruption compared to smaller organisations. Corey and Deitch (2011) found that the education sector experienced the most severe dip in organisational performance following Hurricane Katrina but the construction sector recovered the best on the same factor. Whitman et al. (2013) found that farming organisations suggested that "relationship with neighbours" and "insurance" were the most important factors mitigating earthquake impacts on farmers, but non-farming organisations suggested "financing options" and "supply chain logistics" as being the most helpful. Thus, sectorial differences may determine the importance and helpfulness of mitigation strategies in limiting disruption to business operations and recovery (Whitman et al. 2013).

Organisational resilience

Resilience has been defined in many ways in different fields. Resilience generally refers to the ability of a system to maintain and adapt its essential structure and function in the face of disturbance while maintaining its identity (Holling 1973). Organisational resilience has emerged as an important concept in the organisational behaviour and disaster management literatures. Organisational resilience refers to the capacity of the organisation to adapt to disturbances and seize opportunities emerging from the changed environment (Smit and Wandel 2006; McManus et al. 2008). The organisation's adaptive capacity is an integral constituent of organisational resilience (Smit and Wandel 2006). Some organisations are more adaptive than others post-disaster (McManus et al. 2008). Hence, an emerging research strand links organisational resilience to business recovery (Chang et al. 2001; Bruneau et al. 2003; McManus et al. 2008). This body of research suggests that resilience consists of two dimensions, planned and adaptive. Planned resilience involves the use of existing, predetermined planning and capabilities, as exemplified in business continuity and risk management, which are predominantly pre-disaster activities. Adaptive resilience emerges during the post-disaster phase as organisations develop new capabilities through dynamically responding to emergent situations that are outside of their plans (Lee et al. 2013). For example, post-quake the hospitality sector in Canterbury had the highest number of organisations agreeing that their planning for the unexpected was appropriate, suggesting adequate planned resilience (Kachali et al. 2012). Key indicators of organisational resilience include awareness of issues for roles and responsibilities of key stakeholders, awareness of organisational recovery priorities, and the degree and links between various planning techniques, such as risk and crisis management and business continuity plans (McManus et al. 2008). The need to understand organisational resilience across and within sectors is critical for building resilient communities (McManus et al. 2008).

The survey

A survey was conducted on business behaviours, resilience and recovery following the 2010/2011 Canterbury earthquakes. The data were collected as part of a larger project by Resilient Organisations aimed, a research group at the University of Canterbury, at quantifying the economic implications of vulnerabilities to infrastructure. Earthquake impacts on organisations were measured using 16 items, such as difficulty in accessing premises/sites and perceptions of buildings safety, adapted from the literature (Powell 2010; Kachali et al. 2012; Brown et al. 2014), on a four-point Likert scale (0 = *Not Disruptive* and 3 = *Very Disruptive*). Seventeen factors that helped organisations mitigate the impact of the earthquakes, such as relationship with staff and practiced response to a disaster, were also adapted from the literature (Whitman et al. 2013) and measured on a four-point Likert scale (0 = *Not Important* and 3 = *Very Important*). The extent of disruption caused by the earthquakes on 11 critical basic infrastructures, such as road networks, gas and airport (Wasileski et al. 2011; Whitman et al. 2013) were measured on a four-point Likert scale (0 = *Not Disruptive* and 3 = *Very Disruptive*). Organisational resilience was measured on eight-point Likert scale, anchored on ".00" – *Strongly Disagree* and "1.00" – *Strongly Agree*, using 13 items adapted from the literature, such as the organisation's commitment to practising and testing its emergency plans to ensure they are effective and the barriers stopping the organisation from working well with other organisations (Kachali et al. 2012). Demographics such as age and size of the organisation (Dahlhamer and Tierney 1998), Māori status (i.e. whether the organisation described itself as an iwi corporation or not), and property ownership were also measured (Brown et al. 2014).

The database used to identify the sampling frame of organisations in the region of Canterbury was obtained from a business-to-business marketing company and was divided by sector. Two sampling criteria were used to include companies in the sample: (i) organisations must have premises in one of the three districts (Waimakariri, Christchurch City, and Selwyn District) in the Canterbury region that were directly impacted from the 2010/2011 earthquakes; (ii) the organisations must be classified under the Australian and New Zealand Standard Industrial Classification (ANZSIC). Organisations were initially contacted by telephone and the respondents had the option of completing the survey either over the telephone, online, or on a hard copy that was sent. The data were collected between July and December 2013. From an initial 2176 organisations contacted, 541 complete and valid surveys were obtained. Of these, 154 were included in this study (45 representing the Accommodation sector, 74 representing the Manufacturing sector, and 35 representing the Education/Training sector). The sample was proportionally representative of organisations in these three sectors in the Canterbury region.

Findings

The average age of the organisations participating in this study was 34 years old with an average of 32.7 full time employees in the Canterbury region. On average, no significant differences existed between the three sectors on the number of full-time employees in the Canterbury region ($F = 1.421, p > .05$). However, a significant difference existed on the average age of the organisations ($F = 18.20, p < .001$), whereby organisations in the Accommodation/Food service sectors (M = 19.9, SD = 23.9) and Manufacturing (M = 32, SD = 23.7) were comparatively younger than those in the Education/Training sector (M = 57.6, SD = 39.4).

Earthquake impacts on organisation resources

Analysis of variance (ANOVA) with Hochberg's post-hoc comparisons on the three sectors revealed significant differences on seven of the 16 earthquake impact items (Table 7.1). On average, the earthquake impacts were less disruptive on the Accommodation/Food Service sector (M = 0.57, SD = 0.80) on the item "accessing IT data" compared to the Education/Training (M = 0.99, SD = 1.09) and Manufacturing sectors (M = 1.54, SD = 1.08). A significant difference also existed on the item "difficulty in accessing premises" whereby disruptions were lower for the Accommodation/Food Service sector (M = 0.48, SD = 0.96) in comparison to the Education/Training (M = 1.3, SD = 1.26) sector. On the item "supplier issues", the impact of the earthquakes was less disruptive on the Accommodation/Food Service sector (M = 0.72, SD = 0.79) in comparison to the Education/Training (M = 1.04, SD = 0.91) and Manufacturing (M = 1.19, SD = 0.92) sectors. On the item "customer issues", a similar difference as identified for "supplier issues" was evident. Overall, the earthquake impacts on the Accommodation/Food Service sector were less disruptive compared to the Manufacturing and Education/Training sectors.

Table 7.1 Earthquake impacts on organisational resources

Earthquake Organisational Impacts	Sectors	N	Mean	Std. Dev	F	Sig.
Difficulty accessing IT data	Education and Training	35	1.54	1.094	8.263	0.000*
	Manufacturing	68	0.99	1.086		
	Accommodation and Food Services	37	0.57	0.801		
Structural damage to buildings	Education and Training	34	1.24	1.103	1.717	0.183
	Manufacturing	70	1.29	1.118		
	Accommodation and Food Services	41	0.9	0.995		
Non-structural damage (fittings, etc.)	Education and Training	34	1	1.101	0.189	0.828
	Manufacturing	70	1.09	0.913		
	Accommodation and Food Services	42	0.98	1		
Machinery loss or damage	Education and Training	23	0.65	1.071	2.442	0.091

Earthquake Organisational Impacts	Sectors	N	Mean	Std. Dev	F	Sig.
	Manufacturing	63	1	1.016		
	Accommodation and Food Services	34	0.56	0.96		
Office equipment loss or damage	Education and Training	30	0.87	1.106	1.663	0.194
	Manufacturing	63	0.78	0.906		
	Accommodation and Food Services	37	0.49	0.804		
Damage to inventory or stock	Education and Training	29	0.97	1.085	0.027	0.973
	Manufacturing	67	0.96	0.976		
	Accommodation and Food Services	39	1	0.827		
Damage to ground surface	Education and Training	31	1.06	1.093	0.207	0.814
	Manufacturing	64	0.97	1.098		
	Accommodation and Food Services	41	0.9	0.97		
Damage to or closure of adjacent organisations or buildings	Education and Training	26	1.15	1.347	2.961	0.056
	Manufacturing	57	0.54	0.946		
	Accommodation and Food Services	33	0.67	1.021		
Damage to local neighbourhood	Education and Training	32	1.34	1.181	2.178	0.118
	Manufacturing	61	0.87	1.072		
	Accommodation and Food Services	38	0.92	0.997		
Difficulty accessing premises/site	Education and Training	33	1.3	1.262	5.388	0.006*
	Manufacturing	60	0.8	1.038		
	Accommodation and Food Services	40	0.48	0.96		

(Continued)

Table 7.1 (Continued)

Earthquake Organisational Impacts	Sectors	N	Mean	Std. Dev	F	Sig.
Health and safety issues for employees	Education and Training	32	1.47	1.047	11.732	0.000*
	Manufacturing	65	0.91	0.98		
	Accommodation and Food Services	37	0.41	0.599		
Supplier Issues	Education and Training	26	1.04	0.916	3.502	0.033**
	Manufacturing	70	1.19	0.921		
	Accommodation and Food Services	39	0.72	0.793		
Customer issues	Education and Training	31	1.77	1.055	3.453	0.034**
	Manufacturing	70	1.44	1.085		
	Accommodation and Food Services	43	1.12	1.051		
Availability of staff	Education and Training	32	1.13	0.976	2.536	0.083
	Manufacturing	67	0.99	0.992		
	Accommodation and Food Services	41	0.66	0.794		
Perceptions of building safety	Education and Training	34	1.47	0.961	4.114	0.018**
	Manufacturing	67	1.16	1.053		
	Accommodation and Food Services	37	0.81	0.811		
Changes in staff emotional wellbeing	Education and Training	35	2	0.907	13.38	0.000*
	Manufacturing	66	1.53	0.98		
	Accommodation and Food Services	41	0.88	0.954		

*significant at the p < 0.01 level, ** significant at the p < 0.05 level, 0 = Not Disruptive and 3 = Very Disruptive

Correlations between the items of impact on organisation resources and mitigation strategies revealed several significant relationships. For example, machinery loss or damage was positively correlated with the mitigation strategy 'backup alternatives to basic infrastructure' ($r = 0.23$, $p < 0.05$) and 'relationship with suppliers' (r = 0.285, p < 0.01). The item 'difficulty in accessing IT data' was positively correlated with 'backup alternatives to IT' (r = 0.31, p < 0.01), 'relationship with business advisor' (r = 0.35, p < 0.01), and 'relationship with neighbours' (r = 0.20, p < 0.05) as mitigation strategies. The item 'non-structural damage to buildings' was positively correlated with the mitigation strategy 'spare resources' (r = 0.25, p < 0.01). The item 'changes in emotional wellbeing of staff' was positively correlated with all of the mitigation strategies except for four (relationship with bank/lenders, availability of cash/credit, insurance, and backup or alternative site). Overall, it was evident from the data that positive correlations existed between many of the mitigation strategies and earthquake impacts on organisation resources. As importance levels of mitigation strategies increased, so did disruption levels on organisation resources.

Earthquake impacts on an organisation's basic infrastructure

Following a similar procedure as above (ANOVA and post-hoc comparisons), significant differences were identified between the three sectors of impacts of the earthquake on four of the 11 basic infrastructures (gas, data networks, road networks, and airport) of an organisation. On average, the earthquake impacts on gas were more disruptive for the Accommodation/Food service sector (M = 0.66, SD = 1.03) compared to Manufacturing (M = 0.22, SD = 0.68) and Education/Training (M = 0.12, SD = 0.55) sectors (Table 7.2). On data networks, a significant difference existed between only the Education/Training and Accommodation/Food service sectors. The former (M = 1.63, SD = 0.94) was more heavily disrupted than the latter (M = 0.82, SD = 0.91) on data networks (Table 7.2). A similar finding emerged on road networks for the two aforementioned sectors. However, the Accommodation/Food Services sector (M = 0.78, SD = 0.90) was more heavily impacted by disruptions to the Christchurch airport than the Education/Training sector (M = 0.12, SD = 0.42). The accommodation sector is heavily reliant on visitors arriving by air, with more than 85 per cent of inbound domestic and international visitors using the Christchurch aviation gateway to the South Island (Christchurch International Airport Limited (CIAL) 2012).

Table 7.2 Earthquake impacts on an organisation's basic infrastructure

Impacts on Basic Infrastructure	Sectors	N	Mean	Std. Dev.	F	Sig.
Water supply	Education and Training	35	1.54	1.20	0.558	0.574
	Manufacturing	74	1.34	1.19		
	Accommodation and Food Services	45	1.27	1.21		

(Continued)

Table 7.2 (Continued)

Impacts on Basic Infrastructure	Sectors	N	Mean	Std. Dev.	F	Sig.
Sewage	Education and Training	35	1.46	1.27	1.774	0.173
	Manufacturing	74	1.23	1.22		
	Accommodation and Food Services	45	0.96	1.09		
Electricity	Education and Training	35	1.40	1.04	0.593	0.554
	Manufacturing	73	1.38	1.27		
	Accommodation and Food Services	45	1.16	1.24		
Gas	Education and Training	33	0.12	0.55	5.808	0.004*
	Manufacturing	69	0.22	0.68		
	Accommodation and Food Services	44	0.66	1.03		
Phone networks	Education and Training	35	1.57	0.95	2.382	0.096
	Manufacturing	73	1.25	1.02		
	Accommodation and Food Services	45	1.09	0.97		
Data networks	Education and Training	35	1.63	0.94	6.539	0.002*
	Manufacturing	74	1.15	1.06		
	Accommodation and Food Services	45	0.82	0.91		
Road networks	Education and Training	34	1.65	1.01	6.363	0.002*
	Manufacturing	74	1.30	1.00		
	Accommodation and Food Services	45	0.82	1.11		
Rail	Education and Training	32	0.06	0.35	1.77	0.174

Impacts on Basic Infrastructure	Sectors	N	Mean	Std. Dev.	F	Sig.
	Manufacturing	74	0.30	0.72		
	Accommodation and Food Services	45	0.31	0.67		
Airport	Education and Training	33	0.12	0.42	12.748	0.000*
	Manufacturing	74	0.22	0.58		
	Accommodation and Food Services	45	0.78	0.90		
Port	Education and Training	33	0	0.00	3.03	0.051
	Manufacturing	74	0.22	0.60		
	Accommodation and Food Services	45	0.33	0.77		
Fuel	Education and Training	32	0.19	0.40	1.882	0.156
	Manufacturing	74	0.46	0.78		
	Accommodation and Food Services	44	0.32	0.67		

*significant at the $p < 0.01$ level, 0 = Not Disruptive and 3 = Very Disruptive

Mitigation of earthquake impacts

Organisations were asked to assess the importance of several factors in helping them to mitigate the impacts of the earthquakes. ANOVA results with post-hoc comparisons indicated that significant differences existed between the three sectors on only three of the seventeen factors (Table 7.3). On average, building relationships with staff as a mitigation factor was the least important for the Accommodation/Food Services sector (M = 2.15, SD = 0.98) compared to the Education/Training sector (M = 2.76, SD = 0.50). Practised response to a disaster as a mitigation factor was more important to the Education/Training sector (M = 2.12, SD = 1.16) than the Manufacturing sector (M = 1.34, SD = 1.03). A similar result was also evident between the two aforementioned sectors on installing an emergency kit as a mitigation factor. Overall, the Accommodation/ Food Services sector was on par with the other two sectors on most of the mitigation factors.

Table 7.3 Mitigation strategies of organisations

Mitigation	Sectors	N	mean	Std. Dev.	F	Sig.	Correlation Planned Resilience	Correlation Adaptive Resilience
Backup/alternatives to water, sewerage, electricity, communications	Education and Training	28	1.89	1.10	0.200	0.819	0.247**	0.173
	Manufacturing	61	1.75	1.06				
	Accommodation and Food Services	35	1.86	1.06				
Backup/alternatives to IT	Education and Training	33	1.85	1.06	2.721	0.070	0.126	0.023
	Manufacturing	62	1.95	1.05				
	Accommodation and Food Services	32	1.41	1.19				
Relationship with customers	Education and Training	32	2.63	0.55	2.482	0.087	0.035	-0.014
	Manufacturing	70	2.23	0.98				
	Accommodation and Food Services	42	2.19	1.04				
Relationship with suppliers	Education and Training	26	1.88	1.07	2.824	0.063	0.104	0.040
	Manufacturing	69	2.29	0.93				
	Accommodation and Food Services	40	1.88	1.09				
Relationship with businesses in our sector	Education and Training	32	1.66	1.18	0.35	0.705	0.137	0.027
	Manufacturing	67	1.46	1.06				
	Accommodation and Food Services	41	1.56	1.10				
Relationship with business advisor	Education and Training	22	1.23	1.15	1.797	0.172	0.209*	-0.003

	Manufacturing	42	0.69	1.09				
	Accommodation and Food Services	29	0.86	0.99				
Relationship with staff	Education and Training	33	2.76	0.50	6.012	0.003**	0.173*	0.172*
	Manufacturing	66	2.59	0.76				
	Accommodation and Food Services	39	2.15	0.99				
Relationship with banks or lenders	Education and Training	18	0.83	1.10	1.314	0.273	0.253**	0.088
	Manufacturing	60	1.28	1.20				
	Accommodation and Food Services	34	1.38	1.26				
Relationship with our neighbours	Education and Training	29	1.69	1.04	1.935	0.149	0.166	0.031
	Manufacturing	65	1.23	0.97				
	Accommodation and Food Services	39	1.41	1.19				
Available cash or credit	Education and Training	23	1.30	1.26	0.465	0.629	-0.046	-0.009
	Manufacturing	63	1.52	1.24				
	Accommodation and Food Services	34	1.29	1.36				
Spare resources (e.g. equipment, spare people)	Education and Training	28	1.36	1.22	0.269	0.765	0.241**	0.124
	Manufacturing	63	1.17	0.98				
	Accommodation and Food Services	35	1.23	1.19				
Insurance	Education and Training	28	1.96	1.14	3.185	0.044	0.199*	0.048
	Manufacturing	66	2.03	1.18				
	Accommodation and Food Services	44	2.50	0.82				

(Continued)

Table 7.3 (Continued)

Mitigation	Sectors	N	mean	Std. Dev.	F	Sig.	Correlation Planned Resilience	Correlation Adaptive Resilience
Business continuity, emergency management or disaster preparedness plan	Education and Training	32	1.97	1.03	1.381	0.255	0.330**	0.078
	Manufacturing	67	1.58	1.06				
	Accommodation and Food Services	38	1.71	1.16				
Backup or alternative site	Education and Training	20	1.50	1.40	1.037	0.359	0.134	-0.021
	Manufacturing	52	1.35	1.19				
	Accommodation and Food Services	18	0.94	1.21				
Practiced response to a disaster	Education and Training	33	2.12	1.17	5.403	0.006**	0.382**	0.130
	Manufacturing	61	1.34	1.03				
	Accommodation and Food Services	34	1.53	1.16				
Emergency kit	Education and Training	31	2.10	1.22	7.147	0.001**	0.396**	0.122
	Manufacturing	60	1.20	0.97				
	Accommodation and Food Services	37	1.68	1.18				
Well designed and well built buildings	Education and Training	32	2.34	0.97	0.46	0.632	0.131	0.042
	Manufacturing	67	2.31	0.84				
	Accommodation and Food Services	39	2.15	1.09				

** significant at the $p < 0.01$ level, * significant at the $p < 0.05$ level, 0 = Not Important and 3 = Very Important

Correlations between the earthquake impacts on basic infrastructure and mitigation strategies revealed many significant relationships. For example, backup alternatives for utilities were positively correlated with impacts on water supply ($r = 0.30$, $p < 0.01$), sewage ($r = 0.26$, $p < 0.01$), electricity ($r = 0.23$, $p < 0.05$), data networks ($r = 0.25$, $p < 0.01$), and fuel ($r = 0.23$, $p < 0.23$). The mitigation strategy 'relationship with neighbours' was significantly correlated with the impacts on sewage ($r = 0.19$, $p < 0.05$), data networks ($r = 0.23$, $p < 0.01$), road networks ($r = 0.31$, $p < 0.01$) and fuel ($r = 0.24$, $p < 0.01$). Overall, most of the relationships identified between impacts on basic infrastructure and mitigation strategies were positive, suggesting that the importance of mitigation strategies was higher with increased levels of disruptions on basic infrastructure.

Organisational resilience

The 13 items of organisational resilience were factor-analysed (Table 7.4). Two factors were extracted, explaining 58.2 per cent of total variance. The two factors reflected the dimensions of planning resilience (pre-disaster) and adaptive resilience (post-disaster) as suggested in the literature (McManus et al. 2008; Lee et al. 2013). Both factors had Cronbach's alpha > 0.7 (Hair et al. 2006) indicative of internal consistency and reliability. Composite measures were created prior to analysing whether the three sectors were significantly different on planning and adaptive resilience. The results showed that all three sectors were significantly different on the two factors. On average, the Education/Training sector (M = 0.84, SD = 1.74) was more agreeable than Manufacturing (M = 0.69, SD = 0.20) and Accommodation/Food Services (M = 0.72, SD = 0.15) sectors that their organisations were resilient on planning. The Accommodation/Food Services sector (M = 0.76, SD = 1.39) displayed on average lower agreement than the Education/Training sector (M = 0.85, SD = 1.27) on adaptive resilience. Sectorial differences thus exist on the post-quake resilience of organisations.

Table 7.4 Organisational resilience

Resilience Items	Planning Resilience	Adaptive Resilience	Communalities
We have a focus on being able to respond . . .	0.851	0.191	0.761
Our organisation is committed to practicing . . .	0.840	0.140	0.725
We build relationships with others . . .	0.793	0.159	0.655
We have clearly defined priorities . . .	0.778	0.268	0.677
Given how others depend on us . . .	0.693	0.287	0.563

(*Continued*)

Table 7.4 (Continued)

Resilience Items	Planning Resilience	Adaptive Resilience	Communalities
We proactively monitor our industry . . .	0.618	0.339	0.497
There would be good leadership . . .	0.108	0.851	0.736
People in our organisation are committed resolving problems . . .	0.159	0.765	0.610
If key people are unavailable . . .	0.146	0.690	0.497
We can make tough decisions quickly	0.380	0.685	0.613
Our organisation maintains sufficient resources . . .	0.190	0.669	0.484
We are known for our ability to use knowledge . . .	0.356	0.532	0.410
There are few barriers stopping us . . .	0.239	0.526	0.334
Eigenvalue	3.950	3.611	
% of variance explained	30.388	27.779	
Cronbach's alpha	0.886	0.824	

Planning resilience has significant relationships with most of the mitigation strategies while adaptive resilience has only one significant relationship with the mitigation factor 'relationship with staff' (Table 7.3). As planning resilience improves, so does the importance of the mitigation strategies given that all the significant correlations in Table 7.3 are positive. As adaptive resilience improved so did relationship with staff as a mitigation factor ($r = 0.172$).

Discussion and implications

The main objective of this chapter was to compare three sectors in terms of earthquake impacts, mitigation and organisational resilience following the Christchurch earthquake sequence (2010–2011). Similar to other studies (Whitman et al. 2013), sectoral differences were found on several earthquake impacts and organisational resilience. The Accommodation/Food Services sector was the least impacted by physical impacts of the earthquakes in comparison to the other two sectors, Manufacturing and Education/Training. One plausible explanation for this is that accommodation facilities outside of the CBD were typically single or double-level buildings, which were much less likely to be physically closed due to building damage, hence, these organisations could access buildings and begin their recovery more quickly than for those in the CBD. The earthquakes had greater physical impacts on accommodation and tourism organisations that were closer to the CBD than those located in the periphery regions (Orchiston et al. 2012). The finding of no significant difference between the sectors on the importance of back up for IT facilities, for example, as a mitigation factor contrasts with previous studies (e.g. Orchiston et al. 2012). The contradictory results between the two studies may be partly explained by differences in sampling criteria, since Orchiston et al.'s (2012) study included micro SMEs and other tourism sectors, while the sample in this study includes only accommodation providers.

The Education/Training sector was the most impacted on staff emotional wellbeing. This is likely to be a consequence of the 70 foreign student fatalities in the CTV building in the February 2011 quake, which had major impacts across the whole sector. Education/Training activities were preferentially located within the CBD pre-quake and heavily impacted during the 22 February earthquake. IT data in the education sector was crucially important during the emergency response in terms of contacting the families of foreign students, and the lack of access to these data made their job very challenging. In terms of accessing their workplace to retrieve IT data, businesses in the CBD were locked out because of a cordon. It is therefore not surprising that the education/training sector reported the highest level of disruption on data networks in comparison to the other two sectors. The manufacturing sector, being resource-intensive, experienced a higher level of disruption on physical infrastructure such as structural and non-structural damages to buildings, machinery loss or damage, and supplier issues, but was also highly impacted by damage to basic infrastructure such as fuel. However, organisations in the manufacturing sector reported better mitigation strategies such as back up of IT facilities, relationship with suppliers, and available cash/credit.

From a sector vulnerability perspective, it is not surprising that the Manufacturing and Education/Training sectors were impacted more than the Accommodation/Food Services sector, given the size of these two sectors in the Canterbury region. The amount and size of physical facilities and related infrastructures in these two sectors in comparison to the Accommodation/Food Services sector may explain the higher levels of impact. The impacts are also geographically driven given that some areas were more affected than others. The findings also suggest that disruptions in airport and rail transport infrastructures have a greater impact on the Accommodation/Food Services sector, while disruptions to data and road networks have more of an impact on the Education/Training sector. Utility disruptions have been found in previous studies to impact negatively the entire regional economy (Rose and Liao 2005).

The findings highlight sectorial differences on the impacts of basic infrastructure disruption on organisations. These differences may help in disaster preparedness planning and recovery. For example, disaster preparedness plans for the accommodation sector should include diversification of the transport mode used by customers to strengthen recovery of the sector. Recovery of organisations following a disaster is closely aligned to restoration of basic infrastructure, which also contributes to community resilience (Chang and Shinozuka 2004).

The mitigation strategies used by the three sectors are mostly on par with each other, albeit there were some differences which may well reflect sector-specific requirements and/or varying perceptions of risk. Notably, relationships with staff in the accommodation sector were the lowest compared to the other two sectors. This result is somewhat surprising since hospitality is a 'people oriented' industry. However, this result may reflect the presence of accommodation providers with few staff in the dataset. It may also be related to the high use of seasonal workers in the industry. The hospitality sector in general noted problems with staff availability due to a population outflow after the earthquake, but staff were also not prepared to work in the CBD due to perceptions of the buildings being unsafe (Kachali et al. 2012). There are possibly other reasons contributing to the relationship with staff as a mitigation strategy not being valued as much compared to the other two sectors. The disaster management literature suggests that staff's emotional wellbeing is a major component of industry recovery post-disaster (Brown et al. 2014).

The findings suggest that the Accommodation sector is less likely to plan for disasters, but rely on being adaptive and reacting to situations as they present themselves. This supports the findings of Orchiston et al. (2014), where formal planning was found to be limited in extent, with many providers relying on their ability to react and respond to the events as they happened. This was particularly evident in accommodation types with owner-operator structures that had few or no employees. From a disaster management perspective, this sector is vulnerable with low planning and a reliance on adaptive resilience. Improving resilience is necessary as a risk management technique (Dalziell and McManus 2004). Hence, strategies for improving resilience in the Accommodation sector should include three key aspects (McManus et al. 2008): (i) situation awareness, whereby the sector as a whole and its individual players recognise they are part of a wider network, learning about types of emergency situations; (ii) management of keystone vulnerabilities, including components in the organisational system such as buildings/infrastructures, critical suppliers, relationship with key groups internally and externally, communication structures, and the perception of organisational strategic vision; and (iii) adaptive capacity, which can be built though enhanced decision support systems, governance structures, and robust operations management systems. These strategies may also be relevant to the Manufacturing and Education/Training sectors. Given the importance of the accommodation sector to the Canterbury region, improving its resilience may also have implications for community resilience.

Conclusion

In conclusion, the findings of this chapter confirm that sectorial differences exist for both earthquake impacts on organisation resources and basic infrastructure. The findings also suggest that organisational resilience is different across the three sectors. However, the lack of substantial differences between the sectors on mitigation strategies may suggest that organisational resilience can only partly explain mitigation strategies. This is confirmed by the significant correlations between planning resilience and the seventeen mitigation factors, but only one item with adaptive resilience (relationship with staff). As such, the findings of the study only partially support a relationship between organisational resilience and mitigation factors as suggested in Figure 7.1. However, the data showed that higher levels of disruption on both basic infrastructure and organisation resources had a significant relationship with the importance level assigned by organisations to the seventeen mitigation strategies. Hence, relationships exist between mitigation strategies and felt impacts, while the relationship between organisational resilience and mitigation strategies is more evident on planning rather than adaptive aspects of resilience.

Acknowledgements

The authors are grateful for the comments and suggestions by Charlotte Brown and Erica Seville from Resilient Organisations.

References

Bruneau, M., Chang, S. E., Eguchi, R. T., Lee, G. C., O'Rourke, T. D., Reinhorn, A. M. and von Winterfeldt, D. (2003) 'A framework to quantitatively assess and enhance the seismic resilience of communities', *Earthquake Spectra*, 19(4): 733–752.

Brown, C., Stevenson, J. R., Giovinazzi, S., Seville, E. and Vargo, J. (2014) 'Factors influencing impacts on and recovery trends of organisations: Evidence from the 2010/2011 Canterbury Earthquakes', *International Journal of Disaster Risk Reduction*, doi:10.1016/j.ijdrr.2014.11.009

Canterbury Development Corporation (CDC) (2015) *Sector Profiles*. Online. Available HTTP: <http://www.cdc.org.nz/economy/sector-profiles/> (Accessed 18 February 2015).

Chang, S. E. and Shinozuka, M. (2004) 'Measuring improvements in the disaster resilience of communities', *Earthquake Spectra*, 20(3): 739–755.

Chang, S. E., Rose, A. Z., Shinozuka, M. and Tierney, K. J. (2001) 'Modeling earthquake impact on urban lifeline systems: Advances and integration in loss estimation', in B. Spencer and Y. X. Hu (eds.) *Earthquake Engineering Frontiers in the New Millennium*, Lisse: Swets & Zeitlinger, Lisse.

Christchurch International Airport Limited (CIAL). (2012) *Annual Report 2012*. Online. Available HTTP: <http://www.christchurchairport.co.nz/media/557923/cial_annual_report_2012.pdf> (Accessed 27 November 2012).

Corey, C. M. and Deitch, E. A. (2011) 'Factors affecting business recovery immediately after Hurricane Katrina', *Journal of Contingencies and Crisis Management*, 19(3): 169–181.

Dahlhamer, J. M. and Tierney, K. J. (1996) *Winners and Losers: Predicting Business Disaster Recovery Outcomes Following the Northridge Earthquake*, Newark: Disaster Research Center, University of Delaware.

———(1998) 'Rebounding from disruptive events: Business recovery following the Northridge earthquake', *Sociological Spectrum*, 18(2): 121–141.

Dalziell, E. P. and McManus, S. T. (2004) 'Resilience, vulnerability, and adaptive capacity: Implications for system performance'. Proceedings of the International Forum for Engineering Decision Making (IFED), Stoos, Switzerland, 6–8 December.

Faulkner, B. and Vikulov, S. (2001) 'Katherine, washed out one day, back on track the next: A post-mortem of a tourism disaster', *Tourism Management*, 22(4): 331–344.

Galbraith, C. S. and Stiles, C. H. (2006) 'Disasters and entrepreneurship: A short review', *International Research in the Business Disciplines*, 5: 147–166.

Hair, J. F., Black, W. C., Babin, B. J., Anderson, R. E. and Tatham, R. L. (2006) *Multivariate Data Analysis,* Vol. 6, Upper Saddle River, NJ: Pearson Prentice Hall.

Halvorson, S. J. and Hamilton, P. J. (2010) 'In the aftermath of the Qa'yamat: 1 the Kashmir earthquake disaster in northern Pakistan', *Disasters*, 34(1): 184–204.

Holling, C. S. (1973) 'Resilience and stability of ecological systems', *Annual Review of Ecology and Systematics*, 4: 1–23.

Kachali, H., Stevenson, J. R., Whitman, Z., Seville, E., Vargo, J. and Wilson, T. (2012) 'Organisational resilience and recovery for Canterbury organisations after the 4 September 2010 earthquake', *Australasian Journal of Disaster and Trauma Studies*, 1: 11–19.

Kroll, C. A., Landis, J. D., Shen, Q. and Stryker, S. (1991) *Economic Impacts of the Loma Prieta Earthquake: A Focus on Small Business*, Berkeley: Fisher Center for Real Estate and Urban Economics.

Lee, A. V., Vargo, J. and Seville, E. (2013) 'Developing a tool to measure and compare organisations' resilience', *Natural Hazards Review*, 14(1): 29–41.

Mannakkara, S. and Wilkinson, S. (2014) 'Re-conceptualising "Building Back Better" to improve post-disaster recovery', *International Journal of Managing Projects in Business*, 7(3): 327–341.

McManus, S., Seville, E., Vargo, J. and Brunsdon, D. (2008) 'Facilitated process for improving organisational resilience', *Natural Hazards Review*, 9(2): 81–90.

Orchiston, C., Seville, E. and Vargo, J. (2012) 'Outcomes of the Christchurch earthquake sequence on tourism businesses', *Resilient Organisations Research Report 2012/09*, Christchurch: University of Canterbury.

———(2014) 'Regional and sub-sector impacts of the Canterbury earthquake sequence for tourism businesses', *Australian Journal of Emergency Management,* 29(4): 32–37.

Powell, F. (2010) 'Urban earthquake events and businesses: Learning from the 2007 Gisborne earthquake in New Zealand', *Australian Journal of Emergency Management*, 25(3): 54.

Rose, A. and Liao, S.-Y. (2005) 'Modeling regional economic resilience to disasters: A computable general equilibrium analysis of water service disruptions', *Journal of Regional Science*, 45(1): 75–112.

Rubin, C. B. (1991) 'Recovery from disaster', in T. E. Drabek and G. J. Hoetmar (eds.) *Emergency Management: Principles and Practice for Local Government*, Washington, DC: International City Management Association.

Smit, B. and Wandel, J. (2006) 'Adaptation, adaptive capacity and vulnerability', *Global Environmental Change*, 16(3): 282–292.

Tierney, K. J. (1997) 'Business impacts of the Northridge earthquake', *Journal of Contingencies and Crisis Management*, 5(2): 87–97.

Wasileski, G., Rodríguez, H. and Diaz, W. (2011) 'Business closure and relocation: A comparative analysis of the Loma Prieta earthquake and Hurricane Andrew', *Disasters*, 35(1): 102–129.

Webb, G. R., Tierney, K. J. and Dahlhamer, J. M. (2000) 'Businesses and disasters: Empirical patterns and unanswered questions', *Natural Hazards Review*, 1(2): 83–90.

———(2002) 'Predicting long-term business recovery from disaster: A comparison of the Loma Prieta earthquake and Hurricane Andrew', *Global Environmental Change Part B: Environmental Hazards*, 4(2): 45–58.

Whitman, Z. R., Wilson, T. M., Seville, E., Vargo, J., Stevenson, J. R., Kachali, H. and Cole, J. (2013) 'Rural organisational impacts, mitigation strategies, and resilience to the 2010 Darfield earthquake, New Zealand', *Natural Hazards*, 69(3): 1849–1875.

Part III

Consumer and communication responses

8 From brand love to brand divorce

The effect of a disruption in supply on consumer–brand relationships

Sussie Morrish, Girish Prayag and Matthew Nguyen

Introduction

Consumer–brand relationships can share similar characteristics to those we foster in person-to-person relationships (Fournier 1998; Esch, Langner, Schmitt and Geus 2006) and it is not uncommon for consumers to develop strong bonds with brands (Thomson, MacInnis and Whan Park 2005). This bond has been described as "brand attachment" (Thomson et al. 2005) or "brand love" (Caroll and Ahuvia 2006). At the heart of these concepts is a strong emotional connection to the brand. Research indicates that consumers with strong emotional connection to a brand resist negative information about the brand and often engage in brand forgiveness (Trump 2014). Forgiveness is related to the connection between the self and the brand, whereby a threat to the brand is perceived as a threat to the self (Cheng, White and Chaplin 2012; Lisjak, Lee and Gardner 2012). 'Consumers alleviate the threat by buffering their evaluations of the brand or putting the brand on a pedestal' (Trump 2014: 1825). However, research has also shown that consumers with the strongest relationships with a company can respond the most unfavourably in service failures due to the provider either failing to right a wrongdoing or not holding their end of the relational bargain (Gregoire and Fisher 2008).

Existing consumer–brand relationships research has mainly examined the antecedents and consequences of positive drivers such as attachment, love and passion on the quality of the relationship and the subsequent satisfaction and loyalty (Caroll and Ahuvia 2006). Limited studies exist on how consumers respond when they are personally let down by a loved brand outside of the service failure context (Trump 2014). Many studies have also examined the reasons why the consumer–brand relationship weakens over time as a result of a consumer's changing circumstances or personal choice, such as voluntary simplicity (Huneke 2005) or anti-materialism (O'Shaughnessy and O'Shaughnessy 2002). Likewise, the consumer–brand relationship can also weaken due to changes in perceptions of the brand itself, such as negative brand experience (Aaker, Fournier and Brasel 2004), negative symbolic brand meanings (Hogg, Banister and Stephenson 2009), and incongruent self-brand image (Fournier 1998; Kressman, Sirgy, Herrmann, Huber and Herber 2006). While the consequences of disruption in supply on other firms and supply chain partners have been extensively studied in the operations management literature, the impact on consumer–brand relationship has been rarely examined in the marketing literature.

This study attempts to fill the gap by investigating the impacts of supply disruption on the affective side of the consumer–brand relationship. Specifically, the impact is assessed through consumers' perceptions of the brand identity, personality, attachment and loyalty for Marmite, a yeast extract spread which is an iconic New Zealand brand with a large, devoted community of users. It is produced by the New Zealand Health Association (2012) (commonly known as Sanitarium) in Christchurch with the production being halted by the earthquakes for over a year.

The affective side of consumer–brand relationships

Consumers tend to form special relationships with brands they encounter and several frameworks have been proposed to understand consumer–brand relationships (Fournier 1998; Chang and Chieng 2006). The most popular framework remains the Brand Relationship Quality (BRQ), which encompasses six dimensions, namely love/passion, self-connection, commitment, inter-dependence, intimacy and brand partner quality (Fournier 1998). The antecedents of BRQ include individual experience, shared experience, brand personality, brand image, brand associations, and brand attitude (Chang and Chieng 2006). However, there is no consensus in the literature on the antecedents that have the strongest impacts on perceptions of BRQ among consumers. Accordingly, we selected three antecedents (brand personality, brand identity, brand attachment) and one consequence (brand loyalty) to identify how a disruption in supply impacts consumers' perceptions of BRQ.

Conceptual background

Antecedents of BRQ

Scholars have proposed that brands exhibit different personalities. Brand personality is defined as 'the set of human personal traits that are both applicable to and relevant for brands' (Azoulay and Kapferer 2003: 151). As consumer goods become more homogenous, the brand personality provides a differentiating proposition in consumer choice. Aaker (1997), one of the first scholars in this field, developed a 44-item Brand Personality Scale that encompasses five dimensions called "The Big 5" personality traits of brands. These are: sincerity (domestic, honest, genuine, cheerful); excitement (daring, spirited, imaginative, up-to-date); competence (reliable, responsible, dependable, efficient); sophistication (glamorous, pretentious, charming, romantic); and ruggedness (tough, strong, outdoorsy, rugged).

In a study that is consistent with marketing and consumer researchers' assertions, Sung and Kim (2010) found that certain brand personalities evoke higher brand trust or brand affect than other brand personalities. They suggest that the sincerity and ruggedness brand personality dimensions are more likely to influence the level of brand trust than brand affect, whereas the excitement and sophistication dimensions relate more to brand affect than to brand trust. The competence dimension has similar effects on both brand trust and brand affect.

Brand personality is an important antecedent to brand loyalty as it affects a consumer's attachment towards the brand. The brand's personality 'is a vehicle of consumer self-expression and can be instrumental in helping a consumer express different aspects of his or her self' (Swaminathan, Stilley and Ahluwalia 2009: 985). The brand's personality provides the consumer symbolic value that is central to the establishment of positive attitude and preference for a brand (Biel 1993). By humanising the brand, its personality provides understanding of brand effects as well as the firm's performance in the marketplace (Malär, Nyffenegger, Krohmer and Hoyer 2012). The humanised brand assists consumers in differentiating brands by relating them to human characteristics, enabling consumers to identify the needs the brand satisfies (Park, Jaworski and MacInnis 1986). Consumers use brands to create and communicate their personalities (Sung and Kim 2010); therefore, when the personality and consumer identity align, consumers are more likely to evoke brand loyal behaviours.

Once the brand's personality is recognised, it has been argued that consumers will go through the process of evaluating whether the brand's personality matches the consumer's identity. Brand identification is defined as 'the extent to which the consumer sees his or her own self-image as overlapping the brand's image' (Bergkvist and Bech-Larsen 2010: 506). Brand identification is also known as self-image congruence (Sirgy et al. 1997) and self-connection (Fournier 1998). Brands hold a symbolic value where loved objects are central to people's identity and a consumer is more likely to love a brand the stronger he or she identifies with (Ahuvia 2005). This matches Kressman et al.'s (2006) findings that when the brand significantly reflects the consumer's identity, this positively affects brand loyalty directly and indirectly through functional congruity, product involvement, and brand relationship quality.

Thomson et al. (2005: 77–78) note that 'attachment is an emotion-laden target-specific bond between a person and a specific object.' MacInnis (2012) suggests that the stronger the attachment towards a brand is, the more likely the consumer is committed to the brand, hence attachment is an antecedent to brand loyalty. Essential to one's emotional attachment towards people and objects is one's *love* for them (Thomson et al. 2005); thus, *love* and *attachment* go hand-in-hand. Consumers who are emotionally attached to a brand are likely to have a favourable attitude toward it. Carroll and Ahuvia (2006) suggest that brand love is greater in product categories perceived as more hedonic (vs. utilitarian) and for brands that offer more in terms of symbolic benefits. Consumers who are emotionally attached to an object (brand) also display specific behaviours such as proximity maintenance and *separation distress* similar to a loss in a relationship with a person (Bowlby 1979; Thomson et al. 2005).

Antecedents of brand divorce

'Brand divorce is the act of dissolving the marriage to a brand' (Sussan, Hall and Meamber 2012: 521). Reasons for consumer brand divorce include extrinsic reasons, when consumers terminate their relationship with a brand due to brand transgressions (e.g. negative publicity) (Cheng et al. 2012) that contribute to consumer dissatisfaction (Aaker et al. 2004). Often, the brand personality collapses or the symbolism upon which the brand is built fades over time (Sussan et al. 2012). Brand divorce may also be due to intrinsic reasons, such as when consumers are lured by and switch to a competing brand because of a relatively more attractive product/service offering, leading to the consumer terminating the relationship (Mazursky, LaBabera and Aiello 1987). Relatedly, the consumer can also unintentionally divorce a brand because of self-transformation that eliminates the need for brand attachment (Sussan et al. 2012). While person-brand relationship building requires bilateral commitment and trust, dissolution is more easily initiated unilaterally.

Case and method

On 4 September 2010, a 7.1-magnitude earthquake struck Christchurch, crippling the city's infrastructure, miraculously with no fatalities. On 22 February 2011, another earthquake struck at 6.3 magnitude; this time resulting in a death toll of 185. Already weakened buildings such as the Sanitarium Marmite factory in Papanui suffered further damage, and thousands of full and partial demolitions followed. Damage to the factory and cooling towers halted production. Deconstruction and strengthening work was needed to bring the factory up to new earthquake standards before production was able to resume. On average, the factory produced about 640,000kg of Marmite annually before the earthquakes.

Marmite is unique because it is deeply tied to Christchurch. During the shortage, Sanitarium CEO Pierre van Heerden knew it was critical to resume production on another site. After determining that all New Zealand factories would be too small to keep up with demand, an attempt to temporarily shift production offshore (South Africa) was made while the factory was being repaired; however, it proved impossible to replicate Marmite's distinctive taste. Sending expert staff, importing secret ingredients to South Africa and adjusting South African Pioneer Foods' machinery to Sanitarium's requirements were not enough. Taste, texture and colour were not the same without a particular yeast procured only in Christchurch, and attempts to replicate Marmite elsewhere were deemed futile, resulting in a 12-month shortage.

This shortage sent Marmite users into a panic dubbed 'Marmageddon' by the media (Manhire 2012). Numerous campaigns, giveaways, and advertisements were run and Marmite was a prized item in many charity fundraisers. The value of this 'black gold' was tested on TradeMe (a New Zealand online auction and shopping website) where there were over 400 auctions for jars of Marmite. One charity auction on TradeMe for a 25kg bucket of Marmite along with a 175g jar fetched over $400 (Waikato Times 2012). The highest bid on another auction was $800 for a jar, and other auctions for already-opened jars fetched more than ten times the original value.

These anecdotes illustrate that consumers' emotional attachment to Marmite makes an interesting case to explore the influence that a supply disruption had on the consumer–brand relationship. A multi-method qualitative approach was used, consisting of (i) a content analysis of consumers' posts on Marmite's NZ Facebook page; and (ii) in-depth interviews with six ex-users of Marmite.

Between November 2011 (when the announcement that production had been suspended) and October 2013 (when this study commenced), there were 29,973 comments to 39 Marmite posts. A selection of posts was made that attracted a large number of comments. An analysis of over 5000 randomly selected comments from these posts spread over the 12 months of the shortage period was then conducted. The aim was to get an in-depth understanding of consumers' feelings during the supply disruption. The comments were categorised into (1) personality, (2) brand identity, (3) emotional attachment, and (4) brand loyalty. Further, a temporal perspective was used to understand how general feelings about the brand evolved over the disruption period.

The in-depth semi-structured interviews focused on understanding the process that led to brand divorce and the coping mechanisms adopted over the disruption period. The interviews used two techniques to identify the process: Zaltman Metaphor Elicitation Technique (ZMET) and brand personification. A convenience sampling method was used to recruit participants. The main criteria for inclusion was that they "loved" Marmite, experienced the "Marmageddon", and divorced the brand. The participants were aged between 18 to 45 years old.

Findings

Temporal perspective of the brand divorce

Overall the findings indicate that the supply disruption affected brand personality the most with traits such as sincerity and competence being repeatedly questioned by consumers. In general, the brand's personality, identity, and consumers' attachment changed over the duration of the disruption from an initial "shock" to gradual loss of trust and commitment to the brand, eventuating in consumers becoming less committed, and hence less loyal, over time. As the shortage progressed, anger and frustration toward the brand and the parent company ensued. While there may have been some dislikers venting in these posts, the majority were from people expressing their emotional disconnect with the brand, whether it was comments from consumers who truly missed the brand to people getting fed up about how long it was taking and making threats about switching to a competitor. For example, BB responded to an earlier post on the organisational status of Sanitarium NZ, 'Sanitarium is a joke of a company, milking a tax exempt status no doubt, so Marmite is not a true priority to them' (10/9/13, 6.41pm). The company became increasingly scrutinised online by consumers and the general public, who argued that the corporation should pay income taxes like others and not abuse its 'charity' status: 'If it looks like a duck and quacks like a duck, it probably is a duck. When are you going to admit that you're not a charity . . . start paying corporation tax? How much are you robbing from the average New Zealander by avoiding tax by this ruse?' (PT, 20/10/12, 9.43pm).

Weakened brand personality

The quotes above also suggest a loss in sincerity of the brand from consumers' perspectives. Yet, this was not the only brand personality trait that was affected by the disruption in supply. As seen in online comments, Marmite's personality was no longer *competent*. Aaker (1997) suggests that a brand is competent when it is reliable, responsible, dependable and efficient. Consumers could no longer rely on Marmite: 'It has been 5 months since I was able to have toast for breakfast as the only thing I eat on my toast is Marmite' (LW, 10/12/12, 9.50 pm).

The lack of competence was also evidenced by Sanitarium being perceived to be investing more in communication and promotional activities than in fixing the factory. This was echoed in a growing sentiment among consumers that the company was prioritising the wrong activities. 'I hide my Marmite in my cupboard with all my millions . . . Oh hang on that was a dream . . . I don't have either!!! If you spend the same amount of energy sorting out the production of Marmite as you did creating these silly games we would all be a lot happier!' (SS, 9/8/12, 7.29 pm).

Brand *excitement* also weakened throughout the disruption. CC comments, 'Don't mean to be a hater, but I've gone from oh no I want Marmite to, meh who cares if it never comes back . . .' (18/10/12, 4.04pm). For consumers like CC, the supply disruption was frustrating to the point that they would rather divorce the brand than wait, without a clear return date.

Loss in brand identity

The weakened brand personality impacted negatively on brand loyalty and brand identity for some consumers. During the disruption, Marmite attempted to reinforce their New Zealand identity by launching a new campaign featuring former All Blacks' Coach Sir Graham Henry, as the spokesperson for Marmite's values. The symbolic image they tried to portray, as expressed on Marmite's Facebook page, was 'another Kiwi icon, someone Kiwis have also come to know, trust and love, to reassure all our fans that Marmite will be back' (New Zealand Health Association 2012).

The use of Henry, however, was not well received by many consumers, given that some consumers perceived little brand fit between the celebrity endorser and the brand values. Negative comments confirmed the damaged done to its brand identity: 'If there was a HATE button, I'd be pushing it!!!' (ZMB, 3/4/12, 9.43am); 'What a joke Mr. Henry!!! Just stick to rugby!!!' (JP 6/4/12, 9.37am); 'What a bloody joke! How low will these people go for money?' (DK, 6/3/12, 10.13am). The weakened brand traits seemingly influenced consumers negatively as the brand image of Marmite was no longer what it used to be.

The brand image was further damaged by the parent company in August 2012 when New Zealand customs halted imports of UK Marmite (a similar product to

New Zealand marmite but with a slightly different taste), as Sanitarium claimed it infringed New Zealand's trademark laws. Generally, this was not well-received by consumers; they felt that not only was Sanitarium unable to fulfil consumers' needs, but it was also preventing smaller businesses from accessing the market. JZ pointed out that 'I was looking forward to Marmite (used to be a huge fan and consumer) but after seeing how you are bullying the UK Marmite importer, which coincidently doesn't taste the same and is pretty disgusting to most Kiwis, I've been reconsidering buying anything from Sanitarium . . . I think it's a big rich bullying a little importer. So a few weeks ago I bought Vegemite and I'm starting to get used to the taste. Tax exemption, a lot of your profits going to America, AND bullying little businesses. That's not on. Go Vegemite!' (2/10/12, 9.34pm).

Emotional attachment to the brand

Emotional attachment towards the brand changed over the supply disruption and affected the components of *love, attachment, connection,* and *separation distress.* The *love* for the brand could be easily seen in consumers' comments at the beginning of the shortage. However, as the disruption progressed, this *love* for Marmite either subsided or turned into nostalgia. Some consumers switched to a competitor's brand and hence felt less loving towards Marmite. Others became nostalgic. TS writes: 'Nothing can replace you Marmite, my toast is just not the same, I have been cheating on you just having cereal instead' (19/07/12, 10.45pm).

The sense of loss for consumers manifested itself in two ways: nostalgia and separation distress. For example, DB's comment reflects nostalgia: 'What's Marmite? I know it used to taste pretty good slathered on top of butter on toast . . . but hey we might have to switch to Vegemite . . . Where is Marmite? It's been way too long' (10/08/12, 12.28 am). Separation distress can be seen from this quote: 'Marmite, Marmite, where for art thou Marmite? I have been to Vegemite and back. I have waited days, weeks, it feels like more than a year. I can't handle the separation; I need you back in my life. Please hurry back to me!' (SB, 20/10/12, 1.15pm). For something as mundane as a spread, consumers were attached to Marmite.

The analogy of a divorce

The content analysis findings were generally supported by the consumers we interviewed who divorced the brand. For example, ZMET participants brought images that displayed emotions such as frustration, disappointment, and sadness to voice out how they felt about Marmite. Participant A divorced the brand for intrinsic reasons that included a lack of congruence between brand image and self-identity. For her, while Marmite triggered nostalgic emotions as it had always been a part of her life and who she is, the brand was no longer part of her life because her children would be unable to see the brand the way she did when growing up. The brand no longer had the values it used to have and she did not want to disappoint her children.

The dissipation of brand traits such as competence and sincerity influenced the brand divorce for another participant, reflecting extrinsic reasons for brand divorce.

Participant D felt that maintaining the relationship with Marmite was not important or high on her priority list, as it was no longer available for her son's daily breakfast and school lunches: 'If it's not there, it's not such a big deal as I have grown attached to Vegemite now'. Vegemite was perceived as a more reliable brand.

Brand divorce from the participants' perspectives seems to be the result of: (a) weakened brand personality traits driven by lack of trust and commitment; (b) separation distress often fuelled by nostalgia; (c) incongruent brand/self-identity, and (d) negative emotional attachment to the brand due to loss of emotional connection. All participants stated that their loyalty to the brand was altered in some way or another and weakened overtime. Three participants questioned whether they would be able to truly trust the company again. Overall, the results tend to suggest that the duration of a disruption mediates how consumers' value continuing brand loyalty, and the stronger the negative emotions felt, the higher the sense of loss and lack of trust in the brand.

Discussion and implications

Several theoretical and managerial implications arise from the results of this study. At a theoretical level, the results confirm that brand divorce shares the same characteristics as actual person-to-person divorce. The four phases of divorce that are evident among consumers are shown in Figure 8.1.

The antecedents of the breakdown phase can be related to the effects of the disruption in supply and the lack of communication by the parent company. From the breakdown phase to the decline phase, one important enabler of brand

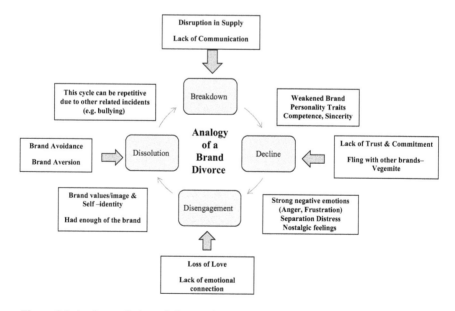

Figure 8.1 Analogy of a brand divorce for Marmite

divorce was the weakened brand personality traits. In the case of Marmite, traits such as competence and sincerity dwindled among the loyal customer base. These were fuelled by declining trust and commitment to the brand. At the same time, consumers engaged in what Alvarez and Fournier (2012) describe as a "brand fling". This refers to consumers switching to other competing brands for self-protection. From the decline to the disengagement phase, consumers increasingly felt negative emotions such as anger and frustration toward the parent company and the brand. They also experienced separation distress, an indicator of brand attachment, fuelled by nostalgic feelings for the brand. As the disruption progressed, consumers felt less emotionally connected to the brand and brand love was quickly dissipating. This encouraged them to disengage completely with the brand. For Marmite, consumers increasingly perceived that the brand image and values were incongruent with their self-identity. In essence the brand identity had weakened. Two typical behaviours associated with this phase of the brand divorce were brand avoidance and brand aversion.

The results also highlight the role and importance of brand personality traits in triggering a brand divorce. The findings of this study indicate that brand personality traits are the most impacted when there is disruption in supply. Weakening brand personality traits can strongly affect the consumer–brand relationship. Aaker et al. (2004) found that relationships with "sincere brands" suffered in the wake of transgressions. As noted by these authors, although transgressions will vary in their severity and cause, all are significant in their ability to affect relationship progress. For Marmite, the disruption in supply was only one antecedent of brand divorce. The lack of communication, seemingly bullying smaller players in the market place, and wrong prioritisation of activities, as perceived by some, were other significant brand transgressions that contributed to brand divorce. These transgressions stand as the hallmark of the relationship, representing perhaps the most significant events in the relationship history (Aaker et al. 2004).

The results also suggest that communication strategies during a crisis are critical for retaining consumer loyalty. For Marmite in particular, the lack of communication and reassurance given to consumers were perceived as significant brand transgressions, weakening brand image and brand values. Reassurance is a precursor to brand competence. Antecedent to brand forgiveness is whether a brand restores high levels of competence (MacInnis 2012). The more a brand is perceived as incompetent, the less likely consumers are to engage in brand forgiveness. Therefore brand managers should develop strategies to rebuild a brand's competence by demonstrating dependability and reliability after a supply disruption. Using these as the foundation, brand managers can attempt to reinforce trust, commitment, and brand loyalty.

References

Aaker, J. (1997) 'Dimensions of brand personality', *Journal of Marketing Research*, 34(3): 347–356.

Aaker, J., Fournier, S. and Brasel, S. (2004) 'When good brands do bad', *Journal of Consumer Research*, 31(1): 1–16.

Ahuvia, A. (2005) 'Beyond the extended self: Loved objects and consumers' identity narratives', *Journal of Consumer Research*, 32(1): 171–184.

Alvarez, C. and Fournier, S. (2012) 'Brand flings: When great brand relationships are not made to last', in S. Fournier, M. Breazeale and M. Fetscherin (eds.) *Consumer–brand Relationships: Theory and Practice*. New York: Routledge.

Azoulay, A. and Kapferer, J. (2003) 'Do brand personality scales really measure brand personality?', *The Journal of Brand Management*, 11(2): 143–155.

Bergkvist, L. and Bech-Larsen, T. (2010) 'Two studies of consequences and action-able antecedents of brand love', *Journal of Brand Management*, 17(7): 504–518.

Biel, A. (1993) 'Converting image into equity', in D. Aaker and A. Biel (eds.) *Brand Equity and Advertising*, Hillsdale, NJ: Lawrence Erlbaum Associates.

Bowlby, J. (1979) *The Making and Breaking of Affectional Bonds*, London: Tavistock.

Carroll, B. and Ahuvia, A. (2006) 'Some antecedents and outcomes of brand love', *Marketing Letters*, 17(2): 79–89.

Chang, P. L. and Chieng, M. (2006) 'Building consumer–brand relationship: A cross-cultural experiential view', *Psychology & Marketing*, 23(11): 927–959.

Cheng, S. Y., White, T. and Chaplin, L. (2012) 'The effects of self-brand connections on responses to brand failure: A new look at the consumer–brand relationship', *Journal of Consumer Psychology*, 22(2): 280–288.

Esch, F. R., Langner, T., Schmitt, B. and Geus, P. (2006) 'Are brands forever? How brand knowledge and relationships affect current and future purchases', *Journal of Product & Brand Management*, 15(2): 98–105.

Fournier, S. (1998) 'Consumers and their brands: Developing relationship theory in consumer research', *Journal of Consumer Research*, 24(4): 343–353.

Grégoire, Y. and Fisher, R. (2008) 'Customer betrayal and retaliation: When your best customers become your worst enemies', *Journal of the Academy of Marketing Science*, 36(2): 247–261.

Hogg, M. K., Banister, E. and Stephenson, C. (2009) 'Mapping symbolic (anti-) consumption', *Journal of Business Research*, 62(2): 148–159.

Huneke, M. (2005) 'The face of the un-consumer: An empirical examination of the practice of voluntary simplicity in the United States', *Psychology & Marketing*, 22(7): 527–550.

Kressmann, F., Sirgy, M., Herrmann, A., Huber, F., Huber, S. and Lee, D. (2006) 'Direct and indirect effects of self-image congruence on brand loyalty', *Journal of Business Research*, 59(9): 955–964.

Lisjak, M., Lee, A. and Gardner, W. (2012) 'When a threat to the brand is a threat to the self. The importance of brand identification and implicit self-esteem in predict-ing defensiveness', *Personality and Social Psychology Bulletin*, 38(9): 1120–1132.

MacInnis, D. (2012) ' "Brands as intentional agents": Questions and extensions', *Journal of Consumer Psychology*, 22(2): 195–198.

Malär, L., Nyffenegger, B., Krohmer, H. and Hoyer, W. (2012) 'Implementing an intended brand personality: A dyadic perspective', *Journal of the Academy of Mar-keting Science*, 40(5): 728–744.

Manhire, T. (2012) 'Marmite shortage leaves New Zealanders spreading them-selves thin', *The Guardian*, 19 March. Online. Available HTTP: <http://www.theguardian.com/world/2012/mar/19/marmite-shortage-new-zealand-spread> (Accessed 24 July 2015).

Mazursky, D., LaBarbera, P. and Aiello, A. (1987) 'When consumers switch brands', *Psychology & Marketing*, 4(1): 17–30.

New Zealand Health Association Ltd. (2012) *Marmite Shortage*. Online. Available HTTP: <http://www.sanitarium.co.nz/about-us/sanitarium-news/2012/marmite-shortage> (Accessed 10 June 2013).

O'Shaughnessy, J. and O'Shaughnessy, N. (2002) 'Marketing, the consumer society and hedonism', *European Journal of Marketing*, 36(5/6): 524–547.

Park, C. W., Jaworski, B. and MacInnis, D. (1986) 'Strategic brand concept-image management', *The Journal of Marketing*, 50(4): 135–145.

Sirgy, M. J., Grewal, D., Mangleburg, T., Park, J., Chon, K., Claiborne, C., Johar, J. and Berkman, H. (1997) 'Assessing the predictive validity of two methods of measuring self-image congruence', *Journal of the Academy of Marketing Science*, 25(3): 229–241.

Sung, Y. and Kim, J. (2010) 'Effects of brand personality on brand trust and brand affect', *Psychology & Marketing*, 27(7): 639–661.

Sussan, F., Hall, R. and Meamber, L. (2012) 'Introspecting the spiritual nature of a brand divorce', *Journal of Business Research*, 65(4): 520–526.

Swaminathan, V., Stilley, K. and Ahluwalia, R. (2009) 'When brand personality matters: The moderating role of attachment styles', *Journal of Consumer Research*, 35(6): 985–1002.

Thomson, M., MacInnis, D. and Park, C. (2005) 'The ties that bind: Measuring the strength of consumers' emotional attachments to brands', *Journal of Consumer Psychology*, 15(1): 77–91.

Trump, R. (2014) 'Connected consumers' responses to negative brand actions: The roles of transgression self-relevance and domain', *Journal of Business Research*, 67(9): 1824–1830.

Waikato Times (2012) *Marmite bucket auction. Bucket of black gold offered on Trade Me*. Online. Available HTTP: <http://www.stuff.co.nz/waikato-times/6617240/Marmite-bucket-auction> (Accessed 31 March 2014).

9 Customer relationships and experiences during times of disaster

A case study of Ballantynes

Jörg Finsterwalder and Hannah Grey

Introduction

On 22 February 2011 the city of Christchurch in New Zealand was hit by a second major earthquake. It killed 185 people, injured many others and, along with destroying many suburbs, devastated the Central Business District (CBD), making it inaccessible to the public for months. Ballantynes, an iconic Christchurch retailer located in the heart of the CBD, sustained significant infrastructural damage, resulting in a period of inaccessibly lasting eight months.

There is little literature on how retailers can maintain customer relationships and experiences in post-disaster situations. This chapter examines how Ballantynes maintained ongoing relationships with its customers by offering unique experiences while their flagship store was out of operation. The chapter describes Ballantynes' challenges after the earthquake, and against the backdrop of key customer service literature, analyses the retailer's measures taken following the earthquake.

Literature review

Customer relationships

> Retaining customers is far more profitable than building new relationships.
> (Chen and Popovich 2003: 681)

Maintaining a loyal customer base can offer an organisation greater stability and provide for improved sales by increasing the volume of purchases from repeat customers (Oliver 1997; Chen and Popovich 2003). Bad experiences with a company can have detrimental effects on customer relationships and affect loyalty. Measures to create repeat patronage are therefore imperative (Payne and Frow 2005).

Product, price, place and promotion – the four Ps of marketing – are still a dominating paradigm in marketing literature. However, this approach does not offer firms the ability to adjust their performance to meet consumer demands (Grönroos 1996). Identifying and establishing, as well as maintaining and enhancing, relationships with customers and other stakeholders, for the benefit of all parties involved, is a more task-oriented approach that focuses on long-term relationships with customers rather than single transactions.

There are three key areas companies can focus on in order to build and maintain customer relationships. First, getting to know their customers better and building trust requires firms to be in direct contact with their customers. Here face-to-face interaction is important (Grönroos 1996). Second, establishing a customer database is another important factor, and it should be kept up to date, readily accessible and easy to use. Databases allow more tailored interactions with customers and also help to maintain relationships and achieve customer loyalty through such activities as tailored marketing campaigns and loyalty programmes (Parvatiyar and Sheth 2001).

For companies to create lasting relationships by means of best meeting customer need, value is a very important third component. The ability for companies to provide continuous superior value can strengthen relationships and offer a strong platform for a competitive advantage over other companies (Ravald and Grönroos 1996).

The development of products, services and effective programmes that are important to customers reinforces the customer relationship and creates return customers. A major component of customer relationship marketing and management is a firm's ability to create continuous and high-quality customer experiences to aid in the creation of enduring customer relationships (Payne and Frow 2005), although these may be severely challenged at a time of natural disaster.

Customer experience

There has been a shift in marketing from focusing on just products and services to customer experiences (Klaus and Maklan 2011). These are important elements of marketing because they contribute to every aspect of a firm's offering, including advertising, service features, reliability, ease of use and quality of customer care (Meyer and Schwager 2007). As all of these components shape a consumer's experience, it is important that the firm has a consistent understanding of what "customer experience" means, to best enable it to deliver superior encounters with customers (Meyer and Schwager 2007). Customers essentially experience satisfaction, or lack thereof, as a result of a series of experiences with a firm, and satisfaction occurs when expectations are equalled with subsequent experiences (Meyer and Schwager 2007; Klaus and Maklan 2011).

The added value that customers receive in a transaction stems from a combination of: pre-consumption experience, such as searching, planning, imagining the experience; the purchase experience itself, such as choice, payment and encounter; the consumption experience, such as sensations, joy and satisfaction; and the post-consumption experience factors, such as remembering and sharing stories (Arnould, Price and Zinkhan 2004; Klaus 2014). Hence, customer experiences are the internal and subjective responses customers have to those direct or indirect contacts with the company (Meyer and Schwager 2007). Successful brands are able to embed their fundamental value in their offering to maximise the experience gained through a variety of "touchpoints" with the company. Customers' expectations and their satisfaction with such experiences are often shaped by previous encounters with the company and its competition, and are judged accordingly (Meyer and Schwager 2007).

Researchers suggest different dimensions of customer experience, including sensory, emotional, cognitive, activity-related, lifestyle-connected and social components (Gentile, Spiller and Noci 2007; Schmitt 2014). Other researchers use the dimensions of passive vs. active participation and immersion vs. absorption to distinguish four realms of an experience: entertainment (passive participation/absorption), educational (active participation/absorption), aesthetic (passive participation/immersion) and escapism (active participation/immersion) (Pine and Gilmore 1998). When customers have satisfying experiences it impacts their level of satisfaction and may create loyalty in repurchasing and spreading positive word-of-mouth (Klaus and Maklan 2011). The type of experience expected to be offered to a customer is dependent on the type of business and the types of products or services it offers.

Department stores

Department stores are more than just retail outlets, and instead often become local institutions (Nelson 2006), often as a result of the wide variety of goods and high level of service provision to customers. Department stores generally carry an extensive assortment of merchandise, with several product lines organised into separate departments. Besides a wide variety of products, many department stores offer additional services to consumers such as credit facilities, merchandise return, gift wrapping, alterations and delivery. Department stores accentuate fashion goods with higher mark-ups, wide-ranging service and an enjoyable shopping experience, with their value propositions focusing on entertainment, service and scale (Davis and Hodges 2012).

Disasters

Major natural disasters such as earthquakes, floods, volcanic eruptions and fire can affect communities on many different levels, such as deterioration of physical and psychological wellbeing and performance (Flin and Paton 1999; Helton and Head 2012; Helton, Ossowski and Malinen 2013), damage to infrastructure, and/or residential displacement (Gray and Oloruntoba 2009). Individuals can experience a lack of basic needs such as food, water, power and accommodation (Finsterwalder 2010). Disasters halt people's abilities to act routinely. From a business perspective, the effects of disasters on infrastructure can create difficulties throughout the supply chain, including retailers' ability to obtain products to sell to consumers (Altay and Ramirez 2010). Even if companies have the ability to stock and offer their products and services, other barriers such as damage to roads can prevent customers from accessing affected retailers. With such a detour from routine life, consumption patterns themselves can be altered in both the short and the longer term (Del Ninno et al. 1998; Lindell and Prater 2003). Shifts in consumers' spending following a disaster can also make it very difficult for a business to recover and survive, making its post-disaster marketing efforts extremely important.

Business recovery and recovery marketing

The way in which individual businesses recover after a natural disaster is a relatively understudied area (Corey and Deitch 2011). The research available is mainly collated from specific business sectors following a natural disaster (Tierney 1997; Corey and Deitch 2011), yet research efforts are increasing, for example, to get a better understanding of an organisation's resilience and its capability to recover (Nilakant et al. 2014; Stevenson et al. 2014; Whitman et al. 2014). Each natural disaster is unique and can differ in terms of how widespread and devastating the damage is, how many people are displaced, and how long vital supply chains are disrupted (Corey and Deitch 2011). Nevertheless, there is some consensus in the literature with respect to some of the key characteristics that impact a business' capacity to recover following a natural disaster. The size of the business is a predictor of recovery (Tierney 1997) as much as it also tends to support a firm's progression during "normal times". Larger businesses have a greater likelihood of recovery because they are more likely to have more than one location (Zhang, Lindell and Prater 2009). Large firm size also suggests greater resources, putting them in a better financial position to recover (Tierney 1997). Moreover, quality of top and middle management's leadership, quality of external linkages and of internal collaboration, ability to learn from experience, and staff wellbeing and engagement influence resilience and recovery (Nilakant et al. 2014; see also Nilakant et al., Chapter 3, this volume).

Industry sector is also a factor in how quickly a business recovers post-disaster. In the construction and manufacturing business, instead of being crippled by a disaster, companies can actually profit from disaster occurrence and be in a better position than pre-disaster (Kroll et al. 1991; Dalhamer and Tierney 1998; Corey and Deitch 2011). The retail and wholesale sector, however, has seen the opposite, being potentially the most vulnerable, and reporting substantial losses (Chang and Falit-Baiamonte 2002), both in sales and customers, so it can therefore be very difficult to return to pre-disaster levels within a short period of time (Corey and Deitch 2011; see also Prayag and Orchistron, Chapter 7, this volume).

The type of physical damage sustained is another inhibiting factor to business recovery. Several studies have found that greater amounts of physical and structural damage increase a business's difficulty in recovering (Tierney 1997; Webb, Tierney and Dahlhamer 2002). Even if the business itself has escaped any damage, there is also the breakdown of infrastructure, such as power, water, and phone lines, that businesses have to contend with to survive. Many roads may be inaccessible, and disruptions in services such as postal delivery and waste removal can heavily affect a business (Corey and Deitch 2011). This type of widespread damage also relates to the issue of forced closure in which a business, its premises and its resources have survived and are ready for operations but because of the surrounding environment, the business cannot reopen, which inhibits any ability to recover (Tierney 1997).

Another factor in business recovery is a disaster's effect on the social structure of a community. Many companies' customer bases derive from the local population. The loss of customers post-disaster is a large contributing factor to business failure (Corey and Deitch 2011), especially as a result of relocation. Importantly, the impact of relocation on a company's ability to recover is not only in terms of customer loss, but also the loss of staff to keep the business running (Corey and Deitch 2011).

Very little research is available that focuses on post-disaster marketing measures of companies. Some literature focuses on the legal aspects of marketing communication (Cook 1998) or on destination marketing after natural disasters (Durocher 1994; Potthorf and Neal 1994; Orchiston and Higham 2014; Walters and Mair 2012). Little research directly relates to customer needs, responses and behaviour and/or the marketing efforts of companies – in particular, retailers – in such situations (Ballantine, Zafar and Parsons 2014; Finsterwalder 2010). Hence, this case study aims at closing some of the existing research gap by analysing post-disaster customer relationship maintenance and customer experience measures of a retailer.

The Christchurch earthquake and Ballantynes

On 4 September 2010 the city of Christchurch in New Zealand was disrupted by a 7.1 Mw earthquake. There were power outages and damage to roads and to properties. Yet, the city was left in awe that there was no loss of life. On 22 February 2011, however, a second earthquake, measuring 6.3 Mw, devastated the city. The second earthquake was more severe, claiming the lives of 185 people (Cubrinovski et al. 2011). The areas of the CBD and the eastern suburbs were affected most severely. Infrastructure was heavily damaged with contaminated water, sewerage systems broke, power disruptions spread to 75 per cent of the city, and entire suburbs flooded, with liquefaction occurring as well as major damage to roads across the city. Christchurch was in a state of emergency for almost ten weeks with large areas of the CBD still cordoned off 20 months later.

Ballantynes

Ballantynes was first established in 1854 as a family-owned business and is still 100 per cent family owned today. The retailer operates with a traditional department store model. Pre-earthquake, Ballantynes' flagship store was an 11,000m² retail space in the City Mall in Christchurch's CBD. Ballantynes also has a store at Christchurch International Airport and in Timaru (two hours south of Christchurch). Ballantynes runs a catalogue business, issuing four catalogues a year, and maintains a website for their customers (www.ballantynes.co.nz). In 2011 Ballantynes employed about 430 staff across the three stores, including members of the Ballantyne family. The company aims to maintain its traditions of service and quality while keeping up to date with times, fashions and brands (Stewart 2011a; Ballantynes 2015a).

Ballantynes' Christchurch store was badly damaged by the February 2011 earthquake (Ballantynes 2015a). The business also faced the closure of the Christchurch CBD, which meant that no one could access the store for eight months, leaving Ballantynes with no accessible "touchpoint" in Christchurch's City Centre. The City Centre closure also denied Ballantynes' staff access to products and information held on site. Damage from the earthquake required the demolition of two of the four buildings that housed Ballantynes, along with the loss of another store the company rented as part of a younger retail offering, The Contemporary Lounge. With approximately 90 per cent of trade coming from the CBD premises, Ballantynes was left in a hugely vulnerable position (Ballantynes 2015a).

Method

To understand how Ballantynes maintained customer relationships, created customer experiences in the aftermath of the earthquake, and successfully reestablished itself while other retailers either moved out of the city to restart their businesses or failed to continue (Canterbury Development Corporation 2015), a qualitative case study based on a range of sources was undertaken. These sources included a semi-structured interview with Mary Devine, the Managing Director of Ballantynes Department Store, as primary data undertaken 4 April 2012 (a follow-up interview was conducted 23 April 2015); examination of information such as marketing material produced by the company; and secondary data research of a variety of sources, such as radio broadcasts, newspapers and magazine articles. This secondary information was not only useful in understanding Ballantynes' post-earthquake measures but also gave insights into some of the firm's prior activities.

Findings

The biggest barrier faced by Ballantynes to keep the business and its customer relationships alive post-earthquake was its location in the heart of the CBD, which was cordoned off from the public for over eight months. The key was the use of relationship marketing activities and the creation of unique customer experiences. Mary Devine (pers. comm.) stressed:

> [What] we focused on really early on – the point of difference – was our relationship we had with a lot of our customers. And that we believed . . . our service ethos was something that had always been important to the brand but really set us aside . . . We said in what ways can we touch the customers?

The role of different touchpoints (Meyer and Schwager 2007) will be drawn on to explain the different measures the company took in the aftermath of the earthquake.

Touchpoint communication

Clear communication is a fundamental aspect of customer relationships (Grönroos 2004). Clear communication was maintained by Ballantynes throughout the recovery phase.

The retailer's initial response was to keep the customers informed. Being known for its page-two advertisements in the local newspaper, it was decided that this would be the channel to articulate actions and intentions with the customers in regard to the department store's situation and recovery efforts (Mary Devine, pers. comm.). The advertisements addressed all types of relationships that Ballantynes was involved in. It was used as a means to communicate with citizens, staff, suppliers and customers and other stakeholders as certain communication channels were not yet available to the entirety of the local population so soon after the earthquake due to power outages or telecommunications infrastructure break downs.

Figure 9.1 shows an example of Ballantynes' communication in the local newspaper post-earthquake. '[T]hat was our initial response. To keep customers informed' (Mary Devine, pers. comm.) about how to contact the department store via phone and which other outlets remained open (i.e. the stores in Timaru and in the International Terminal at Christchurch airport). The newspaper advertisement also mentioned the retailer's catalogue and website.

The catalogue, a relatively small component of previous marketing activities, had been sent out four times a year before the earthquake. This became one of the key means of communication post-earthquake, and Ballantynes very quickly compiled and distributed a catalogue to its customers (Mary Devine, pers. comm.). This was an important measure as immediate and continuous actions were required to continue to generate sales of current season stock held by Ballantynes. Along with the benefit of sales, these catalogues were a main component of Ballantynes' communications to customers in order to maintain relationships. Profile pieces on different elements of Ballantynes' business recovery were incorporated in the catalogue.

In addition, the retailer produced a tabloid publication on specific themes or sales which was inserted into the local newspaper for distribution. Ballantynes moved from minimal use of print publications to producing something nearly every two weeks to keep up communications and customer relationships (Mary Devine, pers. comm.).

With customers informed and reassured about Ballantynes' promises to continue to offer its products and services, other initiatives needed to be developed to continue offering a valuable relationship and experiences to customers. The retailer essentially had to reshape its business model in a short period of time, primarily focusing on its competitive advantages while not having a retail store in the CBD (McGowan 2011).

The company's website, until then a relatively underutilised direct channel, was 'beefed up' and transformed into one of the retailer's 'key lifelines' (Mary Devine, pers. comm.) to support Ballantynes' survival and continuing interaction with the company's customer base. Almost overnight the website was converted from having only a few hundred products to over 2,000, and its online sales capacity was expanded. This extensive range of products online meant the store could continue to cater to its clients. For customers in the region, Ballantynes also aimed at strengthening the value proposition of shopping online by offering free shipping on all purchases in the area (Stewart 2011a).

...a message from Ballantynes

The Board of Directors of Ballantynes, together with Management, wish to convey the following message to its staff, customers and fellow citizens of Christchurch:

- Our sympathies go to the families, friends and relations who have lost loved ones or who have loved ones missing as a result of the earthquake.
- Customers and staff who were present in the Christchurch Shop at the time of the earthquake have been accounted for and apart from minor injuries and one customer whose injury required hospital treatment, all are safe.
- Our immediate concern, like all people in the City, is for the adequate care of people who are badly affected by this calamity and to ensure they are helped properly.

To Our Staff:

- We will continue to communicate via the planned emergency telephone and text network by your immediate manager. This has been working since the event and should there be any difficulties please telephone the General Manager on 021 362 816.
- The Board and management are meeting regularly to review the current status and consider plans for the future operations of the Company. This will be communicated via the Management network and our website.

To Our Customers:

- Telephone calls coming into the business are being routed through our Timaru branch's switchboard. The Timaru and Airport shops are operating normally. In respect of our Christchurch store and online/catalogue business, we will update you all as soon as we have more information to hand.
- We thank the many customers and suppliers from around New Zealand and the world who have conveyed their support for Ballantynes and the people of Christchurch.
- Information, although limited, is available for staff, customers and suppliers, on our website www.ballantynes.com

General:

- We give special thanks to the Police, Fire Service, Armed Forces, Rescue Workers, medical professionals, engineers, other citizens and local body and government leaders who are working around the clock to assist in the rescue and recovery of life.
- The Company is determined to help, in any way it can in the recovery of our treasured city and its future.
- We are absolutely committed to remaining as a cornerstone of inner city retail for Christchurch.

Peter Cox
Chairman

Mary Devine
Managing Director

Ballantynes

City Mall, Christchurch. 03 379 7400 or 0800 656 400. www.ballantynes.com.

Figure 9.1 A message from Ballantynes (2011a)

Apart from heavily relying on above-the-line (mass media) communications in Ballantynes' post-disaster marketing efforts and using Internet marketing and catalogues, e-newsletters and existing email addresses for mail-outs were utilised for below-the-line (niche) communications. Yet, due to limited availability of customers' email addresses, considerable focus was on mass communications.

Touchpoint events

One of the pivotal parts of Ballantynes' creative customer relationship and customer experience measures in their post-disaster recovery were the twice-weekly bus trips the company initiated in April, only a few weeks after the February 2011 earthquake, to the outlet in Timaru, which had increased its merchandise (Mathewson 2011a; Stewart 2011a). Knowing some customers would not respond well to a shift towards online shopping over the traditional retail, the bus trips to the other branch at a safe distance from the earthquakes offered shoppers an alternative way to get 'their Ballantynes fix' (Mathewson 2011a) and allowed them to participate in "escapism", leaving the city and post-earthquake stresses behind to engage in a relaxed retail experience (Mathewson 2011a; Morton 2011). Such a creative response to the earthquakes was recognised by the 2011 Champion Canterbury Business Awards (Stewart 2011b). Figure 9.2 shows one of the advertising examples for these bus trips.

What made these trips so successful was that Ballantynes was creating events that customers could revel in. Consistent with Ballantynes' approach to relationship

Figure 9.2 Girls Day Out (Ballantynes, 2011b)

marketing in-store, the trips were all about customer service, atmosphere and experience. The bus trips themselves involved displays and product tutorials and demonstrations from different suppliers (Cropp 2011). Staff members were hosts on board the buses and entertained the customers (Mathewson 2011a) and, at times stepped out of their own comfort zones to do so (Cropp 2011). Customers were greeted by a glass of sparkling alcohol or juice on arrival, High Tea, and access to exclusive promotions (Mathewson 2011a).

Customers, mostly women aged over 40 years, greatly valued the opportunity to go shopping to Timaru, despite the fact it was 350 km round trip. One business owner, who had chartered a limousine to take some of her own customers along to the store, acknowledged that '[w]e all needed a break from the earthquakes . . . so we thought we should treat ourselves to a bit of fun . . . You've got to indulge yourself . . . we had missed going to Ballantynes' (quoted in The Press, 2011a). Another customer commented: '. . . we're just getting into a stride [of shopping] again' (Morton 2011). This reflects the Ballantynes' perspective: 'people were so stressed. It was just nice to get out of the city and do something light-hearted' (Mary Devine, pers. comm.). Hostess Denise Bird (quoted in Mathewson 2011a) comments: 'It's a fun day to get away from Christchurch'. The incentive of travelling south by bus was very successful. During the six-month period from February 2011 more than 100 buses made the trip, taking more than 5,500 shoppers on this journey (Studholme 2011) with 200–300 people participating each week (Morton 2011). Many of the customers who took part in the bus trips were regular Ballantynes shoppers. This also attracted new customers to Ballantynes, such as a 17-year old girl who had a 'fantastic time' visiting Ballantynes for the first time buying her first cosmetics (Mathewson 2011a). For Ballantynes, sales at the Timaru store nearly doubled (Mary Devine, pers. comm.) with some customers spending over NZ$1,000 on such a trip (Cropp 2011). According to former Managing Director, Richard Ballantyne (in Shadwell 2011), the loyalty of the customers, particularly on the bus trips, enabled Ballantynes to trust in its recovery and in having a continuing basis for business. Hence, these bus trips had a double function: to stay in touch with suppliers and customers and to keep the brand alive (Cropp 2011).

Ballantynes' tradition and exclusivity of events, including sales and one-off retail events (Stewart 2011a; Shadwell 2011), have always been an important component in maintaining relationships and re-creating established experiences with loyal customers. This is also indicated in Figure 9.3. Ballantynes used to offer two major sales a year, and post-disaster the retailer continued the same tradition (Mary Devine, pers. comm.). At a six-day sale held at an enclosed stadium in Christchurch, Ballantynes made available to customers more than 125,000 items that had all been reduced by at least 50 per cent, and the event even had to work around ongoing aftershocks (The Press 2011b). The sale attracted 28,000 people and generated 18,000 transactions (Cropp 2011). It was an 'integral part of the firm's post-earthquake recovery' as it benefited Ballantynes, staff and customers (Mary Devine quoted in The Press 2011b). It allowed the retailer to move products, such as all winter fashion, that had been stuck in the "red-zone",

... a customer update from Ballantynes

Thank you for the overwhelming support that we have received for our company and staff. We do truly appreciate the wonderful loyalty shown by our customers and suppliers.

We would like to take this opportunity to provide an update on the current operations of Ballantynes. At this stage time frame to access the inner city and being able to re-open the business remains uncertain. We do remain confident that we will be opening our doors again; however we do not envisage that this will be within the next few months. We have therefore started to establish various parts of our business on a temporary basis. We now have our administration offices set up alongside our warehousing facility and are able to establish key services for customers:

CUSTOMER SERVICE

- Our Customer Services will be operating from Monday 21 March from 8.00am to 6.00pm seven days Monday to Sunday and are available on 0800 656 400.
- Customer Accounts can be paid to our postal address: PO Box 4648 Christchurch or via Customer Services.
- We are aware that we have gift registers for a number of weddings from late February through to March. If you have any enquiries in respect of the Gift Registry please contact Customer Services.
- Our workroom staff will be working from their homes. Once we can access the building we will complete this work and contact our customers.

CATALOGUE/WEBSITE

- The Autumn Catalogue will be launched at the end of the month. All merchandise will be delivered free of charge to our Christchurch based customers.
- We are working on significant improvements to our website and will keep you informed of progress alternatively visit us on www.ballantynes.com for an update.

BEAUTY SALON

- Temporary premises will be established for our Beauty Salon from late March. The Manager will make direct contact with those customers scheduled for appointments over the previous and coming months.

TIMARU

- Additional brands and products will be available from our Timaru shop, particularly in the areas of Women's Fashion, Footwear, Accessories and Menswear. We will also be introducing into Timaru additional cosmetic brands to enable us to service the requirements of customers.

GENERAL INFORMATION

- We are also in the process of looking at specific one-off retail events to service our customer needs. We will provide more information on this once we have finalised the details.
- We are conscious that there is a demand for personal contact with customers to provide general information on the business and to also assist with valuations for customers. We are looking at options to establish information kiosks to provide a point of contact for customers.

As a company we are determined to help in any way we can in the recovery of the Canterbury community, our treasured city and its future. We are absolutely committed to remaining a cornerstone of the inner city for Christchurch and look forward to reopening our iconic shop.

Thank you for your support.

shop online at www.ballantynes.com

Ph (03) 379 7400 or 0800 656 400. Fax (03) 366 8548.

Figure 9.3 A customer update from Ballantynes (2011c)

the large area in the Central City heavily damaged and cordoned off from public access. It also satisfied customer needs for some "therapeutic" Ballantynes retail experience in Christchurch and enabled staff to service customers again. '[I]t gets them [all] back in that retail environment, which they've been missing' (Mary Devine quoted in The Press 2011b). The event was many customers' first opportunity to shop "at" Ballantynes in Christchurch since the closure of their main outlet in the City Mall four months earlier (Mathewson 2011b); it allowed them to reconnect with the retailer.

Along with events open to any customer, Ballantynes also maintained a focus on the more exclusive events, such as those promoting beauty product brands (Mary Devine, pers. comm.). Pre-earthquake, such exclusive offers were staged during evening events, presenting a variety of experiences for customers to enjoy – from facials, makeovers and product trials, to extensive goodie bags and refreshments – while browsing collections. To continue this strong connection and association with beauty products, Ballantynes ran a series of events at luxury hotels in Christchurch (see Figure 9.4). The availability of a usable part of the database allowed for tailored marketing of these exclusive events. These happenings helped maintain relationships because they were not sales driven; instead, they were about keeping a point of contact with valued customers, and any product sales were an add-on bonus (Mary Devine, pers. comm.).

Touchpoint servicescape

Ballantynes' above-mentioned initiative, as well as key initiatives such as the website, the bus trips and the continuation of their catalogues, helped maintain customer relationships, but other creative approaches were required to continue to interact with the entire customer base. A key component of Ballantynes' business model has always been face-to-face interaction between customers and staff (Mary Devine, pers. comm.). For this, the physical environment of the retailer was important as it enabled face-to-face interactions to occur in a set retail atmosphere.

Ballantynes opened temporary locations in Christchurch to ensure the maintenance of personal relationships throughout the closure of the central city flagship store. The store had previously offered services such as a hair and beauty salon and a café. In order to continue to satisfy customers, both the café and hair salon were temporarily established elsewhere. The hair salon was relocated and operated from a salon in another suburb. The café relocated to one of the biggest malls west of the city centre and included an information kiosk where customers could make inquiries (Cropp 2011).

Another temporary location was established in a second mall north of the city centre. This second kiosk was set up for customers and offered valuation services. The kiosk offered face-to-face contact with experienced Ballantynes staff (McGowan 2011) to help aid with insurance claims and replacement of lost or damaged items, such as broken china. This service was free to anyone, and staff did some 5,000 valuations during the time the kiosk was in the mall. The service

Figure 9.4 M·A·C is back in Christchurch (Ballantynes, 2011d)

offerings in Christchurch allowed customers to have meaningful interaction with experienced Ballantynes staff and created further touchpoints with the retailer, with the information kiosk and café both providing concierges who could answer any questions or concerns customers had along with relaying new information from Ballantynes. Such extra efforts are core to Ballantynes' 'service ethos [and] something that had always been important to the brand but really set [the company] aside' from others (Mary Devine, pers. comm.).

Ballantynes' objective had always been to reopen its iconic central city store. Richard Ballantyne had reiterated that the store would not relocate (Stewart 2011a). A key component in Ballantynes' recovery was the involvement in the so-called Re:Start project (http://restart.org.nz/), which was the initiative of a circle of property owners in the CBD (Gourlay n.d.). With the City Mall already in decline, Ballantynes had been collaborating with these owners prior to the earthquakes, to identify what could be done to revitalise the area (Mary Devine, pers. comm.). The continuation of this collaboration was essential in being able to reopen the central city shopping area ahead of time. The Re:Start precinct was constructed out of shipping containers because they are strong, stackable and relocatable if required. The shipping containers house various shops and allowed retail to move back into the CBD without having to wait for permanent buildings. The area is landscaped, with bright appealing shops in the shipping containers, some in lively colours, and it offers a mix of former central city tenants and big brands anchored by the Ballantynes store.

Ballantynes was instrumental in creating this Re:Start initiative (see also Finsterwalder and Hall, Chapter 15, this volume). The view was that any activity around its store in the deserted central city would be of a significant benefit to the retailer (Mary Devine, pers comm.). The company still had its main location but needed a space for The Contemporary Lounge, their younger retail offering, which was previously leased out in a store next to Ballantynes' main location. This additional space was needed in order to get back to full capacity. The company worked with a construction company that put up two temporary buildings adjacent to the flagship store in the CBD. Parts of the retailer were then housed in 12 temporary containers (Gourlay n.d.).

To create the container mall, retailers had to work together with their competitors in order to co-locate. The notion behind this was customer needs and behaviour. People tend to want to visit a range of shops rather than a single one, even if it is as iconic as Ballantynes. This perception was the reasoning behind Ballantynes being so heavily involved in the Re:Start initiative, as it would take a thriving centre with multiple shops and activity near the department store to get people back into the CBD again and create a symbiosis between the container retailers and the department store (Gourlay n.d.). The Re:Start Mall was officially opened to a crowd of thousands on 29 October 2011 (Gourlay n.d.), in time for the region's Cup and Show Week, a week-long spring festival focusing on horse racing, fashion, entertainment and agriculture. People embraced their new city retail district, with the energy being described as contagious (McGowan 2011).

Ballantynes' reopening campaign 'Back where we belong' emphasised the retailer's perception of its place in the CBD. This campaign was promoted through advertising in the local newspaper (Figure 9.5) and on bus advertisements. A launch party was held with 300 people attending and the Prime Minister re-opening the CBD's retail precinct (Cairns 2011). Customers commented

Figure 9.5 Back where we belong (Ballantynes, 2011e)

that: 'I've been longing for this' and 'It's so great to have it [Ballantynes] back –
I've really missed it' (quoted in Cairns 2011).

Beyond the re-opening, Ballantynes aimed at continuing to improve the in-
store retail experience for their customers by trialling and testing new activities,
such as a homewares week, a fashion week and a beauty week, but also by having
special events, such as cooking demonstrations, tastings and market days, and
continuing with brand-specific events. The objective was to not only provide a
unique experience to make it worthwhile to come into the store but also to offer
a 'total experience the people are not going to get at the malls' (Mary Devine,
pers. comm.).

For Ballantynes, going back into a physical location in the CBD was all about
the "Ballantynes experience". Reopening the store was focused on 'the theatre
we are going to create within the store and within the mall, how we manage our
customer interactions . . . and touchpoints, in any format, not only in our core
city store' (Mary Devine, quoted in McGowan 2011). Not having had the main
physical outlet in the city has helped the retailer to become innovative, flexible

and "fluid", understanding what the real touchpoints were with the customers (McGowan 2011; Mary Devine, pers. comm.).

Discussion

Ballantynes' key motive in the aftermath of the earthquake was to have "the Ballantynes bubble to continue" (Mary Devine, pers. comm.) via other means while there was no CBD store. These means supported the maintenance of customer relationships and enabled the creation of unique customer experiences.

Customer relationships

Communication is the major strategy that precedes other outcomes of relationship marketing, such as trust and commitment (Morgan and Hunt 1994). In order to satisfy customers, information shared should be well organised and timely. Such communication effort was important for Ballantynes (Mary Devine, pers. comm.) and the retailer used a wide range of channels as a means to continue and increase the ability to interact with the customer base when not able to do so face-to-face in the flagship store. These communications started early and were structured, informative, and consistent with Ballantynes' pre-disaster communication strategies but altered to suit the changed context the retailer was operating in.

With the initial breakdown of key infrastructure following the earthquakes, the appropriate selection of key channels in particular newspapers allowed communications to have a large reach. More importantly it was already a type of advertising for which Ballantynes was known. With the main store inaccessible, all other forms of communication offered by Ballantynes were intensified. This included the increased use of the catalogue, website and tabloid publications, and the use of some specific customer databases for more personalised communications. Using established channels meant customers did not have to undertake any search to be subjected to communications from Ballantynes, making this information sharing easier. Catalogue and tabloid publications were increased and more frequent, continuing the flow of information that customers received. Ballantynes' expanded website offered extensive information about the retailer's recovery progress and offerings. However, it required a more active search for information from consumers.

With strong interactions through print and media communications, Ballantynes also recognised the need for face-to-face customer interaction, as this was a key element of the 'Ballantynes experience' (Mary Devine, pers. comm.) that had been lost with the closure of the flagship store. For example, the retailer utilised two concierge desks in conjunction with two temporary locations set up in the north and west parts of the city. This allowed the company's knowledgeable, friendly staff to answer any customer queries in direct and more personal interactions, which offered a stronger sense of (re)connecting and maintaining the relationship than one-way communication can do. Ballantynes' continuous flow of information appears to have been the foundation of stabilising customer trust and commitment (Shadwell 2011). The retailer continued to strengthen this commitment at various touchpoints, which kept drawing customers back to Ballantynes.

The first key initiative was the expansion of the website beyond the informational use mentioned above by creating an additional sales channel. This aided in Ballantynes' recovery because this form of direct distribution mitigated the effects of population dispersion that have been detrimental in the recovery of other retail businesses (Corey and Deitch 2011). To increase value in the relationship for the local customers, Ballantynes offered free shipping to anyone in Christchurch. The use of free shipping may have strengthened the relationship in two ways. First, customers were still able to receive the same products with even greater convenience than venturing to a store and at no additional cost. Second, the free shipping offer may have reinforced the relationship by eliminating some of the emotional cost. This catered to customers with earthquake anxiety about being in a store or surrounded by large groups of people (see Flin and Paton 1999; Morton 2011).

Customer experiences

The unique events were also what drew customers back to Ballantynes and helped maintain customer loyalty by providing customer experiences. Being one of the larger retailers in the city, the company had the option of accessing another location but also had resources available to aid in its recovery.

The defining elements of Ballantynes' impromptu measure of offering bus trips to the out-of-town store created customer experiences that included pre-consumption experience, consumption experience and post-consumption experience. The pre-consumption experience comprised interaction with other customers, staff and sales representatives on the bus on the way to the outlet south of Christchurch. For example, female participants learned 'how to dress [their] man' from a menswear supplier (Cropp 2011). It continued with the experience at the outlet store and finished with the post-consumption experience on the way home, wearing the purchased items and talking about the trip with family, friends or neighbours (Morton 2011). Deemed "escapism" (Mathewson 2011a) the trips were a combination of active participation and immersion (escapism by "getting away"; involvement in shopping, having fun and encounters) and educational experience (active participation/absorption) – for example, through product demonstrations. Ballantynes' customers could have defected to another retail store located in Christchurch. Yet, even though customers had to pay NZ$20 to enjoy a Ballantynes bus trip, it provided added value to them and strengthened customer relationships. This added value was generated by the fact that the location was outside of Christchurch, allowing customers to leave their worries behind. The core component of shopping at Ballantynes Timaru also created value as customers were offered exclusive deals. The final component was the enjoyment factor Ballantynes provided, with product tutorials on the bus, champagne and High Tea offered at the store and the added bonus that customers had the day free to wander the town if they so chose to. The overall experience hence combined elements of sensory experience (for example, food and beverage; the Ballantynes' "smell" of the store), activity (shopping), cognitive involvement (demonstrations), emotional experience (joy and fun) and social experience (for example, connecting with other customers and staff).

The other events Ballantynes offered were cosmetics events. It was important to fulfil promises by offering exclusive products and brands to Christchurch residents to maintain this customer segment. The company also had a range of products available at the events for customers who wished to purchase. Ballantynes' primary motive for these events was to ensure a continuation of face-to-face contacts with these valuable customers by creating another touchpoint with the company (see Meyer and Schwager 2007). The strong cosmetics database aided in the successful running of these events. It allowed Ballantynes to tailor the advertising campaigns directly to current customers of specific cosmetic lines, making them more receptive to the email or advertising campaign preceding the events (see Grönroos 1996).

Enablers for customer relationships and experiences

Ballantynes enhanced and made use of key enablers during the recovery phase that were either underutilised or not part of the company's business strategy prior to the earthquake. This was the use of some databases and of the website for online sales and the addition of and embeddedness in servicescapes.

Databases are a key element in creating success of relationship marketing and customer experience activities as they generate useful information on customers that a company can use to its advantage. Ballantynes' database was in the process of undergoing changes to enhance customer-related activities and enable better data mining. Some departments, such as cosmetics, worked very hard with their respective databases, using the necessity for communication as a way of cleansing and updating the database. The post-disaster need to better communicate with customers required a major clean-up of the main database to make it easier to maintain and monitor activities. In terms of the online sales capacity, Ballantynes increased the number of products available online from a few hundred to over 2,000 (Stewart 2011a).

Besides existing locations Ballantynes could utilise in the aftermath of the earthquake, such as the outlet south of the city and the airport shop, temporary or transitional servicescapes were an integral part of the retailer's recovery efforts. These transitional servicescapes included the service kiosks and café as well as the outsourced hair salon. Later on, when focusing on bringing customers back into the Ballantynes' flagship store, the retailer worked with other businesses in the vicinity to create the Re:Start initiative (see Durocher 1994).

Conclusions

This research bridges the gap between the customer relationship and customer experience literature and the limited research on post-disaster retail marketing.

This case study highlighted several relationship marketing and customer experience techniques that successfully aided in the retention of a customer base during the closure of a company's main operating location. This study has practical implications for retail companies that have experienced a natural or human disaster and are in the process of recovery. Even if a company loses its main source of revenue, by continuing strong relationship marketing techniques and ensuring the continued offering of quality customer experiences, a firm can retain a strong customer base in the recovery phase and continue to be successful in the future. Focusing on the customer through relationships and experiences; being highly communicative; staying fluid in decision-making; using the existing competitive advantage of service, brands and events; testing and trialling new marketing measures; and enabling staff to optimise their contributions (Mary Devine, pers. comm.; see also Nilakant et al. 2014) allowed Ballantynes' recovery efforts to succeed. Some new initiatives may even have made the company more "antifragile"; that is, they took the company further in being robust and resilient (compared to before the earthquake) as 'the antifragile gets better' (Taleb 2014: 3).

With respect to subsequent progress, Ballantynes has since improved online execution by moving to a new e-commerce platform. Additionally, Ballantynes has broadened communication channels by establishing a social media presence (Mary Devine, pers. comm.), a channel that the retailer did not use in the aftermath of the earthquake. Furthermore, Ballantynes established a Beauty Loyalty Programme which has performed very successfully. The company reinforced its existing focus on exclusive brands with a refurbished Fashion Atrium, launched in the main store to display them. The Contemporary Lounge has returned on-site after a major facelift and with a different selection of brands, and a new café has been situated within the lounge (Ballantynes 2015b).

A newly rebuilt CBD may help draw more shoppers back into the city in the future and support this retail destination to continue to be successful in the long term. In such an environment, Ballantynes can continue to focus on what it has been known for – namely, its three areas of competitive advantage: customer service, events and exclusive brands – to maintain customer relationships and create unique customer experiences at all Ballantynes touchpoints.

References

Arnould, E. J., Price, L. and Zinkhan, G. M. (2004) *Consumers* (2nd ed.), Boston: McGraw-Hill/Irwin.

Atlay, N. and Ramirez, A. (2010) 'Impact of disaster on firms in different sectors: Implications for supply chains', *Journal of Supply Chain Management,* 46(4): 59–80.

Ballantine, P. W., Zafar, S. and Parsons, A. G. (2014) 'Changes in retail shopping behaviour in the aftermath of an earthquake', *International Review of Retail, Distribution and Consumer Research,* 24(1): 1–13.

Ballantynes. (2011a) 'A message from Ballantynes', *The Press,* 1 March: A2.

——(2011b) 'Girls Day Out', *The Press,* 8 April: A2.

——(2011c) 'A customer update from Ballantynes', *The Press,* 19 March: A2.

——(2011d) 'M·A·C is back in Christchurch', *Ballantynes E-newsletter,* 24 June.

——(2011e) 'Back where we belong', *The Press*, 29 October: A2.

——(2015a) *Ballantynes History*. Online. Available HTTP: <https://www.ballantynes.co.nz/history> (Accessed 30 March 2015).

——(2015b) *Ballantynes Store Info Christchurch*. Online. Available HTTP: <https://www.ballantynes.co.nz/christchurch> (Accessed 30 March 2015).

Cairns, L. (2011) 'Ravaged retail centre reborn', *Stuff.co.nz*, 30 October. Online. Available HTTP: <http://www.stuff.co.nz/the-press/news/christchurch-earthquake-2011/5877208/Ravaged-retail-centre-reborn> (Accessed 30 March 2015).

Canterbury Development Corporation (2015) *Retail trade sector*. Online. Available HTTP: <http://www.cdc.org.nz/economy/sector-profiles/retail-trade/> (Accessed 30 March 2015).

Chang, S. E. and Falit-Baiamonte, A. (2002) 'Disaster vulnerability of businesses in the 2011 Nisqually earthquake', *Environmental Hazards*, 4(2–3): 59–71.

Chen, I. and Popovich, K. (2003) 'Understanding customer relationship management (CRM) people, process and technology', *Business Process Management Journal*, 9(5): 672–688.

Cook, D. L. (1998) 'Earthquakes and aftershocks: Implications for marketers and advertisers in Reno v. ACLU and the litigation of the Communications Decency Act', *Journal of Public Policy & Marketing*, 17(1): 116–123.

Corey, C. M. and Deitch, E. A. (2011) 'Factors affecting business recovery immediately after Hurricane Katrina', *Journal of Contingencies and Crisis Management*, 19(3): 169–181.

Cropp, A. (2011) "Girls Day Out' bus takes quake shoppers to Timaru', *The New Zealand Herald*, 1 July. Online. Available HTTP: <http://www.nzherald.co.nz/business/news/article.cfm?c_id=3&objectid=10735468> (Accessed 30 March 2015).

Cubrinovski, M., Bradley, B., Wotherspoon, L., Green, R., Bray, J., Woods, C., Pender, M., Allen, J., Bradshaw, A., Rix, G., Taylor, M., Robinson, K., Henderson, D., Giorgini, S., Ma, K., Winkley, A., Zupan, J., O'Rourke, T., DePascale, G. and Wells, D. (2011) 'Geotechnical aspects of the 22 February 2011 Christchurch earthquake', *Bulletin of the New Zealand Society for Earthquake Engineering*, 44: 205–226.

Dahlhamer, J. M. and Tierney, K. J. (1998) 'Rebounding from disruptive events: Business recovery following the Northridge earthquake', *Sociological Spectrum*, 18(2): 121–141.

Davis, L. and Hodges, N. (2012) 'Consumer shopping value: An investigation of shopping trip value, in-store shopping value and retail format', *Journal of Retailing and Consumer Services*, 19(2): 229–239.

Del Ninno, C., Dorosh, P. A., Smith, L. C. and Roy, D. K. (1998) *The 1998 Floods in Bangladesh. Disaster Impacts, Household Coping Strategies and Response*, Washington, DC: International Food Policy Research Institute.

Durocher, J. (1994) 'Recovery marketing: What to do after a natural disaster', *Cornell Hotel and Restaurant Administration Quarterly*, 35(2): 66–70.

Finsterwalder, J. (2010) 'On shaky grounds? Customer needs and service provision after a major disaster in the light of Maslow's hierarchies', *New Zealand Journal of Applied Business Research (NZJABR)*, 8(2): 1–28.

Flin, R. and Paton, D. (1999) 'Disaster stress: An emergency management perspective', *Disaster Prevention and Management*, 8(4): 261–267.

Gentile, C., Spiller, N. and Noci, G. (2007) 'How to sustain the customer experience: An overview of experience components that co-create value with the customer', *European Management Journal*, 25(5): 395–410.

Gourlay, B. (n.d.). 'Devine Inspiration', *Magazines Today*. Online. Available HTTP: <http://www.magazinestoday.co.nz/Features/Interviews/Devine+Inspiration.html> (Accessed 30 March 2015).

Gray, R. and Oloruntoba, R. (2009) 'Customer service in emergency relief chains', *International Journal of Physical Distribution & Logistics Management*, 39(6): 486–505.

Grönroos, C. (1996) 'Relationship marketing: Strategic and tactical implications', *Management Decision*, 34(3): 5–14.

——(2004) 'The relationship marketing process: Communication, interaction, dialogue, value', *The Journal of Business and Industrial Marketing*, 19(2): 99–113.

Helton, W. S. and Head, J. (2012) 'Earthquakes on the mind: Implications of Disasters for Human Performance', *Human Factors*, 54(2): 189–194.

Helton, W. S., Ossowski, U. and Malinen, S. (2013) 'Post-disaster depression and vigilance: A functional near-infrared spectroscopy study', *Experimental Brain Research*, 226(3): 357–362.

Klaus, P. (2014) *Measuring Customer Experience. How to Develop and Execute the Most Profitable Customer Experience*, New York: Palgrave McMillan.

Klaus, P. and Maklan, S. (2011) 'Customer experience: Are we measuring the right things?' *International Journal of Market Research*, 53(6): 771–792.

Kroll, C. A., Landis, J. D., Shen, Q. and Stryker, S. (1991) *Economic Impacts of the Loma Prieta Earthquake: A Focus on Small Business*. Working Paper No. 91–187, Berkley: University of California Transportation Center and the Center for Real Estate and Economics.

Lindell, M. K. and Prater, C. S. (2003) 'Assessing community impacts of natural disasters', *Natural Hazards Review*, 4(4): 176–185.

Mathewson, N. (2011a) 'Hallelujah for Ballantynes' retail therapy', *The Press/Stuff.co.nz*, 01 July. Online. Available HTTP: <http://www.stuff.co.nz/the-press/news/christchurch-earthquake-2011/5216874/Hallelujah-for-Ballantynes-retail-therapy> (Accessed 30 March 2015).

——(2011b) 'Huge queues for Ballantynes sale', *The Press/Stuff.co.nz*, 15 June. Online. Available HTTP: <http://www.stuff.co.nz/the-press/news/5146348/Huge-queues-for-Ballantynes-sale> (Accessed 30 March 2015).

McGowan, R. (2011) 'Balancing the Re:Start plan', *The Press/Stuff.co.nz*, 26 October. Online. Available HTTP: <http://www.stuff.co.nz/the-press/opinion/perspective/5851912/Balancing-the-Re-Start-plan> (Accessed 30 March 2015).

Meyer, C. and Schwager, A. (2007) 'Understanding customer experience', *Harvard Business Review*, 85(2): 117–126.

Morgan, R. M. and Hunt, S. D. (1994) 'The commitment-trust theory of relationship marketing', *Journal of Marketing*, 58(3): 20–38.

Morton, S. (2011) 'Ballantynes Bus', *Radio New Zealand National Broadcast*, 3 September. Online. Available HTTP: <http://www.radionz.co.nz/national/programmes/thiswayup/20110903> (Accessed 30 March 2015).

Nelson, R. (2006) 'A true department store experience', *Minneapolis-St. Paul Star Tribune*. Online. Available HTTP: <http://www.deseretnews.com/article/635184420/A-true-department-store-experience.html?pg=all> (Accessed 30 March 2015).

Nilakant, V., Walker, B., van Heugten, K., Baird, R. and de Vries, H. (2014) 'Conceptualising adaptive resilience using grounded theory', *New Zealand Journal of Employment Relations*, 39(1): 79–86.

Oliver, R. L. (1997) *Satisfaction: A Behavioural Perspective on the Consumer*, New York: McGraw-Hill.

Orchiston, C. and Higham, J. E. S. (2014) 'Knowledge management and tourism recovery (de)marketing: The Christchurch earthquakes 2010–2011', *Current Issues in Tourism*, doi:http://dx.doi.org/10.1080/13683500.2014.990424

Parvatiyar, A. and Sheth, J. (2001) 'Customer relationship management: Emerging practice, process, and discipline', *Journal of Economic and Social Research*, 3(2): 1–34.

Payne, A. and Frow, P. (2005) 'A strategic framework for customer relationship management', *Journal of Marketing*, 69(4): 167–176.

The Press (2011a) 'Ballantynes customers revel in Timaru trip', *The Press/Stuff. co.nz*, 18 April. Online. Available HTTP: <http://www.stuff.co.nz/the-press/news/4899050/Ballantynes-customers-revel-in-Timaru-trip> (Accessed 30 March 2015).

——(2011b) 'Bargains Galore swamp arena floor', *The Press/Stuff.co.nz*, 13 June. Online. Available HTTP: <http://www.stuff.co.nz/the-press/news/5134205/Bargains-galore-swamp-arena-floor> (Accessed 30 March 2015).

Pine, J. B. and Gilmore, J. H. (1998) 'Welcome to the experience economy', *Harvard Business Review*, 76(4): 97–105.

Pottorff, S. M. and Neal, D. M. (1994) 'Marketing implications for post-disaster tourism destinations', *Journal of Travel & Tourism Marketing*, 3(1): 115–122.

Ravald, A. and Grönroos, C. (1996) 'The value concept and relationship marketing', *European Journal of Marketing*, 30(2): 19–30.

Schmitt, B. (2014) 'Experiential marketing: A new framework for design and communications', *Design Management Review*, 25(4): 19–26.

Shadwell, T. (2011) 'All aboard the Big B', *Stuff.co.nz*, 2 June. Online. Available HTTP: <http://www.stuff.co.nz/life-style/fashion/5091308/All-aboard-for-the-Big-B> (Accessed 30 March 2015).

Stevenson, J. R., Chang-Richards, Y., Conradson, D., Wilkinson, S., Vargo, J., Seville, E. and Brunsdon, D. (2014) 'Organizational Networks and recovery following the Canterbury Earthquakes', *Earthquake Spectra*, 30(1): 555–575.

Stewart, T. (2011a) 'Ballantynes to stay in the central city', *The Press/Stuff.co.nz*, 22 March. Online. Available HTTP: <http://www.stuff.co.nz/the-press/news/christchurch-earthquake-2011/4793386/Ballantynes-to-stay-in-the-central-city> (Accessed 30 March 2015).

——(2011b) 'People rose above quake, says Key', *The Press/Stuff.co.nz*, 23 September. Online. Available HTTP: <http://www.stuff.co.nz/the-press/news/christchurch-earthquake-2011/5670893/People-rose-above-quake-says-Key> (Accessed 30 March 2015).

Studholme, R. (2011) 'Ballantynes bus trips returned', *The Timaru Herald/Stuff.co.nz*, 10 November. Online. Available HTTP: <http://www.stuff.co.nz/timaru-herald/news/5939452/Ballantynes-bus-trips-returned> (Accessed 30 March 2015).

Taleb, N. N. (2014) *Antifragile: Things That Gain from Disorder*, New York, Random House.

Tierney, K. J. (1997) 'Business impacts of the Northridge earthquake', *Journal of Contingencies and Crisis Management*, 5(2): 87–97.

Walters, G. and Mair, J. (2012) 'The effectiveness of post-disaster recovery marketing messages – the case of the 2009 Australian Bushfires', *Journal of Travel and Tourism Marketing*, 29(1): 87–103.

Webb, G. R., Tierney, K. J. and Dahlhamer, J. M. (2002) 'Predicting long-term business recovery from disasters: A comparison of the Loma Prieta earthquake and Hurricane Andrew', *Environmental Hazards*, 4(1): 45–58.

Whitman, Z., Stevenson, J., Kachali, H., Seville, E., Vargo, J. and Wilson, T. (2014) 'Organisational resilience following the Darfield earthquake of 2010', *Disasters*, 38(1): 48–177.

Zhang, Y., Lindell, M. K. and Prater, C. S. (2009) 'Vulnerability of community businesses to environmental disasters', *Disasters*, 33(1): 38–57.

10 It's not all dark!

Christchurch residents' emotions and coping strategies with dark tourism sites

Girish Prayag

Introduction

The purpose of this chapter is to understand the emotive experience of residents when visiting post-disaster dark tourism sites. Dark tourism sites generally refer to sites associated with death and suffering and are usually considered a 'must see' attraction by tourists (Biran et al. 2011). Tourism experiences are emotionally laden, and several studies have examined the emotional experiences of tourists consuming destinations. Positive emotions have been prioritised in tourism studies despite the well-accepted notion that visitor experiences can elicit negative emotions (Hosany and Prayag 2013). Studies on emotions at dark tourism sites are recent (Buda et al. 2014; Nawijn and Fricke 2013) and morbidly focused on negative emotions such as anger and fear, almost ignoring that such sites can also elicit positive emotions. Existing studies prioritise tourists' (domestic and international) perspectives of dark tourism while residents' perceptions of dark tourism sites and of tourists consuming the experience of such sites have been lacking. Residents are also visitors to dark tourism sites, but their motives for consuming such sites and their perceptions may be entirely different from those of tourists. Accordingly, this chapter integrates residents' experiences of their visits to disaster sites in the discourse on dark tourism.

The city of Christchurch in New Zealand was shaken by a series of earthquakes in 2010 and 2011. The combined effects of ground shaking and liquefaction significantly impacted people, buildings and infrastructure across the Canterbury region. The earthquakes caused a significant drop in visitor numbers, particularly from the international market (Orchiston et al. 2014). Two-thirds of the existing hotel stock was destroyed, and recovery of tourism infrastructure has been slow. At the end of 2014, total hotel capacity was 55 per cent below pre-earthquake levels. The availability of flights and accommodation beds will be critical to the recovery of visitor numbers (Canterbury and Christchurch Tourism (CCT) 2014). Both domestic and international visitor markets have been slow to recover but, compared to 2012/2013 figures, the international market grew by 15 per cent in 2014 (CCT 2014). The experience of Christchurch differs from some other natural disasters because of the ongoing nature of the aftershocks over a period of 18 months (Orchiston et al. 2014).

Against this backdrop of events, the chapter begins with a general overview of tourism in a post-disaster context, followed by theoretical perspectives on dark tourism and emotions, with a particular emphasis on coping strategies. The results of semi-structured in-depth interviews with a purposive sample of 12 Christchurch residents, selected on a convenience basis in 2014, on their emotive experiences at various dark tourism sites are then reported. The participants were asked to select site(s) they wanted to talk about and then asked a range of questions to elicit their responses to these visits. The sample consisted of seven females and five males. The average age of participants was 47 years old. The chapter concludes with several implications for developing dark tourism in a post-disaster context.

Tourism and disaster sites

The effect of natural disasters on the tourism industry is a growing area of research among both academics and practitioners. Faulkner and Vikulov (2001) proposed a model for tourism disaster management following the 1998 floods at Katherine Gorge in the Northern Territories, Australia, including guidelines for the pre-disaster and post-disaster recovery stages. Their study emphasised the elements of disaster management responses and strategies for tourism recovery. Hystad and Keller (2008) investigated the long-term impacts, recovery strategies and how tourism disaster management had changed following the 2003 forest fire in Kelowna, British Columbia, Canada. They found that marketing and cooperation between stakeholders within and outside of the tourism industry were important components of tourism recovery post-disaster. Focusing on insurance and prevention, Tsai and Chen (2010) proposed several disaster risk management strategies that could be of relevance to the Taiwanese hotel industry in case that the country is impacted by earthquakes.

Ichinosawa (2006) investigated the socio-economic effects of the 2004 Boxing Day tsunami on inbound tourism in Phuket and found risk-induced stigmatisation of the region was a critical factor in the decline and thus affected recovery of tourist numbers. Following the 2011 Queensland floods in Australia, Walters et al. (2015) investigated the motivation, perception, and attitude of tourists toward this destination. They found that visitors who were likely to travel post-disaster were drawn by the need to assist the state of Queensland with its recovery efforts. This body of previous research mainly examines impacts, mitigation and recovery strategies of destinations with a focus on the role of industry stakeholders and tourists' perceptions of place post-disaster.

Several studies also examine the impacts of earthquakes on the tourism industry (Mendoza et al. 2012; Orchiston 2012; Tsai and Chen 2010) with recommendations for risk management, recovery, and marketing. Surprisingly, the voice of residents has been lacking in the tourism literature on disasters, as if industry stakeholders and tourists are the only parties concerned in post-disaster recovery of tourism destinations. With disaster sites increasingly becoming tourist attractions (Biran et al. 2014), raising ethical and moral concerns, the voice of local residents is imperative to understand how they perceive these sites and their potential economic opportunities for the community, as well as the conflicts that may arise between tourists and residents due to these sites being developed and marketed for tourism purposes. Residents' perspectives may also be particularly useful in clarifying the role and purpose of their visits to dark tourism sites, and whether such sites may help in dealing with the trauma and memory of the disaster. Residents' perspectives may, for example, help in shaping community memorialisation sites for disaster victims. Residents' perspectives should, thus, be incorporated in the study of 'dark tourism' as they are the key stakeholders in deciding how disaster remains should be disposed of and represented to others (Coats and Ferguson 2013).

The phenomenon of dark tourism

The term 'dark tourism' (Foley and Lennon 1996) has appeared in the tourism literature since the early 1990s but is not a new phenomenon. Dark tourism refers to the act of travelling to sites associated with death, misery, suffering, and the seemingly macabre (Stone 2006). Terms such as thanatourism (Seaton 1996), black spot tourism (Rojek 1993), grief tourism (Trotta 2006), and morbid tourism (Blom 2000) have been used to describe visitors' interest in such sites. Early definitions of dark tourism relate primarily to the presentation and consumption of real or commodified death and disaster sites by visitors (Foley and Lennon 1996). More recent definitions extend these prior conceptualisations to include sites associated with deviance (e.g. the Red Light District in Amsterdam). For example, Biran and Poria (2012) define dark tourism as the purposeful movement of visitors to spaces displaying acts and sights that can lead to negative social consequences for the visitor if his/her viewing or participation is revealed to those in his/her environment; in other words, tourists may face social sanctions back home for participating in dark tourism. The motives for visiting dark tourism sites are diverse, ranging from curiosity, knowledge about an event, to desire for new experiences (Biran et al. 2011).

Dark tourism has emerged as a significant niche market for the tourism industry, particularly for destinations recovering from natural disasters (Biran et al. 2014). Previous studies stress the need for diversifying the tourism product offer and generating markets following a disaster (Carlsen and Hughes 2008). Newly formed 'dark' attributes that emerge from the disaster may offer another means for the destination to recover, as reflected in the emergence of new tourist segments (Biran et al. 2014). However, given that dark tourism tends to draw from the vortex of immorality and morbidness to create so-called tourism products and attractions, this niche market creates much suspicion among residents and tourism stakeholders when earmarked for tourism development (Stone and Sharpley 2008). Not surprisingly, Christchurch and Canterbury Tourism (CCT), the region's destination marketing organisation, has deliberately avoided developing and promoting the various disaster sites as dark tourism attractions.

Emotions and tourism experiences

Emotions can be characterised as episodes of intense feelings associated with a specific referent that can instigate specific response behaviours (Cohen and Areni 1991). Emotions are ubiquitous to tourism experiences. In particular, holidays are laden with positive emotions, but the intensity of felt emotions varies on a day-to-day basis, depending on, for example, the events of the day, and whether they occur at the beginning or end of a holiday (Nawijn et al. 2013). Despite playing a critical role in tourist encounters, emotions remain an under-researched area in tourism studies (Cohen et al. 2014). Of existing studies, quantitative approaches ascertaining psychological aspects of emotions, including their antecedents (Hosany 2012) and effects on satisfaction and behavioural intentions, dominate (Prayag et al. 2013).

Two criteria are usually used to define emotions: valence and intensity. According to these criteria, an emotion can be either positive or negative and more or less felt by individuals (Izard 1977). Unsurprisingly, the measurement of emotions using a valence approach, conceptualising experiences as consisting of both positive and negative emotions, has become the favoured approach in tourism studies. Recent studies (e.g. Prayag et al. 2013) suggest that measuring basic emotions and their intensity may be more relevant to tourism given its experiential aspects involve a variety of distinct and powerful emotions such as joy and surprise. This approach focuses on a limited number of 'basic emotions' that are innate to all human beings (Izard 1977). Both measurement approaches, valence and basic, are not devoid of criticisms, leading some researchers (e.g. Hosany 2012; Ma et al. 2013) to examine the antecedents of emotions using cognitive appraisal theory (CAT). According to CAT, a situation is influenced by a tourist's pre-existing knowledge and experience and personally relevant information (Ma et al. 2013). The situation is appraised using dimensions relevant to the experience, leading to the discrete emotional reaction being distilled and the relevant emotion elicited (Frijda et al. 1989). In response to the emotion, emotional coping is activated and tourist behaviour such as intentions to revisit a destination occur (Ma et al. 2013).

Emotional experiences and dark tourism

Despite several authors calling for the study of emotions at death and disaster sites (Stone and Sharpley 2008; Biran et al. 2011; Biran et al. 2014), few studies attempt to identify the range and intensity of emotions that such sites elicit. The term 'dark tourism' has been historically criticised for its negative connotations, partly due to the negative emotions associated with dark sites (Biran and Poria 2012). Visits to disaster sites can generate intense emotions (Stone and Sharpley 2008), particularly negative emotions, but such visits can also be enlightening due to identity construction, educational benefits, and feelings of hope (Sharpley 2009). Studying slave trade fortification sites, Austin (2002) uncovered negative emotions of anger, anguish and sorrow among visitors. Lisle's (2004) study of visitors to Ground Zero elicited a mix of positive (hope and love) and negative (anger, sadness and frustration) emotions. The emotional responses of visitors to the Norfolk Islands' convict incarceration settlements included anger, fear, denial, grief, empathy, and pride. More recently, Nawijn and Fricke (2013) uncovered that visitors to the concentration camp memorial at Neuengamme in Germany felt more negative emotions (shock, sadness, anger, scare and negative surprise) than positive emotions (fascination). Positive emotions such as joy, relief and pleasure were hardly felt. Not only the types of emotions, but also the place and context in which these emotions arise, are crucial.

Emotional coping strategies

Coping is a pervasive and complex psychological process that emanates from cognitive, attitudinal and behavioural domains of consumer response. Coping emerges as a consequence of emotion (Duhachek 2005). Folkman and Lazarus (1988) suggest there are two primary ways (problem and emotion-focused) in which coping manifests, but there is no consensus on their relevance to consumption situations (Duhachek 2005). Problem-focused coping involves individuals taking corrective actions intended to resolve or improve the situation eliciting emotion. Emotion-focused coping involves indirect actions intended to minimise experienced emotion. Negatively laden emotion encounters tend to activate both problem and emotion-focused coping strategies (Folkman and Lazarus 1988). Consumption-related coping strategies show that consumers may engage in rational thinking (e.g. try to step back from the situation and be objective), emotional support (e.g. tell others how they feel), emotional venting (e.g. let their feeling out), avoidance (e.g. take off their mind by doing other things), positive thinking (e.g. try to look at the bright side of things), and denial (e.g. deny that the event happened), or a combination of these when negative emotions are elicited (Duhachek 2005).

The negative experiences associated with disaster events may elicit several coping strategies. For example, in a study of the impact of flooding on adults in affected communities in the UK, Mason et al. (2010) found that the most frequently reported coping strategies were rational, detached and avoidant, with the least frequent being emotional coping. Given that events are only traumatic if they are appraised as such, coping styles may play a significant part in response to disasters (Terr 1989). The next section, presents the study's findings.

Emotions are site specific

Despite the prevalence of disaster sites in Christchurch, the 12 residents chose to share their experiences associated with mainly three sites, 'the cathedral', 'the chairs' and the former 'CTV' (Canterbury Television) building. The cathedral site refers to the deconsecrated Anglican Church in the city of Christchurch that was severely damaged during the various earthquakes. The 'chairs' site refers to the 185 empty chairs art installation at another quake-destroyed church site that serve as a tribute to the 185 people killed in the February 2011 earthquakes. The 'CTV' site has become a symbol of the earthquakes because 115 people died when the CTV building collapsed. From participants' perspectives, the experience associated with each site is unique, though the sites are related to the same devastating events. The intensity of emotions elicited by each site is not necessarily the same, with sites where death occurred impacting participants the most. For example one participant mentioned that their visit to the CTV site was:

> . . . because of its significance . . . it was the inconvenience of not being able to drive down there for so long . . . it was just exciting that you can actually get through that way . . . But then as you approached CTV it was, there's just a lot held in that one piece of land and it (pause) . . . gut wrenching to be honest. And each time I drove through there the first few times, I'd cry but I can do it now, I'm staunch now. (Participant 9, F, 47 years old)

The chair site elicited different emotions in participants. For one participant, the site experience was positive because it gave perspective to the event and created an emotional connection with the participant. For others, the site elicited negative emotions because it captured the essence of the disaster by emphasizing the human loss aspect.

> . . . the chair one . . . because it was easy to engage with . . . I really liked the chairs. I thought that that was really, really powerful both visually and . . . (pause) emotionally or a connection to giving some kind of perspective about how many people died. (Participant 2, F, 46 years old)

The findings concur with Mowatt and Chancelor's (2011) view that dark sites and locations are each unique and merit their own research. Disaster sites are not associated with an individual but more with a collective experience of pain and suffering that makes such sites elicit not only different but also intense emotions within the same location or site. The experience is not related to contemplating death per se but rather to contemplating one's life in relation to the disaster and one's mortality as suggested by others (Stone and Sharpley 2008; Biran et al. 2014).

Beyond valence emotions

From residents' perspectives, dark sites are indeed laden with negative emotions. The interviews suggest that sadness and grief were the most commonly felt emotions, as evidenced in this quote from a participant:

> . . . probably more sadness for the people that had to carry on with that loss because you know there's the grief and it always is easier as they say for the people that died because they you know they're dead, they're gone sort of thing. (Participant 7, M, 51 years old)

Other negative emotions such as anger, frustration, emptiness, annoyance, upset, and worry were also identified. Yet it is clear from the transcripts that negative emotions such as anger and annoyance, for example, were not necessarily elicited solely due to the site experience but also related to the post-quake environment within the city. For example, one participant (F, 40 years old) felt angry at the 'cathedral site' because the decision to restore or rebuild the site has not been finalised. Annoyance was elicited due to the ongoing road access issues to the site.

Beyond the negative emotions, the various sites also elicited positive emotions, such as hope, thankfulness, relief, surprise and gratitude. The ability for places to trigger both positive and negative emotional responses is known as co-activation, as evidenced at concentration camp memorials (Nawijn and Fricke 2013) and slave castles (Mowatt and Chancellor 2011). Similar to negative emotions, the positive emotions are not necessarily associated with the site experience only but also with participants' outlook on life and reflections on the impact of the earthquakes on their lives. Two quotes illustrate participants' recall of positive emotions despite initially mentioning negative emotions as being felt at the sites.

> . . . I think there are positives and I am a positive person so I look on the bright side so, I mean, overwhelmingly it was just sadness for what we'd lost . . . and maybe thankful for being alive . . . (Participant 3, F, 35 years old)

> I suppose gratitude to be alive, that I'd made it through it. Gratitude that you've made it through all the aftershocks and gratitude that you still had all those significant loved ones. Gratitude that I, my house wasn't too badly damaged, that I still had my home. (Participant 8, F, 50 years old)

As argued by Buda (2015), it is not unusual for visitors to want to access the "death drive" by travelling to areas associated with traumatic experiences. The experience of both pleasure and fear, for example, is fundamental to human existence. Hence, visitors to warzones tend to disrupt binaries such as fun/fear and life/death by deliberately putting themselves in situations of physical and emotional risks. In the same way, residents are purportedly disrupting the positive/negative emotion binary associated with dark tourism sites given that negative emotions (e.g. sadness) arouse positive emotions (e.g. thankfulness).

Coping strategies

Several of the coping strategies identified in the consumption behaviour literature were evident among the participants. Elicitations of negative emotions unequivocally led to some form of coping by residents such as emotional venting, emotional support, avoidance, positive thinking and rational thinking.

Emotional venting

Emotional venting refers to the tendency for individuals to focus on the situation causing distress and to ventilate the associated feelings. In consumption situations, it is an attempt by consumers to recognise and express one's emotions by talking to others about these emotions (Duhachek 2005). This is shown in one participant's comments on how she coped with the negative feelings at dark sites.

> I just swear every time I feel that way . . . darn it! It's not just here but every time I hit another road block in the city I just let it out, so I deal with it at the time. I don't dwell on it. (Participant 9, F, 47 years old)

Emotional support

Beyond emotional venting, emotional support was another coping strategy used by residents. Emotional support refers to attempts to draw upon social resources (e.g. family, friends, colleagues) to improve one's emotional and/or mental state (Duhachek 2005). As seen from the quote below, this participant utilised friends to share the experience of visiting dark sites in the CBD.

> You know I got a lot of friends . . . so you sit around talking about stuff and people who were killed, people who have left town, people whose houses have been destroyed and of course talking about the places you visit . . . so I talk to them, the experience, how I felt. (Participant 6, M, 48 years old)

Avoidance

The coping behaviour of avoidance is related to attempts by the individual to create psychic or physical distance between oneself and the stressful experience (Duhachek 2005). It was clear from the transcripts that participants' had avoided the sites altogether because of the painful memories associated with the sites. Once on-site, one participant used avoidance strategies by taking his mind off the felt feelings and focusing on other things he had to do for the day.

> I thought about it, processed it and then moved on and you know got on with the rest of the day . . . It was a busy day and there was a lot to get done so . . . it was a case of pay homage, reflect and then move on (Participant 7, M, 51 years old).

Positive thinking

Positive thinking strategies are attempts to psychologically reconstrue a source of stress to make it more tolerable. Consumers try to look at the bright side of things (Duhachek 2005). Despite the CTV site eliciting negative emotions for one participant, she decided to focus on positive things:

> . . . it was almost a feeling of hopelessness . . . nothing can bring those people back. There's no future for those people at all but there is a future for me and so I try to think about where do I go and what do I build into that future . . . you know thinking again of the positive. (Participant 8, F, 50 years old)

Rational thinking

This form of coping involves deliberate attempts by the consumer to prevent subjective emotions from directing behaviour. Consumers try to cope with negative feelings by being rational and trying to control their feelings (Duhachek 2005). This is evident in the two quotes below.

> . . . I think for me I'm always someone that when and if something happens to me, I need three days to think about it and then I'll know how I really feel about it. So I'll have my initial reaction, and my initial reaction was that I was really sad and angry and upset about the state of it. And I guess a few days later you kind of come to terms with the fact that there really isn't a lot that we can do (Participant 11, F, 38 years old)

> I don't have much feelings, I guess I don't, I'm probably a bit desensitised. I'm not naturally strong in empathy or just a probably bit of a sort of practical person thinker. (Participant 5, M, 50 years old)

Conclusion

Despite many studies on tourist emotions in the vacation context, the emotive experiences of residents at dark tourism sites remain under-researched. Of existing studies, negative emotions are almost always recalled at dark sites, but few studies have examined positive emotions. This chapter outlines both positive and negative emotions elicited at dark sites in Christchurch. Beyond the negative emotions of sadness and grief, dark tourism sites emerging from disasters can elicit positive emotions such as hope, gratitude and thankfulness. These positive emotions seem to emerge from a contemplation of one's life in relation to the disaster but also the visual experiences at the site. Hence, understanding the emotive experience of residents at such sites can assist the community and local government in the development of memorialisation sites. Residents' emotive experiences, for example, can be used to identify, design, and refine features of memorialisation and remembrance sites in an engaging and respectful way.

On-site interpretation experiences of both visitors and residents can be enhanced by integrating residents' perspectives and stories of the disaster. The function of dark tourism sites for residents goes beyond commemoration of the event, given that such sites seem to allow residents to contemplate life, deal with emotions, and build personal resilience. Not without controversy, dark tourism sites can use residents' perspectives of the disaster to market dark sites as a co-activation experience (i.e. generate intense positive and negative emotions). This is similar to how tourist destinations use words, slogans and visual imagery in advertising and promotion materials to portray the expected emotional experience to visitors. This may tap into a segment of visitors that is not necessarily attracted by disaster sites but would include such sites as part of a broader trip to the destination. Negative emotions do not necessarily deter visitors, nor do they dampen positive word-of-mouth for sites associated with death and suffering (Nawijn and Fricke 2013).

The chapter also offers insights into coping strategies employed by residents at dark sites. The various strategies such as emotional venting, emotional support and rational thinking noted in this chapter are highly complex and nuanced, but they highlight the symbiotic relationship that exists between the site experience and residents' personal experiences of the disaster. The two experiences can help community support and social agencies in Christchurch, as well as disaster recovery organisations such as Canterbury Earthquake Recovery Authority (CERA), to understand not only how individuals recover from negative experiences but also the personal and community recovery journey from disasters. Seeking emotional support from others is a well-recognised way to build community resilience post-disaster (Gibbs et al. 2013). Positive thinking, for example, is a well-accepted strategy for building personal resilience after traumatic experiences (Gibbs et al. 2013). Overwhelmingly, the results of this study suggest that residents are still emotionally recovering from the trauma of the earthquakes and that dark tourism sites have a role to play in this recovery.

References

Austin, N. (2002) 'Managing heritage attractions: Marketing challenges at sensitive historical sites', *International Journal of Tourism Research*, 4(6): 447–457.

Biran, A., Liu, W., Li, G. and Eichhorn, V. (2014) 'Consuming post-disaster destinations: The case of Sichuan, China', *Annals of Tourism Research*, 47: 1–17.

Biran, A. and Poria, Y. (2012) 'Re-conceptualizing dark tourism', in R. Sharpley and P. Stone (eds.) *The Contemporary Tourist Experience: Concepts and Consequences*, London: Routledge.

Biran, A., Poria, Y. and Oren, G. (2011) 'Sought experiences at (dark) heritage sites', *Annals of Tourism Research*, 38(3): 820–841.

Blom, T. (2000) 'Morbid tourism – a postmodern market niche with an example from Althorp', *Norsk Geografisk Tidsskrift*, 54(1): 29–36.

Buda, D. (2015) 'The death drive in tourism studies', *Annals of Tourism Research*, 50: 39–51.

Buda, D., d'Hausterre, A.-M. and Johnston, L. (2014) 'Feeling and tourism studies', *Annals of Tourism Research*, 46: 102–114.

Canterbury and Christchurch Tourism (CCT) (2014) *Annual Report*, Christchurch: CCT.

Carlsen, J. and Hughes, M. (2008) 'Tourism market recovery in the Maldives after the 2004 Indian Ocean tsunami', *Journal of Travel & Tourism Marketing*, 23(2–4): 139–149.

Coats, A. and Ferguson, S. (2013) 'Rubbernecking or rejuvenation: Post earthquake perceptions and the implications for business practice in a dark tourism context', *Journal of Research for Consumers*, 23: 32–65.

Cohen, J. and Areni, C. (1991) 'Affect and consumer behavior', *Handbook of Consumer Behavior*, 4(7): 188–240.

Cohen, S., Prayag, G. and Moital, M. (2014) 'Consumer behaviour in tourism: Concepts, influences and opportunities', *Current Issues in Tourism*, 17(10): 872–909.

Duhachek, A. (2005) 'Coping: A multidimensional, hierarchical framework of responses to stressful consumption episodes', *Journal of Consumer Research*, 32(1): 41–53.

Faulkner, B. and Vikulov, S. (2001) 'Katherine, washed out one day, back on track the next: A post-mortem of a tourism disaster', *Tourism Management*, 22(4): 331–344.

Foley, M. and Lennon, J. (1996) 'JFK and dark tourism: A fascination with assassination', *International Journal of Heritage Studies*, 2(4): 198–211.

Folkman, S. and Lazarus, R. (1988) 'The relationship between coping and emotion: Implications for theory and research', *Social Science & Medicine*, 26(3): 309–317.

Frijda, N., Kuipers, P. and ter Schure, E. (1989) 'Relations among emotion, appraisal, and emotional action readiness', *Journal of Personality and Social Psychology*, 57(2): 212.

Gibbs, L., Waters, E., Bryant, R. A., Pattison, P., Lusher, D., Harms, L. and Forbes, D. (2013) Beyond bushfires: Community, resilience and recovery-a longitudinal mixed method study of the medium to long term impacts of bushfires on mental health and social connectedness. *BMC Public Health*, 13(1), 1036.

Hosany, S. (2012) 'Appraisal determinants of tourist emotional responses', *Journal of Travel Research*, 51(3): 303–314.

Hosany, S. and Prayag, G. (2013) 'Patterns of tourists' emotional responses, satisfaction, and intention to recommend', *Journal of Business Research*, 66(6): 730–737.

Hystad, P. and Keller, P. (2008) 'Towards a destination tourism disaster management framework: Long-term lessons from a forest fire disaster', *Tourism Management*, 29(1): 151–162.

Ichinosawa, J. (2006) 'Reputational disaster in Phuket: The secondary impact of the tsunami on inbound tourism', *Disaster Prevention and Management: An International Journal*, 15(1): 111–123.

Izard, C. (ed.) (1977) *Human Emotions*, Vol. 17, New York: Plenum Press.

Lisle, D. (2004) 'Gazing at ground zero: Tourism, voyeurism and spectacle', *Journal for Cultural Research*, 8(1): 3–21.

Ma, J., Gao, J., Scott, N. and Ding, P. (2013) 'Customer delight from theme park experiences: The antecedents of delight based on cognitive appraisal theory', *Annals of Tourism Research*, 42: 359–381.

Mason, V., Andrews, H. and Upton, D. (2010) 'The psychological impact of exposure to floods', *Psychology, Health & Medicine*, 15(1): 61–73.

Mendoza, C. A., Brida, J. B. and Garrido, N. (2012) 'The impact of earthquakes on Chile's international tourism demand', *Journal of Policy Research in Tourism, Leisure and Events*, 4(1): 48–60.

Mowatt, R. and Chancellor, C. H. (2011) 'Visiting death and life: Dark tourism and slave castles', *Annals of Tourism Research*, 38(4): 1410–1434.

Nawijn, J. and Fricke, M. (2013) 'Visitor emotions and behavioral intentions: The case of concentration camp memorial Neuengamme', *International Journal of Tourism Research*, 17(3), 221–228.

Nawijn, J., Mitas, O., Lin, Y. and Kerstetter, D. (2013) 'How do we feel on vacation? A closer look at how emotions change over the course of a trip', *Journal of Travel Research*, 52(2): 265–274.

Orchiston, C. (2012) 'Seismic risk scenario planning and sustainable tourism management: Christchurch and the Alpine Fault zone, South Island, New Zealand', *Journal of Sustainable Tourism*, 20(1): 59–79.

Orchiston, C., Seville, E. and Vargo, J. (2014) 'Regional and sub-sector impacts of the Canterbury earthquake sequence for tourism businesses', *Australian Journal of Emergency Management*, 29(4): 32–37.

Prayag, G., Hosany, S. and Odeh, K. (2013) 'The role of tourists' emotional experiences and satisfaction in understanding behavioral intentions', *Journal of Destination Marketing & Management*, 2(2): 118–127.

Rojek, C. (1993) *Ways of Escape: Modern Transformations in Leisure and Travel*, Basingstoke: Macmillan Press.

Seaton, A. (1996) 'Guided by the dark: From thanatopsis to thanatourism', *International Journal of Heritage Studies*, 2(4): 234–244.

Sharpley, R. (2009) 'Dark tourism and political ideology: Towards a governance model', in R. Sharpley and P. R. Stone (eds.) *The Darker Side of Travel: The Theory and Practice of Dark Tourism*, Bristol: Channel View Publications.

Stone, P. (2006) 'A dark tourism spectrum: Towards a typology of death and macabre related tourist sites, attractions and exhibitions', *Tourism: An Interdisciplinary International Journal*, 54(2): 145–160.

Stone, P. and Sharpley, R. (2008) 'Consuming dark tourism: A thanatological perspective', *Annals of Tourism Research*, 35(2): 574–595.

Terr, L. (1989) 'Treating psychic trauma in children: A preliminary discussion', *Journal of Traumatic Stress*, 2(1): 3–20.

Trotta, J. (2006) *Grief Tourism Definition*, Grief Tourism. Online. Available HTTP: <http://www.grieftourism.com/grief-tourism-definition/> (Accessed 13 March 2008).

Tsai, C.-H. and Chen, C.-W. (2010) 'An earthquake disaster management mechanism based on risk assessment information for the tourism industry-a case study from the island of Taiwan', *Tourism Management*, 31(4): 470–481.

Walters, G., Mair, J. and Ritchie, B. (2015) 'Understanding the tourist's response to natural disasters: The case of the 2011 Queensland floods', *Journal of Vacation Marketing*, 21(1): 101–113.

11 Telling tales

Some implications for response agencies from stories of informal personal communication in the aftermath of a devastating earthquake

Colleen E. Mills

Natural disasters, such as earthquakes, floods and tsunamis, provide distinctive communication contexts by virtue of the way they inject danger, disruption, ambiguity, confusion and often urgency into individuals' lives. When we examine the literature addressing communication in disaster contexts (e.g. Barnes, Hanson, Novilla, Meacham, McIntyre and Erickson 2008; Garnett and Kouzmin 2009; Haines, Hulbert and Beggs 1999; Haines, Beggs and Hulbert 2002; Nicholls, Sykes and Camilleri 2010), a curious observation can be made. This literature focuses strongly on message dissemination and the communication media used in the disaster response phase but pays scant attention to the personal communication profiles of those in the disaster zone. Such profiles include the range of ways an individual communicates and the patterns this communication exhibits. By ignoring these profiles, the nexus of informal and casual interpersonal and group communication that exists or emerges between family members, friends, neighbours, customers, colleagues and random people in the community during a disaster phase is largely overlooked.

While we have a limited understanding of how a disaster affects personal communication, we do know the social infrastructure that provides the context for this communication gets tested and may well be dissipated, or at least transformed, immediately following a disaster event such as a severe earthquake. According to Varda, Forgette, Banks and Contractor (2009: 13), disasters

> have the ability to shake up an entire social infrastructure, turning what we know about the way people relate, the way organizations behave, and the system of social and resource support into new questions that, if understood, could greatly impact an entire society's ability to deal with the consequences of disasters.

The devastating earthquakes that struck Canterbury, New Zealand in the middle of the day on 22 February 2011 dramatically shook up the social infrastructure. Communication systems were overloaded or failed altogether, especially when electricity supply was disrupted. The way of life was turned on its head for many people, their families, and the businesses and organisations they ran, worked in, or did business with. The personal communication of residents and business operators across the region changed. Everyone gained an "earthquake story" and over time came to share this with others in ways that manifested existing networks and spawned new patterns of engagement across the region. This situation prompted a study of earthquake narratives in order to tap into the insights such narratives may provide about post-disaster personal communication and its role in responding to the earthquakes.

This chapter discusses findings from an exploratory study of Canterbury's earthquake stories, which highlighted the multifaceted contribution of interpersonal communication to a community's disaster response and suggests that this contribution could be harnessed by public agencies and NGOs to improve the effectiveness of disaster management and response.

Narrativity

Every individual is the middle of a storytelling project, our life story, which is constantly being constructed and reconstructed as we weave new experiences into it. As we narrate our story we give our experiences coherence and direction and, in so doing, create our sense of the world and our place in it (Fisher, 1984, 1985, 1987; Brown, Stacey and Nandhakumar 2008). Brown et al. (2008: 1039) propose 'that sensemaking is a narrative process' and the primary means through which people make their experience meaningful (Polkinghorne 1988). During a crisis, when ambiguity and uncertainty are high and coherence is lacking, it is therefore not surprising that storytelling becomes a particularly prominent constituent of daily interpersonal communication. Storytelling allows people to collaboratively make sense of what is going on and regain a sense of control over their lives, an important task in Christchurch following the devastating February earthquakes, which disrupted many people's lives. For a researcher, these stories not only provide a means of tapping into peoples' sensemaking about their disaster experiences but, by virtue of the nature of a narrative with its emplotment, characterisation and attention to circumstance, they provide a rich source of data about how people interact as they respond across a natural disaster process.

Social support and personal communication during disasters

Research on Hurricane Andrew in the USA suggested physical and mental health outcomes were better for those community members who received the most social support (Haines, Hulbert and Beggs 1999; Haines, Beggs and Hulbert 2002) and that this support can be best understood by examining the social networks available to individuals in a disaster zone. Following Hurricane Katrina, Hurlbert, Beggs and Haines (2005) argued that affluence influenced the quality of pre-disaster social networks and was implicated in the likelihood that these pre-disaster networks would survive. Similarly, pre-disaster inter-organisational networks have also been found to be important because they support trust (Coleman 1990), risk-taking (Fukuyama 1995), social capital (Burt 1997), information dissemination (Kapucu 2005a, 2005b) and effective collective decision-making, and so facilitate post-disaster information flows across organisational boundaries (Kapucu 2005a, 2005b). Existing, rather than emergent networks, provide social capital that can be activated to secure support and assistance at all levels in the community in times when resources are scarce or difficult to access. These networks also provide opportunities for sensemaking conversations. There are therefore good reasons for assuming that social networks, including those that are the main sites of personal communication, are implicated in organisational and community resilience, and that public agencies and NGOs involved in disaster response should be encouraged to find ways to factor strategies that enhance network quality into their disaster management strategies. Curiously, despite the awareness of the importance of networks in disaster response, there is relatively scant research that examines the ways people utilise social networks during disaster (Nagagawa and Shaw 2004), or how personal social network activity articulates with formal community networks, public agencies and NGOs. This is in the face of mounting evidence that social capital derived from social networks is an important resource in disaster situations (Dynes 2006; Chamlee-Wright and Storr 2011), and a sense of community belonging enhances the quality of disaster responses (Kim and Kang 2010).

Social networks

Storytelling is a social performance that relies upon and contributes to a community's social infrastructure. The Insider/Outsider/Seeker/Provider (IOSP) network is a useful framework for examining the social networks that contribute to this social infrastructure during a disaster. This model portrays community members as being within (I) the disaster zone or outside it (O), and as seeking (S) or providing assistance (P). While it does not accommodate the possibility that a person can both seek and provide assistance and move in and out of the disaster zone (Varda et al. 2009), it does highlight the geographical and relational aspects of how individuals relate to each other during a disaster response.

Varda et al. (2009) propose four types of network ties surrounding a disaster: pre-existing, ad hoc, emergent and stable. Pre-existing ties are ones that predate a disaster. These tend to change slowly. *Ad hoc* ties are those that form in temporary networks as seekers and providers come together. Emergent ties are the new relationships formed as people take on new roles or tasks; stable ties are those that persist and are often kinship-based. As discussed below, the narrative data revealed that in the immediate post–22 February response period, some ties were much more significant than others.

Collecting Canterbury tales

The research informing this chapter took advantage of a narrative's ability to reveal both sensemaking and factual details about communication behaviour. Thirty individuals (Female = 20; Male = 10) were invited to participate and agreed to do so. This convenience sample was appropriate as the conditions were not ideal for other forms of sampling at the time the research commenced. Many people were highly traumatised and would have found being approached by an unknown researcher uncomfortable. Of the 30 participants, 13 provided written stories by email, 11 preferred to provide their stories in individual face-to-face interviews, five told their stories in joint face-to-face interviews of two and three people respectively and one was interviewed by telephone. Of those who contributed written stories, four were male. Twenty-eight participants resided in Christchurch and two in a rural area 40 kilometres west of the city. The city dwellers lived in suburbs that ranged from those that were devastated (n = 3) to those where little substantive damage occurred (n = 5). Seven participants had young dependents, three owned their own businesses, one ran a large business, three were retired, and the remainder were employees in private and public organisations. One child was interviewed. Participants ranged in age from 11 years to early 70s. The analysis of their narratives involved identifying accounts of communication and scrutinising these to establish who was involved in the communication, how they were related to the narrator, how the communication was achieved and what purpose it served. Facilitating and inhibiting circumstances were also noted. Where points were only briefly made, additional information was solicited by telephone or in person.

Findings

The remainder of this chapter will focus on findings about personal disaster response communication that have significant implications for initial response agencies such as civil defence, police, armed forces and health authorities.

Elevated levels of personal communication

Participants reported a marked increase in the level of personal communication immediately following the earthquake on 22 February as people addressed their concern for the safety and survival of themselves and others. Some reported that their first post-quake communication was directed toward dealing with the safety and survival of those in the immediate vicinity, particularly when these people were their responsibility. One teacher reported:

> We mulled around for a bit, then once I thought that my professional responsibility bit had been done, I went to check on my kids who were at [a nearby] preschool. I knew intuitively that they would be alright but I still wanted to go to them and see them myself. #8

Getting together with the most important people in one's personal networks was a priority for most even when they knew they were safe. This was particularly evident in the narratives of those with dependent children. Face-to-face personal communication was reassuring and comforting and gave a sense of control even if it introduced tensions, as was this participant's experience.

> I was keen to get in touch with [wife] on the cellphone. I managed to tell her I was OK but my other messages didn't get through till I was already home . . .. [Wife]'s parents were at home when I got there. It was good to have some others to talk to, and share worries, though there were also tensions as the afternoon wore on. [Wife]'s dad was glued to our transistor radio, which dominated the kitchen in a crackly way, and [he] kept relaying the latest horrible news as it came in. #3

As the afternoon of 22 February wore on and people had established that their close family members and friends were safe, they began, to varying degrees, to redirect their communication to establishing the magnitude of what had occurred. For some, this quest kept their level of personal disaster communication high long after the initial peak associated with establishing intimates were safe. This was particularly evident in the narrative of one business operator. His afternoon was spent trying to establish the nature of the quakes' impact on his operators, who were spread across town. The resulting high volume of calls needed to gather information about impacts no doubt contributed to cellphone services becoming overloaded and prompted emergency services to request people to limit their communication. One participant who was away from Christchurch when the earthquakes struck narrated a similar communication pattern. She wrote:

> There were nine of us on the trip and we all huddled around the radio that night to find out more and spent time going over everything that came through with a fine tooth comb, trying to work out what it meant and arguing about our respective interpretations. #5

The participant was not alone in highlighting the sensemaking role interpersonal communication played in the immediate aftermath of the earthquakes. People collaborated on the creation of a macro-disaster narrative that wove all the narrative fragments into a grand and evolving Canterbury earthquake story to help make sense of their situation, assess their prospects, and decide on their course of action (Chamlee-Wright and Storr 2011).

The digital default

Digital communication media were the primary media used to achieve initial connectivity with important people in the participants' networks, and the cellphone was the primary digital device used. Nearly all participants reported employing them to check that others were safe and to reassure others they too were safe, but, as noted previously, cellphones did not supplant personal face-to-face communication. The following participant's story was typical:

I checked via text that my family and friends were OK. As I got home (after about 45 minutes) I found that [husband] was home and received a text from [daughter] which meant she was OK and was going to come around with [her boyfriend]. I picked up a man who was walking down Russley Road and gave him a lift for a short time. It was good to have someone to talk to for part of the journey. #9

As the cellphone system became unreliable and in some districts failed, considerable anxiety was reported and alternative communication means sought. For those who had access to computers and electricity, Facebook and email were used. Old technology landlines became a valuable asset, too, as they connected participants with out-of-region members of their personal networks. Several instances were given of out-of-region friends, relatives and colleagues acting as communication brokers, relaying messages from people in the disaster zone to others elsewhere in Canterbury or overseas. One participant told of a relative in Melbourne relaying messages between two people in Christchurch. These insider-outsider exchanges helped those inside the disaster zone to understand the magnitude of what had happened as the outsiders could follow events on television and online.

Protocol transformation

Participants reported talking to strangers, disclosing information that normally would be shared only with people with closer ties. 'How are you?' became a genuine invitation to share information about oneself rather than the routine phatic formula which usually elicits simple remarks like 'Fine. How about yourself?' This pattern of higher-than-normal disclosure, which began with the first round of quakes in Canterbury in September 2010, was widely evident in reports of interpersonal communication after the February quakes. It was symptomatic of a community drawn together to cope with a situation affecting everyone. A sense of camaraderie and solidarity not evident in the pre-earthquake period prevailed. Talking was therapeutic. One of the business owners in the study illustrated this in her account of one customer's behaviour:

We found like we were counsellors for quite some time. People wanted to come in and talk, and talk about their experiences and the event. And just needed to, like one lady was here, in here when February happened, wasn't she, and she came back maybe a month or so later. She said she just had to come back and stand inside just to make sure it was alright and stuff and put it to bed, like closure, come back and make sure it was alright. #6

Heightened personal communication was sustained through the response period but dissipated somewhat as people picked up the threads of their lives, schools reopened and some businesses started operating again. Participants observed how, as the recovery phase took hold, people withdrew into their own lives to grapple with the consequences of the quakes and balance the new demands in their lives with their regular activities. Those in suburbs without power or water and those who could not return to their homes found the mundane routines of daily life suddenly more difficult and time consuming. Queuing for water at the water truck, cooking on the barbeque or taking household laundry to do at the homes of relatives who had power and water took time. At the same time, the stories reveal that these activities provided new opportunities for interpersonal communication.

The storytelling community

Storytelling became an integral part of the informal relating that occurred, especially in face-to-face situations. People did not wait to be interrogated. They willingly constructed their experiences into a narrative to give them a structure and weave them into conversations. The emplotment (the assembly of a series of historical events into a narrative with a plot) conveyed a coherency and a temporal dimension to the narrated experience. People also told other people's stories as they orally constructed their reality. At times conversations were structured around the trading of personal and second-hand stories. Participants reported this trading served purposes other than establishing the magnitude and impact of the situation the region was dealing with. They provided a common focus that people felt drawn to talk about, a way to gain mastery over their experience and highlight areas of personal need and prospects for the future. Participants' narratives suggest they spent more time than usual talking as a result of this narrativity. They also reported coming to expect narration to be an integral part of most social engagement. For one participant, chatting with neighbours was her only form of communication. She reported:

> We were all without power, water or land lines and, without a cellphone, there was no way for me to communicate with anyone other than the chats with the neighbours. #10

Telling one's own story and soliciting those of others was an integral part of such chats.

The evolving nature of post-disaster communication

The narratives suggested that in the immediate aftermath of the 22 February quakes – commonly termed the response phase – there was a general pattern of moving from personal communication focusing on safety through to communication seeking to understand the disaster process and on to reaching out to others as impacts became known and then, finally, to communication focusing on the future. What complicated the situation in Canterbury was that the region was not dealing with one event, so, while overall this pattern was evident, each sizable quake caused people to refocus on safety and magnitude concerns. It is fair to say that, at the micro level, participants sometimes found themselves addressing all four categories of concern simultaneously in their personal communication. What is significant from a disaster management perspective is that the narratives suggest local authorities and emergency response agencies really only provided information, usually through the mass media, to help individuals to quantify the scale of the disaster and try to establish what was likely to occur next. They urged people to check on others but left personal support for those not needing specialist attention to their friends, family, neighbours and associates. People responded by communicating with people in the immediate location and their personal networks both in the disaster zone and elsewhere in order to meet their safety and comfort-related objectives. Neighbours featured most prominently in the most seriously damaged suburbs. Those in the sample whose homes were uninhabitable, however, were left to make their own arrangements, such as moving in with family or friends. This meant relocating and adding a new communication environment to the earthquake experience.

Revealing social network strength

The narratives revealed how participants prioritised their social networks in the face-to-face and mediated communication. Not surprisingly, spouses and partners, children, parents and siblings were at the top of the list. The following narrative excerpts reveal who was contacted first as the first earthquakes rattled and shook their way through the region:

> I can't remember who called who but it was no time at all before I knew he [husband] was standing beside his car in Antigua Street when the quake struck . . . Our call included pleas from both of us for the other to be careful, then we closed. #1
>
> As soon as we got away from the house we called our daughter on my cellphone. We then gathered with our neighbours on the footpath and called our parents. We were also concerned about other neighbours and there was an informal roll. #12
>
> I had received a text from my daughter who lives in [suburb]. "I'm scared. Can you come?" She had had a knee replacement the week before and was on crutches. Her husband was at work on the south side of Blenheim Road and their daughter, aged seven, was at [name] school. I texted back to say I was on my way . . . The journey to [her suburb] took two and a half hours. How joyful I was to find my son-in-law and granddaughter at home! My son-in-law had managed to get to my granddaughter's school quite quickly as he had gone to work that day on his bike! We were together and unscathed. I made contact with other family members using my mobile phone and was able to establish all were safe. Fellow board members [of the apartment building the narrator lived in] had contacted me to say our building was now red stickered and we could not go in or get anything out. My friends from [nearby town] kept phoning and telling me to "get over here". #13

At first glance, there is nothing surprising in these excerpts. However, only one includes reference to friends. The narratives revealed that in the initial response period, friends mattered most to those who were single. For most participants friends entered the narratives once family networks had been engaged.

Implications for government response agencies

This chapter has highlighted the varied roles personal communication served and how it transformed as Cantabrians coped with the February earthquakes. Their personal communication contributed to the failure of cellphone networks, communication protocols changed, story telling became a more prominent part of personal exchanges even with strangers, media use became much more strategic and differentiated and evolved over time, and personal networks were shown to be a vital part of meeting individuals' needs. Most significantly, close personal networks became a pivotal part of many participants' information processing and decision-making behaviour. Information provided by radio, television and newspapers was processed in face-to-face and mediated interpersonal conversations with people who could be spread across Canterbury, the rest of New Zealand, and the world. Agencies need to appreciate that outsiders had a significant influence on information flow and sensemaking but were not necessarily able to provide on-the-spot company, comfort and assistance. Older participants were those most likely to have geographically dissipated intimate networks yet, ironically, were not always the best placed to access them.

These findings have practical implications for policy makers, local authorities and emergency response agencies as well as communication theorists seeking to develop a more holistic view of disaster communication. Clearly, if informal personal communication and the relationships created and sustained by it are at the heart of successfully coping in the initial response stage of a natural disaster, then ways to recognise and incorporate this understanding into disaster management plans should be sought. Command and control type responses typically superimpose other systems of relating on people (e.g. by installing them in refugee camps or "safe zones", by refusing them access to their homes or businesses) without considering the missed opportunities and costs of doing this.

The media has a role to play in this regard. Instead of dwelling on images of the fleeing refugee or the tragedy unfolding, they can create a more balanced perception by incorporating images capturing how people engage with their personal networks and pull together to resolve issues and adapt to the effects of the disaster. By doing this they will help to encourage people to have faith in personal social capital and local resourcefulness. Coping, after all, is the norm rather than the exception. As Ride and Bretherton (2011: 171) note:

> We have been trained by the Western media and government agencies to look for social problems after disasters, the *unusual story*, not the community resilience, which is the *usual story*.

What this study revealed is that participants' personal highly dispersed networks and mediated communication were the primary resources people activated initially. It has also confirmed that the members of established stable networks, especially kinship networks, were the ones that mattered most. The ties in these networks had considerable influence, even when they were composed mainly of people external to the disaster zone, as they provided moral support and information garnered from the mass media. This is a significant finding because it reinforces the need to make sure the media (i.e. radio, television, newspapers, websites and blogs) have access to sound information. If outsiders are not kept abreast of the situation in the disaster zone, they can provide incorrect or distorted information to those relying on them to make sense of what is happening and to decide how to behave inside this zone.

When digital media failed either through overload or lack of electricity, the value of older-style phones, which typically continued to function, was revealed. Furthermore, if texting had been more strongly advised and people had pre-existing text tree protocols in place with their personal network members, this would also have helped lower the load on cellphone networks. Text trees, for example, were used very successfully by Canterbury police to ensure messages were disseminated in a very economical way across the local police force.

The time of the day when the earthquake struck was significant. It was not until people started regrouping in and around their homes that personal communication became strongly face-to-face. Until then, participants' experiences suggested that interpersonal face-to-face communication in the suburbs was limited, highlighting the fact that many suburbs are sparsely populated during regular working hours. This was especially true of those neighbourhoods without business premises and those located away the city's thoroughfares. This has implications for local authorities' urban planning policy. Perhaps, for example, the desirability of subdivisions devoid of shops and businesses should be reconsidered.

Conclusions

Informal personal communication is the Cinderella of the disaster communication literature, which, with the exception of a nascent interest in the role of social media during disaster response, tends to focus more on public and mass media communication from an information dissemination rather than a dialogic perspective. The findings reported in this chapter suggest a more significant role for informal personal communication than is suggested by this literature, placing it at the heart of disaster response and personal coping strategies. Without doubt, and not surprisingly, stable pre-earthquake networks were the ones individual participants reported turning to in order to satisfy their immediate communication and sensemaking needs. Facebook and other social media platforms played a role in achieving this connectivity when power supply and Internet access allowed. However, except where people were injured or trapped, their primary need was to connect, as personally as possible. This meant face-to-face communication was actively sought by most participants in the immediate post-earthquake period.

This observation is confirmed by evidence from other disasters (e.g. Murphy 2007; Taylor, Priest, Fussell Sisco, Banning and Campbell 2009; Varda et al.

2009). It seems that the ability to cope with the challenges generated by the February earthquakes was, for the participants in this study, built on the quality of social connectivity with both insiders and outsiders as they sought and provided assistance and support. People reported "sorting themselves out", in the first instance, by connecting with other people rather than through access to lots of information. This suggests that agencies concerned with preparing for and coordinating disaster response processes should not set out to impose systems that disrupt the existing relational patterns or inundate people with information. Rather, they should look for ways to encourage robust, stable and efficient local networks that can provide quality informal disaster communication, a sense of belonging (Kim and Kang 2010), and a source of community social capital that will reduce the transaction cost of recovery (Nakagawa and Shaw 2004). Thus, personal networks could be treated not just as personal response management and sensemaking tools but as a community resource that is a worthy focus for policy planning and community development initiatives, which can be designed to enhance constructive community engagement in times of unprecedented disruption and threat. Doing so would be consistent with the finding that informal personal communication, especially face-to-face communication, was vital for providing reassurance and an infrastructure that allowed people to make decisions (Taylor et al. 2009), move forward, and gain control of their personal circumstances.

Overall, this study suggests that agencies should explore how they can encourage closer ties and face-to-face relating among members of the community as well as how they can incorporate these ties into community engagement and emergency response strategies. At the same time, the findings reveal that the network ties people give priority to are not necessarily located in their immediate community. Outsiders also feature significantly in participants' narratives. It seems that in order to empower individuals and their local communities to respond expeditiously and appropriately to natural disasters, network analyses need to be undertaken to ensure the affordances of interpersonal communication can be understood and harnessed.

References

Barnes, M., Hanson, C., Novilla, L., Meacham, A., McIntyre, E. and Erickson, B. (2008) 'Analysis of media agenda setting during and after Hurricane Katrina: Implications for emergency preparedness, disaster response and disaster policy', *American Journal of Public Health*, 8(4): 604–10.

Brown, A. D., Stacey, P. and Nandhakumar, J. (2008) 'Making sense of sensemaking narratives', *Human Relations*, 61(8): 1035–1062.

Burt, R. (1997) 'The contingent value of social capital', *Administrative Science Quarterly*, 42(2): 339–368.

Chamlee-Wright, E. and Storr, V. H. (2011) 'Social capital as collective narratives and post-disaster community recovery', *Sociological Review*, 59(2): 266–282.

Coleman, J. (1990) *Foundations of Social Theory*, Cambridge: The Belknap Press of Harvard University Press.

Dynes, R. (2006) 'Social capital dealing with community emergencies', *Homeland Security Affairs,* 2(11), Monterey: Naval Postgraduate School Center for Homeland Defense and Security. Online. Available HTTP: <http://www.hsaj.org>.

Fisher, W. (1984) 'Narration as a human communication paradigm: The case for public moral argument', *Communication Monographs,* 51: 1–21.

——(1985) 'The narrative paradigm: An elaboration', *Communication Monographs,* 52: 347–367.

——(1987) *Human Communication as Narration: Toward a Philosophy of Reason, Value and Action,* Columbia: University of South Carolina Press.

Fukuyama, F. (1995) *Trust,* New York: Free Press.

Garnett, J. and Kouzmin, A. (2009) 'Crisis communication post Katrina: What are we learning?', *Public Organization Review,* 9: 385–398.

Haines, V., Beggs, J. and Hurlbert, J. (2002) 'Exploring structural contexts of the support process: Social networks, social statuses, social support, and psychological distress', *Advances in Medical Sociology,* 8: 271–294.

Haines, V., Hurlbert, J. and Beggs, J. (1999) 'Taking the environment seriously: A respecification and test of the disaster framing of the stress process', *International Journal of Mass Emergencies and Disasters,* 17: 367–97.

Hurlbert, J., Beggs, J. and Haines, V. (2005) *Bridges Over Troubled Waters: What Are the Optimal Networks for Katrina's Victims?* New York: Social Science Research Council. Online. Available HTTP: <http://understandingkatrina.ssrc.org>.

Kapucu, N. (2005a) 'Interagency communication networks during emergencies: Boundary spanners in multiagency coordination', *American Review of Public Administration,* 36(2): 207–225.

——(2005b) 'Interorganizational coordination in dynamic context: Networks in emergency response management', *Connections,* 26(2): 33–48.

Kim, Y.-C. and Kang, J. (2010) 'Communication, neighbourhood belonging and hurricane household preparedness', *Disaster* 34(2): 470–88.

Murphy, B. (2007) 'Locating social capital in resilient community-level emergency management', *Natural Hazards,* 41: 297–315.

Nakagawa, Y. and Shaw, R. (2004) 'Social capital: A missing link to disaster recovery', *International Journal of Mass Emergencies and Disaster Recovery,* 22(1): 5–34.

Nicholls, S., Sykes, J. and Camilleri, P. (2010) 'The role of the media and communication in recovery from natural disasters', *Australian Journal of Communication,* 37(3): 33–50.

Polkinghorne, D. (1988) *Narrative Knowing and the Human Sciences,* Albany: State University of New York.

Ride, A. and Bretherton, D. (eds.) (2011) *Community Resilience in Natural Disasters,* New York: Palgrave Macmillan.

Taylor, K., Priest, S., Fussell Sisco, H., Banning, S. and Campbell, K. (2009) 'Reading Hurricane Katrina: Information sources and decision-making in response to a natural disaster', *Social Epistemology: A Journal of Knowledge, Culture and Policy,* 23(3/4): 361–80.

Varda, D., Forgette, R., Banks, R. and Contractor, N. (2009) 'Social network methodology in the study of disasters: Issues and insights prompted by post-Katrina research', *Population Research and Policy Review,* 28(1): 11–29.

Part IV

Learning from 'the new normal'

12 'Regeneration is the focus now'

Anchor projects and delivering a new CBD for Christchurch

Alberto Amore and C. Michael Hall

Introduction

The series of strong earthquakes from September 2010 to June 2011 severely damaged the built environment of the Christchurch CBD and the economic core of the city. The rebuild of the central area soon became a major task for the national government authorities, which developed a dedicated strategy for the CBD in conjunction with the Christchurch City Council (CCC) and the main local institutions. This chapter examines urban regeneration practices in a post-disaster context. In particular, it acknowledges that there are common traits between mainstream practices of regeneration and urban redevelopment strategies following disasters. Nevertheless, it suggests that the latter case also resembles features of disaster capitalism, as highlighted in the relevant literature on post-disaster recovery in US cities (e.g. Gotham and Greenberg 2014).

The following section discusses the relevant literature for the purposes of the study. The next section introduces the pre-earthquake situation and the main stages of regeneration that have occurred within the CBD. Broader issues of urban regeneration in suburban areas, including strategies, infrastructure rebuild and housing availability are not discussed, although some relationships are noted, including by policy makers. The chapter then presents an analysis of the rebuilding of the CBD with a focus on the delivery of the anchor projects outlined in the Christchurch Central Recovery Plan (Christchurch Central Development Unit (CCDU) 2012) (hereafter the Plan). The final section summarises the findings of the study and discusses the emerging consequences of the strategy adopted in the light of current events.

Literature review

The literature on urban regeneration and spatial planning provides numerous case studies and findings from hundreds of cities (see Kalandides et al. 2011 for a review). What emerges is that CBDs and the adjacent inner city areas are the foci of different urban redevelopment strategies. These include, but are not limited to, cultural venues, sports facilities, and convention and exhibition centres – all of which are elements of the tourism industry. In particular, the relevance of tourism as urban regeneration strategy is a facet of 'the spatial division of consumption' (Harvey 1989: 9) and the ultimate frontier of capital internationalisation (Britton 1991).

To date, however, the phenomenon of tourism-oriented, urban regeneration strategies in contexts of coping with major crises and disasters is generally overlooked. Major works on disasters, urban resilience and vulnerability (e.g. Pelling 2003; Vale and Campanella 2005) ignore the phenomenon of urban regeneration. Similarly, studies dealing with tourism, as well as crisis and disaster recovery (e.g. Gurtner 2007), seem to overlook the phenomenon of post-disaster recovery of urban tourist spaces. Only a handful of contributions, mostly limited to the U.S. context, address the phenomenon of CBD regeneration, tourism and post-disaster redevelopment (Gotham 2007; Gotham and Greenberg 2008, 2014; Wagner Frisch and Fields 2008; Saxena 2014).

The process of urban regeneration in a context of post-disaster recovery shares a number of essential traits with mainstream urban regeneration as well as showing some significant differences (Figure 12.1). Both forms of regeneration take place in a predominantly de-politicised climate (Swyngedouw 2010; Allmendinger and Haughton 2012) where public-private partnerships pursue the logics of market and competitiveness (Keil 2009). They are also conceived as an opportunity to radically change the urban landscape and tackle perceived economic decline. Both forms of regeneration are often justified through the rhetoric of benchmarking of overseas

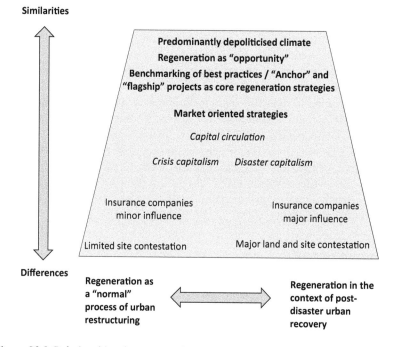

Figure 12.1 Relationships between urban regeneration as usual and post-disaster regeneration

"best practices" (Theodore and Peck 2012) framed by the importance of places being "competitive" in the global economy in order to attract international capital and tourists (Hall 2007; Bristow 2010). Therefore, yet most importantly, both forms of regeneration focus on leisure and tourism-oriented "anchor" or "flagship" projects, such as convention centres, art galleries, museums, stadia, and design or cultural precincts/quarters, all often tied in with the hosting of events, as the best urban redevelopment strategy. Unsurprisingly, there are significant physical and political analogies between the clearances of brownfields in industrial urban areas and the systematic demolition or buildings following urban natural disasters. The latter, in particular, follow the logics of *tabula rasa* (Gotham and Greenberg 2014) for the allocation of land for leisure and tourism spaces (Spirou 2010).

Post-disaster urban regeneration, however, takes place in a more unstable context than mainstream regeneration. Importantly, the phenomenon of regeneration as a process of urban restructuring is an expression of the second circuit of capital (Harvey 1978), also referred to as "fictitious capital" (Becker et al. 2010), which is constituted by real estate, its financial conduits, state regulation of space, and by those distinct social groups that invest in real estate so as to maximise capitalised land rent (Gottdiener 1990). Similarly, the post-disaster regeneration underpinning the phenomenology of disaster capitalism (Klein 2007), as demonstrated in post-9/11 New York (Gotham and Greenberg 2008, 2014), post-Katrina New Orleans (Hartman and Squires 2006; Johnson 2011; Gotham and Greenberg 2014), and post–Van earthquake in Turkey (Saraçoğlu and Demirtas-Milz 2014) also serves to maintain core land rent values, although in the poorer and often most affected suburbs, such state initiatives are usually absent. Mainstream forms of urban regeneration tend to be situated within general market discourse while regeneration in cities following disasters is used by the state to justify market-directed strategies as a solution to quickly fix the dysfunctional climate of "uncertainty" (Porter 2009). Nevertheless, even here substantial similarities occur, with event-led regeneration in particular being used to create a climate of crisis in which normal planning and decision-making are often suspended in order to achieve event deadlines (Hall 2006), while even non–event-led regeneration is often justified within discourses of economic, employment and even aesthetic crisis (Smyth 2005).

Undoubtedly, the role of insurance companies in influencing mainstream regeneration and associated decision-making is less decisive than in a context of post-disaster regeneration, as shown in studies undertaken in New Orleans (Gotham 2012; Adams 2013). In the case of post-disaster regeneration, insurance policies will affect not only how much money is available for rebuild but also, in many cases, the nature of what acts as a replacement for what has been lost or damaged. Finally, mainstream urban regeneration practices tend to take place in land portions that have a unique ownership or have decreased their value over time (Smith 1979). Conversely, the regeneration of urban areas in the aftermath of disasters often occurs in a climate of land contestation, with disputes on clearance and selling of land parcels, although some similarities do exist – for example, with respect to state intervention being used to amalgamate land holdings for specific projects, often in the face of opposition from community groups (Smyth 2005).

Context

The CBD of Christchurch corresponds to the historic core of the city originally designed by Edward Jollie in 1850 (Christchurch Central Development Unit (CCDU) 2012). It comprises the areas of Hagley Park, Cathedral Square and the Avon Loop, with a total surface area of 6.33 km2 (New Zealand Statistics (NZSTATS) 2015a). Before the earthquakes of 2010 and 2011, 8,280 residents lived in the CBD (NZSTATS 2015a), along with 5,989 businesses and 51,280 employees who worked in the CBD (NZSTATS 2015b). Following the earthquakes of 2010 and 2011, the population of the CBD decreased by nearly 40 per cent, the number of businesses dropped by 39 per cent, and the number of workers shrunk by 39.4 per cent (NZSTATS 2015b).

Following an urban strategy oriented toward flagship projects throughout the 1990s, the CBD of Christchurch became the heart of a more organic regeneration strategy in the 2000s (CCC 2001, 2004, 2006). The decentralisation of responsibilities to local level as a result of the *Local Government Act 2002* gave the CCC authority in planning and urban regeneration strategy. During this period, the conversion of warehouses in the south-east frame of the CBD culminated with the creation of the South of Litchfield precinct, a pedestrian area home to leisure and the creative industries (Hall 2008a; New Zealand Historic Places Trust (NZHPT) 2011). On the eve of the first major earthquake, the Christchurch Economic Development Strategy (CEDS) set out a project to 'develop [a] business attraction and retention programme for the city focusing on development opportunities within key industry sectors' (Canterbury Development Corporation (CDC) 2010: 28).

The urban development of Christchurch's CBD, however, took place upon highly unstable geology. The soil beneath the CBD is prone to liquefaction and lateral spreading (Brown and Weeber 1992; Cubrinovski and McCahon 2012). Moreover, much of the original settlement was built upon reclaimed swamps near the Avon River (Brown and Weeber 1992) and the areas of Cathedral Square and the Avon Loop (Hercus 1942). Last, but most importantly, the Christchurch urban region is relatively close to the Alpine Fault and it is subject to major seismic activity (> 7.0 M as measured on the Richter scale) every 200–280 years (Wells et al. 1999). Given that the last earthquake along the Alpine Fault occurred in 1717 (Orchiston 2012), the chances of new major earthquakes hitting the region are relatively high. In fact, the earthquakes registered between 2010 and 2011 are the result of a secondary fault south of Christchurch that had not been recorded before (Quigley 2010).

The first major earthquake in September 2010 (M 7.1) and the following aftershocks between November and December of that year only severely damaged a small amount of CBD's the built environment, with the closure of premises generally only occurring for a limited time. In stark contrast, the earthquake of 22 February 2011 (M 6.3) severely hit the CBD with severe damage to key buildings (Table 12.1). The soil structure of Christchurch CBD heightened the powerful ground acceleration registered at the epicentre of the 22 February earthquake. Seismograms located in the city reported peak accelerations in a range of 1.2 ~ 1.6 G (Holmes Consulting Group (HCG) 2011), along with substantial liquefaction in proximity to the Avon River and several cases of lateral spreading

Table 12.1 Key buildings in the Christchurch CBD and their status after the earth-quakes of February 2011 as of March 2015

Building	Damages following February 201 earthquake	Status (as at March 2015)
AMI Stadium	Severe	Partially demolished Project for eventual new stadium under way
Arts Centre	Severe	3 buildings open to public 19 buildings to open by 2019
Canterbury Museum	Limited	Reopened to public
Christ Church Cathedral	Severe	Partial demolition and rebuilding under scrutiny
Christchurch Art Gallery	Relevant	Closed until the end of 2015
Christchurch Casino	Limited	Reopened
Christchurch Central Police Station	Relevant	To be demolished
Cranmer Court	Relevant	Demolished in 2012
Forsyth Barr	Relevant	Retention underway
Hagley Cricket Oval	Limited	Reopened to public
International Convention Centre	Severe	Demolished in 2012 Building for a new convention centre officially started in August 2014
New Regent Street shops	Relevant	Reopened to public
South of Lichfield district	Relevant	Several buildings demolished Part of High St. currently closed
Isaac Theatre Royal	Relevant	Reopened to public
Town Hall	Severe	Retention underway

(Cubrinovski and McCahon 2012). The end result of the earthquake event was the loss of approximately 60–70 per cent of buildings in the CBD together with severe damage to infrastructure and utilities (Rebuild Christchurch 2012) and the loss of 185 lives.

Delivering a new CBD for Christchurch

The delivery of the CBD recovery plan was far from straightforward. The decision-making process took almost two and a half years to identify which facilities had to be developed in the CBD, where they would be built, the likely partners to involve and the estimated public expenditures (Table 12.2). As a result, the

Table 12.2 Chronology of events from the earthquake of 2010 until the release of the cost-sharing agreement

Date	Event
4 September 2010	A 7.1 earthquakes hits the Canterbury region. Relevant damages in the CBD and lifting of a temporary cordon in some central city premises.
6 September 2010	Appointment of Hon. Gerry Brownlee as interim Minister of the Canterbury Earthquake Recovery.
14 September 2010	Enactment of the *Canterbury Earthquake Response and Recovery Act* (CERR Act 2010), which established the Canterbury Earthquake Recovery Commission (CERC).
September to December 2010	Enactment of orders in council to partially suspend the application of acts as foreseen in Section 6 Par. 4 of the CERR Act 2010. Acts include but are not limited to: the *Building Act 2004*; the *Earthquake Commission Act 1993*; *Historic Places Act 1993*; the *Local Government Act 2002*; the *Resource Management Act 1991*.
October 2010	Mayoral elections in Christchurch. Incumbent Mayor Bob Parker is re-elected for a second term.
22 February 2011	A 6.3 earthquake severely hits Christchurch and its CBD. State of national emergency is declared. Establishment of the red cordon for the CBD.
28 March 2011	Establishment of CERA as Crown as state authority with Order in Council 65/2011. The suspension of legislation is extended over a period of five years.
18 April 2011	Enactment of the *Canterbury Earthquake Recovery Act*. The Act outlines the roles and powers of the Minister for Canterbury Earthquake Recovery, the CEO of CERA, the CCC and the relevant ministers. The Act also establishes the Community Forum and the Canterbury Earthquake Recovery Review Panel as audit bodies. Section 17 of the Act gives the CCC the exclusive power to develop a recovery plan for the CBD within nine months and it recommends a consultation process with the affected communities.
May to June 2011	The CCC holds the *Share an Idea* initiative to collect suggestions for the future of the CBD among the civic society. More than 100,000 suggestions are submitted.
July 2011	The CCC appoints teams of volunteering experts to deliver the first draft of the CBD plan.
August 2011	The CCC submits the first CBD draft to the Minister for Canterbury Earthquake Recovery and the CEO of CERA.
28 September 2011	The Government and the Minister for Canterbury Earthquake Recovery recommend changes to the first draft.
29 September 2011	Government officials and the CCC meet to discuss opportunities for the CBD redevelopment.

Date	Event
October to November 2011	The CCC meets main local stakeholders to elaborate a second draft to submit to the Minister for Canterbury Earthquake Recovery.
December 2011	Submission of the CBD recovery plan for Ministerial approval.
18 April 2012	Minister Gerry Brownlee announces the establishment of the CCDU as dedicated planning unit for the CBD. CCC is disempowered from its planning authority.
April to July 2012	The CCDU establishes a consortium of architects and planners to come with a definitive blueprint of the CBD. Boffa Miskell is the leading firm of the consortium, which includes architects from Woods Bagot, Populous, Sheppard and Rout, RCP, and Warren and Mahoney.
31 July 2012	The CBD Blueprint Plan is officially released.
1 August 2012	Release of the Christchurch Central Recovery Plan and announcement of the lands designated for the 16 anchor projects. Identification of the likely partnerships for each of the projects.
August 2012 to August 2013	Purchase of land parcels for the anchor projects. Controversies arise among landowners and government authorities. After one year, 60 per cent of the land for the anchor projects is secured.
September 2012 to May 2013	The CCC, CERA, the Minister for Canterbury Earthquake Recovery and the New Zealand Government start discussing the budget for the projects and the share of the public expenditures.
June 2013	Complete removal of the red cordon from the CBD.
26 June 2013	Cost-sharing agreement is officially announced. The Government will be key public investor for the Frame, the Avon River Precinct and the Convention Centre Precinct. The CCC will lead the project for the Stadium and the Metro Sports Facility. The total of the public investment (including horizontal infrastructures) is NZD$4.8 billion.

first expressions of interest to attract private investors were only listed in October 2013, when the Minister for Earthquake Recovery, the Hon. Gerry Brownlee, announced the call for international developers for the Convention Centre project (Brownlee 2013c).

The decision-making for the redevelopment of the CBD took place in a context in which "normal" political relationships and procedures were changed and institutional arrangements altered. As Hayward (2013: 37) notes, the National Party–led national government 'used the earthquakes as justification to suspend regional government elections' and established the Canterbury Earthquake Recovery Authority (CERA) as the main body for the management of the early emergency phase and the assessment of buildings for demolition. The *Share an Idea* initiative, run by the CCC to involve the community in the delivery of the draft plans, became a relatively tokenistic form of involvement (Dobbs and Moore 2002) as the Plan, in the end, was delivered by a team of architects and planners led by Boffa Miskell (2013). The same Plan identified the likely partnerships among public and private stakeholders (i.e. the PPPs) for the delivery of the projects. PPPs are very common in mainstream urban regeneration and the redevelopment strategy for the Christchurch CBD identified several opportunities for cost-sharing agreements between national and public authorities and the private sector in June 2013 (CCDU 2013a; CERA 2013a; New Zealand Parliament 2013).

In the post-disaster context, authorities sought to reshape the CBD 'based on international best practice urban design' (Brownlee 2013a: 5). The resulting injection of government funds for the recovery of the CBD (NZD$4.8 billion) (CDC 2013), however, was marked by 'socio-spatial conflicts and political struggles' (Gotham and Greenberg 2014: 95) between public authorities and the local stakeholders. The latter emerged after the announcement of the stadium project in the south-east of the CBD (CCDU 2012; 2013a), which many local residents saw as an unnecessary and expensive project (Gates 2013b). Similar concerns were raised among local arts stakeholders following the CCC decision to fully restore the Town Hall and thus divert most of the budget for performing arts venues to retain a single facility (CCC 2012).

Ideally, the rebuilding of a CBD resembles the conceptualisation of planning as momentum (Nyseth 2012), during which 'systems are open to new insights, ideas and behaviour' (Laws and Rein 2003: 175). Nevertheless, the redevelopment of a CBD is perhaps better characterised by a persisting climate of uncertainty and power struggles within coalitions, especially with respect to where the regeneration cost should lie and the type of projects that should be incorporated. The stadium and the performing arts projects are emblematic of the controversies between national and local authorities. While national authorities pushed for the building of a brand new covered stadium (Stylianou 2012), the CCC argued that the cost-sharing agreement for the stadium forced the council to financially expose its assets to meet the costs not covered by insurance (Cairns 2014). Similarly, the CCC decision to retain the Town Hall was opposed by the Earthquake Recovery Minister, Hon. Brownlee (2013b), who argued that the existing complex was outdated and needed to be replaced with a new international venue for the performing arts. As such the Christchurch CBD rebuild also brought into focus differently political philosophies and policies with respect to state ownership of assets, with the national government encouraging the sale of assets to the private sector and the CCC seeking to retain assets in public ownership where possible. (This situation may of course change in future national and local government elections).

Reliance on the effectiveness of anchor projects as a redevelopment strategy is often paired with the benchmarking of "best practices" overseas (McCann and Ward 2010). For example, the Minister for the Canterbury Earthquake Recovery cited the redevelopment of Lower Manhattan in the aftermath of 9/11 as one of the most prominent examples of redevelopment following a disaster (Brownlee 2012). The CCC held meetings in August 2011 to identify benchmark examples from post-IRA bombings in downtown Manchester (UK) and post-earthquake San Francisco (US) (CCC 2011). Christchurch also joined the network of Resilient Cities pioneered by the Rockefeller Foundation to 'become more resilient to the physical, social and economic challenges that are a growing part of the 21st century' (Rockefeller Foundation 2014).

The rhetoric of anchor projects as best practice in the recovery of the CBD

National and local authorities had diverging ideas with respect to the rebuilding of the CBD. While CERA and the Government identified anchor projects as the preferred urban redevelopment strategy to 'ensure Christchurch's rebuilt and repaired homes retain their value in the future' (Sutton 2014: 54), the CCC envisioned the CBD draft Plan as the opportunity 'to create a distinctive identity for the Central City' (CCC 2011: 62) through the creation of low-rise urban precincts 'to organise and diversify the future development' (CCC 2011: 81). The CCC draft plans were the outcome of local community engagement in the *Share an Idea* initiative and the proactive participation of local and international experts in cultural and creative-led regeneration. On the other hand, the vision of the national authorities was that anchor projects were the best solution 'to streamline the consent process [and] attract private investment into the city' (Steeman and Sachdeva 2012).

With the establishment of the CCDU in April 2012 the national government gave CERA and the Minister for the Canterbury Earthquake Recovery the necessary planning authority to overrule the CCC and deliver a market-oriented urban redevelopment strategy. The Minister for Canterbury Earthquake Recovery asserted that the Plan would 'be vital to achieve a coherent roll-out of a number of anchor projects such as public buildings and strategic city blocks, and [would] provide important guidance to the market' (Brownlee 2012).

Anchor projects were also identified as crucial in the 'reviving of the city's hospitality and tourism sector' (Brownlee 2012). Such a belief was shared among all the key tourism stakeholders (e.g. Tourism Industry Association of New Zealand (TIANZ) 2014). In particular, the building of a new convention centre was seen as 'the key anchor project' (CCDU 2014b) for the new CBD, while the delivery of the Performing Arts Precinct would '[catalyse] development and recovery of the central city' (CCDU 2014c) and 'support tourism and hospitality' (CCDU 2012: 77). Finally, the delivery of the new stadium was seen as 'a world-class option for attracting and hosting events [of] international level' (CCDU 2012: 85).

Demolition and the compulsory purchase of land became the instruments for quickly securing the areas in which anchor projects would be built. By July 2012, CERA and private owners had demolished nearly 70 per cent of the buildings located in the CBD (Rebuild Christchurch 2012). Such systematic demolition was favoured thanks to special legal arrangements included in the *Canterbury Earthquake Recovery Act 2011*, the Plan overruling existing planning legislation

(CCDU 2013b), and the forced eviction of businesses and landowners from the cordoned zones of the CBD (see also Chapter 13, this volume). In the example of South of Lichfield, the state of emergency issued after the earthquakes accelerated the demolition of several buildings that CERA listed as unsafe under Section 38 of the Act. As result, local property developer Lisle Hood lost 11 of the 16 buildings he owned in the area (Schwartz 2013), while other parts of the site were demolished between June 2011 and May 2012 (Platt 2012). In contrast, the purchase of land for anchor projects following the release of the Plan foresaw for owners the possibility of negotiating a sale to the authorities. This was the case of Angus McFarlane, who sold half a hectare of land to CERA for the proposed Performing Arts Precinct for NZD$12.5 million (Gates 2013a). CERA, however, could proceed with the compulsory purchase of land for the anchor projects and issue notices of intention to take land valid for a period of at least three years (CCDU 2013c). In this case negotiation was still possible, but CERA could still proceed with the acquisition without the contentious purchase being resolved (CCDU 2013c). Eventually, many landowners accepted the offer price set by CERA and its real estate auditors (Greenhill 2013) and invested the revenues elsewhere.

CBD regeneration on unstable grounds: emerging traits of disaster capitalism

The redevelopment of the Christchurch CBD exemplifies the disaster capitalism doctrine emerging from empirical evidence in cities affected by natural hazards such as New Orleans (Johnson 2011), L'Aquila (Tiso 2014) and Sendai (Treat 2012). In Christchurch, the earthquake recovery is seen by the national government as a once-in-a-lifetime opportunity to radically change the highly parcelled ownership of land in the CBD and sell allotments to attract major international developers. Despite the willingness of local landowners and developers to reinvest the insurance pay-outs in the CBD, the cordoning of the CBD, the instrumental abuse of demolition assents by CERA and the criteria for the development of private projects in the CBD has "locked in" the trajectory of the CBD rebuilding process (Schwartz 2013). As a result, the majority of local developers invested in the areas surrounding the CBD (i.e. Papanui, Riccarton and Addington), while those who persisted in the re-investment of revenues in the central city faced market and financial constraints. For example, local developer Antony Gough suspended the development of a commercial precinct in the CBD in 2014 due to the reluctance of commercial businesses to return to the CBD (McCrone 2014). This inevitably raises questions as to whose market response the national authorities thought about when they initially released the guidelines for the redevelopment of the CBD.

Insurance is an issue that differentiates post-disaster regeneration from "normal" regeneration processes. Insurance companies are serving to proactively shape the new built environment of the CBD by taking advantage of the market-driven rebuilding climate established by the national government (Hayward 2013). Following the earthquakes, the insurance premiums for some of the buildings nearly tripled (Business Day 2011) along with those of many suburban residences. As the rating agency Standard and Poor's reported (2011), the need for quick re-capitalisation in the light of the relevant loss of liquidity following the earthquakes of 2010 and 2011 resulted in increasing the re-insurance cover costs to owners. The pay-out of premiums with respect to properties was also protracted in many cases. While foreign insurance companies such as ANSVAR decided to withdraw from the New Zealand market following the pay-out of claims (Stewart 2012), local-based insurers like Western Pacific Limited cancelled insurance contracts (Grant Thornton 2015). The insolvency of Western Pacific Limited particularly affected the developers and owners of South of Lichfield, whose claims remain far from being fully settled (Steeman 2014). Even in the case of major public-owned facilities, the pay-outs are far from straightforward. The most prominent example is the debate on the insurance pay-out of the AMI Stadium. The AMI Stadium insurer (Civic Assurance) argues that the facility can be fixed and thus denies the pay-out of NZD$143 million to the CCC (Cairns 2014). The council, on the other hand, is not willing to fully expose its assets to cover the share of the costs for the new stadium (NZD$253 million) without the share from the insurance pay-out and intends to re-negotiate or revoke the cost-sharing agreement originally signed with the Crown (central government) in June 2013 (Cairns 2014). As result, the eventual building and delivery of the new stadium in the south-east frame of the CBD is now postponed to at least 2019 (3 News 2014; CCDU 2014a).

The rebuilding of the CBD is characterised by market-directing strategies (Porter 2009) aimed at attracting international investors. The government is act-ing as the enabler to encourage corporate developers to invest in the anchor projects in Christchurch with conspicuous investments in land purchase and direct infrastructural investment. The decision to appoint international develop-ers (Plenary Group and Accor Hotels) for the delivery of the Convention Centre Precinct (CCDU 2014b) is the most prominent example of the approach sought by authorities for what is seen as the key anchor project for the city (Conway 2014). Policy makers promoted the virtues of "the market" in the achievement of development and competitiveness for the CBD of Christchurch in the long term and the rhetoric of "must do" enables redevelopment strategies that would have not been adopted before the earthquakes (Sutton 2014). The rebuilding is seen as an opportunity to reframe and boost the redevelopment of 'Christchurch into the best little city in the world' (Brownlee 2013d). The role of the market framed the decision-making process that culminated with the release of the Plan. However, since July 2012, authorities have had to downsize the Convention Centre Precinct project (Conway 2014) as well as the plans for the Stadium, the Performing Arts Precinct and the Frame (Stylianou 2015). The search for inter-national investors led to the redevelopment plans of the CBD being regarded as uneconomic by many local developers (Stylianou 2013) and being ostracised by many in the local community (e.g. Sage 2014).

A final feature of the "shock doctrine" in the redevelopment of Christchurch CBD is the land purchase led by the CERA for the anchor projects. The pro-cess consisted of three mechanisms for land acquisition. CERA and the Minister for Canterbury Earthquake Recovery '[could] acquire land compulsorily in the name of the Crown' (CERA 2013b: 3) upon compensation in accordance with the legislation established by the *Public Works Act 1981* for 'current market value of the land' (CERA 2013b: 4). The second option foresaw CERA and the owner negotiating the purchase of parcels in accordance with the *Canterbury Earthquake Recovery Act 2011*. Finally, the area designated for the anchor projects could be negotiated with CERA 'using its own valuations as a base for negotiations' (CCDU 2013c). On the eve of the cost sharing agreement official announcement, CERA had purchased land for anchor projects for a total of NZD$231.6 million (Greenhill 2013). This one-sided scheme of land purchase for anchor projects, however, was often seen by landowners as a process of confiscation and "thievery" (Gates 2013a).

Conclusions

This chapter illustrated the process of urban regeneration in the CBD of Christchurch following the earthquakes of 2010 and 2011. What emerges is a sluggish recovery governance climate where the rhetoric of urban competitiveness and market-driven redevelopment fuelled the redevelopment agenda established by the Minister for the Canterbury Earthquake Recovery, CERA and the CCDU. The decisions taken by these bodies inevitably led to protracted disputes on land use, land value and project feasibility among key stakeholders. Moreover, the national authorities' desire to attract foreign investors in the rebuilding of the CBD hampered a more organic re-investment of insurance pay-outs by local developers. Finally, the prolonged cordoning of the CBD for nearly two years decreased the appeal of commercial investment in the area and eventually encouraged the relocation of offices and retail in the outskirts of the CBD.

The decision to revise the proposals of the CCC and of the wider Christchurch civic society was essentially motivated by concerns 'on the attractiveness and [. . .] the need to future-proof the investment in the city' (CERA 2011: 7). In the words of former CERA CEO, Roger Sutton, the new CBD had to attract 'jobs, businesses, attractive tertiary programmes and facilities' (Sutton 2014: 54) with the anchor projects being regarded by the national government as essential for this. Notwithstanding the highly market-driven approach to regeneration and the use of allegedly consolidated forms of partnerships between public and private stakeholders, the delivery of the anchor projects as originally set in the Plan has almost entirely failed with respect to the purpose of attracting international investors.

The utilisation of anchor projects has already proved its limited applicability and value in mainstream urban regeneration (Hall 1997; Cameron and Gonzalez 2007; Jones and Evans 2008; McCann and Ward 2010). However, it seems to have been appealing to national government policy makers and agencies in the development of post-disaster urban redevelopment strategies in Christchurch. Nevertheless, the adoption of 'property-oriented growth strategies' (Hall 2008b: 200) does not necessarily imply increased competitiveness in real terms. Rather, the adoption of a "low road" urban regeneration strategy (Malecki 2004) only succeeds in replicating what has already been attempted elsewhere. The public vision of a more sustainable city that was promoted in the first wave of city council led planning post the first earthquake, and which built on previous approaches to the regeneration of the central city, was lost in the national government's rebuild strategy. Instead, the focus turned to flagship type developments that were meant to attract international capital, and although public participation has been allowed on specific elements of the rebuild, such as the central city public library and Cathedral Square (albeit with as yet no decision on the future of the Cathedral itself) the community's broader vision of sustainability has been lost. In introducing a new *Greater Christchurch Regeneration Bill* to replace the *Canterbury Earthquake Recovery Act 2011* in 2016, the Canterbury Earthquake Recovery Minister Gerry Brownlee stated, 'It is evident that the community wants a significant step-change in our approach to this rebuild . . . We will work closely with councils and other local stakeholders to progressively pass governance and management of the rebuild to the Canterbury community' (Brownlee 2015). However, by this time the trajectory of the CBD regeneration has already been set. According to the Minister

> We are currently setting up an establishment board which will have a specific focus on ensuring there is greater commercial discipline in [the] delivery [of the Crown's major projects and precincts in the central city]. . . Regeneration is the focus now. It is time to look ahead to the long-term success of the rebuild in order to continue growing confidence in greater Christchurch.
>
> (Brownlee 2015)

However, the success of regeneration is not just measured by the erection of buildings and market confidence. Successful long-term regeneration requires an inclusive approach that also integrates social, environmental and local economic considerations and considers the linkages between the city and the suburbs. This is especially the case in post-disaster cities. By enforcing a neoliberal programme of regeneration projects in the Christchurch CBD, the national government will likely not only manage to make much of the new Christchurch look like elsewhere, but also repeat the same failures.

References

3 News (2014) 'New Christchurch stadium may be delayed again', 25 September. Online. Available HTTP: <http://www.3news.co.nz/nznews/new-christchurch-stadium-may-be-delayed-again-2014092505#axzz3TEIik23J> (Accessed 3 March 2015).

Adams, V. (2013) *Markets of Sorrow, Labors of Faith: New Orleans in the Wake of Katrina*, Durham: Duke University Press.

Allmendinger, P. and Haughton, G. (2012) 'Post-political spatial planning in England: A crisis of consensus?', *Transactions of the Institute of British Geographers*, 37: 89–103.

Becker, J., Jäger, J., Leubolt, B. and Weissenbacher, R. (2010) 'Peripheral financialization and vulnerability to crisis: A regulationist perspective', *Competition & Change*, 14(3–4): 225–247.

Boffa Miskell (2013) *Christchurch Blueprint*. Online. Available HTTP: <http://www.boffamiskell.co.nz/project.php?v=christchurch-blueprint> (Accessed 16 December 2014).

Bristow, G. (2010) *Critical Reflections on Regional Competitiveness: Theory, Policy, Practice,* Abingdon: Routledge.

Britton, S. (1991) 'Tourism, capital, and place: Towards a critical geography of tourism', *Environment and Planning D: Society and Space*, 9: 451–478.

Brown, L. J. and Weeber, J. H. (1992) *Geology of the Christchurch Urban Area*, Wellington: Institute of Geological and Nuclear Sciences.

Brownlee, G. (2012) *New Unit for the Rebuild of Central Christchurch*. Press release. Available HTTP: <http://beehive.govt.nz/speech/launch-central-christchurch-development-unit> (Accessed 13 November 2014).

——(2013a) 'Foreword', in P. Gorman and J. Tewnion (eds.) *A City Recovers: Christchurch Two Years After the Quakes*, Auckland: Random House.

——(2013b) 'Modern city needs new town hall', *The Press*, 17 June, A13.

——(2013c) *International Search for Convention Centre Operator*. Press release. Online. Available HTTP: <http://www.beehive.govt.nz/release/international-search-convention-centre-operator> (Accessed 28 October 2014).

——(2013d) *Anchor Projects Gathering Momentum*. Press release. Online. Available HTTP: <http://beehive.govt.nz/release/anchor-projects-gathering-momentum> (Accessed 18 April 2014).

——(2015) *Regeneration the Focus of Chch Governance*. Press Release. Online. Available HTTP: <https://www.beehive.govt.nz/release/regeneration-focus-chch-governance> (Accessed 28 July 2015).

Business Day (2011) 'Some rates to triple, S&P tells insurers'. Online. Available HTTP: <http://www.stuff.co.nz/business/rebuilding-christchurch/5195169/Some-rates-to-triple-S-P-tells-insurers> (Accessed 28 December 2014).

Cairns, L. (2014) 'Stadium deal critical – Mayor', *The* Press, 1 February, A.3.

Cameron, S. and Gonzalez, S. (2007) *Case Study of the Northern Way and Newcastle. From Redistributive to Neo-liberal Development Policies at Regional and Local Levels*, Newcastle upon Tyne: Newcastle University.

Canterbury Earthquake Recovery Act 2011 (2011 No 12).

Canterbury Earthquake Recovery Authority (CERA) (2011) *Government Response to the August Draft of the Central City Plan*. Online. Available HTTP: <http://cera.govt.nz/sites/default/files/common/government-response-to-august-2011-draft-central-city-plan.pdf> (Accessed 6 July 2013).

——(2013a) *Cost Sharing Agreement*. Online. Available HTTP: <http://cera.govt.nz/sites/default/files/common/cera-crown-ccc-cost-sharing-agreement-2013–12–05.pdf> (Accessed 28 October 2014).

——(2013b) *Landowners Information When Land Is Acquired by Compulsory Acquisition*. Online. Available HTTP: <https://ccdu.govt.nz/sites/default/files/documents/landowners-compulsory-acquisition-info-booklet-20131004.pdf> (Accessed 8 August 2013).

Christchurch Central Development Unit (CCDU) (2012) *Christchurch Central Recovery Plan. Te Mahere Maraka Ōtautahi*. Online. Available HTTP: <https://ccdu.govt.nz/sites/default/files/documents/christchurch-central-recovery-plan-march-2014-a4-pages-version.pdf> (Accessed 4 November 2013).

——(2013a) *Crown and Christchurch City Council Cost Sharing Agreement*. Online. Available HTTP: <http://vimeo.com/69214402> (Accessed 12 October 2014).

——(2013b) *General.* Online. Available HTTP: <https://ccdu.govt.nz/faq/general> (Accessed 8 August 2013).

——(2013c) *Land Acquisition.* Online. Available HTTP: <https://ccdu.govt.nz/faq/land-acquisition> (Accessed 8 August 2013).

——(2014a) *Anchor Projects Overview.* November 2014. Online. Available HTTP: <https://ccdu.govt.nz/sites/default/files/anchor-projects-overview-november-2014.pdf> (Accessed 13 February 2015).

——(2014b) *Convention Centre Precinct Announcement.* Online. Available HTTP: <http://vimeo.com/102805014> (Accessed 27 October 2014).

——(2014c) *Performing Arts Precinct Off to an Exciting Start.* Press release. Available HTTP: <https://ccdu.govt.nz/our-progress/announcements/performing-arts-precinct-off-to-an-exciting-start-12-june-2014> (Accessed 11 September 2014).

Christchurch City Council (CCC) (2001) *Christchurch Central City Strategy Stage 1. Vision, Objectives, Core Principles and Short-Term Priorities for Central City Revitalisation,* Christchurch: CCC.

——(2004) *Urban Leisure. Young People in the Central City,* Christchurch: CCC.

——(2006) *Central City Revitalization Strategy – Stage 2,* Christchurch: CCC.

——(2011) *Central City Plan. Draft Central City Recovery Plan for Ministerial Approval – December 2011.* Online. Available HTTP: <http://resources.ccc.govt.nz/files/CentralCityDecember2011/FinalDraftPlan/FinaldraftCentralCityPlan.pdf> (Accessed 2 February 2014).

——(2012) *Council Votes to Keep Town Hall.* Press release. Available HTTP: <http://www.ccc.govt.nz/thecouncil/newsmedia/mediareleases/2012/201211222.aspx> (Accessed 3 March 2014).

Canterbury Development Corporation (CDC) (2010) *Christchurch Economic Development Strategy 2010.* Online. Available HTTP: <http://resources.ccc.govt.nz/files/ChristchurchEconomicDevelopmentStrategy.pdf> (Accessed 13 February 2015).

——(2013) *The Canterbury Report. Winter 2013,* Christchurch: CDC.

Conway, G. (2014) 'Convention centre plans could be downsized', *The Press,* 28 February. Online. Available HTTP: <http://www.stuff.co.nz/the-press/business/the-rebuild/9773376/Convention-centre-plans-could-be-downsized> (Accessed 1 March 2015).

Cubrinovski, M. and McCahon, I. (2012) *CBD Foundation Damage. Short Term Recovery Project 7,* Christchurch: University of Canterbury.

Dobbs, L. and Moore, C. (2002) 'Engaging communities in area-based regeneration: The role of participatory evaluation', *Policy Studies,* 23: 157–171.

Gates, C. (2013a) 'Owners resisting Govt buy-up; Plan called "thievery" ', *The Press,* 7 May, A.2.

——(2013b) 'Stadium plan least favoured', *The Press,* 10 July, A.1.

Gotham, K. F. (2007) '(Re) Branding the big easy: Tourism rebuilding in post-Katrina New Orleans', *Urban Affairs Review,* 42: 823–850.

——(2012) 'Disaster, Inc.: Privatization and Post-Katrina Rebuilding in New Orleans', *Perspectives on Politics,* 10: 633–646.

Gotham, K. F. and Greenberg, M. (2008) 'From 9/11 to 8/29: Post-disaster recovery and rebuilding in New York and New Orleans', *Social Forces,* 87: 1039–1062.

——(2014) *Crisis Cities: Disaster and Redevelopment in New York and New Orleans,* Oxford: Oxford University Press.

Gottdiener, M. (1990) 'Crisis theory and state-financed capital: The new conjuncture in the USA', *International Journal of Urban and Regional Research,* 14(3): 383–403.

Grant Thornton. (2015) *Update on Western Pacific Insurance Limited*. Online. Available HTTP: <http://www.grantthornton.co.nz/Western-pacific-insurance/index.html> (Accessed 2 February 2015).

Greenhill, M. (2013) 'Landowner says "take the money" ', *The Press*, 31 May. Online. Available HTTP: <http://www.stuff.co.nz/the-press/business/the-rebuild/8739311/Landowner-says-take-the-money> (Accessed 26 April 2014).

Gurtner, Y. (2007) 'Crisis in Bali: Lessons in tourism recovery', in E. Laws, B. Prideaux and K. Chon (eds.) *Crisis Management in Tourism*, Wallingford: CAB International.

Hall, C. M. (1997) 'Geography, marketing and the selling of places', *Journal of Travel and Tourism Marketing*, 6(3/4): 61–84.

——(2006) 'Urban entrepreneurship, corporate interests and sports mega-events: The thin policies of competitiveness within the hard outcomes of neoliberalism', *Sociological Review Monograph*, Sports Mega-events: Social Scientific Analyses of a Global Phenomenon, 54(s2): 59–70.

——(2007) 'Tourism and regional competitiveness', in J. Tribe and D. Airey (eds.) *Advances in Tourism Research, Tourism Research, New Directions, Challenges and Applications*, Oxford: Elsevier.

——(2008a) 'Servicescapes, designscapes, branding and the creation of place-identity: South of Litchfield, Christchurch', *Journal of Travel and Tourism Marketing*, 25(3/4): 233–250.

——(2008b) *Tourism Planning: Policies, Processes and Relationships*, New York, NY: Pearson/Prentice Hall.

Hartman, C. and Squires, G. (eds.) (2006) *There Is No Such Thing as a Natural Disaster: Race, Class, and Hurricane Katrina*, New York, NY: Routledge.

Harvey, D. (1978) 'The urban process under capitalism: A framework for analysis', *International Journal of Urban and Regional Research*, 2: 101–131.

——(1989) 'From managerialism to entrepreneurialism: The transformation in urban governance in late capitalism', *Geografiska Annaler. Series B. Human Geography*, 71: 3–17.

Hayward, B. M. (2013) 'Rethinking resilience: Reflections on the earthquakes in Christchurch, New Zealand, 2010 and 2011', *Ecology and Society*, 18: 37–42.

Hercus, A. (1942) 'A city built upon a swamp: The story of the drainage of Christchurch, 1850–1903', unpublished thesis, University of Canterbury.

Holmes Consulting Group (HCG) (2011) *Detailed Structural Engineering Evaluation of the Christchurch Town Hall for the Performing Arts*. Qualitative assessment. Online. Available HTTP: <http://resources.ccc.govt.nz/files/canterburyearthquake/Engineering-reports-amistadium-townhall-convcentre/106355.01DetailedStructuralAssessment-Qualitative110808.pdf> (Accessed 3 March 2014).

Johnson, C. (2011) *The Neoliberal Deluge: Hurricane Katrina, late capitalism, and the remaking of New Orleans*, Minneapolis: University of Minnesota Press.

Jones, P. and Evans, J. (2008) *Urban Regeneration in the UK: Theory and Practice*, London: SAGE.

Kalandides, A., Kavaratzis, M., Lucarelli, A. and Berg, P. (2011) 'City branding: A state-of-the-art review of the research domain', *Journal of Place Management and Development* 4: 9–27.

Keil, R. (2009) 'The urban politics of roll-with-it neoliberalization', *City*, 13: 230–245.

Klein, N. (2007) *The Shock Doctrine: The Rise of Disaster Capitalism*, New York: Metropolitan Books.

Laws, D. and Rein, M. (2003) 'Reframing practice', in M. A. Hajer and H. Wagenaar (eds.) *Deliberative Policy Analysis: Understanding Governance in the Network Society*, Cambridge: Cambridge University Press.

Malecki, E. (2004) 'Jockeying for position: What it means and why it matters to regional development policy when places compete', *Regional Studies*, 38(9): 1101–1120.

McCann, E. and Ward, K. (2010) 'Relationality/territoriality: Toward a conceptualization of cities in the world', *Geoforum*, 41: 175–184.

McCrone, J. (2014) 'Stalled Terrace project poised for liftoff', *The Press*, 17 May. Online. Available HTTP: <http://www.stuff.co.nz/the-press/business/the-rebuild/10055096/Stalled-Terrace-project-poised-for-liftoff> (Accessed 10 December 2014).

New Zealand Historic Places Trust (NZHPT) (2011) *Heritage Redesigned. Adapting Historic Places for Contemporary New Zealand*, Wellington: NZHPT. Online. Available HTTP: <http://www.heritage.org.nz/resources/books-and-dvds/-/media/e3f14e08d2284b4e9ae7acefe88f04b0.ashx> (Accessed 19 December 2014).

New Zealand Parliament (2013) *Briefing of Christchurch Cost-sharing Agreement*, Wellington: New Zealand Parliament. Online. Available HTTP: <http://www.parliament.nz/resource/en-nz/50DBSCH_SCR5975_1/8fd4c7e4a6bed737ea514c46887a4959c4f12264> (Accessed 28 October 2014).

New Zealand Statistics (NZSTATS) (2015a) *Subnational Population Estimates (TA, AU), by Age and Sex, at 30 June 2006–14 (2013 Boundaries)*, Wellington: NZSTATS.

——(2015b) *Geographic Units by Employee Count Size, Industry and Area Unit 2000–14*, Wellington: NZSTATS.

Nyseth, T. (2012) 'Fluid planning: A meaningless concept or a rational response to uncertainty in planning?', in J. Burian (ed.) *Advances in Spatial Planning*, Rijeka: Intech.

Orchiston, C. (2012) 'Seismic risk scenario planning and sustainable tourism management: Christchurch and the Alpine Fault zone, South Island, New Zealand', *Journal of Sustainable Tourism*, 20: 59–79.

Pelling, M. (2003) *The Vulnerability of Cities: Natural Disasters and Social Resilience*, London: Earthscan.

Platt, S. (2012) *Reconstruction in New Zealand Post 2010–11 Christchurch Earthquakes*, Cambridge: Cambridge University Centre for Risk in the Built Environment (CURBE). Online. Available HTTP: <http://www.carltd.com/sites/carwebsite/files/Reconstruction%20New%20Zealand%20Post%202010–11%20Christchurch%20Earthquakes_0.pdf> (Accessed 27 June 2013).

Porter, L. (2009) 'Whose urban renaissance?' in L. Porter and K. Shaw (eds.) *Whose Urban Renaissance? An International Comparison of Urban Regeneration Strategies*, New York, NY: Routledge.

Quigley, M. (2010) *Greendale Fault: September 4, 2010 Earthquake*. Online. Available HTTP: <http://www.geol.canterbury.ac.nz/earthquake/greendale.shtml> (Accessed 2 May 2014).

Rebuild Christchurch (2012) *Christchurch CBD Recovery Plan*. Online. Available HTTP: <http://www.youtube.com/watch?v=893n—sFilg> (Accessed 7 July 2013).

Rockefeller Foundation. (2014) *About 100 Resilient Cities – Pioneered by the Rockefeller Foundation*. Online. Available HTTP: <http://www.100resilientcities.org/pages/about-us#/-_Yz5jJmg%2FMSd1PWI%3D/> (Accessed 6 January 2015).

Sage, E. (2014) *Time to Review Earthquake Rebuild Costsharing Agreement*. Press release. Available HTTP: <https://home.greens.org.nz/press-releases/time-review-earthquake-rebuild-cost-sharing-agreement> (Accessed 9 February 2015).

Saraçoğlu, C. and Demirtas-Milz, N. (2014) 'Disasters as an ideological strategy for governing neoliberal urban transformation in Turkey: Insights from Izmir/Kadifekale', *Disasters*, 38: 178–201.

Saxena, G. (2014) 'Cross-sector regeneration partnership strategies and tourism', *Tourism Planning & Development*, 11: 86–105.

Schwartz, D. (2013) 'Christchurch rising from the rubble after deadly earthquake', *ABC News*. Online. Available HTTP: <http://www.abc.net.au/news/2013-06-28/christchurch-rises-from-the-rubble/4787884> (Accessed 20 December 2014).

Smyth, H. (2005) *Marketing the City: The Role of Flagship Developments in Urban Regeneration*, London: Taylor & Francis.

Smith, N. (1979) 'Towards a theory of gentrification a back to the city movement by capital, not people', *Journal of the American Planning Association*, 45: 538–548.

Spirou, C. (2010) *Urban Tourism and Urban Change: Cities in a Global Economy*, New York, NY: Routledge.

Standard and Poor's (2011) *Reinsurance Capacity Available for NZ; But at What Cost?* Online. Available HTTP: <http://www.benefitnews.com/news/Standard-Poors-2714976–1.html> (Accessed 20 December 2014).

Steeman, M. (2014) 'Poplar Lane owners still waiting', *The Press*, 10 March. Online. Available HTTP: <http://www.stuff.co.nz/the-press/business/9809331/Poplar-Lane-owners-still-waiting> (Accessed 27 December 2014).

Steeman, M. and Sachdeva, S. (2012) 'New Govt task force to lead city renewal', *The Press*, 19 April. Online. Available HTTP: < www.stuff.co.nz/the-press/news/christchurch-earthquake-2011/6769494/New-Govt-task-force-to-lead-city-renewal> (Accessed 20 July 2015).

Stewart, T. (2012) 'Ansvar fallback scheme worries', *The Press*, 23 June, C.24.

Stylianou, G. (2012) 'Key backs world-class covered arena for Chch', *The Press*, 14 May, A.4.

——(2013) 'Bitterness at CCDU valuations', *The Press*, 13 July. Online. Available HTTP: <http://www.stuff.co.nz/the-press/news/8913714/Bitterness-at-CCDU-valuations> (Accessed 7 July 2015).

——(2015) 'Land for anchor projects reduced', *The Press*, 27 January, A.1.

Sutton, R. (2014) 'A blank canvas for new beginnings' in B. Bennett, J. Dann, E. Johnson and R. Reynolds (eds.) *Once in a Lifetime: City-building after Disaster in Christchurch*, Christchurch: Freerange Press.

Swyngedouw, E. (2010) 'Impossible sustainability and the post-political condition', in M. Cerreta, G. Concilio and V. Monno (eds.) *Making Strategies in Spatial Planning*, New York, NY: Springer.

Theodore, N. and Peck, J. (2012) 'Framing neoliberal urbanism: Translating "commonsense" urban policy across the OECD zone', *European Urban and Regional Studies*, 19: 20–41.

Tiso, G. (2014) 'We weren't laughing: Disaster capitalism and the earthquake recovery in L'Aquila', in B. Bennett, J. Dann, E. Johnson and R. Reynolds. (eds.) *Once in a Lifetime: City-building after Disaster in Christchurch*, Christchurch: Freerange Press.

Tourism Industry Association of New Zealand (TIANZ) (2014) *TIA Applauds Two Wins for Tourism*. Press release. Available HTTP: <https://www.tianz.org.nz/main/news-detail/index.cfm/2014/08/tia-applauds-two-wins-for-tourism/> (Accessed 23 December 2014).

Treat, J. W. (2012) 'Lisbon to Sendai, New Haven to Fukushima: Thoughts on 3/11', *The Yale Review*, 100: 14–29.

Vale, L. J. and Campanella, T. J. (eds.) (2005) *The Resilient City: How Modern Cities Recover from Disaster*, Oxford: Oxford University Press.

Wagner, J., Frisch, M. and Fields, B. (2008) 'Building local capacity: Planning for local culture and neighborhood recovery in New Orleans', *Cityscape* 10: 39–56.

Wells, A., Yetton, M., Duncan, R. and Stewart, G. (1999) 'Prehistoric dates of the most recent Alpine fault earthquakes, New Zealand', *Geology*, 27: 995–998.

13 The governance of built heritage in the post-earthquake Christchurch CBD

Alberto Amore

Introduction

Four years after the earthquake of 22 February 2011, the collapse of iconic heritage buildings in Christchurch, New Zealand, is still a vivid memory for the people of Canterbury. Despite civic initiatives and the recommendations of the New Zealand Historic Places Trust (NZHPT) (as of 2014, Heritage New Zealand Pouhere Taonga), the leading national built heritage agency, national government authorities listed a substantial portion of the built heritage located in Christchurch's CBD for demolition. The controversial speech by the Earthquake Recovery Minister Gerry Brownlee, in which he described Christchurch's heritage architecture as 'old dungas' (Chapman 2011), best synthesises the attitude of the national government towards historic buildings. A handful of sites survived demolition, but their recovery was only possible thanks to a series of favourable conditions.

This chapter is relevant for the understanding of an emerging approach with respect to heritage in post-disaster rebuilding. Following the crisis-driven urbanisation model (Gotham and Greenberg 2014), the study shows how the roots of the systematic demolition of heritage buildings in the CBD of Christchurch are founded on the flaws in governance that existed before the earthquakes. At the same time, the release of the Christchurch Central Recovery Plan (CCRP) (Christchurch Central Development Unit (CCDU) 2012) and the Recovery Strategy for Greater Christchurch (RSGC) (Canterbury Earthquake Recovery Authority (CERA) 2012) disregarded the importance of heritage as tool of economic redevelopment previously highlighted in the CBD draft plans issued by the Christchurch City Council (CCC). This approach eventually changed with the release of the heritage buildings and places recovery programme in November 2014 (Ministry for Culture and Heritage (MCH) 2014), by which time much of the built heritage had already been irreversibly lost.

Literature review

The approach towards built heritage can be broadly divided between strategies for the safeguarding and conservation of historic sites, inaction, and demolition (Ashworth and Tunbridge 2000). The protection of historic buildings is a fairly common practice in urban regeneration strategies around the world. The core principle is that historic buildings 'positively impact economic development' (Spirou 2010: 29) and urban tourism (Park 2013) as well as cultural reasons for heritage conservation (Hall and McArthur 1996). Among the strategies for historic building prevention, facadism (Jones and Evans 2008; Pendlebury 2002) is the most common practice adopted in urban regeneration strategies. The conservation of historic buildings mainly applies to identified heritage buildings, but it can also be implemented along with wider policies of urban sustainability (McCallum 2008), climate change adaptation (Hall et al. 2015), and gradual urban change (Hall 2008), with the emphasis being on preventive strategies aimed at challenging practices of inaction and demolition of the historic built environment.

What happens, however, when built heritage needs to be retained in the aftermath of natural and human-induced disasters? Built heritage is often seen as a means for recovery in post-disaster contexts (Table 13.1). Avrami (2012: 187) asserts that 'heritage can be a very important tool for recovery and rebuilding of community in the face of dramatic change and disasters'. Others suggest that the

Table 13.1 Conservation approaches in post-disaster contexts: findings from the literature

City (country)	Disaster (year)	Strategy adopted
Fulton (USA)	Flooding (1996)	Recovery of historic residential buildings through federal funding scheme (Bigenwald and White 2003).
San Francisco (USA)	Earthquake (1989)	Restoration and re-use of historic buildings through collaboration among public sector and non-government organisations (Al-Nammari 2006; Al-Nammari and Lindell 2009).
Bam (Iran)	Earthquake (2003)	Recovery of the historic centre through international collaboration of heritage authorities to promote the relocation of craftsmanship (Mokhtari, Nejati, and Shad 2008).
Mostar (Croatia)	War (1994)	Reconstruction of destructed key heritage as re-affirmation of urban identity in post-war contexts (Kane 2011).
Arequipa (Chile)	Earthquake (2001)	Restoration and retention of key heritage buildings through the establishment of local coalitions (Rivera Garcia 2011).
L'Aquila (Italy)	Earthquake (2009)	National and local coalitions for the retention of historic centre of the city and its major its key heritage buildings (Platt 2012).

(*Continued*)

Table 13.1 (Continued)

City (country)	Disaster (year)	Strategy adopted
Charleston (USA)	Hurricane (1989)	Local coalition of heritage lobbyists to recover historic properties (Sparks 2012).
Port au Prince (Haiti)	Earthquake (2010)	Co-operation among international and local heritage stakeholders for the recovery of historic properties (Lattig 2012).

allocation of public funds for 'historic buildings endangered by large scale public works, pollution and natural disaster' (Chairatananonda 2009: 65) is valuable for both public and private interests. Clearly, built heritage can be an important resource (Brazendale 2013) that appropriate policy measures can protect (Bigenwald and White 2003). A similar approach towards built heritage recovery in post-disaster contexts is highlighted in several guidelines issued by international bodies, national states and NGOs, such as the World Monuments Fund, the World Heritage Programme and the International Council on Monuments and Sites (ICOMOS) (Lattig 2012). Within integrated approaches towards heritage management (Hall and McArthur 1998), the repair of historic buildings also serves to mitigate sites against hazards (Lattig 2012; Hall et al. 2015).

However, much of the literature seems to overlook the contemporary shift towards market-directing strategies of post-disaster recovery and their influence on the planning process (Le Gales 2011) and the political dimension of heritage management (Hall and McArthur 1996). Developers and government agencies often speculate on the vulnerability of heritage buildings in order to demolish sites with historic value so as to achieve a radical redevelopment of urban form. Examples of such approaches can be found in post-Katrina New Orleans, where a significant portion of historic residential architecture in the heritage core of the city that could have otherwise been conserved or retained was demolished between 2005 and 2008. The example of New Orleans, in fact, suggests that the post-hazard redevelopment undermined the historic traits of the city while advantaging 'the lucrative economics of disaster recovery' (Verderber 2009: 274).

It is suggested here that 'there is no such a thing as a natural disaster' (Smith 2006). Rather, disasters are caused by pre-existing vulnerabilities upon which top-down political and market drivers frame the recovery. Cities affected by natural disasters often become places of neoliberal experimentation in which extraordinary measures are undertaken to boost economic recovery under the principles of market-led policy-making (Gotham and Greenberg 2014). While authorities seek and legitimise their approaches by exploiting the climate of uncertainty and instability caused by disasters (Klein 2007), communities are relatively powerless and subject to political and economic constraints that inhibit *de facto* the quest for a more equitable and collaborative recovery agenda (Harvey and Potter 2009). In such contexts, multiscalar regimes tend to encourage expensive redevelopment projects while downplaying the potentialities of heritage in the wider redevelopment strategies. This may be because of the perceived costs of retaining heritage and/or the desire to amalgamate the land parcels on which built heritage stands for development projects. This process is best synthesised in the crisis-driven urbanisation model (Gotham and Greenberg 2014), which highlights how pre-disaster vulnerabilities and growth coalitions can lead to an uneven recovery governance (see also Amore and Hall, Chapter 12, this volume).

Context

The focus of this analysis is the historic centre of Christchurch. The area is part of what was declared a city by Royal Charter in 1856, thereby making it the oldest city in New Zealand (Christchurch City Libraries (CCL) 2015). The historic centre corresponds to the current CBD, as identified in the dedicated legislation for the recovery of the city after the earthquakes (Section 4(1) (a) of the *Canterbury Earthquake Recovery Act 2011*) (see also Chapter 12, this volume). Before the earthquakes, the CBD was home to remarkable examples of late 19th-century historic sites, such as the Christ Church Cathedral (completed between 1864 and 1904), the Cathedral of the Blessed Sacrament (completed in 1905), the Provincial Council Buildings (completed between 1858 and 1865) and the Arts Centre (formerly the University of Canterbury and completed between 1877 and the late 1920s) (Ansley 2011). Table 13.2 lists an array of the 173 nationally and

Table 13.2 List of key heritage buildings in Christchurch CBD

Site name	Category (NZHPT)	Group (CCC)
ANZ Bank Building	II	2
Arts Centre	I and II	1, 2 and 3
Avon Theatre	II	2
Bridge of Remembrance	I	1
Canterbury Club	II	4
Canterbury Museum	I	1
Canterbury Public Library	II	1 and 2
Canterbury Society of Arts Gallery	I	1
Cathedral of the Blessed Sacrament	I	1
Christ Church Cathedral	I	1
Christ College	I and II	1, 2 and 3
Citizen's War Memorial	I	1
Cook Statue	II	2

(*Continued*)

Table 13.2 (Continued)

Site name	Category (NZHPT)	Group (CCC)
Cranmer Courts	I	1
Durham Street Methodist Church	I	1
Guthrey Centre	I	1
Harald's Building	I	1
Isaac Theatre Royal	I	1
Lyttelton Times Building	I	2
Magistrates Court	I	1
Manchester Courts	I	1
Music Centre of Christchurch	I	1
New Regent Street Historic Area	I	2
Odeon Theatre	I	2
Our City	I	1
Old Government Building	I	n/a
Oxford Terrace Baptist Church	II	1
Peterborough Centre	II	2
Public Trust Office	II	3
Regent Theatre	I	1
Rollerston Statue	II	n/a
St John the Baptist Church	I	1
St Paul's Church	I	1
The Press Building	I	1
Victoria Clock Tower	I	1

Category I refers to buildings and places of special or outstanding historical or cultural significance.

Category II refers to buildings and places of outstanding historical or cultural reference.

Group 1 refers to buildings, places and objects of international or national significance, the protection of which is considered essential.

Group 2 refers to buildings, places and objects which are of national or regional importance, the protection of which is seen as very important.

Group 3 refers to buildings, places and objects which are of regional or metropolitan significance, the protection of which is seen as important.

Group 4 refers to buildings, places and objects which are of regional or metropolitan significance, the protection of which is seen as desirable.

Sources: Derived from NZHPT (2011c, 2013a) and HNZ (2015b)

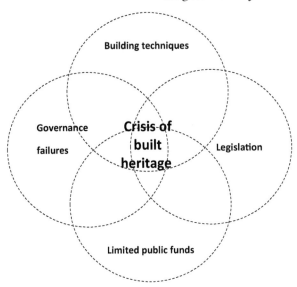

Figure 13.1 Pre-earthquake factors at the basis of the subsequent crisis of built heritage in Christchurch CBD

regionally relevant buildings located in the CBD of Christchurch (Heritage New Zealand (HNZ) 2015).

In light of the crisis-driven urbanisation model, the governance of heritage buildings in Christchurch before the earthquake was decisive in the escalation of the crisis following the earthquakes of 2010 and 2011. Up to four different, yet complementary, pre-earthquake factors eventually persuaded authorities to list a good portion of the built heritage of the CBD for demolition (Figure 13.1). Reports from the NZHPT exhorted the government to address the flaws of governance, promote building retention and upgrade the legislation to prevent the decay of the historic built environment (e.g. McLean 2009). Nevertheless, the government's direct investment for the retention of historic sites remained marginal.

Most of the heritage buildings in Christchurch were built with unreinforced masonry, a technique used in England and Scotland but not suited for an earthquake-prone country like New Zealand (Ingham and Griffith 2011). Only a few heritage buildings were strengthened to sustain moderate or more intense earthquakes (Russell and Ingham 2010). During the earthquakes of 2010 and 2011, unreinforced masonry buildings in the CBD suffered substantial damage (Ingham and Griffith 2011). According to Ingham et al.'s (2011) preliminary report for the NZHPT, 48 per cent of such buildings could be listed for demolition.

The predominance of non-reinforced masonry buildings with historical value is the consequence of an executive default of the CCC in applying the dedicated legislation 'to classify earthquake prone buildings and require owners to reduce or remove the danger' (Russell and Ingham 2010: 197). A report issued by the New Zealand Society of Earthquake Engineering (NZSEE) on the eve of the September 2010 earthquake highlighted the predominantly passive approach of the CCC in promoting masonry building reinforcement among private owners (Russell and Ingham 2010). A prominent exception was the refurbishment of warehouses in South of Litchfield in the early 2000s (New Zealand Historic Places Trust (NZHPT) 2011a). In this case, in fact, the change of use foresaw a mandatory earthquake-strengthening of historic buildings above 33 per cent of that required in the Building Code, but the legislation did not make provision for fiscal incentives to owners who sought to retain and strengthen such buildings, including those listed in the NZHPT registry. Finally, many historic sites were owned by religious organisations (NZHPT 2013a) that did not have the financial means or the willingness to undertake earthquake strengthening works to their properties. Consequently, a large number of historic buildings did not meet the minimum requirement of 33 per cent recommended by the NZSEE, when Christchurch was hit by the earthquakes (Holmes Consulting Group 2011).

The national legislation with respect to heritage before the earthquakes (i.e. HPA 1993) established the NZHPT as an independent Crown agency of the Ministry of Culture and Heritage (MCH) (Section 39) with limited budget allocations and roles at national level. The NZHPT could not acquire new historic properties, and the budget for the 48 sites under its direct responsibility was very limited (NZD$1.05 million in 2010). The NZHPT could assist the owners of buildings enlisted in the national registry with practical guidelines (NZHPT 2007), but the latter were not enforceable mandatory requirements as in other countries. The *Resource Management Act* (RMA) 1991 represented the main legal instrument to protect heritage 'from inappropriate subdivision, use and development' (Section 6(f)). Under this Act, the NZHPT could require the designation of heritage orders and thus rescue sites of historic relevance from immediate demolition and radical reconstruction.

The CCC only had limited financial and jurisdictional authority to encourage private owners to retain historic sites. The management guidelines in the CCC's *Heritage Conservation Policy* were only applicable to sites owned or run by the Council. To cope with such restrictions, the CCC established a policy to 'work with building owners, developers and community to find compatible new uses for under-utilised heritage buildings and heritage buildings at risk of demolition' (CCC 1999: 11). Focusing on financial instruments, the CCC had established two funding schemes in support of heritage: the Historic Building Emergency Fund 'for the retention of significant-listed buildings under imminent threat of demolition' (CCC 2000); and the Heritage Retention Incentive Fund to assist private owners who sought 'the conservation, protection and maintenance' (CCC 1999: 12) of their historically valuable properties. These initiatives, however, were far from meeting 'the need for substantial seismic upgrading' (Nahkies 2011: 16). The recovery and retention of historic sites instead depended on the proactive involvement and goodwill of private developers and investors.

Wreck the old dungas!

Early inspections in the aftermath of the 4 September 2010 earthquake reported damage to several historic buildings in the CBD. Of the 173 historic sites in central Christchurch, Manchester Courts was the first building listed for demolition (CCC 2010a), followed by four other buildings (Heather 2011b). In contrast, the 22 February 2011 earthquake represented the turning point for the governance of heritage in Christchurch's CBD. Between March and November 2011, 45 per cent of listed heritage buildings had been demolished within the Central City (CCC 2011b: 69). As of March 2015, 76 heritage buildings of national relevance have been demolished (Table 13.3).

Local and national heritage advocates agree that the public pronouncement by the Minister for Canterbury Earthquake Recovery against what he termed as 'old dungas' synthesises the disregard of heritage by national government authorities and its potential role as a means for post-disaster recovery and redevelopment (Halliday 2014). There are, nevertheless, three different elements that should be considered in order to critically analyse the socio-spatial conflicts of post-earthquake heritage governance in Christchurch and in the CBD in particular. These include the market drivers, particularly insurance and real estate; heritage and planning policies and legal instruments; and the final decision to demolish or restore.

The recovery of Christchurch is strongly influenced by the role of the insurance sector, and the governance of built heritage in the CBD is no exception. The NZHPT reported inadequate private insurance of heritage buildings and argued that, with hindsight, the insurance coverage provided by the EQC should have also been applied to public heritage buildings (NZHPT 2011b). On the other hand, the Insurance Council of New Zealand argued that the earthquake strengthening of heritage buildings to the level required of new ones would increase the costs of reinsurance and thus compromise 'the willingness of insurers to invest in the New Zealand' (*The Insurance Council of NZ Incorporated v Christchurch City Council* 2012).

The pay-out of premiums for heritage properties were particularly troubling. While ANSVAR, a UK-based company specialising in heritage insurance, cancelled coverage to several key heritage sites in Christchurch and proceeded with

Table 13.3 Listed heritage buildings before and after the earthquakes of 2010 and 2011

NZHPT Category	As at September 2010	As at March 2015	Demolished and partially demolished	%
I	61	32	29	47.5%
II	112	65	47	42%
Total	173	97	76	44%

Sources: HNZ 2015b; NZHPT 2011b, 2013a.

insurance claims case by case (KPMG 2012; Stewart 2012), national insurance companies such as Western Pacific Insurance became insolvent in the immediate aftermath of the February 2011 earthquake (Grant Thorton 2015). The lack of a solid insurance basis, the rocketing of seismic strengthening costs (City Owners Rebuild Entity (CORE) 2011), and the evacuation of many historic properties after the earthquake of February 2011 hampered asset values. This generated a climate of greater uncertainty among building owners.

Under a market-driven post-earthquake governance regime, 'the future for remaining heritage buildings [lay] with the owners and insurers' (Christchurch Central Development Unit (CCDU) 2013) as the District Plan legislation was suspended under the *Canterbury Earthquake Recovery Act* 2011. Despite efforts among engineers and architects to obtain solutions for historic buildings, many owners pursued the demolition of their properties in order to gain compensation from the Canterbury Earthquake Recovery Authority (CERA) and re-invested elsewhere.

The emergency management tools deployed in the aftermath of the earthquakes heightened the vulnerability of heritage buildings. The state of emergency issued after the earthquake of February 2011 (Carter 2011) culminated with the cordoning of the CBD areas for several months. Particularly during the first weeks of the cordon, owners had to comply with safety measures set by CERA and other authorities. The cordoning of premises within the CBD and the repeated aftershocks exasperated local developers and business people seeking to assess the damage to their properties (Robinson 2011b). The adoption of emergency measures to conserve heritage buildings was not among the priorities of either the Civil Defence or CERA (Waikato Times 2011). Rather, the controversial application of "red stickers" (a notice to display the safety level of a building) to list historic buildings as unsafe caused frictions between CERA and heritage stakeholders. On the one hand, the NZHPT reported that 27 of the demolished historic buildings could have been retained (Platt 2012). On the other, San Francisco–based Miyamoto International provided alternative reports in which it was shown that some heritage buildings tagged as highly unsafe by CERA were instead safe and could be retained with limited expenses (Miyamoto International 2014).

The special legislation established in the aftermath of the September 2010 earthquake and further strengthened following the earthquake of February 2011 was also adverse to the retention of heritage buildings. According to the *Canterbury Earthquake Recovery Act 2011*, the Chief Executive of CERA had overruling authority on buildings listed as unsafe. In particular, Section 38 of the Act empowered CERA to commission works where the owner failed to provide a satisfactory retention plan for his or her property. Particularly with respect to heritage buildings in the CBD, the Act gave CERA and the Chief Executive the power to overrule pre-established national legislation supporting the safeguarding of heritage (i.e. the *RMA 1991* and the *HPA 1993*) and the CCC planning authority as foreseen by the *Local Government Act 2002* (Section 71 (2) (3)). CERA also had no legal obligation to consult heritage stakeholders and could carry out demolitions without resource consents.

The rebuilding of the CBD progressively overlooked the relevance of heritage as means for economic recovery. While the first central city draft plans acknowledged the economic importance of restoring heritage buildings (CCC 2011a) and identified the funding solutions available for the recovery of key landmarks (CCC 2011b), the CCRP only recommended the retention of the remaining heritage buildings in specific areas of the CBD (CCDU 2012). The CCDU referred to the *Built Heritage Recovery Plan* under the *Greater Christchurch Recovery Strategy* (GCRS), but the plan was only released in November 2014 (MCH 2014). This Plan broadly underpins what was originally foreseen in the CCC's CBD plans but states that 'heritage recovery is an integral part of the recovery of Greater Christchurch, not a roadblock to [it]' (MCH 2014: 6), but by this time much of the built heritage of the CBD had been lost. The reality is that apart from some isolated cases (e.g. the Arts Centre, the New Regent Street precinct), heritage was not seen as an economic driver and was instead regarded as an obstacle to the recovery of Christchurch to be demolished where necessary.

The systematic demolition of heritage buildings aroused fierce opposition from heritage stakeholders and owners. Between February and December 2011 a local heritage lobbying group known as IConIC provided the Civil Defence national controller and CERA a list of 40 'heritage buildings, the retention of which was deemed essential' (IConIC 2011). A group of heritage building owners also recommended that both CERA and the CCC provide timely advice to owners on the work needed to retain heritage buildings and suggested a system of fiscal incentives to encourage the recovery of historic properties (CORE 2011). Despite the efforts of these groups to prevent the demolition of heritage buildings, and the availability of funds through the Canterbury Earthquake Heritage Buildings Fund (CEHBF) and the CCC Heritage Grants, the strong pressures of the market and the role played by national authorities led to several owners accepting the compensation from CERA and thus the demolition of their properties, as with the case of the Guthrey House (Heather 2011c).

There are nevertheless exceptions where heritage was successfully retained. The Canterbury Heritage Trust (CHT) successfully managed to rescue the Excelsior Hotel, built in the late 19th century, from the demolition scheduled by CERA and proceeded with its restoration (Heather 2011a). The Old Governor's Building and the Spanish Mission style shops in New Regent Street from 1932 were similarly spared from demolition (NZHPT 2013b). The following subsection focuses on the main heritage restoration project currently underway in the Christchurch CBD: the Arts Centre of Christchurch (see also Amore, Chapter 6, this volume).

The Arts Centre of Christchurch

The Arts Centre of Christchurch is a complex of 23 Category I and II sites built between the 1880s and the 1920s (HNZ 2015a). Together with the Canterbury Museum, and the Christchurch Art Gallery, it was the core feature of the Cultural

Precinct of Christchurch (CCC 2006) and one of the main tourist attractions of the city. Originally home to the University of Canterbury, the Arts Centre was converted to a facility for cultural exhibitions and businesses following the takeover by the Arts Centre Trust in 1978.

After a first round of earthquake strengthening during the 1980s (Crean 2008), the Trust launched a new programme of further earthquake strengthening commencing in late 2007 (Crean 2007; Le Couteur 2011). To fund these works, the Trust intended to lease part of the land for the building of the National Conservatorium of Music but a planning commission hearing eventually refused the building consent in March 2010 (CCC 2010b). The earthquake of September 2010 caused approximately NZD$25 million worth of damage and required extraordinary measures to retain the Observatory building (Copeland 2010). The complex was eventually re-opened, but the earthquake of 22 February 2011 caused severe damage to the complex and forced the Trust to close the complex and evict all but one of the tenants (Gates 2011). At the time of writing (July 2015), only two of the 22 cordoned units are fully repaired. The damage was estimated to cost NZD$200 million to repair (The Arts Centre of Christchurch Incorporated (ACC) 2012).

The recovery of the Art Centre was possible thanks to four favourable conditions. First, the Arts Centre area was only cordoned until 6 March 2011 (Robinson 2011a). Access was therefore granted before the official establishment of CERA and the promulgation of the *Canterbury Earthquake Recovery Act 2011* at the end of March 2011. Moreover, the Trust did not apply to CERA for engineering assessments for the complex and instead hired its own team of engineers to assess the damages to the buildings, collect broken masonry, remove unstable sections of the roofs and pile into wooden crates for later reinstatement (Le Couteur 2011).

Insurance also played a decisive role in the decision to recover the Arts Centre. Following the earthquake of September 2010, the then Chief Executive of the Trust, Ken Franklin, started talks with the primary insurer (ANSVAR) to raise the insurance cover from NZD$95 to NZD$116 million (Barton 2012). Despite concerns about ANSVAR's financial instability, Franklin was able to negotiate close to NZD$40 million pay-out of earthquake insurance proceeds for business interruption and material damage by the end of 2011 (ACC 2012) and, later, secured a further NZD$122 million claim with its primary insurer (ACC 2013b). The settlement with ANSVAR enabled the Arts Centre Trust to quickly begin the first major recovery works on the Clock Tower and College Hall in late 2011 (ACC 2012). Most importantly, it gave the Trust the possibility to cover most of the restoration costs for the whole complex (Dally 2012a) and negotiate a settlement with its secondary insurer (Lumley NZ Limited) (ACC 2013b).

A third decisive factor was the firm intention of the Trust to proceed with the full physical recovery of the Arts Centre and strengthen the buildings in accordance with the earthquake standards established by legislation, the NZSEE and NZHPT (ACC 2013b). The key challenge was 'to rebuild the damaged structures and bring the buildings up to building code requirements' (ACC 2012: 5).

One of the tasks of André Lovatt, who was appointed as new Chief Executive in October 2012, is to continue to pursue the full restoration and strengthening of the Arts Centre 'so it survives the next few hundred years' (Dally 2012a: 4). The Trust aims to retain the heritage of the Arts Centre, as reiterated in the *Arts Centre of Christchurch Trust Bill* that was promulgated as private act on June 2015 'to provide legal foundations for the Trust board to continue to be able to respond to, and recover from, the impact of the earthquakes'(New Zealand Parliament 2015). The ultimate vision of the Trust is 'to recast the future of the Arts Centre [...], ensure its relevance for generations to come' (ACC 2013d), re-establish its centrality as a heritage site (ACC 2012), and as a major cultural resource (ACC 2013b) for the new Christchurch.

Finally, fundraising campaigns for the retention of heritage in Christchurch after the earthquakes were quite favourable for the Arts Centre. Given the importance of this heritage complex, the Trust managed to obtain significant contributions from national and international charities in the immediate aftermath of the February earthquake. Among these, the American Robertson Foundation, the Lion Foundation, Fletcher Building and the Canterbury Earthquake Heritage Building Fund donated NZD$14.8 million for the recovery of the Clock Tower and the Great Hall building (ACC 2014; Christchurch Earthquake Appeal Trust (CEAT) 2011). These sums allowed the Trust to commence the recovery of its main heritage building and therefore run the various rounds of negotiations with its insurance companies with relatively little pressure compared to many other local entities.

At the time of writing, the restoration of the Arts Centre is still underway. The budget for restoration programme is approximately NZD$290 million (Dally 2012b) and it will be 'developed in accordance with the requirements of the Resource Management Act [...] the Historic Places Act [and] the principles of the International Council for Monuments and Sites New Zealand Charter' (ACC 2013e). Some of the units are fully recovered and reopened to public (ACC 2013c), but it will take at least 15 years for the Arts Centre to fully recover. In the meantime, the Trust has adopted a new Trust Deed which includes the possibility of winding up the current Trust and transferring the property of the site under the Crown (i.e. the NZHPT) if the Trust fails to carry out the objective of 'conserving and maintaining the heritage integrity of the land and buildings of the Arts Centre' (*Arts Centre of Christchurch Trust Bill* 2014: 9). This sort of exit strategy was included in the bill in order to safeguard the Arts Centre in the event of major earthquakes in the near future.

Conclusions

The earthquakes of 2010 and 2011 severely changed the governance of built heritage in Christchurch and its CBD. While the flaws of pre-earthquake governance were integral to creating the crisis of post-disaster built heritage conservation, the period following the earthquake of 22 February 2011 led to an unprecedented top-down demolition process that erased nationally relevant buildings that the minister responsible for earthquake recovery referred to as 'old dungas'. Despite international reports and the expertise of local heritage stakeholders that repeatedly stressed 'the long-term benefits of heritage architecture and the historic environment' (Halliday 2014: 210), the approach to recovery run by the authorities (CERA *in primis*) resembled the speculative post-disaster governance for heritage buildings that occurred in New Orleans in the aftermath of Hurricane Katrina (e.g. Verderber 2009). The main purpose of the leading authorities was to allocate new spaces in the CBD to locate the anchor projects foreseen in the CCDU's CCRP (see Chapter 12, this volume). Such an approach underpinned the crisis framing stage in which 'political coalitions [. . .] seize opportunity for political intervention' (Gotham and Greenberg 2014: 12). A similar approach followed the earthquake of April 2009 in L'Aquila (Italy); the national authorities and key developer lobbies launched a €833 million project for brand-new residential areas rather than retaining homes and commercial premises in the historic area, where repairs were economically feasible (Tiso 2014). In the same way, the post-9/11 relief funds were mainly awarded to the Port Authority of New York and New Jersey, with the remainder allocated to properties in the eastern edge of Lower Manhattan rather than on the western premises, where most of the middle and low-income residents and businesses were located (Gotham and Greenberg 2014).

Undoubtedly, the climate of persisting uncertainty and the repeated aftershocks shaking Christchurch became the pretext for {or was it simply the unavoidable reality which led to} the adoption of zealous safety measures that impeded private owners to access cordoned buildings, evaluate the damages to their properties and timely budget repair costs. The issue of safety annihilated the principle of heritage retention as an obligation towards future generations. The President of NZSEE, Prof. Stefano Pampanin, acknowledged that engineers took speedy decisions under the persisting concern of safety heralded 'by a number of stakeholders' (Pampanin and Hare 2012) and did not provide adequate advice on feasible techniques of heritage retention. The result is what local architectural historian Jessica Halliday (2014) described as 'urbicide'. In sum, political factors potentially caused more destruction to heritage than the series of earthquakes between 2010 and 2011 combined.

What emerges from the experience in Christchurch is a predominantly market-led approach to heritage appraisal and management. The earthquakes made the financial sustainability of heritage places highly vulnerable and left owners with only one option: the acceptance of the compensation from CERA. The example of the Arts Centre should not mislead. In this case the recovery program of the complex is mainly funded by insurance pay-outs and the donation of trusts and foundations from New Zealand and overseas. New Zealand's central government and its agencies do not provide recovery funding of any kind, even for what is considered 'one of the most unique heritage sites in the Southern Hemisphere' (ACC 2013a). As Auckland-based barrister Nicola Jane Brazendale (2013: 245) states, the conservation of heritage in New Zealand remains 'a matter of market economics'.

References

Al-Nammari, F. (2006) 'Sustainable disaster recovery of historic buildings: The case of San Francisco after Loma Prieta earthquake', unpublished thesis, Texas A&M University.

Al-Nammari, F. and Lindell, M. (2009) 'Earthquake recovery of historic buildings: Exploring cost and time needs', *Disasters*, 33: 457–481.

Ansley, B. (2011) *Christchurch Heritage: A Celebration of Lost Buildings and Streetscapes*, Auckland: Random House.

The Arts Centre of Christchurch Incorporated (ACC) (2012) *Annual Report 2011*, Christchurch: ACC. Online. Available HTTP: <http://www.artscentre.org.nz/assets/arts-centre-annual-report-2011.pdf> (Accessed 6 August 2013).

———(2013a) *About Us*. Online. Available HTTP: <http://www.artscentre.org.nz/about-us.html> (Accessed 19 June).

———(2013b) *Annual Report 2012*, Christchurch: ACC. Online. Available HTTP: <http://www.artscentre.org.nz/assets/ac-annual-report-1213.pdf> (Accessed 6 August 2013).

———(2013c) *First Art Centre Building Restoration Complete – Open Day Sunday 7 July*, Christchurch: ACC. Online. Available HTTP: <http://www.artscentre.org.nz/assets/3_registry-building-opening-media-advisory – arts-centre-media-release—-3-july-2013.pdf> (Accessed 19 November 2013).

———(2013d) *Our Vision*. Online. Available HTTP: <http://www.artscentre.org.nz/looking-ahead.html#ourvision> (Accessed 19 October 2013).

———(2013e) *Rebuild and Restore*. Online. Available HTTP: <http://www.artscentre.org.nz/rebuild – restore.html> (Accessed 19 October 2013).

———(2014) *Lion Foundation Assists Clock Tower and Bell Restoration*, Christchurch: ACC. Online. Available HTTP: <http://www.artscentre.org.nz/assets/arts-centre-clock-tower-restoration-media-release-12-june.pdf> (Accessed 5 February 2015).

Arts Centre of Christchurch Trust Bill (2014) Wellington: House of Representatives.

Ashworth, G. and Tunbridge, J. (2000) *The Tourist-Historic City. Retrospect and Prospect of Managing the Heritage City*, London: Routledge.

Avrami, E. (2012) 'A systems approach to historic preservation in an era of sustainability planning', unpublished thesis, Rutgers University.

Barton, C. (2012) 'Legacy at risk as city crumbles', *The New Zealand Herald*, 14 January, A.18.

Bigenwald, C. and White, R. (2003) 'Heritage preservation and disaster management: United States and Canada', *Policy Options*, 24: 36–40.

Brazendale, N. (2013) 'Preservation of heritage buildings in the wake of the Canterbury Earthquakes', *The New Zealand Journal of Environmental Law*, 17: 237–289.

Canterbury Earthquake Recovery Act 2011 (2011 No 12).

Canterbury Earthquake Recovery Authority (CERA) (2012) *Recovery Strategy for Greater Christchurch. Mahere Haumanutanga o Waitaha*, Christchurch: CERA. Online. Available HTTP: <http://cera.govt.nz/sites/default/files/common/recovery-strategy-for-greater-christchurch.pdf> (Accessed 10 April 2013).

Carter, J. (2011) *Minister of Civil Defence Statement to Parliament That State of National Emergency Declared*. Press release. Available HTTP: <http://www.bee-hive.govt.nz/speech/minister-civil-defence-statement-parliament-state-national-emergency-declared> (Accessed 12 June 2013).

Chairatananonda, P. (2009) 'Review of conservation guidelines in relation to land use planning aspects of buffer zone affective urban heritage places', unpublished thesis, Silpakorn University.

Chapman, K. (2011) 'Lives before Christchurch earthquake damaged historic buildings', *The Press*, 1 March. Online. Available HTTP: <http://www.stuff.co.nz/national/christchurch-earthquake/4715003/Lives-before-Christchurch-earthquake-damaged-historic-buildings> (Accessed 20 February 2014).

Christchurch Central Development Unit (CCDU) (2012) *Christchurch Central Recovery Plan. Te Mahere Maraka Ōtautahi*, Christchurch: CCDU. Online. Available HTTP: <https://ccdu.govt.nz/sites/default/files/documents/christchurch-central-recovery-plan-march-2014-a4-pages-version.pdf> (Accessed 4 November 2013).

———(2013) *The Recovery Plan*. Online. Available HTTP: <https://ccdu.govt.nz/faq/the-recovery-plan> (Accessed 4 November 2013).

Christchurch City Council (CCC) (1999) *Heritage Conservation Policy*, Christchurch: CCC. Online. Available HTTP: <http://resources.ccc.govt.nz/files/Heritage-ConservationPolicy-docs.pdf> (Accessed 27 February 2015).

———(2000) *More Moves to Save Heritage Buildings*. Online. Available HTTP: <http://archived.ccc.govt.nz/CityScene/2000/April/HeritageBuildings.asp> (Accessed 25 March 2015).

———(2006) *Central City Revitalization Strategy – Stage 2*, Christchurch: CCC.

———(2010a) *Christchurch Earthquake – Building Demolition*. Press release. Available HTTP: <http://www.ccc.govt.nz/thecouncil/newsmedia/mediare-leases/2010/201009074.aspx> (Accessed 22 November 2014).

———(2010b) *Decision on a Publicly Notified Resource Consent Application. RMA 90014850 National Conservatorium of Music*, Christchurch: CCC.

———(2011a) *Draft Central City Plan – August 2011 — Volume 1*, Christchurch: CCC. Online. Available HTTP: <http://static2.stuff.co.nz/files/ChristchurchCityCouncilDraftCentralCityPlan.pdf> (Accessed 31 January 2014).

———(2011b) *Central City Plan. Draft Central City Recovery Plan for Ministerial Approval – December 2011*, Christchurch: CCC. Online. Available HTTP: <http://resources.ccc.govt.nz/files/CentralCityDecember2011/FinalDraftPlan/FinaldraftCentralCityPlan.pdf> (Accessed 2 February 2014).

Christchurch City Libraries (CCL) (2015) *City of Christchurch European Settlement: Historical Note*. Online. Available HTTP <http://my.christchurchcitylibraries.com/christchurch-european-settlement/> (Accessed 20 July 2015).

Christchurch Earthquake Appeal Trust (CEAT) (2011) *Christchurch Appeal Trust – Heritage and Culture. The Arts Centre*. Online. Available HTTP: <http://christchurchappealtrust.org.nz/Heritage-and-Culture#TheArtsCentre> (Accessed 21 January 2015).

City Owners Rebuild Entity (CORE) (2011) *Initial Submission for the Rebuilding of Christchurch Central City*. Facebook. Available HTTP: <https://www.facebook.com/notes/178343008885628/> (Accessed 27 December 2014).

Copeland, J. (2010) 'Strengthening the Christchurch Arts Centre against earthquakes', *TV3 News*, 8 December. Online. Available HTTP: <http://www.holmesgroup.com/strengthening-the-christchurch-arts-centre-against-earthquakes/> (Accessed 31 January 2014).

Crean, M. (2007) 'Centre of attention', *The Press*, 11 April, D.2.

———(2008) 'Renovations mean best of both worlds', *The Press*, 22 November, D.11.

Dally, J. (2012a) 'Arts Centre redux', *The Press*, supplement 3 November, 4.

———(2012b) 'Arts Centre set to host summer market stalls', *The Press*, 26 October, A.3.

Gates, C. (2011) 'Centre evicts tenants, lays off staff', *The Press*, 24 March, A.3.

Gotham, K. and Greenberg, M. (2014) *Crisis Cities: Disaster and Redevelopment in New York and New Orleans*, Oxford: Oxford University Press.

Grant Thornton (2015) *Update on Western Pacific Insurance Limited*. Online. Available HTTP: <http://www.grantthornton.co.nz/Western-pacific-insurance/index.html> (Accessed 2 February 2015).

Hall, C. M. (2008) *Tourism Planning: Policies, Processes and Relationships*, New York: Pearson.

Hall, C. M., Baird, T., James, M. and Ram, Y. (2016) 'Climate change and cultural heritage: Conservation and heritage tourism in the Anthropocene', *Journal of Heritage Tourism*, 11(1), 10–24.

Hall, C. M. and McArthur, S. (eds.) (1996) *Heritage Management in Australia and New Zealand: The Human Dimension*, Auckland: Oxford University Press.

Hall, C. M. and McArthur, S. (1998) *Integrated Heritage Management: Principles and Practice*, London: HMSO.

Halliday, J. (2014) 'Losing our collective memory: The importance of preserving heritage architecture', in B. Bennett, J. Dann, E. Johnson and R. Reynolds (eds.) *Once in a Lifetime: City-building after Disaster in Christchurch*, Christchurch: Freerange Press.

Harvey, D. and Potter, C. (2009) 'The right to the just city', in P. Marcuse (ed.) *Searching for the Just City: Debates in Urban Theory and Practice*, New York, NY: Routledge.

Heather, B. (2011a) 'Excelsior Hotel to rise again in heritage style. Earthquake recovery', *The Press*, 4 August, A.7.

———(2011b) 'Heritage advocates call for calm', *The Press*, 7 February, A.6.

———(2011c) 'Heritage losing battle to bulldozers', *The Pres*, 2 August. Online. Available HTTP <http://www.stuff.co.nz/the-press/news/christchurch-earthquake-2011/5373378/Heritage-losing-battle-to-bulldozers> (Accessed 3 March 2015).

Heritage New Zealand (HNZ) (2015a) *Arts Centre of Christchurch*. Online. Available HTTP: <http://www.heritage.org.nz/the-list/details/7301> (Accessed 20 March 2015).

———(2015b) *New Zealand Heritage List*. Online. Available HTTP: <http://www.heritage.org.nz/the-list> (Accessed 20 March 2015).

Historic Places Act 1993 (1993 No 38).

Holmes Consulting Group (HCG) (2011) *Christchurch Town Hall for the Performing Arts. Seismic Repair & Retrofit Evaluation*. Online. Available HTTP: <http://resources.ccc.govt.nz/files/TheCouncil/councilfacilities/2013/11TownHallSeismicRepairandRetrofit.pdf> (Accessed 10 November 2014).

IConIC (2011) *Interests in Conserving the Identity of Christchurch (IConIC)*, Christchurch: IConIC.

Ingham, J., Biggs, D. and Moon, L. (2011) 'How did unreinforced masonry buildings perform in the February 2011 Christchurch earthquake?', *Structural Engineer*, 89: 14–18.

Ingham, J. and Griffith, M. (2011) *The Performance of Unreinforced Masonry Buildings in the 2010/2011 Canterbury Earthquake Swarm*, Christchurch: Canterbury

Earthquake Royal Commission. Online. Available HTTP: <http://canterbury.royalcommission.govt.nz/documents-by-key/20110920.46/$file/ENG.ACA.0001F.pdf> (Accessed 20 January 2015).

The Insurance Council of NZ Incorporated v Christchurch City Council (2012) CIV 2012-409-2444 (New Zealand High Court).

Jones, P. and Evans, J. (2008) *Urban Regeneration in the UK: Theory and Practice*, London: Sage.

Kane, L. (2011) 'Rebuilding to remember, rebuilding to forget: The tangible and intangible afterlife of architectural heritage destroyed by acts of war', unpublished thesis, Rutgers University.

Klein, N. (2007) *The Shock Doctrine: The Rise of Disaster Capitalism*, New York, NY: Metropolitan Books.

KPMG (2012) *ACS (NZ) Limited. Examination of Reserve Uncertainty at 31 December 2011*, Sydney: KPMG. Online. Available HTTP: <http://www.rbnz.govt.nz/regulation_and_supervision/insurers/publications/4891142.pdf> (Accessed 27 February 2014).

Lattig, J. (2012) 'Calamities, catastrophes, and cataclysms: Current rends in international disaster risk management practices for cultural heritage sites', unpublished thesis, University of Pennsylvania.

Le Couteur, C. (2011) 'A unique complex', *Engineering Insight*, Institute of Professional Engineers New Zealand, 16–19.

Le Gales, P. (2011) 'Policy instruments and governance', in M. Bevir (ed.) *The SAGE Handbook of Governance*, London: Sage.

Local Government Act 2002 (2002 No 84).

McCallum, D. (2008) 'Regeneration and the historic environment', in M. Forsyth (ed.) *Understanding Historic Building Conservation*, Oxford: Blackwell.

McLean, R. (2009) *Toward Improved National and Local Action on Earthquake-prone Heritage Buildings*. Historic Heritage research paper No 1, Wellington: New Zealand Historic Places Trust – Pouhere Taonga. Online. Available HTTP: www.heritage.org.nz/resources/research-and-papers/-/media/15ff965c325c4a5cbfa251e01be47a71.ashx (Accessed 20 January 2015).

Ministry of Culture and Heritage (MCH) (2014) *Heritage Buildings and Places Recovery Programme for Greater Christchurch – Ko te Hōtaka Haumanu e aro ana ki Ngā Whare me Ngā Wāhi Tuku Iho*, Wellington: MCH. Online. Available HTTP: <http://www.mch.govt.nz/files/Heritage%20Recovery%20Programme%20%28D-0588813%29.PDF> (Accessed 20 February 2015).

Miyamoto International. (2014) *Cashmere Hills Presbyterian Church*. Online. Available HTTP: <http://miyamotointernational.co.nz/projects/cashmerehillspresbyterianchurch/> (Accessed 27 November 2014).

Mokhtari, E., Nejati, M., and Shad, S. (2008) 'Lesson learned from recovery project of Bam's Cultural Heritage (RPBCH)', paper presented at the Fourteenth World Conference on Earthquake Engineering, Beijing, 12–17 October 2008.

Nahkies, P. B. (2011) 'Retrofitting – CPR for the Central City?', paper presented at the 17th Annual Conference of the Pacific Rim Real Estate Society, Gold Coast, 16–19 January 2011.

New Zealand Historic Places Trust (NZHPT) (2007) *Sustainable Management of Historic Heritage – Guidance Series*, Wellington: NZHPT. Online. Available HTTP: <http://www.heritage.org.nz/resources/sustainable-management-guides> (Accessed 21 February 2014).

———(2011a) *Heritage Redesigned. Adapting Historic Places for Contemporary New Zealand*, Wellington: NZHPT. Online. Available HTTP: <http://www.heritage.org.nz/resources/books-and-dvds/-/media/e3f14e08d2284b4e9ae7acefe88f04b0.ashx> (Accessed 19 December 2014).

———(2011b) *NZHPT Submission to the Canterbury Earthquakes Royal Commission*, Wellington: NZHPT. Online. Available HTTP: <http://canterbury.royalcommission.govt.nz/documents-by-key/20120730.4861/$file/ENG.NZHPT.0005.pdf> (Accessed 3 March 2015).

———(2011c) *Appendix Two: Damage to Significant Buildings in Central Christchurch (as at 13 October 2011)*, Wellington: NZHPT. Online. Available HTTP: <http://canterbury.royalcommission.govt.nz/documents-by-key/20111017.402/$file/GEN.NZHPT.0001B.SUB.pdf> (Accessed 4 March 2015).

———(2013a) *Heritage Lost Canterbury Earthquakes*. Online. Available HTTP: <http://www.historic.org.nz/theregister/heritagelost/lostheritagecantyearthquakes.aspx> (Accessed 21 February 2014).

———(2013b) *New Regent St Shops Preserve Streetscape*. Online. Available HTTP: <http://www.historic.org.nz/publications/canterburytales/artscentre.aspx> (Accessed 8 August 2014).

New Zealand Parliament (2015) *Arts Centre of Christchurch Trust Bill*. Online. Available HTTP: <http://www.parliament.nz/en-nz/pb/legislation/bills/00DBHOH_BILL56364_1/arts-centre-of-christchurch-trust-bill> (Accessed 23 July 2015).

Pampanin, S. and Hare, J. (2012) *Seismic Assessment of Earthquake Damaged Heritage Buildings*. Press release. Available HTTP: <http://historicplacesaotearoa.org.nz/assets/IPENZ-SESOC-Seismic-Assessment-of-heritage-buildings.pdf> (Accessed 6 January 2015).

Park, H. (2013) *Heritage Tourism*, Hoboken: Taylor & Francis.

Pendlebury, J. (2002) 'Conservation and regeneration: Complementary or conflicting processes? The case of Grainger Town, Newcastle upon Tyne', *Planning Practice and Research*, 17: 145–158.

Platt, S. (2012) *Reconstruction in New Zealand post 2010–11 Christchurch Earthquakes*, Cambridge: Cambridge University Centre for Risk in the Built Environment (CURBE). Online. Available HTTP: <http://www.carltd.com/sites/carwebsite/files/Reconstruction%20New%20Zealand%20Post%202010–11%20Christchurch%20Earthquakes_0.pdf> (Accessed 27 June 2013).

Resource Management Act 1991 (1991 No 69).

Rivera Garcia, A. (2011) 'Heritage conservation and tourism in the Historic Center of Arequipa, Peru', unpublished thesis, University of Oregon.

Robinson, V. (2011a) 'Eased cordon gives public first access', *Waikato Times*, 5 March, A.2.

———(2011b) 'Uncertain future for eateries', *The Press*, 11 March, A.2.

Russell, A. and Ingham, J. (2010) 'Prevalence of New Zealand's unreinforced masonry buildings', *Bulletin of the New Zealand Society of Earthquake Engineering*, 43: 182–202.

Smith, N. (2006) *There's No Such Thing as a Natural Disaster*. Online. Available HTTP: <http://understandingkatrina.ssrc.org/Smith> (Accessed 12 January 2015).

Sparks, K. (2012) 'The relationship between changes in business structure and tourism growth and development in Charleston, South Carolina, 1899–1999', unpublished dissertation, Clemson University.

Spirou, C. (2010) *Urban Tourism and Urban Change: Cities in a Global Economy*, New York, NY: Routledge.

Stewart, T. (2012) 'Ansvar fallback scheme worries', *The Press*, 26 March: C.24.Tiso, G. (2014) 'We weren't laughing: Disaster capitalism and the earthquake recovery in L'Aquila', in B. Bennett, J. Dann, E. Johnson and R. Reynolds (eds.) *Once in a Lifetime: City-building after Disaster in Christchurch*, Christchurch: Freerange Press.

Verderber, S. (2009) 'The un building of historic neighbourhoods in post-Katrina New Orleans', *Journal of Urban Design*, 14: 257–277.

Waikato Times (2011) 'Businesses face weeks of waiting', *Waikato Times*, 28 February: 2.

14 Disasters, insurance and accounting

Rob Vosslamber

Introduction

This chapter considers financial statement disclosures concerning insurance cover for disasters. Specifically, it addresses the following questions:

1   What are the requirements of current accounting standards for reporting an organisation's insurance cover for operational losses (i.e. material damage and business interruption)?
2   What did a sample of Christchurch organisations actually disclose concerning their insurance in their annual reports before, during and after the 2010–2011 earthquakes?

Insurance should be a key component of any organisation's disaster preparedness and resilience (Brown et al. 2013). By converting uncertainty to measured risk, and transferring this risk from an individual or organisation to a larger group (Bernstein 1996), insurance reduces the risk of loss or business failure following a catastrophe. It is not surprising that insurance has played a major role in the recovery of Christchurch following the severe earthquakes of 2010 and 2011 (Insurance Information Institute 2015).

Information about how an organisation has mitigated the risk of future losses through insurance cover provides an indication of an entity's likely resilience if a disaster were to strike. Although directors and management who are responsible for the organisation have access to this information, other stakeholders, including external shareholders, have limited control over the quantity and quality of information they are able to obtain about the entity. Their primary source of information about an entity's financial affairs, including its preparedness for disaster, is usually the entity's publicly available annual reports and financial statements.

Financial statements of larger entities are prepared in accordance with legally enforced financial reporting standards, commonly referred to as International Financial Reporting Standards (IFRS). These comprise two series of standards with equal authority: the earlier International Accounting Standards (IAS) and the more recent IFRS. According to these standards, the objective of financial reporting is to assist users in making decisions. In locations where there is a high risk of natural disaster, information in financial statements relating to insurance cover for disasters can assist users to evaluate their level of involvement with the entity.

There are no requirements in accounting standards for organisations to disclose their insurance cover for future operating losses. Organisations report little, if any, information concerning their insurance cover, perhaps because this information is considered to be commercially sensitive. Given the potential significance of insurance in reducing potential future losses, this chapter suggests that accounting standards should require enhanced disclosure of a reporting entity's insurances to help users to assess how the entity has addressed the operating risks, including natural disasters, that organisations face. Although this research focuses on a New Zealand context, it has international relevance, since large organisations with stringent reporting requirements such as those reviewed here usually must comply with IFRS, which also apply in many international jurisdictions.

The next section outlines the requirements of relevant accounting and auditing standards related to insurance cover for future events. The following section then reviews the insurance disclosures of a sample of Christchurch organisations in their financial statements for the year preceding, during and following the most significant Canterbury earthquakes. The findings are then discussed and conclusions drawn.

Reporting requirements

Shimizu and Fujimura (2010) distinguished between *ex post* and *ex ante* accounting for disaster. *Ex post* accounting involves the measurement and reporting of the losses actually incurred by a disaster-affected entity. This is little different from accounting for an entity's routine activities. In contrast, *ex ante* accounting involves assessing the probability that a disaster will occur and the likely loss to be incurred, and making provision for this loss. If a disaster is likely to happen and the estimated loss can be estimated reliably, an organisation can make a financial provision for the disaster or obtain insurance to provide for the potential loss. Organisations are unlikely to record a financial provision for infrequent and unpredictable future disasters such as earthquakes, although conceptually this might be appropriate (Amernic et al. 2012). Instead, organisations usually prepare for disasters by purchasing insurance cover for material damage and business interruption.

The context of accounting

New Zealand is one of 114 jurisdictions that require IFRS for all or most domestic publicly accountable entities (such as listed companies and financial institutions) (International Financial Reporting Standards Foundation 2015). IFRS are issued by the International Accounting Standards Board (IASB). IFRS govern general purpose financial reports, which are 'intended to meet the needs of users who are not in a position to require an organisation to prepare reports tailored to their particular information needs' (External Reporting Board, 2011e, para. 7). Since general purpose financial reporting does not and cannot provide all the information that users need, accounting standards are intended to ensure that financial statements will meet the needs of the maximum number of users (External Reporting Board 2011i).

According to the IASB conceptual framework, the objective of financial reporting is 'to provide financial information about the reporting organisation that is useful to existing and potential investors, lenders and other creditors in making decisions about providing resources to the organisation' (External Reporting Board 2011i, para. OB 2). Although financial statements provide information concerning an organisation's *past* activities and results, they are intended to have a *prospective* focus and inform users' decision-making. Financial reporting information should be relevant, as well as reliable – that is, complete, neutral and free from error. Reliable information concerning risks from natural disasters, and measures taken by those charged with governance and management to mitigate these risks, would be relevant and useful for users of financial statements of the many organisations which operate in areas that are particularly susceptible to disasters.

Financial statements of larger entities are audited. According to International Standards on Auditing (ISA), auditing is intended to enhance the usefulness of financial statements for decision-making and increase the degree of confidence of intended users in the financial statements by ensuring that, as a whole, they are free from material misstatement (External Reporting Board 2011a). Auditors should consider misstatements through omissions of information that could reasonably be expected to influence the decisions users take on the basis of the financial statements. To provide a fair representation, organisations may need to make disclosures beyond those required by financial reporting standards. As part of their audit, auditors must consider the risks that organisations face. However, neither accounting standards nor auditing standards specifically address disclosure of an entity's insurances. As discussed below, this is surprising given requirements to assess and report on an entity's going concern status, financial risk and liabilities.

Going concern

A fundamental assumption in financial reporting is that the reporting organisation is a going concern; that it 'will continue in operation in the foreseeable future [and] has neither the intention nor the need to liquidate or curtail materially the scale of its operations' (External Reporting Board 2011i, para. 4.1). If the going concern assumption is invalid, the values at which assets and liabilities are reported may need to be restated, since an entity would then be unlikely to realise its assets and discharge its liabilities in the normal course of business. The relevant timeframe for assessing whether an organisation is a going concern is 12 months from the end of the reporting period (External Reporting Board 2011e), during which time a natural disaster could occur. This was the experience in Christchurch, which suffered several catastrophic earthquakes within twelve months of the first and largest earthquake of 4 September 2010. In fact, it was the aftershock on 22 February 2011 which caused the most damage and resulted in the loss of 185 lives.

Organisations are required to disclose material uncertainties which could cast significant doubt upon their ability to continue as a going concern (External Reporting Board 2011e). Likewise, auditors must obtain sufficient evidence that the going concern assumption remains valid (External Reporting Board 2011d). In evaluating the going concern assumption, auditors must consider 'uninsured or under-insured catastrophes' (Ibid. para. A2), but not until they occur. This seems inconsistent with an assessment of going concern given the 12-month prospective timeframe noted above.

Financial risk

According to IFRS 7 *Financial Instruments Disclosures* (External Reporting Board 2011h), users of financial statements need information about an organisation's exposure to risks and how those risks are managed, since this information may influence a user's assessment of the organisation's financial situation. Increased disclosure concerning the risks an organisation faces would allow users to make better informed judgements. However, IFRS 7 is focused on *financial* risk, and specifically excludes insurance contracts. Likewise, while risk is a major focus in any audit (External Reporting Board 2011b, 2011c), auditing standards make little mention of either natural disasters or insurance.

Management recognises the existence of significant risks when it purchases insurance; otherwise, it would not do so. If users had information concerning operating risks and how the organisation mitigated these risks by insurance they would be better informed to make economic decisions concerning the organisation's future prospects and its ability to continue as a going concern. However, unlike detailed requirements to disclose financial risk, there is no explicit requirement for an organisation to disclose the operating risks it faces, or how it has addressed these risks – for example, by taking out insurance. The focus on disclosures of *financial* risk in financial statements suggests that accounting continues to be focused on numerical and financial matters, rather than providing additional information that would also be useful for decision-making (Davis et al. 1982).

Liabilities

According to IFRS, a liability is 'a present obligation of the organisation arising from past events, the settlement of which is expected to result in an outflow from the organisation of resources embodying economic benefits' (External Reporting Board 2011i, para. 4.4). This definition excludes any potential liabilities resulting from a future disaster, since by definition liabilities only arise from *past* events. Even if the risk of a disaster and consequent loss is probable, contingent liabilities need not be disclosed since a contingent liability is defined as 'a possible obligation that arises from *past* events' (External Reporting Board 2011g, para. 10), and the disaster has not yet occurred at the reporting date.

If the organisation is based or operates in a location that is susceptible to frequent natural disasters, it could be argued that the choice of location, rather than disaster itself, could be considered a relevant past event. Although the liability would only crystallise when the disaster struck, the potential (i.e. contingent) liability could be considered to have arisen well before the event. Where an organisation has a contingent liability, it should provide a brief description of the nature of the contingent liability, an estimate of its financial effect, an indication of the uncertainties relating to the amount or timing of any outflow, and the possibility of any reimbursement, such as from insurance (External Reporting Board 2011g). This disclosure would provide similar information of an organisation's operating risks as is currently required by accounting standards in respect of financial risks. It would assist readers of financial statements in evaluating 'the nature and extent of risks arising from financial instruments to which the organisation is exposed during the period and at the end of the reporting period, and how the organisation manages those risks' (External Reporting Board 2011h, para. 1). This would, however extend well beyond the current interpretation of the standard.

Summary

The stated objective of financial reporting is to assist decision-making by those who are not able to obtain information directly from the reporting organisation. However, financial reporting standards focus on the numerical representation of past financial transactions. Notwithstanding the relevance for decision-making, how organisations which are exposed to the risks of natural disasters have addressed these risks is not addressed in financial reporting standards. While reporting organisations may prefer not to disclose these risks, failure to do so reduces the usefulness of financial reporting for users who have limited ability to obtain the information they need to make decisions concerning the organisation.

Insurance reporting by Christchurch entities

What information can readers obtain about insurance cover for disasters from an organisation's financial statements? The Canterbury earthquake sequence provides an occasion to consider how, or even whether, organisations disclose their insurance cover for operating losses, and whether the nature and extent of disclosure changed following the earthquakes. This section discusses the disclosures made by a sample of Christchurch-based entities.

The financial statements of 15 large Christchurch-based organisations, which are required to report in terms of IFRS, were reviewed. Each entity had received an unqualified audit report on its financial statements, which indicates that their financial statements complied in all material respects with reporting standards and generally accepted accounting practice. The sample included the nine Christchurch-based companies listed on the Deloitte South Island Index (Deloitte 2014), which is an index of listed companies whose head office is in the South Island of New Zealand and/or where a substantial portion of their operations is focused in the South Island. The sample also included three public bodies and three publicly owned trading organisations.

The financial statements of each organisation for the three years of 2010 to 2012 reflected the periods before the first Christchurch earthquake of 4 September 2010, during the earthquakes, and after the last major aftershock on 23 December 2011. Audited financial statements for each organisation were downloaded from the Internet and scanned using the Microsoft Word "find" function to locate the key word "insurance". Since the focus was on disclosures of current insurance cover for *future* events, any references to insurance recoveries on claims in respect of past events were disregarded, as were disclosures related to an entity's insurance business (if it had one). The following discussion is impressionistic, but indicates a gap in disclosure.

2010: pre-earthquake

Based on the date of the audit opinion, about half of the sample had completed their 2010 financial statements prior to the first Canterbury earthquake on 4 September 2010. All but one of the remainder were finalised during September 2010, and disclosed the September earthquake as an event subsequent to balance date in terms of NZ IAS 10 *Events after the Reporting Period* (External Reporting Board 2011f), and/or mentioned it in the Directors' Report. The exception was the University of Canterbury (University) which had a 31 December balance date; so the University's 31 December 2009 financial statements were used to reflect the University's pre-earthquake reporting practice.

The pre-earthquake financial statements contained little or no disclosure related to insurance cover. Only one organisation disclosed its total insurance expense and named its insurance broker. A few organisations discussed their operating risk management policies, but only in very general terms. This level of disclosure would not enable a user to make any prospective assessments of the financial effects of a future disaster on the organisation. Nor would a user be able to assess whether the organisation had acted prudently in securing insurance cover at all, or at what cost.

This lack of disclosure contrasts with the detailed note related to *financial* risk which all organisations provided. This is required under NZ IFRS 7 (External Reporting Board 2011h), and in some cases extended to several pages. It also contrasts with the detailed disclosures of directors' indemnity insurance as required under section 211 of the *New Zealand Companies Act 1993*. It appears that where there is a specific legal and reporting standard requirement, detailed disclosures will be made. In the absence of a detailed prescription, limited information is provided, as in the case of general insurances.

2011: during the earthquakes

For most entities, the 2011 financial year included the two main earthquakes: the initial earthquake of 4 September 2010, and the major (and deadly) aftershock of 22 February 2011. Each of the annual reports in the sample referred to these earthquakes and discussed the effects of the earthquakes on the entity's results and financial position. However, there continued to be little disclosure of organi-sations' *ex ante* provision for future disasters.

Three entities disclosed their insurance expense. This had trebled for the Uni-versity. Three entities also reported their policy deductible. For the University this had increased to the rather significant amount of $20 million per earthquake event. Given the ongoing aftershocks at the time, unavoidable self-insurance at this level could be relevant to a user of the financial statements.

Several organisations also provided some discussion on their operating risk pol-icy, but this was in very general terms. The University disclosed the investment rankings of its insurers. However, this was only in respect of insurers where there was a financial risk due to existing outstanding claims (i.e. *ex post*), rather than the University's exposure to the risk that an insurer would be able to pay out on future claims (i.e. *ex ante*).

The limited disclosure is surprising given the significant insurance-related issues that the earthquakes caused, and the increased risk (or reality) of material damage and business interruption losses that entities faced. This is evident in the finan-cial statements of the Lyttelton Port Company (LPC), which sustained severe earthquake damage to its wharves and other assets. LPC was confident that the damage would be covered by insurance. However, it also reported that while it had obtained limited insurance cover for the Port going forward, it had not been able to obtain cover for natural disasters, including earthquakes, or business interruption cover (Lyttelton Port Company 2011). Since such disclosures are not required by accounting standards, the financial statements were not qualified by the auditor in respect of going concern, and readers were not provided with details of the Port's actual insurance cover.

Despite the serious and ongoing effects of the earthquakes, reporting of insur-ance cover in financial statements remained limited. The information provided was discursive rather than numerical, and piecemeal rather than comprehensive. The limited disclosures appeared to be designed more to reassure than to inform readers. The lack of detail concerning the scope and level of insurance cover, deductibles, and the names and financial ranking of insurance providers would not allow a user to make an informed decision concerning the organisation's exposure to operational risks, or to make comparisons with other entities.

2012: post-quakes

By the time organisations reported for the 2012 year, it was evident that Christch-urch's recovery from the earthquakes would be protracted. These delays could directly affect shareholders. As an example, the directors of LPC suspended the payment of dividends until insurance matters had been resolved (Lyttelton Port Company 2012).

The insurance market had also changed. The cost of insurance had escalated, and policy deductibles had increased significantly, at least in respect of earthquake losses. Smiths City Group, a large retailer, noted that the deductible in respect of its central city building was now $3.5 million (Smiths City Group 2012), and

Christchurch International Airport's insurance costs had risen by more than 400 per cent since the start of the earthquakes (Christchurch International Airport 2012). Likewise, the University advised that it was responsible for excesses ranging from $10 million to $20 million, depending on the reinsurer (University of Canterbury 2012). This affected the validity of the going concern assumption, a matter emphasised in the University's 2012 audit report, and discussed in detail in the accounts themselves. However, detailed information concerning the University's actual insurance cover was not disclosed.

Moreover, insurance cover was not always obtainable, or obtainable to the extent desired. The Canterbury District Health Board (CDHB) noted that their post-quake policies significantly reduced cover for earth movement and were on less favourable terms, which materially limited insurance coverage and therefore likely recoveries (Canterbury District Health Board 2012). In other cases, insurance cover had always been unaffordable, such as for the underground cables owned by Orion, an electricity supply company (Orion 2011), or was simply unobtainable, at least for a time, as previously noted concerning the Lyttelton Port Company. The post-quake situation was aptly summarised by Christchurch City Holdings Limited, the Christchurch City Council-owned holding company:

> There is a risk that the group will have insufficient coverage for its assets and operations in the event of another natural disaster. Following the Canterbury earthquakes, insurance companies have been reluctant to provide full insurance cover. It is likely that, when insurance policies are renewed, some companies within the Group may not be able to obtain cover for natural disasters.
> (Christchurch City Holdings Limited 2012: 45).

This indicates a significant risk that would be of interest to readers of financial statements. However, reporting standards do not require disclosure of operating risks and their mitigation, and the financial statements in the sample provide little information in respect of these matters. The Christchurch earthquakes did not result in any significant increase in *ex ante* insurance disclosures.

Discussion

This review considered how a sample of organisations disclosed their insurance cover for natural disasters in the context of the Canterbury earthquakes. Although some entities provided limited information, in no case could a user of the financial statements ascertain the amount or adequacy of insurance cover held by an organisation in the event of a future disaster. Despite this, the limited disclosure provided was consistent with the requirements of financial reporting standards.

Prior to the earthquakes, disclosures related to insurance were generally those required by law (i.e. directors' indemnity insurance). Following the earthquakes there was some increased disclosure concerning insurance. However, most disclosures were of the earthquakes and their effects, and particularly of insurance recoveries in respect of material damage or business interruption that had been incurred. This is consistent with the emphasis of financial reporting on past trans-actions. Disclosures of current insurance policies for future losses were limited, despite the considerable risks arising from a changed and changing insurance envi-ronment. Limited additional information was provided by some organisations, in part to explain increased costs, but also to advise limitations on insurance cover.

Information concerning natural disaster cover would be useful to users of the financial statements of organisations operating in a disaster-prone area to help them make decisions about whether to provide resources to the organisation. Full disclosure could include the following information for each type of cover held (e.g. business interruption, material damage):

- Sum insured, and, in the case of business interruption cover, length of indemnity.
- Contingencies covered by each policy.
- Excesses applying to each asset.
- Insurers' financial strength ratings.
- Policy review dates and likelihood that the policy will be renewed and any changes to the terms of renewal.
- Potential costs of lodging claims.
- Policy exclusions, and risks that the organisation has chosen to self-insure.
- Uninsurable risks, and how these are addressed (e.g. by way of a disaster recovery or resilience plan, off-site back-ups).

Given the significance of adequate and effective insurance in ensuring the sur-vival and facilitating the recovery of organisations following a disaster, this infor-mation would help users to reliably estimate the effect of a future disaster on the organisation, and to assess how effectively management and governance have prepared for such a contingency.

Conclusion

A review of the financial statements of a sample of large organisations at the time of the Canterbury earthquakes found that disclosures of insurance cover for operating risks, including disasters, were limited. Although this level of disclosure was consistent with the requirements of accounting and auditing standards, it was insufficient to enable a user to assess the adequacy of the organisation's insurance cover in the event of a future event.

Several implications are drawn. First, unless something is prescribed by statute or reporting standard it seems unlikely to be reported. This is evident from a comparison of the lack of disclosures concerning operational risk with the exten-sive disclosures concerning financial risk. Even though IFRS are said to be prin-ciples rather than rules based (Agoglia et al. 2011), clear rules seem to result in more detailed disclosures.

Secondly, while there was some increase in disclosure following the earth-quakes, this disclosure was piecemeal, appeared to serve a promotional rather than an informational purpose, and focused on the past disaster, rather than a future event. Although financial reporting is intended to assist users in making decisions for the future, the information provided was historical rather than prospective. The stated objective of accounting conflicts with the actual practice of accounting and the limited disclosures actually made.

The limited disclosure discussed in this chapter suggests a gap in accounting standards. Additional guidance and requirements concerning how a reporting organisation has addressed operational risk provisions, including by insurance, would enhance consistency and completeness of disclosure and would assist users in assessing the ability of an organisation to endure the shock of a disaster and continue as a going concern in an environment where a disaster is more than a remote possibility.

This chapter is based on the assumption of accounting standards that financial reporting actually provides useful information. It is possible that this assumption is unfounded, and that an entity's stakeholders do not place much reliance on financial reporting, and this may explain why there is no call for enhanced reporting in this area. This begs the question of who actually reads financial reports and for what purposes, and whether it is the users who actually call for changes in accounting standards.

References

Agoglia, C. P., Doupnik, T. and Tsakumis, G. (2011) 'Principles-based versus rules-based accounting standards: The influence of standard precision and audit committee strength on financial reporting decisions', *Accounting Review*, 86(3): 747–67.

Amernic, J., Craig, R. and Tourish, D. (2012) 'Reflecting a company's safety culture in 'fairly presented' financial statements: The case of BP', *CPA Journal*, 82(4): 6–10.

Bernstein, P. (1996) *Against the Odds: The Remarkable Story of Risk*, New York: Wiley.

Brown, C., Seville, E. and Vargo, J. (2013) *The Role of Insurance in Organisational Recovery Following the 2010 and 2011 Canterbury Earthquakes: Resilient Organisations Research Report 2013/04*, Christchurch: Resilient Organisations, University of Canterbury.

Christchurch City Holdings Limited (2012) *Annual Report 2012*, Christchurch: Christchurch City Holdings Limited.

Canterbury District Health Board (2012) *Annual Report*, Christchurch: Canterbury District Health Board.

Christchurch International Airport Limited (2012) *Annual Report*, Christchurch: Christchurch International Airport Limited.

Davis, S., Menon, K. and Morgan, G. (1982) 'The images that have shaped accounting theory', *Accounting Organizations and Society*, 7(4): 307–318.

Deloitte (2014) *The Deloitte South Island Index*. Online. Available HTTP: <http://www2.deloitthttp://www2.deloitte.com/nz/southislandindexe.com/nz/south-islandindex> (Accessed 4 December 2014).

External Reporting Board (2011a) *International Standard on Auditing (New Zealand) 200 Overall Objectives of the Independent Auditor and the Conduct of an Audit in Accordance with International Standards on Auditing (New Zealand) (ISA (NZ) 200), compiled to 02/2014*, Wellington: External Reporting Board.

——(2011b) *International Standard on Auditing (New Zealand) 315 Identifying and Assessing the Risks of Material Misstatement through Understanding the Organisation and Its Environment (ISA (NZ) 315) compiled to 12/2013*, Wellington: External Reporting Board.

——(2011c) *International Standard on Auditing (New Zealand) 330 The Auditor's Response to Assessed Risks (ISA (NZ) 330) compiled to 12/2013*, Wellington: External Reporting Board.

——(2011d) *International Standard on Auditing (New Zealand) 570 Going Concern (ISA (NZ) 570) compiled to 02/14*, Wellington: External Reporting Board.

——(2011e) *New Zealand Equivalent to International Accounting Standard 1 Presentation of Financial Statements (NZ IAS 1, complied 09/ 2014)*, Wellington: External Reporting Board.

——(2011f) *New Zealand Equivalent to International Accounting Standard 10 Events after the Reporting Period (NZ IAS 10, complied to 11/2012)*, Wellington: External Reporting Board.

——(2011g) *New Zealand Equivalent to International Accounting Standard 37 Provisions, Contingent Liabilities and Contingent Assets (NZ IAS 37, complied to 02/2014)*, Wellington: External Reporting Board.

——(2011h) *New Zealand Equivalent to International Financial Reporting Standard 7 Financial Instruments: Disclosure (NZ IFRS 7, complied to 12/12)*, Wellington: External Reporting Board.

——(2011i) *New Zealand Equivalent to the IASB Conceptual Framework for Financial Reporting 2010 (NZ Framework, issued 03/2014)*, Wellington: External Reporting Board.

Insurance Information Institute (2015) *Earthquakes: Risk and Insurance Issues*. Online. Available HTTP: <http://www.iii.org/issue-update/earthquakes-risk-and-insurance-issues> (Accessed 30 March 2015).

International Financial Reporting Standards (IFRS) Foundation (2015) *IFRS Application around the World*. Online. Available HTTP: <http://www.ifrs.org/Use-around-the-world/Pages/Analysis-of-the-IFRS-jurisdictional-profiles.aspx> (Accessed 31 March 2015).

Lyttelton Port Company Limited (2011) *Annual Report*, Christchurch: Lyttelton Port Company Limited.

——(2012) *Annual Report*, Christchurch: Lyttelton Port Company Limited.

Orion New Zealand Limited (2011) *Annual Report*, Christchurch: Orion New Zealand Limited.

Shimizu, Y. and Fujimura, S. (2010) 'Accounting *in* disaster and accounting *for* disaster: The crisis of the Great Kanto Earthquake, Japan, 1923', *Accounting, Organisation and Financial History*, 20(3): 303–16.

Smiths City Group (2012) *Annual Report*, Christchurch: Smiths City Group.

University of Canterbury (2012) *Annual Report*, Christchurch: University of Canterbury.

15 Disasters, urban regeneration and the temporality of servicescapes

Jörg Finsterwalder and C. Michael Hall

Introduction

Regeneration has been a major urban planning and policy theme in much of the developed world since the late 1970s (Porter and Shaw 2013). The impacts of ongoing global economic, technological and policy changes have meant that many urban economies have been fundamentally restructured. These areas have been characterised by physical decline and/or new forms of production and consumption, as well as related social changes with respect to exclusion and deprivation as a result of changing labour markets and the welfare role of the state. Cities are required to respond to change, with some able to adapt to rapid change better than others. The effects of economically-induced change, such as industry closures or changes in transport modes, on specific locations bear a number of similarities to the impacts of natural disasters in terms of physical impacts and associated socioeconomic effects. Not surprisingly this can also lead to common planning responses under the rubric of regeneration (Garr 2001; Reece 2006; Cox and Reece 2007; Pallagst et al. 2009; Hall 2013a; Mannakkara and Wilkinson, 2014; Saraçoğlu and Demirtaş-Milz 2014; see also Amore and Hall, Chapter 12, this volume). As Couch and Fraser (2003: 2) argue, urban regeneration is 'concerned with the re-growth of economic activity where it has been lost; the restoration of social function where there has been dysfunction, or social inclusion where there has been exclusion; and the restoration of the environmental quality or ecological balance where it has been lost'.

Regeneration includes both physical (i.e. concerned with material architecture and image, infrastructure, and urban design and form) and social/immaterial dimensions (i.e. concerned with improving the quality of life of areas targeted for regeneration and/or attracting new permanent and temporary migrants, as well as the attraction of business and capital) (Hall 2013a). The material and intangible aspects of regeneration are increasingly woven together as part of the marketing and promotion of place and the conscious commodification and development of spaces of consumption (Jessop and Sum 2001).

The design and use of the physical environment to provide particular experiences and services for consumers is wrapped up in the idea of a "scape" (Hall 2008). The word "scape" refers to a view or a scene as well as to realist and abstract representations of a view (Aldrich 1966; Gold 2002). In marketing and related literature, the notion of a scape has been utilised to refer to the physical environment that a consumer experiences and which is, often, deliberately produced so as to encourage consumption, provide a specific set of experiences, or at least satisfy a consumer's desires (e.g. Julier 2005). Central to these notions is the idea of a servicescape (Bitner 1992). Yet, very little attention has been paid to the temporal dimension of servicescapes and other forms of designed scapes that are an increasingly important part of urban form in post-disaster or crisis regeneration environments. The post-earthquake recovery in the city of Christchurch provides a unique environment within which to examine the role of servicescapes in regeneration (De Nisco and Warnaby 2013). This chapter explores the temporal dimension of servicescapes in a post-quake environment and their use as a regeneration tool, supplies examples to illustrate the different facets of temporary "transitional servicescapes", and suggests that a deeper understanding of the temporal character of spaces and scapes is required in understanding the nature of change in the urban environment.

Servicescapes

Servicescapes refer to the physical facility or surroundings in which a service is delivered and in which the service provider (firm or other organisation, including employees) and the customer interact, and to any material or tangible commodities that facilitate the service (Bitner 1992). The term "servicescape" was first defined by Booms and Bitner (1981) as the environment in which the service is assembled for the customer and where they interact with the service provider. Bitner (1992) views the 'total configuration of environmental dimensions [as defining] the servicescape' (Bitner 1992: 67) and influencing customer and employees alike within the scape. The servicescape of an organisation usually comprises elements of the facility's exterior (such as exterior design, parking, signage, landscape, surrounding environment) and interior physicality (such as interior design/layout, décor, signage, equipment, air quality, temperature, sound, scent and lighting) (Bitner 1992).

The servicescape concept builds upon well-established research in marketing, especially in relation to retailing, that the design of the physical environment is an extremely important element in influencing consumption patterns and practices (e.g. Kotler 1973; Booms and Bitner 1981; Donovan and Rossiter 1982). Marketing research on servicescapes is also heavily influenced by, or in some cases runs parallel to, research on place and the built environment in architecture, environmental psychology, geography and planning (Hall 2008). Thus, although originally primarily focused on the internal environment of buildings, the service-scape context has been extended to include the external built environment and concept of place experience (Clarke and Schmidt 1995; Sherry 1998a; Rosenbaum and Massiah 2011), as well as the social environment created in and by spaces of consumption, otherwise referred to as the social-servicescape (Tombs and McColl-Kennedy 2003). A summary of some of the perspectives on servicescapes and exemplar studies within the marketing literature is provided in Table 15.1.

Table 15.1 Perspectives on the role of servicescapes in marketing

Perspective	Focus and exemplar studies
Consumers	Consumers as co-builders of the service space (Aubert-Gamet 1996)
	Impact on cognition, affect and behaviour after remodelling (Brüggen, Foubert and Gremler 2011)
	Influence on the formation of customer experiences (Pareigis, Echeverri and Edvardsson 2012)
	Influence on quality perceptions (Reimer and Kuehn 2005)
	Role of place attachment in the consumption of servicescapes (Debenedetti and Oppewal 2009)
	The social connectedness of individuals as a determinant of service provider (and scape) choice (Johnstone 2012).
	Role as spaces to satisfy the needs for companionship and emotional support (Rosenbaum 2006; Rosenbaum, Sweeney and Smallwood 2011)
	Perceived level of comfort as a result of the social servicescape (Tombs and McColl-Kennedy 2010)
Cultural Identity	Mediation of ethnic identity construction public and private urban servicescapes (Veresiu and Giesler 2012)
Provider	Architect design and visualisation (Holopainen 2010)
	Creative design and retail store environments (Kent 2007)
	Effect of servicescape on employees (Parish, Berry, and Lam 2008)
	Commercial activity at home (Grayson 1998; Hall 2009)
Place and Place Marketing	Design of hard and soft place marketing infrastructure and relationship to servicescape (Hall 2008)
	Wilderness (Arnould, Price and Tierney 1998)
Sectoral/Industry	Hospitality and leisure (Wakefield and Blodgett, 1996; Hall, Tipler, Reddy and Rowling, 2010; Spielmann, Laroche and Borges 2012)
	Healthcare (Rosenbaum and Smallwood 2013)
	Retailing (Parish, Berry and Lam 2008)

Yet, none of the marketing literature elaborates on the temporality of service-scapes, a notion that has received considerable attention in urban design, where it is referred to as temporary architecture, and which is discussed in further detail below. However, where the concept has been expanded is in connection with the development of internal and external symbolic spaces and urban regeneration and renewal. Sherry (1998b: 112) uses the term "brandscape" to refer to the 'material and symbolic environment that consumers build with marketplace products, images, and messages, that they invest with local meaning, and whose totemic significance largely shapes the adaptation consumers make to the modern world.' In a similar fashion Guliz and Belk (1996) refer to a "consumptionscape".

Broader spatial understandings of servicescapes are found in the notion of "experiencescapes", which are staged physical spaces 'of pleasure, enjoyment and entertainment' (O'Dell 2005: 16) that are planned and designed with market imperatives at the forefront of the design process. Examples include themed waterfronts and former industrial precincts, although many previously existing distinct communities, such as ethnic districts in urban areas, e.g. Chinatowns, may also be repackaged and designed as experiencescapes (Hall 2008). Similarly, Julier (2005) uses the term "urban designscapes" to describe the regeneration of areas within cities that attempt to create a distinctive place-identity. Urban designscapes are 'the pervasive and multilevel use of the symbolic capital of design in identifying and differentiating urban agglomerations' (Julier 2005: 874), with reference not only to brand design, architecture, events and urban planning, but also the productive processes of design promotion and governance. The designscape concept is therefore not only significant for the post-earthquake rebuild experience of Christchurch with its emphasis on precincts (see Amore and Hall, Chapter 12, this volume), but also because it explicitly recognises the role of events, which are by definition temporary features, in the urban design process and the production of scapes.

Temporary architecture

Temporary architecture has been a significant architectural device for many years. Chabrowe (1974) contends that temporary architecture has its roots in antiquity, and temporary structures have been erected at least since the Renaissance for the sake of public celebrations and public mourning. When the events were over, the structures served no further purpose and were dismantled (Chabrowe 1974). Bonnemaison (1990) also noted similar roots for the importance of events in the urban fabric and argued that 'cyclical events, such as markets, fairs and festivals – temporary urbanism – appear and disappear like apparitions or television images, visible when on and invisible when off' (1990: 25). This also suggests that such temporary use of space, vital as it is, is so taken for granted that its significance may sometimes not be recognised in urban design and planning processes.

To describe impermanent *structures* or *scapes* within urban developments, terms such as "pop-up" (Lähdesmäki 2013; Schwarz and Rugare 2009; Greco 2012), "time-based" (Anastasopoulos 2003; Leupen and van Zwol 2005), "temporary" (Charbrowe 1974; Jodidio 2011; Leitner 2011;), "ephemeral" (Coar 2011; Glade 2011) or "portable architecture" (Kronenburg 2003; Siegal 2002); as well as "temporary environment" (Caballero 2013) and "temporary urbanism" (Tardiveau and Mallo 2014) have been coined. Such has been the degree of recognition of the importance of temporary structures in urban design, and hence cityscapes, that terms such as the "temporary city" (Bishop and Williams 2012; Dovey 2014), "portable city" (Austin 1983), "instant city" (Kiib 2013) and "DIY urbanism" (Finn 2014) are also in use.

The recognition of the role of temporary structures also influences understanding of ways in which the temporal dimension can also be applied to *space* (Ruoppila 2004; Colomb 2012). The German term "Zwischennutzung" (literally: in-between use) has been coined (Teder 2011; Colomb 2012) to refer to temporal spatial gaps in urban development and their associated scapes. MacArthur (2012) provides an agricultural analogy and introduces the notion of "fallow time" with respect to urban landscape regeneration. Other authors denote it as "meanwhile", "temporary", "informal" or "interim" use of land in urban areas (Blumner 2006; Bishop and Williams 2012; Oswalt et al. 2013). 'Interim suggests a fluidity of temporality, rather than an understanding of time measured and designated as insignificant or as located between the "real" times of before development and after development' (Till 2011: 106). In fact the term "drosscape" has been applied to the redesign and adaptive re-use of "waste" landscapes of defunct industrial areas within urban areas (Hall 2013b). Nevertheless, Till's comment is salutary as it also highlights the ways in which the mobile and the temporary have historically been discriminated against in urban planning in favour of "permanency" (Hall 2014, 2015). Permanent urbanism is typically portrayed as "real" development; temporary urbanism is unreal – and unwanted – by virtue of its ephemerality.

The interim use of scape and space can be defined as 'the temporary activation of vacant land or buildings' (Blumner 2006: 4). Haydn and Temel (2006: 17) suggest that temporary uses are 'planned from the outset to be impermanent' and 'seek to derive unique qualities from the idea of temporality'. In the context of thematising servicescapes and their temporality, this chapter introduces the term "transitional servicescape" to denote the temporary production of scape and space. The following section provides a brief overview of the work on temporality of scape and space in the aftermath of disasters.

Disasters and the temporality of space and scape

Work conducted in connection with the temporally specific usage of structures and land in a post-disaster context is primarily architecture and construction related. Caballero (2013), for example, investigated the effect of temporary environments on cities which have been damaged environmentally and/or economically. Most other literature focuses on housing issues after disasters (Comerio 1997, 1998) rather than the urban fabric of the Central Business District (CBD) or industrial districts. Mouclier (2010) examined temporary architecture in the recovery phase of an earthquake and shelters as temporary structures. El-Anwar and Chen (2014) investigated the optimal decision-making process for temporary housing solutions in the aftermath of environmental disasters. Similarly, Johnson (2007a) analysed problems of temporary housing projects in Turkey in the aftermath of the 1999 earthquakes. In extending this work, she reviewed five more sites with temporary post-disaster housing projects (Colombia (1999), Japan (1995), Greece (1986), Mexico (1985), Italy (1976)) (Johnson 2007b).

McIntosh (2013) studied temporary emergency housing in the wake of Hurricane Katrina with a focus on trailers and prefabs.

Japanese architect Ban Shigeru used paper tubes for the structural elements to construct temporary relief housing and a church for victims of the Hanshin-Awaji earthquake in 1995 (McQuaid 2003). He later applied the same technique in India (2001), Haiti (2010), Italy (2011), and the Philippines (2014) (Ban and Shodhan 2003; Ban 2015; see also Preston and Banks 2012). Parr (2013), referring to the Christchurch earthquakes, studied the temporary use of land in the context of planning for disaster recovery and highlights various initiatives, such as Gap Filler, an initiative to activate vacant spaces for temporary projects. This work will be further expanded on below.

Temporality of servicescapes

Bitner (2000) pointed out that the notion of servicescape could be expanded to include the natural, political, cultural and *temporal* environment, but neither she nor other researchers elaborate on these factors. No research has therefore been undertaken to explore the connection of servicescapes and temporality in disaster-stricken environments. Some research has highlighted the *temporality of consumption* in general (Arnould and Thompson 2005), and investigated, for example, the existence of temporary or recurrent markets in public squares (Warnaby 2013). Although there is also a very substantial literature on urban events and markets, these have not usually been studied from a broader design and planning perspective, including differences between short-term, recurrent and permanent market spaces (Hall 2016). The following section therefore examines some of the "new spatiotemporal interactions" (McFarlane 2011: 733) of contemporary urbanism, providing examples from post-disaster Christchurch with a focus on *temporary* (vs. permanent) (Dovey 2010) scapes and spaces.

On the temporality of urban space

As noted above, one of the clearest indications of the temporality of urban space is the occurrence of vacant land or empty *space* where buildings or other forms of the permanent built environment would otherwise be located. Such vacant or "waste" land became available after the Christchurch earthquakes because in urban areas, particularly in the central city, many damaged buildings had to be deconstructed or demolished. Thus, spaces normally occupied by buildings or other forms of urban infrastructure, such as car parks, became vacant for varying periods of time. The locations of these empty spaces varied, with their number increasing (deconstruction) or decreasing (rebuild) depending on the stage of activities taking place in the recovery phase of the earthquakes. Moreover, the dimensions and shapes of these spaces also changed depending on the nature of the rebuild activities that were occurring and the extent to which cordons and bureaucracy affected their accessibility. Furthermore, an empty space could host one or several scapes simultaneously or sequentially.

In regeneration strategies, including those in post-disaster urban environments, unoccupied space is usually viewed negatively, often because it is regarded as non-productive (Hall 2013b). Therefore, given the interrelationships between use and exchange value, temporary use of space is often sought by urban planners to enliven areas that consumers otherwise avoid (Schwarz and Rugare 2009; Lähdesmäki 2013). Such short-term use strategies reflect the "fluidity of space" and the way in which transitional servicescapes are often rather "liquid" and flexible in nature. In addition, transitional servicescapes may themselves also shift across space, adding another layer of fluidity to the regeneration of the built environment especially in early periods of rebuild.

Examples

One of the main initiatives in post-earthquake Christchurch was to set up a pop-up retail precinct called the Re:Start Mall (http://www.restart.org.nz/; https://www.youtube.com/watch?v=R3NyfO4PRAg) in the central city in 2011. Retailers set up shops in shipping containers converted into retail outlets. This innovative initiative was instigated to bring shoppers back into the city before permanent structures would go up to finally house retailers and other businesses. The available space for the Re:Start Mall was located next to one of Christchurch's iconic retailers, Ballantynes (see Finsterwalder and Grey, Chapter 9, this volume), which integrated its store into the container mall (Figure 15.1). Due to permanent structures being established on parts of the space of the Re:Start Mall in 2014,

Figure 15.1 Re:Start Mall.

Source: Photograph by Jörg Finsterwalder

Figure 15.2 Relocated Re:Start Mall.
Source: Photograph by C. Michael Hall

the structure allowed for parts of the containers to be shifted to new locations (Figure 15.2).

The success of the mall as part of the rebuild has also raised questions as to whether it will be moved again to another site as the rebuild continues. In April 2015 property developer Antony Gough stated he would offer 1000 m² of land to house the Re:Start mall near his new central city development, The Terrace, for at least a further ten years. However, the long-term future of the mall is controversial as while present tenants are in favour of retaining the mall in some form, other central city tenants in permanent developments have indicated that they do not want the competition (Meier 2015). Lichfield Holdings developer Nick Hunt said that the Re:Start mall should go once permanent buildings were completed and he did not expect to have to compete with the Re:Start for tenants: 'The whole idea was for the Re:Start to maintain the central city as a retail area on a temporary basis. That was the basis for my decisions and for a lot of other people's decision making' (quoted in Meier 2015). However, the nature of the Re:Start mall structure enables it to move from one temporary space to another, allowing it to take advantage of the availability of space over time during the rebuild process. One possibility in the longer term, of course, is that the extended use of a temporary space may become permanent because of consumer demand, the financial success of the project and/or the lack of a viable economic alternative.

Figure 15.3 Pallet Pavilion and arches.
Source: Photograph by Jörg Finsterwalder

The nature of a space can also enable the hosting of a variety of different service-scapes on one site. For example, through the initiative of the Gap Filler project, a Pallet Pavilion was established on the site of the former Crown Plaza Hotel in late 2012 with the help of volunteers using thousands of used wooden packaging pallets painted in blue (https://www.youtube.com/watch?v=ibO-Xi_HRGQ). This pavilion was used to host events until it was deconstructed in early 2014 (see Figure 15.3).

As a follow-on project, volunteers established other impermanent art installations in the form of arches (see Figure 15.3 left side). Both the pallet pavilion and the arches existed simultaneously in the same space for some time.

On the temporality of urban scapes

The use of impermanent servicescapes in Christchurch as part of the recovery process and the economic regeneration of the CBD following the earthquakes allowed for interim usage of a structure in a space which awaited rebuild activities. A pop-up structure can be a substituted in a different location for an existing structure which had become unusable for a certain period of time. A temporary servicescape can alter its shape to suit the changes in available space. Moreover, a servicescape's lifespan can be designed flexibly with the knowledge that it is temporary from the outset, including with respect to whether it is a one-off use or may be required to be reusable. For example the Re:Start Mall can, and has, changed location depending on the space available and its relocatability, yet maintaining many of its servicescape characteristics. The Re:Start Mall is a good example of the fluidity of a servicescape as the scape itself can be changed and altered (see Figures 15.1 and 15.2). The shipping containers are stackable and easily relocatable and hence different shapes of servicescapes can be designed and assembled while retaining their design integrity.

The temporal dimension of servicescapes helps capture the "fluidity of scape", in that the transitional servicescape as such is rather "liquid" as it can usually be disassembled and reassembled or changed in a short timeframe. There is also the possibility of "fluidity of scape across spaces", as in the case of the Re:Start Mall, if the scape is "liquid" across locations and can be adapted to a new destination.

Examples

As a one-off transitional servicescape, the central city saw a football field established for a limited period of time near one of the main hotels (Figure 15.4). Another example was Smash Palace, an initiative of a bar owner whose bar was destroyed during the 2011 earthquakes (http://thesmashpalace.co.nz/). Unlike other bar and hospitality rebuilds that occurred on the same site they previously occupied, Smash Palace is a deliberately flexible and relocatable servicescape in form of a former school bus turned into a bar. The owner occupies vacant spaces and relocates the bar when the occupied space is about to be converted to fit a permanent structure. Since its inception, Smash Palace has found its third location. Figure 15.5 shows the bar in its second space. Smash Palace is a good example for a very high level of "fluidity of the scape across spaces" as it is mobile and relocatable but essentially the same servicescape, i.e. the bus can be driven elsewhere and set up in a new vacant space. The mobility of a businesses with a significant loyal following is valuable not only to the business itself but also the locations to

Figure 15.4 Transitional football field servicescape.

Source: Photograph by Jörg Finsterwalder

Figure 15.5 Smash Palace at its second location.

Source: Photograph by Jörg Finsterwalder

Figure 15.6 Dance-o-Mat transitional servicescape.

Source: Photograph by Jörg Finsterwalder

which it moves as it can help bring people back to spaces that have not been able to be used for several years as a result of rebuild activity. In so doing, such flexible businesses, as with activities like farmers' markets, can also help provide custom for their surrounds (Hall et al. 2008; Hall 2013c).

A similar portable idea is the Dance-o-Mat, a project that provides an outdoor dance floor, four speakers and a washing-machine-turned-music-player, where enthusiasts can plug in their smartphones and for some small change can play their music via the speaker system and dance on the concrete dance floor. This project has been relocated several times because the vacant spaces have been gradually occupied by permanent structures. Figure 15.6 shows the Dance-o-Mat at its second location.

A temporary scape can be used as a substitute for a structure in a different location if the permanent but damaged structure has not yet been removed from

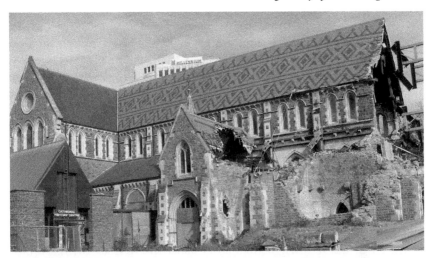

Figure 15.7 Damaged Christchurch Cathedral (above) and transitional servicescape Cardboard Cathedral (below) in different spaces.

Source: Photograph by Jörg Finsterwalder

its original space. Based on his previous work, Japanese architect Shigeru Ban designed a cathedral made out of cardboard, containers and plastic to temporarily replace the heavily damaged Christ Church Cathedral. Figure 15.7 upper part shows the damaged Christ Church Cathedral in its original location and the transitional servicescape Cardboard Cathedral in a different location (lower part of Figure 15.7).

Conclusions

The theoretical underpinning of the concept of transitional servicescapes and servicespaces shows different options of fluidity of scape and space that are hallmarks of urban regeneration, whether they be brownfield or post-disaster sites. Examples from post-earthquake urban Christchurch demonstrate that different scapes and spaces were used as part of the renewal process, with temporary spaces being used to increase or maintain use values that would otherwise be diminished, especially in the initial recovery and response phase. Temporary transitional servicescapes therefore helped utilise space and provide for commercial transition from one stage of post-disaster reconstruction to another. The role of transitional servicescapes in the Christchurch rebuild is therefore arguably as much a strategy for property-led urban regeneration as is the broader redevelopment plan for the CBD and its precinctification (see Amore and Hall, Chapter 12, this volume). The difference is that much of the use of transitional servicescapes in Christchurch was relatively bottom-up in initiation (Wesener 2015). Furthermore, it could be argued that the specific earthquake context of Christchurch also shaped the role of temporary servicescapes. A prolonged aftershock sequence and associated uncertainty, risk aversion by insurers and rebuild bureaucracy may also have ensured that transitional servicescapes were utilised longer than one might expect in other post-disaster contexts.

Although many of the temporary community-driven initiatives for the use of space were undoubtedly driven by a desire to help maintain people's relationship to the CBD as a place, they nevertheless acted to serve economic and commercial goals as well. Indeed, a longer-term issue with respect to community-initiated use of post-disaster space is how this fits into market-directed planning strategies (Gotham and Greenberg 2014) so that the vitality they bring to a location is not lost as the city is rebuilt. Arguably the required approach may simply be one of good design, i.e. ensuring that public spaces and squares are incorporated into urban design practice (Carmona 2014), and good governance, i.e. ensuring that the space is genuinely public and can be utilised for markets, exhibits and events that are art- and community-based rather than commercial and fee-paying. Regardless of their rationale and motivation, the role of temporality of servicescape remains an underdeveloped and under-researched area in the understanding of place and especially business districts post-disaster that needs further exploration.

This chapter has focused on the spatio-temporal dimension of scape and space without including the *temporality of usage of existing scapes or spaces*. For example, the '"empty spaces" movements to occupy abandoned buildings for a range of purposes' (Iveson 2013: 941) was neglected. Furthermore, actors as an important part of the servicescape has only been lightly touched on in this work. In this context Schwarz and Rugare (2009: 5) write of 'temporary users'. Future research needs to refine and verify the variations of temporary and transitional servicescapes and expand on these concepts.

Finally, the notion of transitional servicescapes raises broader questions of understanding change in the city, and especially in areas affected by rapid change, as in the case of natural disasters or even industry closure. We are transitioning from what to what? Change, even rapid change, is part of the lifecourses of cities and urban areas. Yet many of the common understandings of place are surprisingly static unless challenged by events such as the Christchurch earthquakes. Scapes are integral to the development of a deeper understanding of place and individuals' sense of place. To what extent may transitional servicescapes serve to cushion the effects of change and the impacts of solastalgia, the psychological impact of rapid environmental change? This is especially significant given that many of the transitional servicescapes in the Christchurch CBD allowed a reengagement of people with the (lost) spaces of the city as well as providing for continued consumption in what was the retail, nightlife and business heart of the region.

References

Aldrich, R. (1966) 'The development of "-scape"', *American Speech*, 41(2): 155–157.

Anastasopoulos, N. (2003) 'Time-based architecture: Techniques of time, ephemeral structures: Eternal moments or monumental eternities', *Archis Magazine*, 2: 34–37.

Arnould, E. J., Price, L. and Tierney, P. (1998) 'The wilderness servicescape: An ironic commercial landscape', in J. F. Sherry (ed.) *Servicescapes: The Concept of Place in Contemporary Markets,* Chicago: NTC/Contemporary Publishing.

Arnould, E. J. and Thompson, C. (2005) 'Consumer culture theory (CCT): Twenty years of research', *Journal of Consumer Research*, 31(4): 868–882.

Aubert-Gamet, V. (1996) 'Twisting servicescapes: Diversion of the physical environment in a re-appropriation process', *International Journal of Service Industry Management*, 8(1): 26–41.

Austin, D. (1983) *The Portable City,* Vancouver: Arsenal Editions.

Ban, S. (2015) *Disaster Relief Projects.* Online. Available HTTP: <http://www.shigeru banarchitects.com/works.html#disaster-relief-projects> (Accessed 10 June 2015).

Ban, S. and Shodhan, K. (2003) 'Paper-tube housing', *Perspecta*, 34: 154–159.

Bishop, P. and Williams, L. (2012) *The Temporary City,* London: Routledge.

Bitner, M. J. (1992) 'Servicescapes: The impact of the physical surroundings on customers and employees', *Journal of Marketing,* 56(2): 57–71.

——(2000) 'The Servicescape', in T. Swartz and D. Iacobucci (eds.) *Handbook of Services Marketing and Management.* Thousand Oaks: Sage.

Blumner, N. (2006) *Planning for the Unplanned: Tools and Techniques for Interim Use in Germany and the United States.* Berlin, Deutsches Institut für Urbanistik. Online. Available HTTP: <http://www.difu.de/dokument/planning-for-theunplanned-tools-and-techniques-for-interim.html#3> (Accessed 10 June 2015).

Bonnemaison, S. (1990) 'City policies and cyclical events', in *Celebrations Urban Spaces Transformed*, Design Quarterly 147, Cambridge: Massachusetts Institute of Technology for the Walker Art Center.

Booms, B. and Bitner, M. J. (1981) 'Marketing strategies and organizational structures for service firms', in J. Donnelly and W. George (eds.) *Marketing of Services,* Chicago: American Marketing Association.

Brüggen, E., Foubert, B. and Gremler, D. (2011) 'Extreme makeover: Short- and long-term effects of a remodelled servicescape', *Journal of Marketing*, 75(September): 71–87.

Caballero, D. (2013) *Filling the Gap: The Effect of Temporary Environments on Deteriorated Cities*, Syracuse, Syracuse University. Online. Available HTTP: <http://surface.syr.edu/cgi/viewcontent.cgi?article=1225&context=architecture_tpreps> (Accessed 10 June 2015).

Carmona, M. (2014) 'Re-theorising contemporary public space: A new narrative and a new normative', *Journal of Urbanism: International Research on Placemaking and Urban Sustainability*, doi:10.1080/17549175.2014.909518

CCDU (2015) *Popular Container Mall on the Move*. Online. Available HTTP: <https://ccdu.govt.nz/our-progress/announcements/popular-container-mall-on-the-move-6-march-2014> (Accessed 10 June 2015).

Chabrowe, B. (1974) 'On the significance of temporary architecture', *The Burlington Magazine*, 116(856): 385–391.

Clarke, I. and Schmidt, R. (1995) 'Beyond the servicescape: The experience of place', *Journal of Retailing and Consumer Services*, 2(3): 149–162.

Coar, L. (2011) 'The lasting meaning in ephemeral architecture', *Design Principles & Practice: An International Journal*, 5(6): 667–678.

Colomb, C. (2012) 'Pushing the urban frontier: Temporary uses of space, city marketing, and the creative city discourse in 2000s Berlin', *Journal of Urban Affairs*, 34(2): 131–152.

Comerio, M. (1997) 'Housing issues after disasters', *Journal of Contingencies and Crisis Management*, 5(3): 166–178.

Comerio, M. (1998) *Disaster Hits Home. New Policy for Urban Housing Recovery*, Berkeley: University of California Press.

Couch, C. and Fraser, C. (2003) 'Introduction: The European context and theoretical framework', in C. Couch, C. Fraser and S. Percy (eds.) *Urban Regeneration in Europe*, Oxford: Blackwell Science.

Cox, D. and Reese, L. (2007) 'Natural disasters, local economic development and the chocolate city', paper prepared for the Annual Meeting American Society for Public Administration, Washington DC, March. East Lansing: Michigan State University.

De Nisco, A. and Warnaby, G. (2013) 'Shopping in downtown: The effect of urban environment on service quality perception and behavioural intentions', *International Journal of Retail & Distribution Management*, 41(9): 654–670.

Debenedetti, A. and Oppewal, H. (2009) 'Place attachment and the consumption of servicescapes', in S. Luxton (ed.) *Proceedings of the Australian & New Zealand Marketing Academy (ANZMAC) Conference 2009, Sustainable Management and Marketing*. Melbourne, 30 November–2 December 2009.

Donovan, R. and Rossiter, J. (1982) 'Store atmosphere: An environmental psychological approach', *Journal of Retailing*, 58: 34–57.

Dovey, K. (2010) *Becoming Places: Urbanism / Architecture / Identity / Power*, Abingdon: Routledge.

——(2014) 'The temporary city', *Journal of Urban Design*, 19(2): 261–263.

El-Anwar, O. and Chen, L. (2014) 'Maximizing the computational efficiency of temporary housing decision support following disasters', *Journal of Computing in Civil Engineering*, 28(1): 113–123.

Finn, D. (2014) 'DIY urbanism: Implications for cities', *Journal of Urbanism: International Research on Placemaking and Urban Sustainability*, 7(4): 381–398.

Garr, D. J. (2001) 'Disaster recovery in a progressive community: Santa Cruz, California', in M. A. Burayidi (eds.) *Downtowns: Revitalizing the Centers of Small Urban Communities*. New York: Routledge.

Glade, P. (2011) *Black Rock City, NV: The Ephemeral Architecture of Burning Man*, San Francisco: Real Paper Books.

Gold, D. L. (2002) 'English nouns and verbs ending in -scape', *Revista alicantina de estudios ingleses*, 15: 79–94.

Gotham, K. F. and Greenberg, M. (2014) *Crisis Cities: Disaster and Redevelopment in New York and New Orleans*, Oxford: Oxford University Press.

Grayson, K. (1998) 'Commercial activity at home: Managing the private services-cape', in J. F. Sherry (ed.) *Servicescapes: The Concept of Place in Contemporary Markets*, Chicago: NTC/Contemporary Publishing Company.

Greco, J. (2012) 'From pop-up to permanent', *Planning*, 78(9): 14–18.

Guliz, G. and Belk, R. W. (1996) 'I'd like to buy the world a Coke: Consumption-scapes in the less affluent world', *Journal of Consumer Policy*, 19: 271–304.

Hall, C. M. (2008) 'Servicescapes, designscapes, branding and the creation of place-identity: South of Litchfield, Christchurch', *Journal of Travel and Tourism Marketing*, 25(3/4): 233–250.

——(2009) 'Sharing space with visitors: The servicescape of the commercial exurban home', in P. Lynch, A. McIntosh and H. Tucker (eds.) *The Commercial Home*, London: Routledge.

——(2013a) 'Regeneration and cultural quarters: Changing urban cultural space', in M. Smith and G. Richards (eds.) *The Routledge Handbook of Cultural Tourism*, Abingdon: Routledge.

——(2013b) 'The ecological and environmental significance of urban wastelands and drosscapes', in M. J. Zapata Campos and C. M. Hall (eds.) *Organising Waste in the City. International Perspectives on Narratives and Practices*, Bristol: Policy Press.

——(2013c) 'The local in farmers markets in New Zealand', in C. M. Hall and S. Gössling (eds.) *Sustainable Culinary Systems: Local Foods, Innovation, and Tourism & Hospitality*, Abingdon: Routledge.

——(2014) 'Mobile second homes or cheap permanent homes? The problematic fluidity of caravans and motor homes as second homes', paper presented at *New Perspectives on Second Homes*, 9–11 June 2014, Stockholm, Sweden.

——(2015) 'Second homes: Planning, policy and governance', *Journal of Policy Research in Tourism, Leisure & Events*, 7(1): 1–14.

——(2016) Heirloom products in heritage places: Farmers Markets, local food, and food diversity', in D. Timothy (ed.) *Heritage Cuisines: Traditions, Identities and Tourism*, Abingdon: Routledge.

Hall, C. M., Mitchell. R., Scott, D. and Sharples, L. (2008) 'The authentic market experiences of farmers' markets', in C. M. Hall and L. Sharples (eds.) *Food and Wine Festivals and Events Around the World: Development, Management and Markets*, Oxford: Butterworth Heinemann.

Hall, C. M., Tipler, J., Reddy, R. and Rowling, K. (2010) 'Coffee servicescapes: The design of café culture in New Zealand', in L. Joliffe (ed.) *Coffee Culture, Destinations and Tourism*, Bristol: Channelview.

Haydn, F. and Temel, R. (eds.) (2006) *Temporary Urban Spaces: Concepts for the Use of City Spaces*, Berlin: Birkhäuser.

Holopainen, M. (2010) 'Exploring service design in the context of architecture', *The Service Industries Journal*, 30(4): 597–608.

Iveson, K. (2013) 'Cities within the city: Do-it-yourself urbanism and the right to the city', *International Journal of Urban and Regional Research*, 37(3): 941–956.

Jessop, B. and Sum, N. L. (2001) 'Pre-disciplinary and post-disciplinary perspectives', *New Political Economy*, 6: 89–101.

Jodidio, P. (2011) *Temporary Architecture Now!* Cologne: Taschen Verlag.

Johnson, C. (2007a) 'Impacts of prefabricated temporary housing after disasters: 1999 earthquakes in Turkey', *Habitat International*, 31(1): 36–52.

——(2007b) 'Strategic planning for post-disaster temporary housing', *Disasters*, 31(4): 435–458.

Johnstone, M. (2012) 'The servicescape: The social dimensions of place', *Journal of Marketing Management*, 28(11/12): 1399–1418.

Julier, G. (2005) 'Urban designscapes and the production of aesthetic consent', *Urban Studies*, 42(5/6): 869–887.

Kent, T. (2007) 'Creative space: Design and the retail environment', *International Journal of Retail and Distribution Management*, 35(9), 734–745.

Kiib, H. (2013) *Instant City Design*, Aalborg: Dansk Arkitektur Center. Online. Available HTTP: <http://vbn.aau.dk/ws/files/76587608/Instant_City_Design_ Small.pdf> (Accessed 10 June 2015).

Kotler, P. (1973) 'Atmospherics as a marketing tool', *Journal of Retailing*, 49: 48–64.

Kronenburg, R. (2003) 'Introduction', in R. Kronenburg (ed.) *Portable Architecture* (3rd ed.), Oxford: Elsevier.

Lähdesmäki, T. (2013) 'Pop-up architecture as urban revitalization', in 4th Global Conference – Space and Place, University of Oxford, 9–12 September 2013. Online. Available HTTP: <http://www.inter-disciplinary.net/critical-issues/ wp-content/uploads/2013/09/L%C3%A4hdesm%C3%A4ki-SP4-2013.pdf> (Accessed 10 June 2015).

Leitner, B. (2011) *Temporary Architecture,* Stuttgart: AVEdition.

Leupen, B. and van Zwol, J. (2005) *Time-Based Architecture,* Rotterdam: 010 Publishers.

Mannakkara, S. and Wilkinson, S. (2014) 'Re-conceptualising "Building Back Better" to improve post-disaster recovery', *International Journal of Managing Projects in Business*, 7(3): 327–341.

McArthur, H. (2012) 'Regenerating the urban landscape. An architectural journey through fallow time'. Unpublished masters thesis, Carleton University, Ottawa.

McFarlane, C. (2011) 'Encountering, describing and transforming urbanism: Concluding reflections on assemblage and urban criticality', *City,* 15(6): 731–739.

McIntosh, J. (2013) 'The implications of post disaster recovery for affordable housing', in J. Tiefenbacher (ed.) *Approaches to Disaster Management – Examining the Implications of Hazards, Emergencies and Disasters.* Rijeka, Croatia: InTech. Online. Available HTTP: <http://www.intechopen.com/books/approaches-to-disaster-management-examining-the-implications-of-hazards-emergencies-and-disasters/ the-implications-of-post-disaster-recovery-for-affordable-housing> (Accessed 10 June 2015).

McQuaid, M. (2003) *Shigeru Ban.* New York: Phaidon Press.

Meier, C. (2015) 'Re:Start mall in Christchurch may stay another 10 years', *The Press,* 23 April. Online. Available HTTP: <http://www.stuff.co.nz/business/small-business/67962367/Re-Start-mall-in-Christchurch-may-stay-another-10-years> (Accessed 24 April 2015).

Mouclier, C. (2010) 'Injecting architecture in the post-earthquake reconstruction phase? Temporary architecture within the shelter phase', thesis, Politecnico di Milano, Milan.

O'Dell, T. (2005) 'Experiencescapes: Blurring borders and testing connections', in T. O'Dell and P. Billing (eds.) *Experiencescapes: Tourism, Culture and Economy,* Copenhagen: Copenhagen Business School Press.

Oswalt, P., Overmeyer, K. and Misselwitz, P. (2013) *Urban Catalyst,* Berlin: DOM Publishers.

Pallagst, K., Aber, J., Audirac, I., Cunningham-Sabot, E., Fol, S., Martinez-Fernandez, C., Moraes, S., Mulligan, H., Vargas-Hernandez, J., Wiechmann, T., Wu, T. and Rich, J. (eds.) (2009) *The Future of Shrinking Cities: Problems, Patterns and Strategies of Urban Transformation in a Global Context,* Institute of Urban & Regional Development Monograph Series, Berkeley: Institute of Urban & Regional Development, University of California Los Angeles.

Pareigis, J., Echeverri, P. and Edvardsson, B. (2012) 'Exploring internal mechanisms forming customer servicescape experiences', *Journal of Service Management,* 23(5): 1–35.

Parish, J., Berry, L. and Lam, S. (2008) 'The effect of the servicescape on service workers', *Journal of Service Research,* 10(3): 220–238.

Parr, W. (2013) 'Investigating the role of temporary land uses in the Christchurch earthquake recovery', unpublished masters thesis, University of Otago, Dunedin.

Porter, L. and Shaw, K. (eds.) (2013) *Whose Urban Renaissance? An International Comparison of Urban Regeneration Strategies,* Abingdon: Routledge.

Preston, S. and Bank, L. (2012) 'Portals to an architecture: Design of a temporary structure with paper tube arches', *Construction and Building Materials,* 30: 657–666.

Reese, L. (2006) 'Economic versus natural disasters: If Detroit had a hurricane . . . ', *Economic Development Quarterly,* 20(3): 219–231.

Reimer, A. and Kuehn, R. (2005) 'The impact of servicescape on quality perception', *European Journal of Marketing,* 39(7/8): 785–808.

Rosenbaum, M. (2006) 'Exploring the social supportive role of third places in consumers' lives', *Journal of Service Research,* 9(1): 59–72.

Rosenbaum, M. and Massiah, C. (2011) 'An expanded servicescape perspective', *Journal of Service Management,* 22(4): 471–490.

Rosenbaum, M. S. and Smallwood, J. (2013) 'Cancer resource centers as third places', *Journal of Services Marketing,* 27(6): 472–484.

Rosenbaum, M., Sweeney, J. and Smallwood, J. (2011) 'Restorative cancer resource center servicescapes', *Managing Service Quality: An International Journal,* 21(6): 599–616.

Ruoppila, S. (2004) 'Eastern European cities in the making – temporary land use as a tool for cultural projects', *Journal for Northeast Issues,* 3: 24–26. Online. Available HTTP: <http://www.kaupunkikettu.fi/temporary2004.html (Accessed 10 June 2015).

Saraçoğlu, C. and Demirtaş-Milz, N. (2014) 'Disasters as an ideological strategy for governing neoliberal urban transformation in Turkey: Insights from Izmir/Kadifekale', *Disasters,* 38(1), 178–201.

Schwarz, T. and Rugare, S. (2009) *Pop up City,* Urban Infill, Vol. 2, Ohio: Kent State University.

Sherry, J. F., Jr. (ed.) (1998a) *Servicescapes: The Concept of Place in Contemporary Markets,* Lincolnwood: Nike Town Chicago Business Books.

——(1998b) 'The soul of the company store: Nike Town Chicago and the emplaced brandscape', in J. F. Sherry, Jr. (ed.) *Servicescapes: The Concept of Place in Contemporary Markets,* Lincolnwood: Nike Town Chicago Business Books.

Siegal, J. (ed.) (2002) *Mobile: The Art of Portable Architecture*, Princeton: Princeton Architectural Press.

Spielmann, N., Laroche, M. and Borges, A. (2012) 'How service seasons the experience: Measuring hospitality servicescapes', *International Journal of Hospitality Management*, 31(2): 360–368.

Tardiveau, A. and Mallo, D. (2014) 'Unpacking and challenging habitus: An approach to temporary urbanism as a socially engaged practice', *Journal of Urban Design*, 19(4): 456–472.

Teder, M. (2011) 'Transitional use – approaching temporary spatial gaps in urban landscapes'. European Network on Housing Research (ENHR) Conference, 5–8 July 2011, Toulouse, France, University of Toulouse. Online. Available HTTP: <http://www.enhr2011.com/sites/default/files/Paper-Maria%20Teder-02-03.pdf (Accessed 10 June 2015).

Till, K. (2011) 'Interim use at a former death strip? Art, politics and urbanism at Skulpturenpark Berlin-Zentrum', in M. Silberman (ed.) *The German Wall; Fallout in Europe*, Basingstoke: Palgrave Macmillan.

Tombs, A. G. and McColl-Kennedy, J. (2003) 'Social-servicescape conceptual model', *Marketing Theory*, 3(4): 447–475.

——(2010) 'Social and spatial influence of customers on other customers in the social-servicescape', *Australian Marketing Journal*, 18(3): 120–131.

Veresiu, E. and Giesler, M. (2012) 'Ethnic entrepreneurship: Creating an identity-enhancing assemblage of public and private servicescapes in the global city', in R. Ahluwalia, T. Chartrand and R. Ratner (eds.) *Advances in Consumer Research, Building Connections 2011*, Vol. 39, Duluth: Association for Consumer Research.

Wakefield, K. and Blodgett, J. (1996) 'The effect of the servicescape on customers' behavioural intentions in leisure service settings', *The Journal of Service Marketing*, 10(6): 45–61.

Warnaby, G. (2013) 'Synchronising retail and space: Using urban squares for competitive place differentiation', *Consumption, Markets and Culture*, 16(1): 25–44.

Wesener, A. (2015) 'Temporary urbanism and urban sustainability after a natural disaster: Transitional community-initiated open spaces in Christchurch, New Zealand', *Journal of Urbanism: International Research on Placemaking and Urban Sustainability*, doi:10.1080/17549175.2015.1061040

Part V
Conclusions

16 Undertaking business, consumer and organisational research in a post-disaster setting

C. Michael Hall, Sanna Malinen,
Venkataraman Nilakant, Rob Vosslamber,
Bernard Walker and Russell Wordsworth

One area of post-disaster research that is substantially underreported and studied is the actual process of undertaking research in a disaster and post-disaster setting. Researcher reflections on the research process are extremely limited in the rapidly growing social science literature on crisis, disasters, and the accompanying recovery stages (Tierney 2007; Hall 2010; van Heugten 2014). Undertaking research on disasters is not just a case of being aware of sensitive topics for individuals, but also needing to be aware that, as a researcher, one is also operating in a sensitive physical and political environment (Reed 2012). Arguably this is even more the case for social scientists, as opposed to engineers, geologists, and health researchers who, in the case of many natural disasters, have an "obvious" justification for doing *in situ* research. The role of social scientists will often not be so clear to many agencies and policy makers, at least not in the short term, thereby potentially creating a significant set of personal and institutional research challenges (O'Mathúna 2012). Disaster situations are often regarded as providing a "unique laboratory" in which to explore behaviour and change through a different lens (e.g. Arnold et al. 1982; Forthergill 1998; Shoaf et al. 2004; Fussell and Elliott 2009). But what are the ethics of gaining from the suffering of others?

In many ways social science research in disaster settings possibly has much in common with the conduct of research in conflict settings (Ford et al. 2009; El-Khani et al. 2013; Jayawickrama 2013) and public and humanitarian emergencies (Tansey et al. 2010; de Jong et al. 2011; Tehrani 2011; O'Mathúna et al. 2014). It therefore brings with it special ethical and safety challenges, as well as a desire to produce relevant results, such as the chapters in this book. In addition, unlike research in the health sciences, and perhaps to a lesser extent in the physical sciences, there are often few research programmes running before a disaster event at an appropriate scale providing good, robust and relevant, pre- and post-event data sets. The one exception for this is some very general economic and business data, yet the spatial scale of such information, i.e. at a national level, may still not provide a good match for the business impact of disaster events.

Unlike physical or health science research, social science research is open to a much wider range of research paradigms and approaches. Nevertheless, there is potential, if not the likelihood, that post-disaster social science research will also produce results which may be inherently contested not only by other researchers but also by policy makers and those responsible for disaster management in the short term, and the recovery process in the longer term. Yet, as the various chapters in this book suggest, social science research can have an enormously positive role in assisting individuals, organisations, businesses, policy-makers and places in post-disaster recovery.

Undertaking research in post-disaster contexts is much more than doing research in the "real world" (Gray 2014). For whoever directly experienced the Christchurch earthquakes and their aftermath – as all the authors did – the disaster event and the response and recovery period are probably better described as initially "unreal" or even "hyperreal" in terms of the effects on their personal lives, encounters with others, working life, careers and, of course, research. Then, in time, the earthquakes became part of the lifecourse and came to be seen, as the Christchurch saying goes, as "the new normal". We survive. We adapt. Life goes on. (This is sometimes also called "resilience" by outsiders or people trying make positive statements – one of us wanted to have a T-shirt made up with "Please stop calling me resilient" on it!). And then it's time to do research on the experience.

The purpose of this chapter is to draw on the experiences of the authors in carrying out research in the post-earthquake environment of Christchurch and the surrounding region. As a result the style of this chapter is more personal and reflective than other chapters in the book and relies more heavily on personal insights than published works, although relevant literature will be noted where significant. The lessons learned are presented thematically, with particular insights and issues provided as boxed text. The individual source(s) of the observations and reflections are anonymised; it should be emphasised that although we take collective responsibility for the chapter, its contents are not presented as a consensus as we have different experiences and perspectives.

Dealing with stakeholders

Conducting research in the post-disaster setting involved a complex set of interactions among numerous individuals and groups. It meant dealing with a range of stakeholders, including disaster-affected individuals, leaders of organisations, government agencies and external funders. Each had its own agenda and this produced both tensions and areas of collaboration between the groups and with researchers.

Although these dynamics are typical of other research settings, the complexity was exacerbated by the urgency of the needs of the individuals and groups in the disaster-affected areas. This was a community experiencing a sustained period of continuing aftershocks, extreme stress and ongoing change and uncertainty. The community desired very immediate assistance. Information was of value to them when it could inform the emergency response, address their pressing needs and aid them in handling the uncertainty of the unfamiliar world of recovery.

In contrast, some of us were involved in research which partly overlapped and partly clashed with stakeholder needs. We were following a process that investigated aspects of their situation, but that process had longer timeframes, with the systematic analysis and rigour of research, as well as sharing and writing our findings for different audiences. At times this situation could facilitate research opportunities, while at other times it only served to heighten the barriers and problems. A number of issues emerged from this situation.

Timelines and tensions

One of the most significant research challenges with sudden-onset disasters is that they are usually unexpected. From a research perspective, the situation they present is unique and there is only a narrow "window" in which to develop a research design and gather data. This means disasters are important for academic research in terms of documenting and analysing the situation, given that disasters tend to have relatively long intervals between reoccurrence (longer than many living personal or organisational memories). Thus there was a perceived need (which was supported by a number of co-ordinating agencies) to do research with scholarly written outcomes. Nevertheless, there is tension between this scholarly research and the desire to intervene to assist the disaster-affected communities directly in the immediate moment – what might be termed 'researcher versus consultant/helper tension'. Furthermore, this leads to differing agendas and outcomes, with academic research tending to be a longer-term process, intended for the good of other disaster situations and future generations. Such concerns also raise interesting and complicated issues with respect to intellectual property because there are tensions between making findings available early for the benefit of locals versus the need to safeguard intellectual property with the aim of making it available for international outlets.

Another dimension of the timing challenge is related to research funding. A disaster does not necessarily occur at a convenient time that matches regular research funding rounds that occur on a yearly or two-yearly basis, and there may be months or years until the next funding round becomes available. This has significant implications for funders around creating rapid responses and flexibility for disaster-related funding, including how they handle ethical considerations, as well as implications for researchers in learning how to create business cases for funding.

Issues of timing

One of the key issues I came across in my PhD was when exactly to collect data. While I understand that most often this will be dictated by the nature of the research question/project, I did come across some common issues. While it is desirable to collect data as soon as possible following a disaster, this is not always possible or ideal. Our circumstances were exacerbated by the fact that we were not dealing with a "static" disaster but rather an ongoing, unfolding and uncertain set of circumstances, and this made the timing

(*Continued*)

of data collection a little difficult. In my case, I chose to delay data collection significantly (18 months after the first earthquake in September 2010) in order to capture the full and cumulative impacts of the ongoing situation. This, however, raised concerns regarding memory decay and recall bias, and also sample selection (see, for example, van den Berg et al. 2012). I was able to address some of these concerns with counter arguments and evidence that delayed self-reports of traumatic events often demonstrate remarkable stability and reliability over time (see, for example, Norris and Kaniasty 1992; Lee et al. 1999; Norris et al. 2002; Krinsley et al. 2003).

The interface between practitioner-initiated forums and formal research

We had to work in parallel with various locally initiated gatherings of practitioners or business groups, comprising people such as organisational leaders, Human Resources, and welfare staff who initially wanted to informally share their experiences and create their own ways of learning about disaster and recovery. This continued to varying degrees, with some even conducting their own debriefings months or years later. There were challenges around managing those interfaces, and for us as researchers there were important issues around discovering how to utilise synergies when those did not come easily, given the differing agendas. Associated with this are issues around survey fatigue as those informal forums engaged in their own, very loosely structured, data gathering exercises using low-level, descriptive semi-surveys, collecting information from members about their circumstances. When our research commenced, this created difficulties as organisational leaders felt that they had already shared their accounts through those informal information-sharing processes.

This situation is also linked to issues around timeframes and tensions between consultancy versus long-term formal research. Initially the practitioner groups and organisations were looking for immediacy and instant advice. Their own semi-formal meetings involved information-sharing sessions that provided very immediate information for members, learning from each other and gaining reinforcement from knowing that others were encountering similar issues and approaching them in similar ways. In contrast, our research timeframes were measured in weeks or months in the early projects, and this turned into months or years with the larger project. There was a tension between organisations' expectations of instant answers and our systematic processes of data gathering and in-depth analysis.

The number and types of other parties involved

In undertaking post-disaster research in a business and organisational setting, there tends to be a wide range of stakeholders and interested parties. For example, in the human resource area this includes the loose associations mentioned earlier – of business leaders, groups of human resource staff, and welfare workers, as well as employees – meeting together to learn from each other and gain support from knowing others are dealing with similar challenges. These groups typically were seeking rapid answers, advice and support from researchers. Similar clusters of individuals came together in a range of organisational specialisations such as finance, accounting, marketing, information technology and communication.

Researchers operating in a post-disaster setting should, however, take cognisance of the fact there will be a plethora of others doing research of various sorts which may intersect with their own research in various ways, including with respect to *research fatigue* (discussed below). In addition to the local forums, this other research might include brief descriptive data gathered by nationwide professional bodies and business groups (surveying their members and/or other organisations), school and tertiary student projects, formal academic research by external tertiary researchers (internationally and from elsewhere in New Zealand) and specialist centres (e.g. centres for small business studies), as well as specialist researchers in their own fields, including education and health. In the background, emergency services such as the Fire Service (NZFS), disaster agencies such as the Canterbury Earthquake Recovery Authority (CERA) and the Ministry of Civil Defence and Emergency Management (MCDEM), and other central government organisations, along with regional and local councils (see for example Vallance 2015), were all doing their own retrospective formal reviews of the disaster response, and gathering information about the situation in the recovery phase.

This meant that there were a variety of *overlapping and competing* activities these other parties engaged in, ranging from information gathering, to bringing in external experts as advisors, and even creating their own advisory resources (booklets and websites) in the subsequent months/years after the disaster events as retrospective learning to assist in future disasters. All of these overlapped to some degree with academic research, and in some areas duplicated it. Researchers also had to work amidst a *lack of co-ordination* and awareness of different groups regarding each others' activities, although there were government and other official attempts to deal with this. For example, controls were placed on the capacity and nature of research being undertaken in the first months following the earthquakes. According to van Heugten (2014) when writing of her experiences with respect to human service organisation research post-earthquake:

> Much of the social science research in Christchurch has been undertaken by or advised on by so-called insiders. This may be somewhat unusual and, in part, reflects the number of tertiary institutions based in the city. In addition, following the February 2011 earthquake, the national controller for the civil

emergency placed a moratorium on the undertaking of research that could not be shown to be immediately beneficial to the emergency response.

(van Heugten 2014: 8)

The moratorium lasted for the duration of the national emergency and Van Heugten suggests that this may have prevented international researchers from initiating research before locals were able to regroup sufficiently to do so (see also Crothers 2011).

The rather unusual official constraints that were placed on research in the immediate aftermath of the February 2011 earthquake were imposed to protect disaster-affected people. The *Review of the Civil Defence Emergency Management Response to the 22 February Christchurch Earthquake* provides some valuable insights into the advantages and disadvantages of such an approach:

> During the response, social science researchers were banned from interviewing people affected by the earthquake. This was done in a desire to avoid extra stress for people suffering ongoing trauma caused by living in damaged homes without sanitation, and with their normal activities, social contacts and communications disrupted. In addition, some extra stress was being imposed by the multiplicity of agencies, official and unofficial, calling and offering help to families in a largely uncoordinated manner. Such a ban was a highly unusual occurrence, and may have meant that some important information available shortly after the disaster was lost. In the case of physical sciences, efforts were made to gather such time sensitive information (such as on liquefaction). With adequate planning before an event it should be possible to gather important social data in a strictly controlled manner as happened with research into physical science and engineering.
>
> (McLean et al. 2012: 173)

Interestingly, Beaven et al. (2015), in discussing their role in managing the post-earthquake research effort, comment that 'active coordination of research engagement after disasters has the potential to maximise research opportunities, improve research quality, increase end-user engagement, and manage escalating research activity to mitigate ethical risks posed to impacted populations'. They suggest that the focus on the coordination of research activity after the February 2011 Christchurch earthquake by the then newly formed national research consortium, the Natural Hazards Research Platform, which included the social science research moratorium during the state of emergency, reinforced the need for systematic approaches to the management of post-disaster research, in collaboration with the response effort. They also highlight the importance of involving an existing, broadly-based research consortium, ensuring that this consortium's coordination role is fully integrated into emergency management structures, and ensuring that all aspects of decision-making processes are transparent and easily accessed. Local groups, such as the Researching the Health Implications of Seismic Events (RHISE) group that developed in Christchurch, were also important for research coordination. However, the activities of institutionally-sanctioned research groups, no matter how well intentioned, may also serve to stifle other research issues or perspectives that do not fit into the official response effort. In addition, research moratoriums may also mean that some difficult but vital questions may not be asked or information gained. This is clearly not to suggest that there should be an insensitive, ethicsless research free-for-all, but to highlight that there are winners and losers in the approach taken in institutional responses to post-disaster research.

Access to organisations and individuals

Access to organisations and individuals is clearly vital for social science post-disaster research. Organisations' appetites to participate in such research varied between enthusiasm and resistance. In the first year of the recovery phase, organisations and individuals perceived the value of learning from the unique experience they had gone through or were going through, and wanted to contribute to the research effort. However, this initial openness rapidly dissipated as, in some instances, they were over-used as sources by the broad range of uncoordinated research endeavours. Their own business-as-usual demands began to take over and they questioned what value was in the research for them. They also sought to protect their own long-running internal data-collection efforts, such as staff engagement surveys, and preserve the response rates on those, rather than risk staff "turning off" to research altogether and not responding. Nevertheless, *research fatigue* and over-exposure to research did occur. In some cases, this made maintaining organisational interest and getting groups to consider implementing research findings challenging. Christchurch organisations (and individuals within some parts of the community) were inundated with requests for data collection following the earthquakes. While organisations were initially open and responsive, this changed, and organisations such as the emergency services and the key infrastructure businesses would not engage in research with other groups after a while.

As access to organisations and people was often difficult, a range of strategies was used to encourage participation in research. These centred upon using pre-disaster professional networks to identify key contacts within the organisations, meeting with those persons and then negotiating wider access to the organisation. Without these, access may not have always been possible. This process also illustrates the value for researchers of having *insiders* from within the local community, so that established trust and relationships could be utilised in the post-disaster setting.

Issues of access

Researcher A: Compared to other research projects I have conducted, I found participants quite eager and willing to participate in my study. I also found gaining access to organisations not overly problematic, and

(Continued)

I think this is partly attributable to the fact that organisations could see the value in the research (given their own lack of knowledge and understanding of how to deal with the situation). This made businesses and individuals more receptive to research participation (at least initially). I have, however, also heard of accounts where researchers had difficulty gaining any traction, mainly due to survey/research fatigue, since a lot of studies were going on at once. Thus, while researchers should not necessarily rush in the moment the dust settles, data collection needs to be timed carefully.

Another issue I encountered with access was actually obtaining reliable contact information for participants, given that many people had moved within Christchurch, moved within New Zealand, or left the country altogether. This added a new dimension to communicating with participants and meant that I gathered data via face-to-face interviews, phone interviews and Skype interviews. It also meant that a large percentage of invitations to participate were undeliverable. Not a biggie for a qualitative study like mine, but this could be an issue for survey research. It was also a significant issue for another colleague's study, which looked at whether businesses were still operating. Some were, although no trace of the "old" business could be found: some had relocated, some had folded and opened under a new name elsewhere, some had relocated out of town, etc.

Researcher B: Some organisations, such as the emergency services, were very quickly swamped by research requests, covering everything from school projects to formal academic research. Consequently, this closed off access very early for other researchers like us, who had to go through a more lengthy process around ethics and funding and overcome other hurdles before we could even start talking to these organisations. In the case of one vital infrastructure organisation, we got in early and so all subsequent research requests to that organisation were referred on to us – the organisation's leaders felt they had spent a lot of time sharing information in detail, and didn't want to repeat that process.

The process for gaining research access becomes very significant in a post-disaster situation. We created a process for identifying entry through a key individual and establishing them as a liaison person within their own organisation. There were many negotiation topics here, around what would be the returns for the participants/organisations, and the demands upon them. Promises made in the course of access negotiations then created obligations that have to be honoured. In short, I had to become a salesperson and relationship-manager, which was a time-intensive but critical role, for the research to proceed.

Having established business and community networks also has other research benefits. There is a policy choice for government agencies in a disaster situation regarding the criteria for choosing researchers to support. In post-earthquake recovery Christchurch, local researchers were often used in many government-supported research initiatives. This had benefits of not pushing aside local researchers with an invasion of enthusiastic outsiders, although this did happen in some cases. Nevertheless, on the whole it permitted the sensitivity of using people who themselves had an understanding of what residents had experienced, and it allowed the development of expertise in disaster studies at local institutions and research centres.

The earthquakes clearly provided incredibly valuable opportunities for some local researchers; however, this was again contingent upon being able to access *funding* and support. In a number of cases, researchers had to negotiate with funders to allow a special one-off funding grant for their work, leaving the funders with the challenge of reconciling this with their predetermined annual budgets. Special disaster-related funding did become available, but it was important to be proactive in seeking this and learning about the new landscape of funders in the post-disaster situation.

Funding

What was surprising and wonderful to [some of] us was that the calls for proposal didn't just include physical science research, but that social science research was also recognised. Yet, I would still argue that funding bodies need to have a broad lens when thinking of research priorities (i.e. to include areas outside of physical sciences).

Researcher wellbeing

As residents in the city, many of the insider researchers were also affected by the disaster. Researcher wellbeing is therefore an important consideration. Some of us faced considerable personal stress dealing with loss of housing, displacement, repairs, insurance companies and the Earthquake Commission (EQC). Researchers therefore had to manage their own stress and fatigue over an extended period of time. The researchers' workplace (for the most part, the University of Canterbury) was also damaged. In some cases, during the first months, researchers often had no physical base to work from, and when temporary work-space was eventually built, it involved working in large open-plan rooms where it was difficult to even do basic tasks such as making phone calls. Added to this were also employment concerns associated with the loss of students as a result of the earthquakes. This created further financial pressures on departments along with threats of programme closure and redundancies as the University sought to refocus its activities. While perhaps creating empathy with research participants in some contexts, this situation is likely to potentially colour the research process in various ways (van Heugten 2014), or perhaps even influence what will be examined as part of individual and institutional research programmes. Not only do we study organisations, but we also work within them.

Researcher wellbeing

There is plenty of anecdotal evidence, including from our research group, of how challenging doing post-disaster research can be. Listening to people's stories can be taxing for the researchers, and exposure to these types of data is repetitive (i.e. in the analysis phase, writing up, member checking). The fact that the participants may have been more significantly affected does not lessen the importance of researcher wellbeing (i.e. "how can I complain when they have lost their home/job/loved one?"). Researcher self-care and wellbeing is vital. We found a couple of things important: Planning to make sure that support is available if/when needed and having regular debriefs with fellow researchers (without jeopardising participant confidentiality).

The dynamic research environment

Due to the unique earthquake and aftershock sequence experienced in Christchurch (see Chapter 1 of this book), the post-earthquake research environment was dynamic and constantly changing. The volatile and uncertain nature of the continuing seismic activity was confounded by ongoing organisational, institutional and regulatory changes. This affected the ability to plan on a long-term basis for data collection. Data collection had to be improvised and adaptive. Changes to key staff and business situations mirrored this context. There was often sudden, significant turnover of the key staff in respondent organisations who had entered into verbal agreements with the researchers regarding the research projects. This affected the ability to retain those organisations' involvement in the studies. Some organisations experienced significant structural changes and leadership changes in the recovery phase while others had radically changed business situations, including moving premises. Travel times to some of these organisations were also quite long because of damaged infrastructure and altered traffic flows.

Indeed, the practicalities of undertaking research are significant in a highly dynamic post-disaster environment. Even basic issues of being able to start the research process, especially in terms of the timeframes around consents and funding, as well as issues around ethics and confidentiality, became more challenging in earthquake impact research. These issues produced trade-offs and constraints around the timing of projects, forcing hard decisions around the optimal time for data gathering, including the dilemmas around potential for recall and bias. Yet the situation was unpredictable; it was not possible to know how long the earthquake sequence would continue, and this meant that, due to timing issues, projects developed their own strengths and weaknesses. Nevertheless, in some cases, earlier projects could be used as pilots that then informed the later ones.

The ability to *improvise and be flexible* in research planning became essential. All sorts of unplanned issues emerged with organisations and research. There was a need to keep to the strategic plan, yet not get involved in specific issues for organisations.

However, in the case of Nilakant et al. (Chapter 3, this volume), the Resilient Organisations Group that conducted the interviews and focus groups ended up completing the Stronger Christchurch Infrastructure Rebuild Team (SCIRT) internal Peak Performance Review as a condition of access. This Review largely covered the same content and subject matter as the research and so it would have been impractical to have consultants and then researchers gathering the same data. This unplanned opportunity gave Nilakant et al. (Chapter 3) much richer data on an organisation that had a finite existence, so they had to move quickly to capture it. In other cases, when they saw the needs of the organisations, it was tempting to enter into greater depth of involvement; however, they had to keep to the focus on their agreed contract and address all of the organisations within the agreed timeframe.

Another aspect of the dynamic environment was the effect it had on the timing and co-ordination of the different subgroups of research teams. For example, in one case it would have been preferable to first complete the qualitative data collection prior to moving on to the quantitative work as the next stage in a sequence. In practice, however, there was a need to capture data before recall bias affected responses, and the quantitative work needed to be started almost concurrently in order to meet the timeframes and expectations of the funders and organisations involved in the project.

(Not) raising expectations

Researcher A: This is perhaps related not just to post-disaster context, but when doing research with employees there may be an implicit assumption that something will be done with that data, i.e. employees will expect a change if they have reported something negative. We were very clear from the beginning that we were simply collecting information, and while we recommended potential 'solutions' to organisational leaders, it was up to these leaders whether anything would be done. Most participants were quite happy with this, and were just glad to be able to discuss their experiences.

Researcher B: I suspect it depends on how intensely you are involved with an organisation. Researcher A's team was intensely involved in a smaller number of organisations, whereas we were dealing at a broader level with a larger number of organisations. In both scenarios there are expectations – Researcher A may have been more around individuals or subgroups within the organisation/s having expectations that change would occur, whereas we had to deal with the problem that we were covering so many interviews and processes that there were delays between gathering data and finally returning to those organisations, in the way we had promised, to share findings and frameworks that they could implement. This is part of managing a very large project in a post-disaster setting, with multiple stakeholders, and the timeframes, expectations and ownership of the outcomes.

Issues of risk and reciprocity when dealing with sensitive topics

In a disaster and post-disaster situation, clearly one of the most important issues is that participants are telling their personal stories, and often share personal, intimate and sometimes traumatic accounts. One dimension, noted above, was the need to obtain trust and rapport with participants and the importance of a 'shared common experience' between researcher and participants. This shared experience also undoubtedly influences the creation and interpretation of meaning both during interview situations as well as when examining transcripts and even survey responses. The fact that researchers have shared the experience that underlies the changes they are studying is potentially a mixed blessing. On the one hand it creates significant empathy and provides the basis for the start of many conversations and stories. On the other, it can be a challenge to researcher detachment and focus. Also associated with disaster research is the risk, and often reality, of arousing strong emotional responses from participants, and the possibility that research may cause distress for the participants as well as for the researchers. As Dominey-Howes (2015) observes, post-disaster research is tightly bounded by ethics and professional codes of conduct requiring researchers to be vigilant about the impact of their work on participants. However, there are also direct and vicarious impacts on researchers (Dominey-Howes 2015). There is therefore a need for the utmost sensitivity in undertaking disaster research, even several years on from the event, which requires good preparation on behalf of the researcher, including guaranteeing preservation of anonymity and confidentiality, as well as the capacity to create space for participants when needed (see Corbin and Morse (2003) for a valuable paper that provides insights into such issues in unstructured interview situations). Researchers should not cause participants further distress.

With respect to more organisationally-oriented research, there is a need for multiple staff perspectives which includes front-line staff as well as management, but there are issues around locating staff-participants when organisational managers help to identify relevant roles and individuals and provide access to them. In such situations there are challenges in maintaining a degree of anonymity and confidentiality in the post-disaster context, perhaps above and beyond what would normally be expected. As discussed above, to undertake research one needs to gain access to organisations, and then work with key contacts to identify the relevant people who hold central roles during the disaster and recovery. It becomes a greater challenge, then, to conceal their identities. Moreover, there are also practical problems of accessing participants if this usually occurs during work hours and the researchers are known to all the staff. In such a situation it could then be very obvious when a colleague is being interviewed, and so new tactics had to be devised to work around these challenges.

There are also specific issues involved in interviewing front-line staff. They are often describing a holistic situation that includes both their home and work situations, so emotional issues can emerge, and their accounts can also contain details that refer to the shortcomings of organisational leaders. These staff usually also have to be interviewed during work hours. In some early phases, researchers could see the difficulty in very controlling organisations when staff linked up with the researchers for interviewing but were afraid to say anything! As a result we had to rapidly come up with new methods for recruiting and protecting participants.

The ethical issues involved in post-disaster research are clearly considerable (e.g. risk of harm, mitigation strategies, informed consent). One significant lesson from the disaster research experience is the extreme importance of interview protocols and learning to 'tread lightly' in the interview process. In addition there is a clear need to thoroughly debrief participants. Corbin and Morse (2003), describe a helpful four-phase protocol in this regard, which involves a pre-interview phase, tentative phase, immersion phase, and emergence phase. Although Corbin and Morse intended this protocol for qualitative researchers, it also provides important insights for quantitative studies, especially with respect to the preparation of surveys, how they are administered, and feeding back the results to participants. In fact, the notion of reciprocity and the value of the research to participants and other stakeholders arguably become even more important in post-disaster situations given the sensitivity of the subject matter – really letting people know that some of the stress involved in being participants has potentially valuable results and insights.

Quantitative research

You only get a limited amount of information with quantitative measures. Understanding the context (of each organisation, division, team or individual) is imperative, and protecting the wellbeing of the participants should be the priority. It is also vital to ensure that all participants have access to the findings.

Another lesson to emerge from our studies relates to the "consultancy" element of research – the need to share findings so that practitioners can be informed and guided. Researchers who were involved with large research projects were often mandated to collaborate with organisations in working towards the implementation of findings and recommendations. Yet that in itself creates a new pressure for researchers and ways of working with which they will not necessarily be familiar. It involves changing one's role from data-gatherer and analyst to supplier of information, and doing this in ways that are not perceived as inappropriate or making further impositions.

The question we perhaps need to ask as researchers is: have we exploited vulnerable participants in the sense that we have benefited more from the research than the participants, or have we taken steps to ensure that the balance of power is shared more equally between participants, stakeholders and researchers? Researchers in disaster contexts might want to reflect on the fact that as researchers we need to be opportunistic, i.e. the earthquake sequence provided us with a very unique set of circumstances, from which the seeds of serendipity often sprout; however, treading lightly is essential. We need to seize the opportunity but do so responsibly and ethically.

Research impact

A major concern of researchers, participants and sponsors is the impact of research. In the case of post-disaster research, this desire for impact appears to be greater than at other times. Anecdotal experience suggests that the impact is felt more quickly than in other research, and audiences are eager for research results, at least earlier in the recovery period. Disasters can expose gaps in organisational knowledge and disaster-preparedness, and organisations respond by demanding answers, as soon as possible. An obviously important aspect of this is that academics are not the only audience for disaster-related research. Therefore, a very important consideration in thinking of the audience is to consider how the publication and dissemination strategy can be integrated so that both academic and wider impact goals can be achieved.

Unusually high interest in research

We found that employers realised that they needed to do something to care for their staff, but they didn't necessarily know what. Seminars on stress and coping were popular, but more was needed. [The research] was almost like a "health-check" for many organisations that pushed them to think about employee wellbeing.

An interesting caveat with respect to disaster research and its impact is the question of the extent to which the findings are unique to a disaster context. How did the research and the findings differ from other (more "ordinary") contexts? In responding to these questions we can consider the broader relevance of disaster research. Are researchers simply learning about disasters so that in future people can be better prepared and/or respond better, or are they using a disaster as an opportunity to learn about crises and capacity for adaptation as a more generic processes? As a group of researchers we believe that 'good' research should have relevance for contexts outside of disasters, although clearly this raises its own set of challenges of comparison and applicability. Despite the positive reception of our feedback and results, the impacts of research – like the impacts of disasters – may not be enduring. For example, a recent graduate study looked at the extent to which human resource-related changes initially occurred following the earthquakes; some continued for several years, but others gradually faded.

Who do researchers serve: society, organisations and/or the individual?

Finally, we come to a question that is relevant to any research context and that all researchers should consider regardless of research context, but which was magnified in our disaster context: who was the research for? Were we helping and supporting organisations, individuals within them, or was this research for academic journals and the enhancement of our own personal interests? Within the framework of some of our research, the sponsor's end-user engagement was central, so there were relatively clear pathways for dissemination, including individual organisations and individuals. However, while there are clear lines of provision of research in some areas of business and management research, in others these lines might not be so clear. In the case of more policy-oriented research, for example, do politicians and policy-makers actually want to support research that may criticise post-disaster policy and planning settings, or the suspension of normal democratic processes, even if it relates to issues of urban resilience? (Hayward 2013). One of the meta-problems of disaster research, and one which is extremely sensitive for some stakeholders and institutions, is research that examines the political process surrounding disaster management and recovery, especially of public agencies that have a clear link to political decision-making and responsibilities. This is difficult because of the desire to avoid being partisan, as well as how research findings may be treated, but at the same time there is recognition in social science research that there are methodological and paradigmatic issues in dealing with sensitive political subjects, the results of which may be divisive (Reed 2012).

The political dimension can also create difficulties for researchers, including graduate students, who may find information that, while extremely relevant for a better understanding of the policy response to disasters, may not be able to be made public because of concerns over retaining source confidentiality, access to future research funding, or even careers. While there may be an espoused desire for university researchers to be 'speaking truth to power' (Wildavsky 1979), it also needs to be remembered that at the same time there may be significant ethical and institutional constraints in doing so (Hall 2011). This situation is likely only to be made worse after a natural disaster when the extent of future government funding for universities affected by the disaster may be uncertain. As was commented at an internal research day on earthquake-related research held at the University of Canterbury: 'Do you engage in public debate when you have lost your house and are fighting insurance companies; the University is cutting jobs while awaiting news on government funding; you are being encouraged by the University to provide "positive" messages and news stories because of student decline and earthquake damage; and you want to criticise the same Government for their rebuild strategy?'

Conclusion

This chapter provides a range of lessons and insights from the experiences of conducting business and organisational research on the impacts of the Christchurch earthquakes and their aftermath. Many of the issues raised also occur in the conduct of "normal" research, yet some of these concerns, especially with respect to increased sensitivity to participant welfare, as well as researcher welfare, are heightened. In addition, there are clear issues of timeliness of research which affect not only how research is conducted but also how it is disseminated. Stakeholder relationships, collaboration and communication become more important areas of research management than usual given time-related pressures as well as the nature of the wider recovery and rebuild process. Finally, there is a range of ethical issues that researchers need to examine and reflect upon. These affect methodological decisions, protocols, stakeholder engagement, choice of research topic and how conclusions and findings are framed and communicated.

The introduction to this chapter noted the potential relationships between disaster research and research in conflict and post-conflict settings. In both cases social science research is justified by the need to improve the quality of assistance provided in these settings and to collect high-quality data to inform policy and long-term recovery (Ford et al. 2009) as part of an evidence-based research approach (Banatvala and Zwi 2000). Nevertheless, the heightened vulnerability of populations, organisations and researchers caught in such dynamic and potentially unstable environments calls for careful consideration of and reflection on the research methods employed, the levels of evidence sought, and the ethics of undertaking and communicating research. It is hoped that these personal reflections will help inform others faced with similar research settings.

References

Arnold, C., Eisner, R., Durkin, M. and Whitaker, D. (1982) 'Occupant behavior in a six-storey office building fallowing severe earthquake damage', *Disasters*, 6(3): 207–214.

Banatvala, N. and Zwi, A. (2000) 'Public health and humanitarian interventions: Developing the evidence base', *British Medical Journal*, 321(7253), 101–105.

Beaven, S., Wilson, T., Johnston, L., Johnston, D. and Smith, R. (2015) 'Research engagement after disasters: Research coordination before, during, and after the 2010–2011 Canterbury Earthquake Sequence, New Zealand', *Earthquake Spectra*, doi:http://dx.doi.org/10.1193/082714EQS134MCorbin, J. and Morse, J. (2003) 'The unstructured interactive interview: Issues of reciprocity and risks when dealing with sensitive topics', *Qualitative Inquiry*, 9(3): 335–354.

Crothers, C. (2011) 'Sociological tales of two cities – Christchurch and Auckland: An editorial', *New Zealand Sociology*, 26(1): 3–11.

de Jong, S. L. V. Z., Dominey-Howes, D., Roman, C., Calgaro, E., Gero, A., Veland, S., Bird, D., Muliaina, T., Tuiloma-Sua, D. and Afioga, T. (2011) 'Process, practice and priorities – key lessons learnt undertaking sensitive social reconnaissance research as part of an (UNESCO-IOC) International Tsunami Survey Team', *Earth-Science Reviews*, 107(1): 174–192.

Dominey-Howes, D. (2015) 'Seeing "the dark passenger" – Reflections on the emotional trauma of conducting post-disaster research', *Emotion, Space and Society*, doi:10.1016/j.emospa.2015.06.008

El-Khani, A., Ulph, F., Redmond, A. and Calam, R. (2013) 'Ethical issues in research into conflict and displacement', *The Lancet*, 382(9894), 764–765.

Ford, N., Mills, E., Zachariah, R. and Upshur, R. (2009) 'Ethics of conducting research in conflict settings', *Conflict and Health*, 3(7), doi:10.1186/1752-1505-3-7

Fothergill, A. (1998) 'The neglect of gender in disaster work: An overview of the literature', in E. Enarson and B. H. Morrow (eds.) *The Gendered Terrain of Disaster: Through Women's Eyes*, Westport: Praeger.

Fussell, E. and Elliott, J. (2009) 'Introduction: Social organization of demographic responses to disaster: Studying population – environment interactions in the case of Hurricane Katrina', *Organization & Environment*, 22(4): 379–394.

Gray, D. (2014) *Doing Research in the Real World*, London: Sage.

Hall, C. M. (2010) 'Crisis events in tourism: Subjects of crisis in tourism', *Current Issues in Tourism*, 13(5): 401–417.

Hall, C. M. (2011) 'Researching the political in tourism: Where knowledge meets power', in C. M. Hall (ed.) *Fieldwork in Tourism: Methods, Issues and Reflections*, Abingdon: Routledge.

Hayward, B. M. (2013) 'Rethinking resilience: Reflections on the Earthquakes in Christchurch, New Zealand, 2010 and 2011', *Ecology and Society*, 18(4), 37.

Jayawickrama, J. (2013) 'If they can't do any good, they shouldn't come': Northern evaluators in southern realities', *Journal of Peacebuilding & Development*, 8(2): 26–41.

Krinsley, K., Gallagher, J., Weathers, F., Kutter, C. and Kaloupek, D. (2003) 'Consistency of retrospective reporting about exposure to traumatic events', *Journal of Traumatic Stress*, 16(4): 399–409.

Lee, T. W., Mitchell, T., Holtom, B., McDaniel, L. and Hill, J. (1999) 'The unfolding model of voluntary turnover: A replication and extension', *Academy of Management Journal*, 42(4): 450–462.

McLean, I., Oughton, D., Ellis, S., Wakelin, B. and Rubin, C. (2012) *Review of the Civil Defence Emergency Management Response to the 22 February Christchurch Earthquake, June 2012*, Wellington: Ministry of Civil Defence & Emergency Management.

Norris, F. H., Friedman, M., Watson, P., Byrne, C., Diaz, E. and Kaniasty, K. (2002) '60,000 disaster victims speak: Part I. An empirical review of the empirical literature, 1981–2001', *Psychiatry: Interpersonal and Biological Processes*, 65(3): 207–239.

Norris, F. and Kaniasty, K. (1992) 'Reliability of delayed self-reports in disaster research', *Journal of Traumatic Stress*, 5(4): 575–588.

O'Mathúna, D. (2012) 'Roles and challenges for IRBs with disaster research', *Research Practitioner*, 13(5): 167–174.

O'Mathúna, D., Gordijn, B. and Clarke, M. (eds.) (2014) *Disaster Bioethics: Normative Issues When Nothing Is Normal*, Public Health Ethics Analysis, Vol. 2, Dordrecht: Springer.

Reed, R. (2012) 'Researching Ulster loyalism: The methodological challenges of the divisive and sensitive subject', *Politics*, 32(3): 207–219.

Shoaf, K., Sauter, C., Bourque, L., Giangreco, C. and Weiss, B. (2004) 'Suicides in Los Angeles County in relation to the Northridge earthquake', *Prehospital and Disaster Medicine*, 19(4): 307–310.

Tansey, C., Herridge, M., Heslegrave, R. and Lavery, J. (2010) 'A framework for research ethics review during public emergencies', *Canadian Medical Association Journal*, 182(14): 1533–1537.

Tehrani, N. (ed.) (2011) *Managing Trauma in the Workplace: Supporting Workers and Organisations*, Hove: Routledge.

Tierney, K. (2007) 'From the margins to the mainstream? Disaster research at the crossroads', *Annual Review of Sociology*, 33: 503–525.

Vallance, S. (2015) 'An evaluation of the Waimakariri District Council's integrated and community-based recovery framework following the Canterbury Earthquakes: Implications for urban resilience', *Urban Policy and Research*, doi:10.1080/0811 1146.2014.980401

van den Berg, B., Wong, A., van der Velden, P., Boshuizen, H. and Grievink, L. (2012) 'Disaster exposure as a risk factor for mental health problems, eighteen months, four and ten years post-disaster–a longitudinal study', *BMC Psychiatry*, 12(1): 147.

van Heugten, K. (2014) *Human Service Organizations in the Disaster Context*, New York: Palgrave Macmillan.

Wildavsky, A. (1979) *Speaking Truth to Power*, New Brunswick: Transaction Publishers.

17 Putting ecological thinking back into disaster ecology and responses to natural disasters

Rethinking resilience or business as usual?

C. Michael Hall

Introduction

The transfer and translation of concepts and models from one discipline to another is an inherent part of the development of academic knowledge. Concept transfer can help shed new light on a range of research issues as well as encourage shifts in the way that problems are defined or framed and, hence, the selection of solutions. So it is also with concepts in ecology which have been utilised as core ideas in a range of areas of business, economics and disaster studies (e.g. Mirowski 1994). Some of these ideas have been applied in a "soft" fashion, in which they are utilised as an analogy or a metaphor, i.e. in business and organisation studies, the metaphor of a business adapting to its environment or developing a strategy so as to be more competitive is used often without an awareness of its biological and ecological foundations (Hannan and Freeman 1977, 1989; Aldrich 1979, 1999; Dobrev et al. 2006; Abatecola 2012; Dollimore 2014). Ecological ideas have also been applied in a "hard" form, whereby they have been used to develop significant new insights using natural scientific methods in areas such as, for example, industrial ecology, in which industrial systems are treated in a similar fashion to ecological systems (Isenmann 2003; Levine 2003; Røpke 2005), or the development of ecological economics (Common and Perrings 1992; Arrow et al. 1995) and evolutionary economics (Nelson and Winter 1982; Foster 1997; Laurent and Nightingale 2001; Hodgson 2002, 2004a). There are, however, concerns that the use of some of these ecological ideas, including such significant concepts as resilience, do not just morph into a crude form of social Darwinism (Hodgson 2004b) or environmental determinism, with the translation of ideas also creating issues of interpretation.

Pendall et al. (2010), for example, point to continued "fuzziness" of the idea of resilience in social science, and caution with respect to the rapid and simplistic transfer of an ecological systems concept into the public policy arena. In the case of resilience, Cutter et al. (2010) observe that:

Lingering concerns from the research community focus on disagreements as to the definition of resilience, whether resilience is an outcome or a process, what type of resilience is being addressed (economic systems, infrastructure systems, ecological systems, or community systems), and which policy realm (counterterrorism; climate change; emergency management; long-term disaster recovery; environmental restoration) it should target.

(Cutter et al. 2010: 1)

Similarly, in reflecting on the post-Christchurch earthquake experience, Hayward (2013) observes, 'the idea of resilience as a personal quality must be treated with caution':

Given that human resilience is best understood as the interrelationships among the individuals and their community, environment, and social institutions, it has been disturbing to witness the plethora of consultancies that have sprung up in the wake of our local disaster to offer courses in personal resilience, aimed at helping employees to adapt to the "new normal" of life lived in ongoing aftershocks. The implicit subtext of many of these self-help resilience courses appears to be to restore individuals to their roles as willing workers to aid an economic recovery as quickly as possible.

(Hayward 2013: 37)

This chapter therefore examines the concept of resilience as a way of examining how ecological ideas may better inform understanding of disaster recovery and preparedness. It also highlights the need to question the way in which concepts are transferred, without a full appreciation of the intellectual history of an idea, from one academic context to another and the implications for potential abuse and misuse.

Disaster and disturbance ecology

Disaster ecology examines the interrelationships and interdependence of the social, psychological, anthropological, cultural, geographic, economic, and human context surrounding disasters and extreme public health events such as severe storms, earthquakes, acts of terrorism, industrial accidents, and disease epidemics (Kaplan 1999). Schultz et al. (2007) note that the concept is part of a broader approach within public health that seeks to understand the social and environmental context, including the impact of disasters on human populations. They utilise the epistemological triad of host, agent (vector) and environment in relation to pre-, during and post-event phases to emphasise that disasters occur within an environment that provides a multilayered structural context (individual/family, community, societal/structural). The ecological model hypothesises that these levels interact and that these dynamic interactions determine disaster planning, preparedness, response, and recovery outcomes (Beaton et al. 2008; Radhakrishnan and Jacelon 2009; Anåker and Elf 2014). These environmental dimensions are also regarded as significant risk and resilience factors (Schultz 2013). However, while the disaster ecology literature highlights the importance of structure for the resilience of communities and the individuals within them, the utilisation of ecological ideas is only partial at best.

Disturbance is an extremely important concept in ecology. Disturbance was once viewed largely as damaging the "balance of nature" and seen as synonymous with habitat destruction (Botkin 1990; Worster 1990). This has meant, for example, that in Australia and the United States, some fire-adapted landscapes, which depend on fire for regeneration, have been severely affected by the suppression of fire under a cultural perspective that sees fire as "unnatural" (Pyne 1982, 1991). However, certain forms of ecosystem disturbance are now recognised as playing a fundamental and creative role in maintaining 'the natural heterogeneity in environmental conditions that organisms experience through space, time, or both' (Brawn et al. 2001: 252). This means that in many environments, disturbance has been recognised as essential for biodiversity conservation (Kreutzweiser et al. 2012; Spies et al. 2012; Seidl et al. 2014), and for any attempt at system restoration (Walker 2012).

Disturbance ecology refers to the disruption of the function of ecosystems by discrete events. One of the most widely used definitions of disturbance is that of Pickett and White (1985: 7) who defined it as 'any relatively discrete event in time that disrupts ecosystem, community, or population structure and changes resources, substrate availability, or the physical environment.'

One of the important elements in seeking to understand the role of disturbance in either ecosystems or socio-economic systems is the assumption of long-term stability in the system prior to disturbance. In ecological thinking, the concept of succession has been extremely important. Succession is 'an orderly unidirectional process of community change in which communities replace each other until a stable (self-reproducing) community is reached' (Johnson and Miyanishi 2010: 1). This very influential concept, which has been a part of the history of ecological ideas since the 19th century (Worster 1990), is based on the notion that, for each type of environment, species are adapted to different stages in a succession and in some way make the environment unsuitable for themselves and better suited for the species in the next stage until a stable "climax" is reached, i.e. a representation of environmental histories and futures in which there is 'sequential invasion and replacement of dominants driven by facilitation' (Johnson and Miyanishi 2010: 3) as the natural order of things.

Despite substantial evidence that traditional ideas of succession are not well-supported by research results, the concept of succession persists. Change does definitely occur, of course; ecological communities are constantly changing, but species assemble and reassemble in different, and sometimes novel or unfamiliar, combinations, often as a result of the effects of change in the physical environment.

This does not mean that succession is without value as an ecological concept. However, as Prach and Walker (2011: 119) observe, 'the questions of how species assemble into communities or how ecosystems change following a disturbance are still not fully resolved. Prediction of trajectories is still difficult'. Succession appears rarely predictable at the level of species composition but is sometimes predictable at the level of functional groups of species (Prach and Walker 2011). The trajectories of ecological succession from one state to another are complex and problematic, especially as assumptions of long-term stability without disturbance usually do not hold. Community assembly is therefore neither entirely predictable nor completely random. As Johnson and Miyanishi (2010: 11) argue, 'All disturbances have differential impacts on different populations within communities and also on different ecological processes. Therefore, to advance our understanding of the ecological effects of disturbances, we must couple the disturbance process with ecological processes'.

Can business survival in post-disaster recovery be explained ecologically?

Within business and organisational adoption of the notion of resilience, the term is usually used with respect to the survival of an organisation (Davoudi et al. 2012; Shaw and Maythorne 2013) and, related to this, its capacity to adapt without losing its identity (Biggs et al. 2014). Much research tends to focus on internal organisational characteristics rather than the structures and systems within which they are embedded and the spaces that such organisations occupy within systems, especially other organisations that may also occupy the same space (de Oliveira Teixeira and Werther Jr. 2013; Johnson et al. 2013; Limnios et al. 2014). For example, Lengnick-Hall et al. (2011: 243) suggest 'that an organization's capacity for resilience is developed through strategically managing human resources to create competencies among core employees, that when aggregated at the organizational level, make it possible for organizations to achieve the ability to respond in a resilient manner when they experience severe shocks'.

One area of ecology that may help shed light on the importance of system dynamics for organisational survivability is that of island biogeography. The concept of island biogeography examines the relationships between species and a given area (MacArthur and Wilson 1963, 1967). The conventional expression of the species–area relationship is $S = CAz$ where S and A are species count and area, respectively, and C and z are fitted species-specific constants. However, significantly for the wider applicability of the species–area relationship, an 'island' can be regarded as any appropriate bounded space (Whittaker and Fernández-Palacios 2007).

The number of species that are found on an island depends on several factors, including its area, diversity, shape, spatial and temporal isolation, environmental characteristics, accessibility, and the equilibrium rate of colonisation by new species and the rate of extinction of existing species. The equilibrium model of the biota of a single island proposes that the equilibrial species number is reached at the intersection between the curve of the rate of new species immigration, not already on the island, and the curve of extinction of species previously on the island (Figure 17.1). MacArthur and Wilson favoured logarithmic transformations of both axes, thereby enabling the constants C and z to be determined by least squares (linear) regression (Whittaker and Fernández-Palacios 2007). The model is highly significant in that, even though it has substantial heuristic value without it, it has provided a high degree of rigour with respect to dynamic modelling of ecological population processes. Nevertheless, it has three main limitations (Lomolino 2000a):

1   As the spatial and temporal scales are broadened, it becomes increasingly clear that many systems are not only dynamic in species composition, but that they may seldom attain an equilibrium number of species, especially as

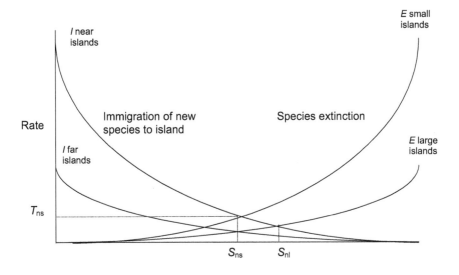

Number of species present

The equilibrial species number is reached at the intersection between the curves of the rate of immigration of new species, not already on the island, and the curve of extinction of species on the island. Immigration rates are postulated to vary as a function of distance, and extinction rate as a function of island area (increased competition for finite natural resources). The model predicts different values for S (number of species), which can be read off the ordinate and for turnover rate (T) (the number of species that become extinct and are replaced by immigrants and speciation over unit time). Each combination of island area and isolation should produce a different and unique combination of S and T. For reasons of uncluttered illustration only limited values are shown. The equilibrium point at which I equals E is never completely constant as it will shift over time in relation to a range in external and internal factors, including disturbance; however, the key point is that there is a 'capacity' to how many species can successfully inhabit a finite area over time because of availability and stability of habitat and/or resources at the same trophic level (Whittaker & Fernández-Palacios 2007; Hall 2010).

Figure 17.1 Equilibrium model of single island biota

a result of disturbances that either modify the species pool or alter immigration and extinction rates before an equilibrium can be achieved. Figure 17.2 provides a representation of some of these issues with respect to the different findings on equilibrium (Whittaker and Fernández-Palacios 2007).

2   The theory assumes that insular habitats and immigration filters (intervening opportunities) are homogeneous. However, much of the observed richness and variation in insular species composition may result from variations in habitat and other environmental conditions.

3   The theory is species-neutral and assumes that all species are independent and equivalent. Yet, in complex systems, the structure and dynamics of insular communities are also influenced by feedback, i.e. interactions among species and other system components. The theory therefore insufficiently addresses the potential role of inter-species interactions and patterns in species composition.

Although the model is limited in terms of its predictive capacity for equilibrium, it is valid in suggesting that, although fluctuations will occur over time, there is a limit to the species diversity of a given area (Cox and Moore 2010). This is highly significant for species survival; because every species runs the risk of extinction, the more species that arrive in a location, the more species there are at risk. Furthermore, 'as more species arrive, the average population size of each will diminish as competition increases – and a smaller population is at greater risk of extinction than a larger population' (Cox and Moore 2010: 240).

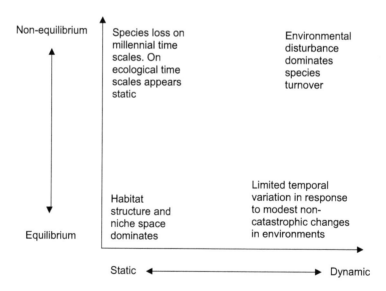

Figure 17.2 Representations of dominant factors in island species turnover

Islands are extremely dynamic, and their characteristics change over time (Lomolino 2000a, 2000b; Warren et al. 2015). Therefore, Figure 17.3 presents a tripartite model of island biogeography with respect to the three fundamental processes of immigration, extinction and evolution as a function of island characteristics. Immigration rates should increase with proximity to a source region and the ability of species to travel across immigration filters. Extinction rates

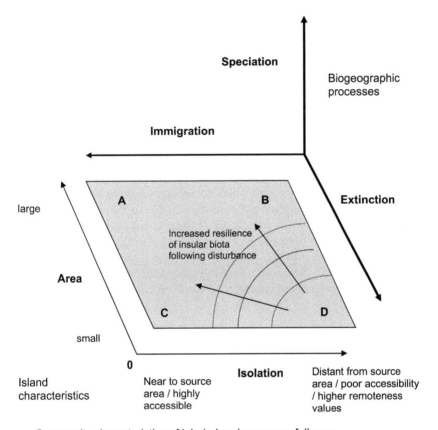

Community characteristics of labeled regions are as follows:
A: Moderate to high species richness, low endemicity and low turnover;
B: Moderate to high species richness, high endemicity and low turnover;
C: Moderate to low species richness, low endemicity and high turnover;
D: Low species richness, low endemicity and high turnover – a depauperate island.
Species richness is the number of different species represented in a set or collection of individuals. It does not take into account the abundance of the species or their relative abundance distributions.
Endemism is the ecological state of being unique to a defined location. Species are not endemic if they are also found elsewhere (after Lomolino 2000a, 2000b; Hall 2010, 2012).

Figure 17.3 Relationships between biogeographical processes and island characteristics

should decrease as area increases or, obversely, increase with growing resource requirements of the focal species. Speciation, the evolutionary process by which new species arise, should be most important where extinction and immigration are lowest. Speciation should therefore increase in relation to area and isolation and decrease with respect to resource requirements and the capacity of species to move or disperse within their environments (Lomolino 2000a).

The model also suggests the importance of both independent and interacting effects of a disturbance on species (Whittaker et al. 2008; Jackson and Sax 2010; Yackulic et al. 2011; Warren et al. 2015), with a disturbance sometimes providing colonisation opportunities for new species in the long-term. However, depending on the nature of the impact, in the short term it can provide opportunities for members of some indigenous species because they face less competition for habitat and/or resources. The characteristics of disturbances are critical to understanding their impact on species (Figure 17.4): the time scale over which a disturbance's impacts are being assessed (as a species identified as adaptive at point T1 may not be recognised as such at point T2 because of reasons such as the growth rate of a species), especially given that many ecological processes occur in evolutionary time, and the extent to which a system is relatively open or closed (therefore affecting the extent to which competitors may be able to migrate to take advantage of the ecological niches made available via disturbance). The clear lesson is that survivability and adaptation are the result of a complex and dynamic interplay between many individuals of the same and of different species and of the habitats and resources they use.

Hall (2012, 2015) used island biogeographical theory to illustrate issues of adaptation, resilience, and vulnerability of island economies (although, as noted

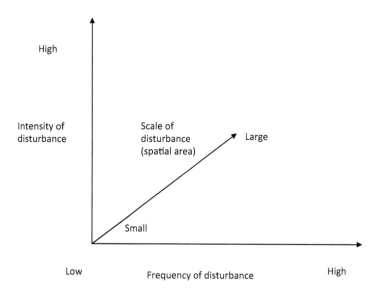

Figure 17.4 Characteristics of disturbance: intensity, scale and frequency

above, this can refer to any bounded space). From this approach the "equilib-rial" number of businesses and organisations for a given set of resources in a specific space is reached at the intersection of the rate of immigration of new firms and capital, and the emigration or closure (extinction) of businesses, along with the capacity of businesses and organisations to innovate and adapt (which is analogous to species evolution over time and the occupation of new ecological niches) (Figure 17.5). Immigration rates are postulated to vary as a function of

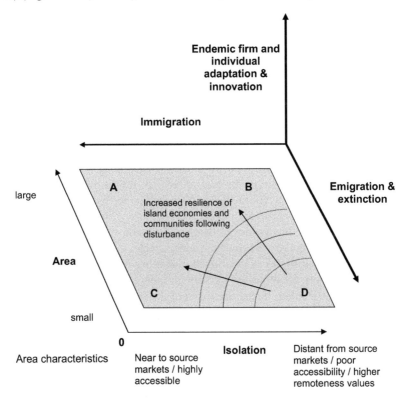

Community characteristics of labeled regions are as follows:
A: Moderate to high economic richness, low endemicity and low turnover;
B: Moderate to high economic richness, high endemicity and low turnover;
C: Moderate to low economic richness, low endemicity and high turnover;
D: Low economic richness, low endemicity and high turnover – a depauperate island economy
Economic richness is the number and variety of different businesses. it is used here in the sense of diversity of business and organisations.
Endemicity is the development of businesses unique to the location as a result of adaptation and innovation.
Immigration refers to the inflow of firms, people and/or funds and remittances.
Emigration refers to the departure of firms, people and/or funds.
Extinction refers to firm's ceasing to operate (after Hall 2012, 2015).

Figure 17.5 Island biogeographical perspectives on business endemism, immigration, emigration and extinction

distance (which may be regulatory, economic, cultural or perceptual rather than Euclidean) and closure rates are functions of island area and resources that determine the competition for finite capital in its various forms, e.g. economic capital, human capital, natural capital. Although heuristic, the model can potentially predict different values for S (e.g. number of firms and/or capital) (in substituting values for Figure 17.1), and for turnover rate (T) (the number of firms that close and are replaced by immigrants and innovation over unit time) given assumptions about the equilibrium nature of the bounded space. The equilibrium point at which I equals E is, of course, never completely constant as it will shift over time in relation to external and internal factors. Nevertheless, there is a 'capacity' limit as to how many businesses and organisations, as well as individuals – can inhabit a finite area over time (Hall 2015) or, in broader ecological economic terms, without there being substantial importing of external resources, e.g. energy, food, water and/or economic capital, to maintain a given population base (Hall 2010, 2012).

In island economies, as with many island species, some businesses occupy a specialised niche in order to survive. In ecology the more specialised a species is, the less adaptable it tends to be to disturbance or new species interactions (Poisot et al. 2011; Concepción et al. 2015). In the case of the loss of habitat or co-evolutionary interactions due to disturbance, for example, species survival may be linked to the capacity to disperse to patches with reduced levels of competition (thereby reducing specialisation). However, in other cases disturbance may reduce the number of inter- and extra-species competitors and potentially increase the survival rates of individuals, assuming resource levels stay constant. In such a situation, the increased capacity for individual survival may have very little to do with the inherent characteristics of the individual or the species (except luck), and is instead a function of wider system characteristics. The system analogy here is that firms that have survived an initial disturbance have a survival advantage, at least in the short run, before new firms emerge to enter the market and increase levels of competition and the rate of firm death.

The factors that underlie species turnover and ecosystem change are complex, dynamic, multi-scaled and often stochastic. Moreover, in drawing an analogy between species turnover and the birth and death of organisations, significant issues of scale arise. From an ecological perspective, is it the death of individuals that is significant? Or, as Holling (1973: 1) posed in his seminal paper on resilience, is it 'the numbers of organisms and the degree of constancy of their numbers? These are two very different ways of viewing the behavior of systems, and the usefulness of the view depends very much on the properties of the system concerned'.

But to what extent does this issue transfer to our understanding of resilience?

Resilience to disturbance

Resilience is 'the capacity of a system to absorb disturbance and reorganise while undergoing change so as to retain essentially the same function, structure, identity and feedbacks' (Walker et al. 2004: 6) that existed before the disturbance event. By its very nature, resilience assumes disturbance. When transferred to the social world, this means that uncertainty, variability in the environment, and surprise are 'part of the game and you need to be prepared for it and learn to live with it' (Folke 2006: 255). However, ecological resilience and socio-economic resilience have two fundamentally different dimensions.

First, in ecology, resilience is neither a positive nor a negative: while longer-term survival may be appreciated by an individual of a species (if they are cognisant enough to appreciate such things), it may make no difference to the survival of a species or to ecosystem stability. Following on from this initial observation, the second key difference is that of the role of human agency in not only formulating notions of resilience but also their application and value, especially when the focus shifts from the resilience of a system to the resilience or survival of a firm, organisation or individuals. This shift in thinking also moves from the more stochastic understanding of change in ecology to one which is often much more deterministic and in which communities, organisations and individuals supposedly possess the attributes with which to adapt to external change. As Maguire and Cartwright (2008) argue with respect to community capacity to manage change in Australia, resilience:

> . . . recognises the powerful capacity of people to learn from their experiences and to consciously incorporate this learning into their interactions with the social and physical environment. This view of resilience is important because it acknowledges that people themselves are able to shape the trajectory of change . . . and play a central role in the degree and type of impact caused by the change.
>
> (Maguire and Cartwright 2008: 5)

If resilience is translated as a normative goal of being the capacity to generate ecosystem or economic services, it raises significant issues as to how resilience is to be maintained. For example, resilience could be maintained through an inequitable social and economic system in which the distribution of services falls unevenly among the population (Ernston 2008). In incorporating human agency into notions of resilience (and following Ernston's observations as to the importance of considering how resilience is defined and achieved), a more critically-formulated definition of resilience would therefore suggest that resilience is the capacity of a system to sustain a certain set of services, in face of disturbance, uncertainty and change, for a certain set of humans. Applying such an approach to research suggests that researchers need to analyse not just how systems are managed, but also which services are prioritised (Daily and Matson 2008) and who benefits from them. Questions of power in the determination of the role, agenda setting and interpretation of resilience in policy making are often unaddressed (Hudson 2010), as are the distributional effects of the promotion of particular interpretations of resilience (Cutter et al. 2010; Yoon 2012; Vale 2014). Indeed, following on from Lasswell's (1936) dictum of politics as the study of who gets what, where and how, it can also be suggested that the question of 'resilience for whom and for what' (Armitage and Johnson 2006) needs to be asked.

Overly simplistic interpretations of resilience as equated to the survival of people or organisations, without appreciating the complex and heterogeneous nature of the regional systems they are embedded in, has led to significant criticisms (Hudson 2010). As a review of resilience in regional policy argues, 'there is a need to proceed with caution and ensure that policy fixes do not exceed the capability of the research base to justify them' (Christopherson et al. 2010: 9). Therefore, a key issue in determining policies is the understanding of the nature of the system that is meant to become resilient.

System characteristics and scale

In ecology the portrayal of ecosystems as inherently stable, in equilibrium and predictable has given way to a much more complex understanding of ecological system dynamics. Resilience is a 'framework for understanding how complex systems self-organise and change over time' (Anderies et al. 2013: 3). Holling's (1973) much cited, but probably increasingly little-read, seminal paper on the resilience and stability of ecological systems, contributed to this transition by demonstrating that because ecosystems are complex adaptive systems, they potentially have multiple states in which, post-disturbance, they can be fully functional without returning to their previous equilibrium. Building upon early understandings of complexity theory, Holling suggested that rather than a single equilibrium point of stability, there were multiple 'domains of attraction' (1973: 9) in which numerous possible behaviours of a system exist. Holling emphasised the difference between resilience and stability:

> Resilience determines the persistence of relationships within a system and is a measure of the ability of these systems to absorb changes of state variables, driving variables, and parameters, and still persist. In this definition resilience is the property of the system and persistence or probability of extinction is the result. Stability, on the other hand, is the ability of a system to return to an equilibrium state after a temporary disturbance. The more rapidly it returns, and with the least fluctuation, the more stable it is. In this definition stability is the property of the system and the degree of fluctuation around specific states the result.
>
> (Holling 1973: 17)

Holling's work was expanded by Gunderson and Holling (2002), who showed how systems move through adaptive renewal cycles consisting of the four stages of "conservation" (stability), "release" (impact of a disturbance), "reorganisation" (change after the disturbance), and "growth" (transition into a new stable state) (Walker et al. 2004). They also demonstrated that complex social-ecological systems are made up of multiple nested adaptive cycles with cross-scalar dimensions (Gunderson and Holling 2002). This approach is far from the static equilibrium models of early ecology and has significant implications for how systems are designed and managed (Folke 2006). According to Holling (1996), a static equilibrium approach to resilience seeks to create "fail-safe" systems that are stable, efficient, and predictable, whereas a dynamic resilience approach accepts change and unpredictability and designs systems to be safe to fail (Meerow and Newell 2015). A key point here for the wider analysis and understanding of resilience is that these different approaches to resilience also characterise the literatures on resilience in different disciplines. Meerow and Newell's (2015) bibliometric analysis indicates that dynamic resilience predominates in studies related to complexity. However, research in disaster management, economics, and engineering, tends to follow equilibrium models of resilience (Colbourne 2008; Pendall et al. 2010).

In providing a think piece for the UK Sustainable Development Commission, Colbourne (2008) noted the development of different disciplinary approaches to resilience, but ignored different understandings of equilibrium in attempting a synthetic conclusion:

> Resilience appears to involve *purposive* change in response to the opportunities and demands created by a disturbance . . . Resilient systems . . . have a capacity for self-organisation, which enables structures and processes to be re-*configured* to ensure long-term survival. In practical terms, this implies that a resilient person, household, organization or community would have the ability to change practices and structures in the aftermath of a major event or change. As a result, the person or entity is not only able to function in the new environment, but also has the capacity to anticipate and prepare for the possibility of similar shocks and surprises in the future.
>
> (Colbourne 2008: 3, emphasis in the original)

One of the issues, among many, arising from Colborne's comments is the scaled nature of the person or entity that is responding to change; that is, a person lives in a household or works within organisations that are in turn embedded in a community (which may be part of a larger urban setting and so on). Scale is therefore important in dealing with complex systems (Berkes et al. 2003). Ecological scales are context-sensitive and difficult to define in practice, but are generally viewed as hierarchically and dynamically linked (Gunderson and Holling 2002), where interactions between parts of a system are nonlinear and local and constrained by larger scales, but where local interactions could have emergent effects influencing other scales and the system as a whole (Pickett et al. 2008). The capacity to understand, anticipate and prepare for the potential of emergent effects is related to different ontological positions on the relationship between the parts and the whole and which, in turn, influences how knowledge of ecological/system entities is framed (Table 17.1). Recognising the implications of ontological positions

Table 17.1 Ontologies and epistemologies of ecological systems

Methodological Approach	Ontology	Epistemology
Reductionism	Properties of wholes are always found among the properties of their parts	Knowledge of the parts is both necessary and sufficient to understand the whole
Mechanism	Properties of wholes are of the same kind or type of those parts	Knowledge of the kind or type of the cause suffices to understand the type of kind of the effect
Emergentism	There is at least one property of some wholes not possessed by any of their parts. Parts can exist independently of the whole, and novel properties of wholes can be lost via submergence when a system is reduced to its parts	Knowledge of the parts and their relations is a necessary but not a sufficient condition to understand the whole
Organicism	Recognise the existence of emergent properties of wholes. Once a whole has appeared, its parts cannot exist or be understood independently of a whole	Knowledge of the whole is a necessary condition to understand the parts and vice-versa
Holism	The emergent novel properties of the whole can be understood without further consideration of the parts and their relationships. The basic unit is the whole – wholes are independent of parts	Knowledge of the parts is neither necessary nor sufficient to understand the whole

Source: After Blitz 1992: 175–178; Keller and Golley 2000.

is extremely important in generating awareness of the different order effects of disturbance within a system amid the complexity of interactions between different actors and institutions.

Although many management agencies and organisations have embraced resilience as a concept, concrete examples of actual management for resilience remain rare, perhaps because of issues of time-scale, or difficulties in quantifying resilience and the factors that affect it, or because the concept can be interpreted in multiple ways (Hughes et al. 2010; Suding and Hobbs 2009). The possibility remains therefore that the concept of resilience may share the same fate as "sustainability" in that, though widely adopted, the range of its application may affect its utility in that if it comes to mean everything, then it potentially means nothing (Hall 2011). As research from many environments illustrates, knowing what the stressors of a system are does not necessarily lead to appropriate intervention to reduce disturbance and therefore the likelihood of significant change in ecosystem properties (Laurence et al. 2011; Brodie and Waterhouse 2012; Nyström et al. 2012). Applications of resilience thinking in restoration ecology usually focus on associated factors, such as diversity, connectivity and heterogeneity, that are assumed to contribute to greater resilience (Millar et al. 2007; Sudling 2011). Ecological redundancy in critical functional groups that allow for a diversity of responses to different forms of disturbance and environmental variability but maintain similar effects on ecosystem function have also been identified as leading to increased ecological resilience (Elmqvist et al. 2003; Nyström 2006; Brand and Jax 2007; Suding 2011). However, such ecological thinking does not transfer very well to dominant modes of engineering and economic thought that focus on efficiency and return time as being the key characteristics of resilience (Colbourne 2008), and that usually seek to remove any perceived system redundancies or inefficiencies. Indeed, Hayward (2013), in commenting on the Christchurch earthquakes, observes

> . . . the rhetoric of resilience is used to justify authorities making decisions quickly and measuring their impact on recovery by the speed with which the city returns to a "new normal" or experiences "certainty" as firm centralized decision making, . . . the drive for efficiency is all too frequently used to justify expert command-and-control decision making with little or no meaningful local scrutiny or community leadership in decision making.
>
> (Hayward 2013)

Hayward (2013) notes the formal depoliticalisation of much of post-earthquake Christchurch by the transfer of authority to central government and by the suspension of elections on the regional council. She also argues, along with others such as Brown (2012), that resilience research itself often appears depoliticised because of the dominance of policy paradigms that frame economic resilience in relation to greater engagement with the global market economy – even when that itself is often a major shock for local economies. Furthermore, at a community level, any discussion of resilience also needs to go hand-in-hand with a better understanding of vulnerabilities (Miller et al. 2010). According to Birkmann (2006: 30), building on the work of Wisner et al. (2004), the "root causes" of vulnerability, such as lack of access to power, structures, and resources, or the presence of certain political and economic systems, can give way to more "dynamic pressures", which may include a lack of institutions, training, appropriate skills, investment, and ethical standards in public life at the local level, or macroforces such as rapid population change or urbanisation. These combine with unsafe conditions, for example dangerous locations, low income levels, special groups at risk, lack of local institutions, and lack of disaster preparedness to mean that the level of risk for a location is equivalent to the nature of the hazard times the level of vulnerability.

Vital in understanding these vulnerabilities, as well as in capturing the experience of ecosystem change, is the role of community debate and community-based decision-making. According to Folke et al. (2005) these are a very important source of resilience that can be used to guide and frame collective action in times of crisis and reorganisation. Similarly, Adger et al. (2005) also emphasise the value of local memory and knowledge in relation to ecosystem management and adaptive capacities. Arguably, the resilience of Christchurch before the 2010–2011 earthquake sequence was limited by the loss of institutional memory of the impacts of previous earthquake and liquefaction events, as well as by planners choosing to ignore such evidence (see Clayford 2011 for a good overview of pre-2010 earthquake information). Similarly, others have argued that the lack of public participation in the rebuild post the February 2011 earthquake and in the policies developed by the national government for Christchurch have also failed to contribute to increased resilience in Christchurch, especially for some of the most vulnerable (Hayward 2013).

Conclusions

This chapter has explored the concepts of disaster ecology and resilience, and their application to understanding how organisations, places, and communities respond to natural disasters and change. In particular, the notion of "resilience" is used in a wide range of pre-, during- and post-disaster settings, including the case of the Christchurch earthquakes, where the term was utilised by numerous stakeholders. However, as this chapter has made clear, there is often a significant divergence between how the concept is used in an ecological sense and how it has been transferred into other knowledge domains. Nevertheless, it is argued that a reconsideration of the ecological roots of resilience may assist in a better understanding of disaster ecology.

The chapter highlighted the significance of disturbance for ecological thinking. Importantly, it stressed how the role of disturbance has shifted from being regarded as affecting the balance of nature to now being seen as integral to the maintenance of many ecosystem qualities. Such considerations are also important in considering the pre and post states of a system following a major disturbance as they frame how resilience is understood; for example, dynamic understandings of resilience dominate in studies related to complexity (e.g. ecological systems and socio-ecological systems). However, research in disaster management, economics, and engineering tends to follow equilibrium models of resilience (Meerow and Newell 2015). Issues of equilibrium and disturbance were also examined with specific reference to island biogeographic research. Here it was pointed out that the survival of individuals of a species, following a disturbance, may be due to stochastic factors rather than any particular internal attribute of individual resilience. This analogy provides a significant challenge for business and organisational thinking on resilience with respect to the need simultaneously to understand internal and external factors of firms and their embeddedness in place. In so doing greater attention needs to be placed on the complex set of interactions between actors in a system; the development of competitive, cooperative and co-evolutionary relations; and the resource limitations that exist in any location. In studying such factors, assumptions that organisations and individuals that survive a disturbance are then better equipped to tolerate subsequent perturbations may need to be challenged. Important factors here also include better defining *disturbance* (Figure 17.4), as well as the time spans in which response and survival are examined. Indeed, an important consideration is the need to differentiate between the influence on actors of natural variation in a system versus a high-magnitude, low-frequency, disturbance.

The chapter also highlighted a number of important considerations that emerge from the original grounding of resilience thinking in ecological system dynamics as a means to understanding how complex systems self-organise and change over time. This includes a need to be better aware of the ontological and epistemological implications of systems, especially with respect to emergent properties, as more reductionist approaches may not be sufficient to explain such properties. A further issue is that if resilience is concerned with the dynamic relationships within a system – that is, "adaptive renewal" – then the survival (sometimes termed resilience) of a particular organisation or member of a specific species may not be particularly relevant. It is necessarily neither a positive nor a negative to the system *per se*. What is significant is adaptation and self-organisation in the system as it moves between states.

The attribution of the survival of a system element as a positive also reinforces the role of human agency in socio-ecological systems. But perhaps it also highlights the way in which understandings of resilience have diverged from many of the ecological insights into system dynamics as resilience has been translated into other contexts, including serving particular policy goals. Therefore, the assumptions underlying certain uses of resilience in academic studies and policy pronouncements need to become better defined, and the underlying assumptions, including the nature of the system, less opaque. Indeed, as discussed above, issues of system redundancy, diversity, and connectivity that are significant for ecological resilience do not fit well with political-economic approaches in which resilience is used to provide a framework for regional transformation characterised by further downsizing of public services, privatisation, greater government austerity, stronger links to the global economy and a mantra of personal responsibility (Hudson 2010; Brown 2012; Hayward 2013).

There is no intrinsic relationship between organisational resilience and improving the resilience of a community *per se*. Not all organisations need to survive for a community to be resilient. At the community level the issue becomes more *which* organisations need to survive and which organisations will be born with what characteristics and values to replace those that have died in order to maintain or enhance system properties and develop a system that accepts change and unpredictability and is designed to be safe to fail. This undoubtedly includes ensuring that the system is able to respond to the needs of the most vulnerable (Birkmann 2006; Cutter 2006; Miller et al. 2010; Cutter et al. 2014). As noted above, from a community perspective the question of 'resilience for whom and for what' (Armitage and Johnson 2006) needs to be asked. This is not to suggest that organisational survival is unimportant (it usually is to the organisation and those within it!), but it is to highlight that, from the functioning of the system within which the organisation is embedded, different sets of questions need to be asked other than those *just* concerned with organisational survival. For each level of a system different concerns arise, and so the emergent nature of a system means that different questions need to be asked at each level and of the system as a whole. When dealing with the disturbance of complex dynamic systems, business and organisational studies, as well as researchers from all fields who respond to the impacts of natural disasters, need to better reflect on the questions they are asking and the assumptions on which their questions are based.

This book has sought to relate the significance of the Christchurch post-earthquake experience to a wider audience. In reflecting on how resilience and disaster ecology are framed, this chapter has sought to emphasise the implications of a broader ecological perspective, from which the concept of resilience was derived, to our understanding of systems that have been or will potentially be affected by major disturbance. Which, in an age of global change, means every ecosystem, every socio-economic system and everybody. It is therefore appropriate to finish with reference to the seminal work of Holling (1973) and how he understood the implications of resilience:

> A management approach based on resilience . . . would emphasize the need to keep options open, the need to view events in a regional rather than a local context, and the need to emphasize heterogeneity. Flowing from this would be not the presumption of sufficient knowledge, but the recognition of our ignorance; not the assumption that future events are expected, but that they will be unexpected. The resilience framework can accommodate this shift of perspective, for it does not require a precise capacity to predict the future, but only a qualitative capacity to devise systems that can absorb and accommodate future events in whatever unexpected form they may take.
>
> (Holling 1973: 21)

The challenge for business and organisational studies is to contribute to the understanding and development of such systems.

References

Abatecola, G. (2012) 'Organizational adaptation: An update', *International Journal of Organizational Analysis*, 20(3): 274–293.
Adger, N., Brown, K. and Tompkins, E. (2005) 'The political economy of cross-scale networks in resource co-management', *Ecology and Society*, 10: 9.
Aldrich, H. (1979) *Organizations and Environments*, Englewood Cliffs: Prentice Hall.

——(1999) *Organizations Evolving,* London: Sage.

Anåker, A. and Elf, M. (2014) 'Sustainability in nursing: A concept analysis', *Scandinavian Journal of Caring Sciences,* 28(2), 381–389.

Anderies, J. M., Folke, C., Walker, B. and Ostrom, E. (2013) 'Aligning key concepts for global change policy: Robustness, resilience, and sustainability', *Ecology and Society,* 18(2): 8.

Armitage, D. and Johnson, D. (2006) 'Can resilience be reconciled with globalization and the increasingly complex conditions of resource degradation in Asian coastal regions?', *Ecology and Society,* 11(1): 2.

Arrow, K., Bolin, B., Costanza, R., Dasgupta, P., Folke, C., Holling, C. S., Jansson, B-O., Levin, S., Mäler, K-G., Perrings, C. and Pimentel, D. (1995) 'Economic growth, carrying capacity, and the environment', *Ecological Economics,* 15(2): 91–95.

Beaton, R., Bridges, E., Salazar, M., Oberle, M., Stergachis, A., Thompson and Butterfield, P. (2008) 'Ecological model of disaster management', *Workplace Health & Safety,* 56(11), 471–478.

Berkes, F., Colding, J. and Folke, C. (2003) 'Introduction', in F. Berkes, J. Colding and C, Folke (eds.) *Navigating Social-Ecological Systems: Building Resilience for Complexity and Change,* Cambridge: Cambridge University Press.

Biggs, D., Hall, C. M. and Stoeckl, N. (2014) 'The resilience of formal and informal tourism enterprises to disasters: Reef tourism in Phuket, Thailand', *Journal of Sustainable Tourism,* 20(5): 645–665.

Birkmann, J. (2006) 'Measuring vulnerability to promote disaster-resilient societies: Conceptual frameworks and definitions', in J. Birkmann (ed.) *Measuring Vulnerability to Natural Hazards: Towards Disaster Resilient Societies,* New Delhi: TERI Press.

Blitz, D. (1992) *Emergent Evolution: Qualitative Novelty and the Levels of Reality,* Boston: Kluwer.

Botkin, D. B. (1990) *Discordant Harmonies,* Oxford: Oxford University Press.

Brand, F. and Jax, K. (2007) 'Focusing the meaning(s) of resilience: Resilience as a descriptive concept and a boundary object', *Ecology and Society,* 12: 23.

Brawn, J. D., Robinson, S. K. and Thompson III, F. R. (2001) 'The role of disturbance in the ecology and conservation of birds', *Annual Review of Ecology and Systematics,* 32: 251–276.

Brodie, J. and Waterhouse, J. (2012) 'A critical review of environmental management of the "not so Great" Barrier Reef', *Estuarine, Coastal and Shelf Science,* 104: 1–22.

Brown, K. (2012) 'Policy discourses of resilience', in M. Pelling, D. Manuel-Navarrete and M. Redclift (eds.) *Climate Change and the Crisis of Capitalism: A chance to reclaim self, society and nature,* New York: Routledge.

Christopherson, S., Michie, J. and Tyler, P. (2010) 'Regional resilience: Theoretical and empirical perspectives', *Cambridge Journal of Regions, Economy and Society,* 3: 3–10.

Clayford, J. (2011) *Faulty Thinking About Christchurch. Reflections on Auckland Planning.* 26 June. Online. Available HTTP: <http://joelcayford.blogspot.com/2011/06/faultythinkingaboutchristchurch.html> (Accessed 1 April 2015).

Colbourne, L. (2008) *Sustainable Development and Resilience. Think Piece for the Sustainable Development Commission,* London: Sustainable Development Commission. Online. Available HTTP: <http://www.sd-commission.org.uk/data/files/publications/SD_and_Resilience_thinkpiece1LC.pdf>.

Common, M. and Perrings, C. (1992) 'Towards an ecological economics of sustainability', *Ecological Economics*, 6(1): 7–34.

Concepción, E. D., Moretti, M., Altermatt, F., Nobis, M. and Obrist, M. (2015) 'Impacts of urbanisation on biodiversity: The role of species mobility, degree of specialisation and spatial scale', *Oikos*, doi:10.1111/oik.02166

Cox, C. and Moore, P. (2010) *Biogeography: An Ecological and Evolutionary Approach* (8th ed.), Hoboken: John Wiley.

Cutter, S. L. (ed.) (2006) *Hazards Vulnerability and Environmental Justice*, London: Earthscan.

Cutter, S. L., Ash, K. and Emrich, C. (2014) 'The geographies of community disaster resilience', *Global Environmental Change*, 29: 65–77.

Cutter, S. L., Burton, C. and Emrich, C. (2010) 'Disaster resilience indicators for benchmarking baseline conditions', *Journal of Homeland Security and Emergency Management*, 7(1), doi:10.2202/1547–7355.1732

Daily, G. and Matson, P. (2008) 'Ecosystem services: From theory to implementation', *Proceedings of the National Academy of Sciences*, 105: 9455–9456.

Davoudi, S., Shaw, K., Haider, L., Quinlan, A., Peterson, G., Wilkinson, C., Fünfgeld, H., McEvoy, D., Porter, L. and Davoudi, S. (2012) 'Resilience: A bridging concept or a dead end? "Reframing" resilience: Challenges for planning theory and practice Interacting traps: Resilience assessment of a pasture management system in Northern Afghanistan urban resilience: What does it mean in planning practice? Resilience as a useful concept for climate change adaptation? The politics of resilience for planning: A cautionary note: Edited by Simin Davoudi and Libby Porter', *Planning Theory & Practice*, 13(2), 299–333.

de Oliveira Teixeira, E. and Werther Jr., W. (2013) 'Resilience: Continuous renewal of competitive advantages', *Business Horizons*, 56(3): 333–342.

Dobrev, S., van Witteloostuijn, A. and Baum, J. (2006) 'Introduction: Ecology versus strategy or strategy and ecology?' in J. Baum, S. Dobrev and A. Van Witteloostuijn (eds.) *Advances in Strategic Management: Ecology and Strategy*, Bingley: Emerald.

Dollimore, D. (2014) 'Untangling the conceptual issues raised in Reydon and Scholz's critique of organizational ecology and Darwinian populations', *Philosophy of the Social Sciences*, 44(3): 282–315.

Elmqvist, T., Folke, C., Nyström, M., Peterson, G., Bengtsson, J., Walker, B. and Norberg, J. (2003) 'Response diversity, ecosystem change, and resilience', *Frontiers in Ecology and the Environment*, 1(9): 488–494.

Ernston, H. (2008) 'In Rhizomia – Actors, networks and resilience in urban landscapes', doctoral dissertation, Department of Systems Ecology, Stockholm University.

Folke, C. (2006) 'Resilience: The emergence of a perspective for social-ecological systems analyses', *Global Environmental Change*, 16: 253–267.

Folke, C., Hahn, T., Olsson, P. and Norberg, J. (2005) 'Adaptive governance of social-ecological systems', *Annual Review of Environment and Resources*, 30: 441–473.

Foster, J. (1997) 'The analytical foundations of evolutionary economics: From biological analogy to economic self-organization', *Structural Change and Economic Dynamics*, 8: 427–451.

Gunderson, L. H. and Holling, C. S. (eds.) (2002) *Panarchy: Understanding Transformations in Human and Natural Systems*, Washington, DC: Island Press.

Hall, C. M. (2010) 'An island biogeographical approach to island tourism and bio-diversity: An exploratory study of the Caribbean and Pacific Islands', *Asia Pacific Journal of Tourism Research*, 15: 383–399.

——(2011) 'Policy learning and policy failure in sustainable tourism governance: From first and second to third order change?' *Journal of Sustainable Tourism*, 19: 649–671.

——(2012) 'Island, islandness, vulnerability and resilience', *Tourism Recreation Research*, 37(2): 177–181.

——(2015) 'Global change, islands and sustainable development: Islands of sustain-ability or analogues of the challenge of sustainable development?', in M. Redclift and D. Springett (eds.) *Routledge International Handbook of Sustainable Develop-ment*, Abingdon: Routledge.

Hannan, M. and Freeman, J. (1977) 'The population ecology of organizations', *The American Journal of Sociology*, 82(5): 929–964.

——(1989) *Organizational Ecology*, Cambridge, MA: Harvard University Press.

Hayward, B. (2013) 'Rethinking resilence: Reflections on the earthquakes in Christch-urch, New Zealand, 2010 and 2011', *Ecology and Society*, 18(4): 37.

Hodgson, G. M. (2002) 'Darwinism in economics: From analogy to ontology', *Jour-nal of Evolutionary Economics*, 12(3): 259–282.

——(2004a) *The Evolution of Institutional Economics: Agency Structure and Darwin-ism in American Institutionalism*, London: Routledge.

——(2004b) 'Social Darwinism in Anglophone academic journals: A contribution to the history of the term', *Journal of Historical Sociology*, 17(4): 428–463.

Holling, C. S. (1973) 'Resilience and stability of ecological systems', *Annual Review of Ecology and Systematics*, 4: 1–23.

——(1996) 'Engineering resilience versus ecological resilience', in P. Schulze (ed.) *Engineering Within Ecological Constraints*, Washington, DC: The National Acad-emies Press.

Hudson, R. (2010) 'Resilient regions in an uncertain world: Wishful thinking or prac-tical reality', *Cambridge Journal of Regions, Economy and Society*, 3: 11–25.

Hughes, T., Graham, N., Jackson, J., Mumby, P. and Steneck, R. (2010) 'Rising to the challenge of sustaining coral reef resilience', *Trends in Ecology & Evolution*, 25: 633–642.

Isenmann, R. (2003) 'Industrial ecology: Shedding more light on its perspective of understanding nature as model', *Sustainable Development*, 11(3): 143–158.

Jackson, S. and Sax, D. (2010) 'Balancing biodiversity in a changing environment: Extinction debt, immigration credit and species turnover', *Trends in Ecology & Evo-lution*, 25(3): 153–60.

Johnson, E. and Miyanishi, K. (2010) 'Disturbance and succession', in E. Johnson and K. Miyanishi (eds.) *Plant Disturbance Ecology: The Process and the Response*, New York: Academic Press.

Johnson, N., Elliott, D. and Drake, P. (2013) 'Exploring the role of social capital in facilitating supply chain resilience', *Supply Chain Management: An International Journal*, 18(3): 324–336.

Kaplan, G. (1999) 'What is the role of the social environment in understanding ine-qualities in health?' *Annals of the New York Academy of Sciences*, 896: 116–119.

Keller, D. and Golley, F. (eds.) (2000) *The Philosophy of Ecology. From Science to Syn-thesis*, Athens: University of Georgia Press.

Kreutzweiser, D. P., Sibley, P., Richardson, J. and Gordon, A. (2012) 'Introduction and a theoretical basis for using disturbance by forest management activities to sustain aquatic ecosystems', *Freshwater Science*, 31(1): 224–231.

Lasswell, H. (1936) *Politics: Who Gets, What, When, How?* New York: McGraw-Hill.

Laurance, W. F., Dell, B., Turton, S., Lawes, M., Hutley, L., McCallum, H., Dalee, P., Bird, M., Hardy, G., Prideaux, G., Gawne, B., McMahon, C., Yu, R., Hero, J-M., Schwarzkopf, L. Krockenberger, A., Douglas, M., Silvester, E., Mahony, M., Vella, K., Saikia, U., Wahren, C-H. Xu, Z., Smith, B. and Cocklin, C. (2011) 'The 10 Australian ecosystems most vulnerable to tipping points', *Biological Conservation*, 144(5): 1472–1480.

Laurent, J. and Nightingale, J. (eds.) (2001) *Darwinism and Evolutionary Economics*, Cheltenham: Edward Elgar.

Lengnick-Hall, C., Beck, T. and Lengnick-Hall, M. (2011) 'Developing a capacity for organizational resilience through strategic human resource management', *Human Resource Management Review*, 21(3): 243–255.

Levine, S. (2003) 'Comparing products and production in ecological and industrial systems', *Journal of Industrial Ecology*, 7(2), 33–42.

Limnios, E. A. M., Mazzarol, T., Ghadouani, A. and Schilizzi, S. (2014) 'The resilience architecture framework: Four organizational archetypes', *European Management Journal*, 32(1): 104–116.

Lomolino, M. (2000a) 'A call for a new paradigm of island biogeography', *Global Ecology and Biogeography*, 9: 1–6.

Lomolino, M. (2000b) 'A species-based theory of insular zoogeography', *Global Ecology & Biogeography*, 9: 39–58.

Macarthur, R. H. and Wilson, E. O. (1963) 'An equilibrium theory of insular zoogeography', *Evolution*, 17: 373–387.

——(1967) *The Theory of Island Biogeography*, Princeton: Princeton University Press.

Maguire, B. and Cartwright, S. (2008) *Assessing a Community's Capacity to Manage Change: A Resilience Approach to Social Assessment*, Canberra: Bureau of Rural Sciences.

Millar, C., Stephenson, N. and Stephens, S. (2007) 'Climate change and forests of the future: Managing in the face of uncertainty', *Ecological Applications*, 17: 2145–2151.

Miller, F., Osbahr, H., Boyd, E., Thomalla, F., Bharwani, S., Ziervogel, G., Walker, B., Birkmann, J., Van der Leeuw, S., Rockström, J., Hinkel, J., Downing, T., Folke, C. and Nelson, D. (2010) 'Resilience and vulnerability: Complementary or conflicting concepts?' *Ecology and Society*, 15(3): 11.

Mirowski, P. (ed.) (1994) *Natural Images in Economic Thought: "Markets Read in Tooth and Claw"*, New York: Cambridge University Press.

Nelson, R. and Winter, S. (1982) *An Evolutionary Theory of Economic Change*, Cambridge, MA: Harvard University Press.

Nyström, M. (2006) 'Redundancy and response diversity of functional groups: Implications for the resilience of coral reefs', *Ambio*, 35: 30–35.

Nyström, M., Norström, A., Blenckner, T., de la Torre-Castro, M., Eklöf, J., Folke, C., Österblom, H., Steneck, R., Thyresson, M. and Troell, M. (2012) 'Confronting feedbacks of degraded marine ecosystems', *Ecosystems*, 15(5): 695–710.

Pendall, R., Foster, K. and Cowell, M. (2010) 'Resilience and regions: Building understanding of the metaphor', *Cambridge Journal of Regions, Economy and Society*, 3: 71–84.

Pickett, S. T., Cadenasso, M., Grove, J., Groffman, P., Band, L., Boone, C., Burch, W., Grimmond, C., Hom, J., Jenkins, J., Law, N., Nilon, C., Pouyat, R., Szlavecz, K., Warren, P. and Wilson, M. (2008) 'Beyond urban legends: An emerging framework of urban ecology, as illustrated by the Baltimore Ecosystem Study', *Bioscience*, 58: 139–150.

Pickett, S. T. and White, P. (1985) 'Natural disturbance and patch dynamics: An introduction', in S. T. Pickett and P. White (eds.) *The Ecology of Natural Disturbance and Patch Dynamics*, Orlando: Academic Press.

Poisot, T., Bever, J. D., Nemri, A., Thrall, P. and Hochberg, M. (2011) 'A conceptual framework for the evolution of ecological specialisation', *Ecology Letters*, 14(9), 841–851.

Prach, K. and Walker, L. (2011) 'Four opportunities for studies of ecological succession', *Trends in Ecology & Evolution*, 26(3): 119–123.

Pyne, S. J. (1982) *Fire in America. A Cultural History of Wildland and Rural Fire*, Princeton: Princeton University Press.

——(1991) *Burning Bush: A Fire History of Australia*, Sydney: Macmillan.

Radhakrishnan, K. and Jacelon, C. (2009) 'Synthesis of literature on strategies for chronic disease management post disasters', *Journal of Nursing and Healthcare of Chronic Illness*, 1(4): 294–302.

Røpke, I. (2005) 'Trends in the development of ecological economics from the late 1980s to the early 2000s', *Ecological Economics*, 55(2): 262–290.

Schultz, J. (2013) 'Perspectives on disaster public health and disaster behavioral health integration', *Disaster Health*, 1(2): 1–4.

Seidl, R., Rammer, W. and Spies, T. (2014) 'Disturbance legacies increase the resilience of forest ecosystem structure, composition, and functioning', *Ecological Applications*, 24(8): 2063–2077.

Shaw, K. and Maythorne, L. (2013) 'Managing for local resilience: Towards a strategic approach', *Public Policy and Administration*, 28(1): 43–65.

Shultz, J., Espinel, Z., Galea, S. and Reissman, D. B. (2007) 'Disaster ecology: Implications for disaster psychiatry', in R. Ursano, C. Fullerton, L. Weisaeth and B. Raphael (eds.) *Textbook of Disaster Psychiatry*, Cambridge: Cambridge University Press.

Spies, T., Lindenmayer, D., Gill, A., Stephens, S. and Agee, J. (2012) 'Challenges and a checklist for biodiversity conservation in fire-prone forests: Perspectives from the Pacific Northwest of USA and Southeastern Australia', *Biological Conservation*, 145(1): 5–14.

Suding, K. N. (2011) 'Toward an era of restoration in ecology: Successes, failures, and opportunities ahead', *Annual Review of Ecology, Evolution, and Systematics*, 42(1): 465–487.

Suding, K. N. and Hobbs, R. (2009) 'Threshold models in restoration and conservation: A developing framework', *Trends in Ecology & Evolution*, 24: 271–279.

Vale, L. (2014) 'The politics of resilient cities: Whose resilience and whose city?' *Building Research & Information*, 42(2): 37–41.

Walker, B., Holling, C. S. Carpenter, S. and Kinzig, A. (2004) 'Resilience, adaptability and transformability in social-ecological systems', *Ecology and Society*, 9(2): 5.

Walker, L. R. (2012) *The Biology of Disturbed Habitats*, Oxford: University Press.

Warren, B. H., Simberloff, D., Ricklefs, R., Aguilée, R., Condamine, F., Gravel, D., Morlon, H., Mouquet, N., Rosindell, J., Casquet, J., Conti, E., Cornuault, J., Fernández-Palacios, J., Hengl, T., Norder, S., Rijsdijk, K., Sanmartin, I., Strasberg,

D., Triantis, K., Valente, L., Whittaker, R., Gillespie, R., Emerson, B. and Thébaud, C. (2015) 'Islands as model systems in ecology and evolution: Prospects fifty years after MacArthur-Wilson', *Ecology Letters*, 18(2): 200–217.

Whittaker, R. J. and Fernández-Palacios, J. (2007) *Island Biogeography: Ecology, Evolution, and Conservation* (2nd ed.), Oxford: Oxford University Press.

Whittaker, R. J., Triantis, K. A. and Ladle, R. J. (2008) 'A general dynamic theory of oceanic island biogeography', *Journal of Biogeography*, 35(6): 977–994.

Wisner, B., Blaikie, P., Cannon, T. and Davis, I. (2004) *At Risk: Natural Hazards, People's Vulnerability, and Disasters* (2nd ed.), London: Routledge.

Worster, D. (1990) 'The ecology of order and chaos', *Environmental History Review*, 14(1–2): 1–18.

Yackulic, C., Sanderson, E. and Uriarte, M. (2011) 'Anthropogenic and environmental drivers of modern range loss in large mammals', *Proceedings of the National Academy of Sciences*, 108(10): 4024–4029.

Yoon, D. K. (2012) 'Assessment of social vulnerability to natural disasters: A comparative study', *Natural Hazards*, 63(2): 823–843.

Index

accommodation and food services sector 102–14; *see also* hospitality; tourism
adaptation 201, 264, 276–7, 285; consumer 233; organisational 35–6, 44
agenda setting 7, 279
AMI Stadium 9, 185, 187, 188, 189, 191
Anchor Projects 181–93, 212; disaster capitalism 190–2; rhetoric 189–90
ANSVAR 191, 207, 210
ANZ Bank building 203
Arequipa 201
Arts Centre 65, 66, 71, 72, 74, 185; gentrification processes 79, 83–92; restoration 209–11, 212
Avon Loop 184
Avon Theatre 203

Ballantynes 132–54, 236; advertising 139–40, 142, 144, 146; earthquake impact 136; history 136–7
Bam 201
Barcelona 81–2
Boxing Day tsunami 156
brands 121, 133, 136, 141, 233; attachment 123, 127; brand love 121, 123, 129; brand relationship quality 122–3; consumer-brand relationships 121–2; divorce 123, 127–9; fling 129; forgiveness 129; identity 126–7; personality 123, 126; rebranding 73; and service 145; temporal perspectives 125
brandscape 232–3; *see also* servicescape
Bridge of Remembrance 203
Brownlee, Gerry 186, 187, 188, 189, 191, 193; attitudes towards heritage 200

Building Code 89, 206, 210
business continuity 99, 100, 110
business turnover 25

Canterbury Cheesemongers 86, 87
Canterbury Club 203
Canterbury District Health Board 10, 48, 226
Canterbury Earthquake Heritage Buildings Fund (CEHBF) 209
Canterbury Earthquake Recovery Act 2011 186, 192, 193, 203, 208
Canterbury Earthquake Recovery Authority (CERA) 10, 38, 164, 187, 200, 208, 255
Canterbury earthquakes *see* Christchurch earthquake sequence
Canterbury Heritage Trust (CHT) 209
Canterbury Museum 67, 69, 72, 73, 74–5, 90, 185, 203
Canterbury Public Library 203
Canterbury Society of Arts Gallery 203
Canterbury Wellbeing Index 10–11
Cardboard Cathedral 73, 74, 241
Cathedral of the Blessed Sacrament 65, 203
Cathedral Square 184, 193
Central Business District (CBD) 80–2; Christchurch 8–9, 11, 74, 85, 91, 113, 114, 132, 136, 162, 203–12; regeneration of Christchurch CBD 181–93
Charleston 202
Christchurch Art Gallery 185, 209
Christchurch Arts Centre *see* Arts Centre
Christchurch and Canterbury Tourism 67, 68, 70, 71, 73, 74, 157
Christchurch casino 185

Christ Church Cathedral 65, 74, 159, 185, 241; emotional attachment 159, 161
Christchurch Central Development Unit (CCDU) 187, 189, 192, 209, 212
Christchurch Central Police Station 185
Christchurch Central Recovery Plan (CCRP) 181, 200, 209, 2012
Christchurch City Council (CCC) 79, 84, 86, 181, 186–9, 192, 209–10; heritage conservation policy 203–4, 206, 207; *see also* Christchurch City Holdings Limited
Christchurch City Holdings Limited 226
Christchurch City Public Library 193
Christchurch Convention Centre 185, 189, 191; precinct 191
Christchurch earthquake sequence 8–9, 10, 24, 48, 52, 53, 55, 112
Christchurch Economic Development Strategy (CEDS) 184
Christchurch International Airport 105, 136, 138, 226
Christchurch Town Hall 185, 188
Christchurch Tram 67–8, 69, 72, 73, 74
Christ College 203
circuit of capital 183
Citizen's War Memorial 203
City Care 38
City Owners Rebuild Entity (CORE) 208, 209
Civic Assurance 191
civil defense 86, 170, 208, 209, 256
climate change 8, 201
collaboration 35, 39, 40–2, 44, 72, 135, 145, 252, 256
communication 37, 39–40, 42, 44, 71, 114, 167, 170–7, 255, 256; marketing communication 128, 129, 136, 137–40, 147–9; social support and personal communication during disasters 168–9; *see also* social media
construction sector 28, 97, 99
Consumer Price Index 9
consumptionscape 233; *see also* servicescape
Cook Statue 203
Cranmer Courts 185, 204
crisis management 23, 48, 100
CTV Building 113
Cultural Precinct of Christchurch 83, 90, 209–10

cultural precincts 183
cultural quarter 183
cultural services 65–76; *see also* heritage; tourism
customer experience 133–4, 136, 147, 148–9; escapism 148
customer relationships 147–8

Dance-o-Mat 240
democratic processes 265
Department of Labour 10, 48
disaster: definition 3, 4–5; growth in 3; *see also* disaster research
disaster capitalism 181, 182, 183, 190–2
disaster ecology 270–2, 284, 286
disaster management 3, 23, 36–7, 67, 98, 100, 114, 156, 168–9, 175, 252, 265, 281
disaster research 3–4, 251; access to organisations and individuals 257–9; dynamic research environment 260–1; ethics 251, 257, 258, 260, 262, 266; expectations 261; impact 264; issues of risk and reciprocity when dealing with sensitive topics 262–4; major themes in business literature 4–8; relationships practitioner forums and formal research 254; relevance 265; researcher wellbeing 259–60; social science research 251–2; stakeholder relationships and involvement 252–3, 255–7; timeliness of research 253–4
disturbance ecology *see* disaster ecology
Downer 38
Durham Street Methodist Church 204
Dux de Lux 83, 87, 89

Earthquake Commission (EQC) 9, 207, 259; dealing with 57, 58
education and training sector 102–14
employee turnover 48–61
empowerment 40, 44, 177
experiencescape 233; *see also* servicescape

fictitious capital 183
Fletcher 38
foot and mouth disease 24
Forsyth Barr 185
framing 82, 212, 286
Fulton 201
Fulton Hogan 38

Gap Filler 73, 74, 235, 238
gentrification 79–92; defined 80–1;
    retail gentrification 81–3; *see also*
    regeneration
global environmental change 3, 36
governance 4, 8, 192–3; of built
    heritage 200–12
Greater Christchurch Recovery Strategy
    (GCRS) 209; built heritage recovery
    plan 209
grounded theory 25, 35, 37, 51
Guthrey Centre 204

Hagley Cricket Oval 185
Hagley Park 184
Hanshin-Awaji earthquake 235
Harald's Building 204
heritage 65, 79–82, 85–91;
    conservation in post-disaster context
    201–3; cultural tourism 65–6, 69–75;
    governance of built heritage in
    Christchurch 200, 203–12
Heritage New Zealand Pouhere Taonga
    83, 203–5
hospitality sector 26, 27, 33, 68, 79,
    85, 90, 91, 99, 100, 101, 189, 232,
    239; *see also* accommodation and food
    services sector; tourism
human resource management 254, 255,
    264, 272; customisation 40
Hurricane Katrina 13, 24, 99, 168,
    183, 202, 212, 235; *see also*
    New Orleans

IConIC 209
inflation 9
infrastructure 8–9, 24, 29, 31, 37–8,
    68–9, 98, 104–7, 113–15
Inland Revenue Department (IRD)
    10, 48
insurance 156; Christchurch
    earthquakes 9, 10, 13, 27, 30, 31, 99,
    105, 109, 210; financial statement
    disclosures 219–28; heritage 207,
    208; urban regeneration 182, 183,
    188, 190–1
Insurance Council of New Zealand
    207
International Council On Monuments
    and Sites (ICOMOS)
International Financial Reporting
    Standards (IFRS) 219–21
Isaac Theatre Royal 185, 204
island biogeography 272, 275

Japanese tsunami 9, 13

Katrina *see* Hurricane Katrina
Kirkgate Market 80

L'Aquila (Italy) 190, 201, 212
leadership 35, 39–42, 44, 112, 135,
    260, 283
Leeds 80, 82
local government 35, 37, 163, 188
Local Government Act 184, 186,
    208
London 81
Lyttleton Port Company 225, 226
Lyttleton Times Building 204

Magistrates Court 204
Manchester 80, 81
Manchester Courts 207
Manhattan 188, 212; *see also*
    New York
manufacturing sector 26–7, 97, 99,
    101–15
marketing 69, 75, 122, 132, 156; area
    of disaster research 6, 8, 135–6; place
    marketing 232; relationship 132–50;
    social 8; tourism 67, 157; *see also*
    servicescape
Marmite 122, 125–9
McConnell Dowell 38
mental health 11, 40, 168
Minister for the Canterbury Earthquake
    Recovery 186, 188, 189, 193, 200;
    see also Brownlee, Gerry
Ministry of Civil Defence and
    Emergency Management
    (MCDEM) 255
Mostar 201
Music Centre of Christchurch 204

National Conservatorium of
    Music 210
natural disaster *see* disaster
neoliberalism 80, 193, 202; neoliberal
    urbanism 80
Newcastle Upon Tyne 81
New Orleans 13, 80, 81, 183, 190,
    202, 212
New Regent Street Historic Area 185,
    204, 209
New York 80, 81, 82, 183, 212
New Zealand Historic Places Trust
    see Heritage New Zealand Pouhere
    Taonga

New Zealand Society of Earthquake
   Engineering 206
New Zealand Transport Agency 38
9/11 183, 188, 212
Northridge (California) earthquake
   13, 27

Odeon Theatre 204
Old Government Building 204
organisational adaptation to disasters
   36–44; *see also* resilience
Orion (electricity supply company) 226
Our City 204
Oxford Terrace Baptist Church 204

Pallet Pavilion 238
Peterborough Centre 204
population change 283
Port au Prince 202
Port Authority of New York 212
Portland 82
post-disaster management *see* disaster
   management
power 188, 263, 265
pre-disaster inter-organisational
   networks 168–9
Press Building, The 204
public-private partnership 182, 188
Public Trust Office 204

Quake City *see* Canterbury Museum

real estate 82, 84, 183, 207
recovery marketing 8, 135–6
Recovery Strategy for Greater
   Christchurch (RSGC) 200
Red Bus Tour 73, 74
Red Zone 9, 69, 73, 74, 141
regeneration *see* urban regeneration
Regent Theatre 204
relationship management 132–50
residential displacement 80
resilience 8, 74, 76, 135, 219, 227, 272;
   adaptive 35, 100–15; community 66,
   114, 164, 169, 175; definition 23,
   100, 252, 269–70, 285–6; disaster
   4, 11; ecological 272–86; firm 7;
   fuzziness 269; governments 13;
   organisational 35–44, 97–115, 272;
   personal 30–2, 163, 270; planned
   100–15; politics of 283–4; research
   6; resilience to disturbance 278–80;
   small firm 23–30; supply-chain 7;

system characteristics and scale 280–4;
   urban 182, 265
Resilient Cities (network) 189
Resilient Organisations (research group)
   100
Resource Management Act (RMA) 86,
   186, 206, 211
Re:Start Mall 74–5, 76, 88, 145, 149,
   236–8
retail sector 26–30, 99; Ballantynes
   132–50; gentrification 79–82; *see also*
   Arts Centre
Review of the Civil Defence Emergency
   Management Response to the 22
   February Christchurch Earthquake
   256
risk management 100, 114, 156, 224
Rockefeller Foundation 189
Rolleston Statue 204
Rugby World Cup 9

San Francisco 189, 201, 208
Sanitarium (New Zealand Health
   Association) *see* Marmite
seasonal workers 114
Seoul 82
servicescape 143, 149; defined 231–3;
   transitional 233–44
Seville 82
social marketing 8
social media 66; disaster response 176;
   firm's post-disaster 150
social networks 10, 168–9; strengths
   174–5
small firms 23; resilience 23–34
Smash Palace 239–40
Smith's City Group 225–6
social capital 76, 169, 175, 177
South of Litchfield 80, 206
St Catharine 82
St John the Baptist Church 204
St Paul's Church 204
Stronger Christchurch Infrastructure
   Rebuild Team (SCIRT) 38
strategy 33, 72, 89, 149, 164;
   communication 147; competitive
   33; coping 162; disaster research
   area 6, 7; mitigation 104–5, 111,
   114
supply chain 23, 100, 122, 134;
   disruption 7, 134, 135
Swiss Re 3, 13
Sydney 81

temporality 233–42; and disasters 234
temporary architecture 233–4; urban
    space 235–6
temporary housing 234
Timaru 136, 138, 140–1
Toronto 82
touchpoints 133, 137, 144, 146–7, 148
tourism 9, 67–76, 97; anchor projects
    189; cultural tourism 65–6; dark
    155–64; gentrification 80, 82;
    historic neighbourhoods 80; impact
    of foot and mouth disease 24;
    infrastructure damage 68, 113, 115;
    long-term recovery planning 71;
    operational responses and strategies
    71–5; regeneration 181–3; safety
    and security 69–70; short-term
    emergency response 70–1; urban
    201; visitor perception 69; *see also*
    accommodation and food services;
    cultural services; hospitality
transport 35, 66, 74, 76, 99, 113–14,
    230; public 9

UN International Strategy for Disaster
    Reduction 3

University of Canterbury xiii, 10, 48,
    83, 85, 88, 91, 259, 265; insurance
    224, 226
urban design 188, 230, 232, 233, 242
urban designscapes 233; *see also*
    servicescape
urban development 80, 184, 233–4
urban regeneration 66, 79, 181,
    184–93, 201, 230, 232; disaster
    capitalism 190–2; post-disaster 182–3;
    retail gentrification 80–2
urbanisation 3, 79, 283; crisis-driven
    model 84, 200, 203, 205
urbicide 212

Van earthquake 183
Victoria Clock Tower 204
vulnerability 8, 98, 113, 182, 266,
    283; heritage buildings 202, 208;
    intensification 83; island economies
    276; reduction 13, 76; research on
    6, 7

Western Pacific Insurance 208
World Heritage 202
World Monuments Fund 202

For Product Safety Concerns and Information please contact our EU
representative GPSR@taylorandfrancis.com
Taylor & Francis Verlag GmbH, Kaufingerstraße 24, 80331 München, Germany